# The Political Thought
# of Justice Antonin Scalia

*Binford*
1363 Logans Way
Blanco, Texas 78606

# The Political Thought of Justice Antonin Scalia

## A Hamiltonian on the Supreme Court

James B. Staab

ROWMAN & LITTLEFIELD PUBLISHERS, INC.
*Lanham • Boulder • New York • Toronto • Oxford*

ROWMAN & LITTLEFIELD PUBLISHERS, INC.

Published in the United States of America
by Rowman & Littlefield Publishers, Inc.
A wholly owned subsidiary of The Rowman & Littlefield Publishing Group, Inc.
4501 Forbes Boulevard, Suite 200, Lanham, Maryland 20706
www.rowmanlittlefield.com

PO Box 317
Oxford
OX2 9RU, UK

British Library Cataloguing in Publication Information Available

**Library of Congress Cataloging-in-Publication Data**

Staab, James Brian.
  The political thought of Justice Antonin Scalia : a Hamiltonian on the Supreme Court /
James B. Staab.
    p. cm.
  Includes bibliographical references and index.
  ISBN-10: 0-7425-4310-2 (cloth : alk. paper)
  ISBN-13: 978-0-7425-4310-2 (cloth : alk. paper)
  ISBN-10: 0-7425-4311-0 (pbk. : alk. paper)
  ISBN-13: 978-0-7425-4311-9 (pbk. : alk. paper)
  1. Scalia, Antonin—Political and social views. 2. United States. Supreme Court—
Biography. 3. Constitutional law—United States. 4. Constitutional history—United
States. I. Title.

  KF8745.S33S73 2005
  342.73—dc22                                               2005030662

Printed in the United States of America

To Renée

# Contents

# Acknowledgments

I am grateful to have the opportunity to thank and acknowledge the many people who helped me with this book project. Henry J. Abraham and David M. O'Brien, my two graduate advisers at the University of Virginia, provided invaluable support and assistance during all stages of this project. Several other colleagues provided helpful comments on particular aspects of the book, including Martha Derthick, James V. Young, James W. Ceaser, A. E. Dick Howard, Miles Williams, and Paul McCartney. I wish to extend a special thanks to John Dinan and Don Wallace, each of whom read the entire manuscript and provided sage advice on how to improve it. The library staff at Central Missouri State University acquired the countless articles and books that allowed me to conduct the research for the manuscript. I would like to thank, in particular, Vanessa Chappell, Patti Morrison, Lori Fitterling, Marian Davis, Teresa Heater, Jim Agee, Scott Norwood, and Mark Love. I am indebted to Kirk Randazzo for his able and patient assistance in conducting research on Harold Spaeth's Supreme Court databases. For the chapters discussing Justice Scalia's views on federalism, *The Journal of Law & Politics* and *Roger Williams University Law Review* kindly allowed me to reprint portions of articles I had previously published with them. Christopher Anzalone, my editor at Rowman & Littlefield, was a superb collaborator on this project who believed in the book's thesis from the beginning and made many excellent and necessary editorial suggestions. Karen Ackermann and Molly Ahearn, production editors at Rowman & Littlefield, also provided valuable editorial assistance. Finally, I would like to thank my wife, Renée, for her patience and encouragement during the time I was working on this project, as well as for her helpful suggestions on how to improve the substance and style of the book. It is to her that this book is dedicated.

# Abbreviations

BOR—Bernard Schwartz, ed., *The Bill of Rights: A Documentary History*, 2 vols. (New York: Chelsea House Publishers, 1971).

CA—Herbert J. Storing, ed., *The Complete Anti-Federalist*, 7 vols. (Chicago: University of Chicago Press, 1981).

Commentaries—Joseph Story, *Commentaries on the Constitution of the United States*, 2 vols, 5th ed. (Boston: Hilliard, Gray, and Company, 1905).

Debates—John Elliot, ed., *The Debates in the Several State Conventions on the Adoption of the Federal Constitution*, 5 vols. (Salem, NH: Ayer Co. Publishers, 1987).

FP—Isaac Kramnick, ed., *The Federalist Papers* (New York: Penguin Books, 1987).

HABP—Harry A. Blackmun Papers (Washington, DC: Library of Congress, Manuscript Division, 2003).

L&OWJM—*Letters and Other Writings of James Madison*, 4 vols. (Philadelphia: J. B. Lippincott & Co., 1865).

LPAH—Julius Goebel Jr., ed., *The Law Practice of Alexander Hamilton: Documents and Commentary*, 5 vols. (New York: Columbia University Press, 1964).

PAH—Harold C. Syrett et al., ed., *The Papers of Alexander Hamilton*, 27 vols. (New York: Columbia University Press, 1961–1987).

PJM—William T. Hutchinson et al., ed., *The Papers of James Madison*, 17 vols. (Chicago and Charlottesville: University of Chicago Press and University of Virginia Press, 1962–1991).

Records—Max Farrand, ed., *The Records of the Federal Convention of 1787*, 3 vols. (New Haven, CT: Yale University Press, 1966).

SWEB—*Select Works of Edmund Burke*, 3 vols., new imprint of the Payne Edition (Indianapolis, IN: Liberty Fund, 1999).

WJM—Gaillard Hunt, ed., *The Writings of James Madison*, 9 vols. (New York: G. P. Putnam's Sons, 1900–1910).

WTJ—Albert Ellery Bergh, ed., *The Writings of Thomas Jefferson*, 20 vols. (Washington, DC: Thomas Jefferson Memorial Association, 1903–1904).

*Investiture ceremony of Chief Justice William Rehnquist and Justice Antonin Scalia at the Front Plaza. The retiring Chief Justice Warren Burger is in the center.*
*Photographer: Joel Richardson*
*Courtesy of the Supreme Court of the United States*

*Justices Antonin Scalia and Ruth Bader Ginsburg on an elephant in India*
*Courtesy of the Supreme Court of the United States*

*Justice Antonin Scalia at an April 2004 address in Hattiesburg, Mississippi*
*Courtesy of the Hattiesburg American*

# Introduction: Scalia's Distinctive Brand of Conservatism

To his enthusiasts, Antonin Scalia is probably the greatest judge to sit on the United States Supreme Court since Chief Justice John Marshall. To his detractors, he is a conservative activist bent on turning back the progress made during the Warren and Burger courts. But on one thing both sides can agree: Justice Scalia is one of the most provocative and controversial public officials in modern times. Since his appointment to the Supreme Court in 1986, a cottage industry of scholarship has been produced on Scalia. Whether it be his sharp and witty sense of humor, his take-no-prisoners approach to deciding cases, or his keen and wide-ranging intellect, Court watchers seem to draw near when he speaks on or off the bench. But what has not been examined very closely is Scalia's political philosophy. True, Scalia is usually referred to as a conservative, but the nature of *his* conservatism has not been well defined.

## VARIETIES OF LEGAL CONSERVATISM

At least six major schools of conservative jurisprudence can be identified in the legal community today: Burkean traditionalism, conservative pragmatism, Legal Process, libertarianism, natural law, and originalism. The Burkeans are the "traditional" conservatives. Following in the footsteps of the eighteenth-century English philosopher and statesman Edmund Burke, who is regarded by many as the father of modern conservatism, traditional conservatives exhibit a profound distrust of abstract reasoning, are skeptical about modern social contract theory and the idea of "founding" political regimes, and place great reliance on tradition or precedent. According to traditional conservatives, constitutions are not made; they grow. Judges who follow this perspective reject an originalist interpretation of the Constitution and instead utilize a common law approach to interpreting law. The late Yale law professor Alexander Bickel subscribed to a Burkean approach to the law, as did former Supreme Court justices John Marshall Harlan II, Lewis F. Powell, and Sandra Day O'Connor.[1]

Conservative pragmatism represents the second school of modern conservative legal philosophy. Tracing its origins back to the political philosophy of John Dewey, pragmatists (whether liberal or conservative) are skeptics about absolute truths and stress the indeterminacy of law. The impetus for a pragmatic approach to law was a deep hostility toward the conceptual jurisprudence of the *Lochner* era, which regarded law as a closed, self-contained logical system whereby judges, trained in the science of the law, deduce legal conclusions from preexisting rules of law.[2] Pragmatists reject such a conception of the law and instead candidly admit the element of discretion involved in the judicial craft. For the pragmatist, the process of judging is not sterile or mechanical, but contextual, adaptive, innovative, and creative. Since the fundamental purpose of law is social utility, the pragmatic judge weighs all of the various interests presented in a case and tries to reach the best socially desirable result. Former federal judges who used a pragmatic approach to the law include Oliver Wendell Holmes, Benjamin Cardozo, and Learned Hand. On the federal judiciary today, a conservative-leaning pragmatism is represented in the prolific and eclectic writings of Seventh Circuit Court of Appeals judge Richard A. Posner.[3]

The third type of modern conservative legal thought represented on the federal judiciary today is the Legal Process School. Widely popular in the 1950s, the Legal Process School generally agreed with the pragmatic critique of classical jurisprudence but did not believe the pragmatists paid sufficient attention to the "nihilistic" tendencies of such a critique. In reaction to the atrocities committed in Nazi Germany during World War II, the Legal Process theorists sought to bring more "objectivity" back into the legal enterprise and emphasized two major concepts about the law: "institutional settlement" and a judicial decision-making process called "reasoned elaboration." According to the first concept, if the procedures used by the majoritarian branches of government are conducive to well-informed and wise decisions, then their substantive outcomes are regarded as presumptively valid. This view of the majoritarian process counsels considerable deference and restraint by judges, where the legitimacy of law is not based primarily on the content of legal doctrine but on whether established procedures are followed. A federal judge who followed this particular tenet of the Legal Process School was former Supreme Court justice Felix Frankfurter, who was exceedingly solicitous of the democratic process. With respect to the second concept—reasoned elaboration—the Legal Process theorists contended that judicial discretion could be curbed if judges based their decisions on reasons or principles that transcend the particular case. For example, former Columbia law professor Herbert Wechsler criticized the Supreme Court's decision in *Brown v. Board of Education*[4]—which struck down segregation in public schools—for placing reliance upon psychological studies showing that black children were marked by a badge of inferiority because of segregated schools. According to Wechsler, because those findings were disputable or could change over time, they diminished the Court's attempt to arrive at a more principled decision.[5] While the focus on institutional settlement clearly implied a restraint-oriented conception of the federal judiciary, the emphasis on "reasoned" or "principled" decisions laid the groundwork for closer judicial inspection of both the process and *substance* of institutional decisions in the areas of statutory, administrative, and constitutional law. Even though germinations of the Legal Process School predate Henry Hart and Albert Sacks, it was their casebook materials,[6] as well as the "Legal Process" course they taught at Harvard in the 1950s and 1960s, which are credited with galvanizing this movement. On the Supreme Court today, the most prominent exponent of a reasoned elaboration approach to the law is represented in the cautious conservatism of Anthony Kennedy, a 1961 graduate of Harvard Law School. While Kennedy exhibits many of the trademark qualities of Burkean traditionalism,[7] his utilization of a reasoned elaboration methodology in deciding cases (which is not necessarily anti-Burkean[8]) distinguishes him from Justice O'Connor and prior Burkean Supreme Court justices, who arguably placed greater weight on precedent. Kennedy's use of a reasoned elaboration technique in cases running the gamut from abortion to political patronage[9] points to important differences between him and the other conservative members of the Court, including Scalia.[10]

The libertarians are the fourth major school of conservative thought represented in the legal academy today. Comprising an eclectic group of thinkers, this school emphasizes natural rights and a limited-government philosophy. In some ways, calling libertarians "conservative" misses the mark because many of their believers (e.g., Stephen Macedo and Randy Barnett[11]) defend basic freedoms across the political spectrum, including the "liberty of contract" doctrine seen during the *Lochner* era and a woman's right to obtain an abortion in the modern era. Having said this, however, the conservative feature of libertarianism is represented by some of their adherents' single-minded defense of economic and property rights. For example, Bernard Siegan, a law professor at the University of San Diego, has argued that the federal judiciary should apply a higher level of scrutiny to claims of economic and property deprivation under the Due Process Clauses of the Fifth and Fourteenth Amendments. Such an interpretation of these clauses, as Siegan readily admits, would return the Court's jurisprudence to the type of substantive economic due process witnessed during the *Lochner* era.[12] Meanwhile, University of Chicago law professor Richard Epstein, who desires the same end as Siegan—that is, a dismantling of many of the federal programs begun during the New Deal—would rather see the Court protect property rights under the Fifth Amendment's Takings Clause. Epstein has advocated a higher level of judicial scrutiny to a host of local, state, and federal regulations that arguably burden proprietary interests, including rent controls, minimum wages, landmark preservation, zoning, civil rights, and collective bargaining.[13] Clarence Thomas, Associate Justice of the Supreme Court, Douglas Ginsburg, Chief Judge of the D.C. Court of Appeals, and Alex Kozinski, judge of the Ninth Circuit Court of Appeals, could all properly be called libertarian conservatives, who support greater judicial protection of economic and property rights.[14] In court opinions or extrajudicial writings, Thomas and Kozinski have defended closer judicial scrutiny of regulations impeding commercial speech and have either strongly suggested or argued that the Second Amendment confers a personal right "to keep and bear Arms."[15] Thomas has distinguished himself from some of his conservative colleagues on the Court by criticizing governmental efforts to regulate same-sex sodomy and the medicinal use of marijuana,[16] and has defended a formalistic, strict constructionist interpretation of Congress's commerce power as a way of restricting federal authority to regulate the economy.[17] Nonetheless, Thomas's libertarian streak is limited by the fact that he denies that a general right of privacy exists under the Constitution.[18]

A fifth group of legal conservatives supports a natural law interpretation of the Constitution. Conservative natural law theorists believe in immutable and eternal moral truths, derived from a divine source or the natural order, that are superior to civil law. In contrast to the rights defended by "liberal" natural rights theorists, such as Ronald Dworkin,[19] these conservative followers of natural law emphasize such moral precepts as the innate equality of individuals, religious freedom, and the right to life. They are also willing to use natural law arguments both to oppose and support legislation. For example, political scientist Harry Jaffa and Justice Thomas have used natural law arguments to call for the overturning of affirmative action programs. For Jaffa and Thomas, affirmative action violates the moral dignity of individuals as promised by the Declaration of Independence.[20] By contrast, in *Beyond the Constitution*, political scientist Hadley Arkes defends a natural law reading of the Constitution to support congressional efforts to regulate private discrimination and the practice of abortion.[21] Similarly, Ninth Circuit Court of Appeals judge John T. Noonan Jr. and philosophy and religion professor Russell Hittinger have defended a natural law reading of the Free Exercise Clause of the Constitution. According to Noonan, "religion, untrammeled by government restraints, has been the foremost of our political institutions," and both he and Hittinger have criticized the Court's 1997 *City of Boerne v. Flores* decision,[22] which overturned the Religious Freedom Restoration Act of 1993.[23] Depending on the issue involved, then, and how it is being dealt with in the legislative process, natural law conservatives can be prudential supporters of judicial activism, but they are not opposed to government regulation (including federal regulation) of such issues as obscenity, discrimination, religion, abortion, physician-assisted suicide, violence against women, and homosexuality.[24] Because conservative natural law theorists believe in immutable principles of justice, they are sharp critics of positivistic interpretations of the Constitution.

Finally, the sixth school of conservative thought represented in the legal community today is originalism. As a method of constitutional interpretation, originalism has roots that run deeper than the 1980s, but as a conservative movement, it gained a head of steam during the Reagan administration. In 1985, U.S. Attorney General Edwin Meese announced that in all federal cases involving the administration, it would defend a constitutional interpretive approach based on original intent.[25] While some originalists look to the intentions of the framers for guidance in interpreting the Constitution, and others are more concerned about the popular meaning of a constitutional provision when it was adopted, both sides agree that the Constitution should not be read to reflect current social values and attitudes. For the originalist, the Constitution is not a living but static document and can be amended only by the process prescribed under Article V of the Constitution. Originalists contend that when judges update the Constitution to conform with modern values and attitudes, they subvert the democratic process and violate separation of powers principles. Accordingly, while originalists concede that judges can and should defend the rights clearly listed in the Constitution, they adamantly reject that judges can defend any others.

What, then, makes this school of thought conservative? In one sense, insistence upon Article V's amendment process is neutral, since the people can decide for themselves what they want to do with such hot-button issues as abortion, capital punishment, the right to die, and homosexual rights. The conservative nature of originalism, however, is evident in several ways. First, as a method of constitutional interpretation, originalism places a presumption against the creation of new rights. Because the Constitution is so difficult to amend—we've only had seventeen amendments since 1791!—a mode of constitutional interpretation that denies judges the ability to update its often broad and ambiguous provisions necessarily places a presumption against the recognition of new rights. In a common law system in which judges have historically "made" law, and when dealing with a legal document whose framers differed over how it should be interpreted, the conservative purpose of such a mode of constitutional interpretation should be apparent.

The second way in which originalism is conservative is that many of its adherents support an authoritarian legal system, which is reflected in their positivistic reading of the Constitution. Originalists-positivists, such as Antonin

Scalia, the late Chief Justice William H. Rehnquist, and former federal judge Robert Bork, draw a sharp distinction between law and morality. In order for someone to be required to follow a law, it does not have to meet some "moral" test. As John Austin, the father of legal positivism, put it, "The existence of law is one thing; its merit or demerit is another."[26] The strength of such a conception of law, the originalist-positivist will contend, is that it not only limits judicial discretion, but it makes the law more predictable and understandable, and thus gives those subject to its sanctions clear guidelines of legal obligation. "If you express or intimate a wish that I shall do or forebear from some act, and if you will visit me with an evil in case I comply not with your wish, the *expression* or *intimation* of your wish is a *command*," wrote Austin.[27]

Finally, the originalists' support of the structural principles of the Constitution reveals an elitist conception of the democratic process and a preference for *moderate* decision making. Here the originalist gives credence to the Progressive critique of the founding generation, that is, that the framers were reactionaries who were acting against the democratic excesses unleashed after the Revolutionary War and whose conservative principles were embedded in the Constitution. These conservative principles included a republican form of government, which recognizes that the ultimate source of authority resides with the people but which discourages people from actively participating in the affairs of government, and an infinitely complex structural system—bicameralism, separation of powers, federalism, and staggered terms—which places a premium on deliberation, compromise, and moderate decision making. For the originalist, the values of the framers and the structure of the U.S. political system are what is most sacrosanct and in need of preserving in this country.

It should be noted that not all originalists are alike. Because of their support of the common man or states' rights, some originalists, such as former Supreme Court justice Hugo Black, Chief Justice Rehnquist, and Justice Thomas, reveal a Jeffersonian streak.[28] Others, such as the late legal historian Raoul Berger and Judge Robert Bork, demonstrate more of a Madisonian influence because of their emphasis on the political process and a more balanced approach to separation of powers and federal-state relations.[29] Still others, including political scientists Harvey Mansfield and Walter Berns, Seventh Circuit Court of Appeals Judge Frank Easterbrook, and Justice Scalia, are Hamiltonians, because of their support of national power and a strong executive.[30]

## SCALIA'S CONSERVATIVE JURISPRUDENCE

If we were to examine Justice Scalia's political views purely from a policy perspective, there would be little difficulty concluding that he is a conservative. He has been a staunch opponent of affirmative action, abortion rights, the right to die, and homosexual rights. At the same time, he has strongly favored a more pervasive role for religion in society, capital punishment, regulations of libel and obscenity, deregulation of private industry, and property rights. But when we move from the realm of policy into the area of political philosophy, his classification becomes less clear. Although some have questioned the relevance of Edmund Burke's political philosophy to modern conservatism[31] and, more fundamentally, its distinctiveness as a branch of philosophical inquiry,[32] it is clear that Burke still has a significant influence on modern political and legal thought.[33] Justice Scalia and Edmund Burke, however, are fundamentally different thinkers. They not only exhibit different temperaments, but they differ over such basic issues as the importance of theory to politics, the possibility of founding political regimes, the respect owed to precedent, and the desirability of change in a political regime. The true Burkeans on the Supreme Court have been the moderate traditional conservatives. At least since John Marshall Harlan II, there has been a conservative on the Supreme Court who has used a common law approach to interpreting the Constitution and who has exhibited the sense of moderation, balance, and humility that was a central characteristic of Burke's thought.

Justice Scalia, by contrast, is a classical liberal—a classical liberal in the tradition of Thomas Hobbes, David Hume, John Locke, Charles de Secondat Montesquieu, and Niccolo Machiavelli. His realistic view of human nature is similar to Hobbes's and Hume's;[34] he would agree with Locke that government is based on consent and has the primary responsibility of securing rights;[35] he is an enthusiastic disciple of Montesquieu, who, prior to James Madison, provided the most comprehensive treatment of the doctrine of separation of powers;[36] and he would agree with Machiavelli that executive power is absolutely crucial to the stability of republican government.[37] But what is equally clear is that Justice Scalia is a Hamiltonian.

## HAMILTONIAN POLITICAL PRINCIPLES

Alexander Hamilton, like Burke, was a man of action rather than a speculative philosopher, but he was much more receptive of "political science" and of its utility in the formation of political regimes than Burke was. Hamilton believed that government could be established based on "reflection and choice" and not simply be the consequence of "accident and force."[38] In *Federalist* 9, he confidently claimed that "the science of politics . . . has received great improvement. The efficacy of various principles is now well understood, which were either not known at all, or imperfectly known to the ancients" (FP, 119). Many political philosophers influenced Hamilton's view of politics, but none more so than David Hume. From Hume, Hamilton learned "[t]hat politics may be reduced to a science."[39] He also learned from Hume that the policies and institutions of a political regime must conform to a clear understanding of human nature.[40] Of all the framers, Hamilton had perhaps the darkest view of human nature. In *Federalist* 6, he told his readers that men are "ambitious, vindictive, and rapacious" (FP, 104). Human nature was at its worst, Hamilton believed, in popular assemblies, where "[r]egard to reputation has a less active influence" on the actions of men and where there is a tendency for mob rule (FP No. 15). "The ancient democracies, in which the people themselves deliberated," Hamilton wrote, "never possessed one feature of good government."[41] While Hamilton did not always speak so dismally about the human condition, his view was a sober realism:

> The true politician . . . takes human nature . . . as he finds it, a compound of good and ill qualities of good and ill tendencies—endued with powers and actuated by passions and propensities which blend enjoyment with suffering and make the causes of welfare the cause of misfortune.
>
> With this view of human nature he will not attempt to warp or distort its natural direction—he will not attempt to promote its happiness by means to which it is not suited . . . ; but he will . . . favour all those institutions and plans which tend to make men happy according to their natural bent.[42]

Hamilton's generally dark understanding of human nature did contain an important exception, however. He believed that "a few choice spirits" could rise above their own self-interest and make decisions on behalf of the people. "The supposition of universal venality in human nature is little less an error in political reasoning than the supposition of universal rectitude," reasoned Hamilton. "The institution of delegated power implies that there is a portion of virtue and honor among mankind which may be a reasonable foundation of confidence" (FP No. 76). Harking back to a classical idea of honor, Hamilton regarded the "love of fame" as "the ruling passion of the noblest minds," and that which provides the greatest stimulus for "arduous enterprises for the public benefit" (FP No. 72). Hamilton was thus the founding generation's chief defender of an aristocracy built upon republican principles.

In terms of an ideal form of government, Hamilton supported a limited elective monarchy. At the Constitutional Convention, he praised the British government as "the best in the world," because it was "the only Govt. . . . 'which combines public strength with individual security.'"[43] But Hamilton was a realist and fully realized that the American people would not tolerate any system of government based on monarchical principles. Since the American people would only accept a republican system of government, he sought "to go as far in order to attain stability and permanency, as republican princi-ples will admit."[44] Of all the delegates assembled at Philadelphia in 1787, Hamilton's plan of government was the most nationalistic. He boldly pro-posed that the president and U.S. senators be elected for life, and that the "Governor . . . of each state . . . *be appointed by the general government*" who would then have "a *negative* [veto] upon the laws about to be passed in the state."[45] Some have suggested that this was a tactical strategy by Hamilton to make the Virginia Plan seem more palatable,[46] which, of course, is quite plau-sible. But Hamilton's plan of government is also consistent with a central component of his constitutional system: a unitary administration. Unlike Thomas Jefferson, who wanted the national government to promote an agrar-ian economic system, Hamilton wanted the United States to become a vibrant and diversified commercial republic. In order to achieve this goal, he made the case for a strong executive. In framing a system of government, Hamilton claimed there must be two objects:

> Safety for the people, and energy in the administration. When these two objects are united, the certain tendency of the system will be to the public welfare. If the latter object be neglected, the people's security will be as certainly sacrificed, as by disregarding the former. Good constitutions are formed upon a comparison of the liberty of the individual with the strength of government: If the tone of ei-ther be too high, the other will be weakened too much.[47]

In contrast to Jefferson, who was distrustful of national power and sought to place limits on the authority of national officials, Hamilton encouraged the people to place confidence in their national leaders. In order for these officials to perform their "numerous, extensive and important" functions,[48] Hamilton argued that they should be afforded ample discretion. To those who com-plained that the national government was given too much power, Hamilton ar-gued that once a system of separation of powers is put into place, the people ought to be willing to give power. In a speech delivered at the New York Rat-ifying Convention in June 1788, Hamilton stated, "When you have divided and nicely balanced the departments of government; when you have strongly connected the virtue of your rulers with their interest; when, in short, you have rendered your system as perfect as human forms can be; you must place con-fidence; you must give power."[49] And none of the framers spoke as favorably about power as Hamilton: "It might be said that too little power is as danger-ous as too much, that it leads to anarchy, and from anarchy to despotism. . . . Powers must be granted, or civil Society cannot exist; the possibility of abuse is no argument against the *thing*; this possibility is incident to every species of power however placed or modified."[50] In sum, Hamilton's unique contribu-tion to the science of politics consisted of: (1) a proper arrangement of power into distinct departments, where the two weaker branches of government (the executive and judiciary) would be able to protect themselves from encroachment by Congress, and where the executive branch would have the capacity to act independently and with authority; (2) an "energetic" executive that, through a broad construction of Article II, has substantial implied and inherent authority, and which is the nation's "sole organ" in foreign affairs; (3) a theory of administration that views agency action as a matter of politics, not science, and which is distinguishable by its emphasis on unity, discretion, and policy making; (4) a strong and independent national judiciary, which has the fortitude to place checks on the republic's most powerful branch, the Congress, as well as on the "dangerous innovations" by the people themselves, but which is still regarded as the least dangerous branch of government; and (5) a federal system in which the national government is unquestionably supreme and where the states are primarily protected by the political process and the structural provisions of the Constitution, such as the original method of selecting U.S. senators by state legislatures.

## SCALIA'S HAMILTONIAN PRINCIPLES

Justice Scalia has conspicuously aligned himself with Hamilton on each of these political principles. In contrast to modern-day libertarians, Scalia has a rather positive view of governmental power. At a 1982 conference on federalism, Scalia challenged conservatives to reexamine what he regarded as their hostile view toward national power. At a time when the presidency and Senate were controlled by Republicans, Scalia maintained that a "do nothing" approach toward national policy making was "self-defeating" for purposes of achieving conservative policy goals. In order to place limits on novel state court created theories of liability, and to restrict state and city laws that impose rent controls, building codes, and penalties on businesses for creating monopolies, Scalia argued that *positive* legislation by the federal government was required. Scalia urged the members of the audience—"as Hamilton would have urged you—to keep in mind that the federal government is not bad but good. The trick is to use it wisely."[51] In a speech delivered in 1988 titled "Reflections on the Constitution," Scalia again embraced a favorable view of national power when he paraphrased Hamilton on the subject of authority: "It's not a good argument against the existence of power that it can be abused; every power can be abused. The question is how it will be used or exercised."[52] As a judge, Scalia has coupled his optimistic view of governmental power with a defense of the aforementioned Hamiltonian political principles, that is, a formalistic view of separation of powers, an energetic executive, a "political" conception of public administration, a strong and independent federal judiciary, and a political process approach toward federalism.[53] The basic purpose of this book is to demonstrate how Scalia's jurisprudence is guided by these Hamiltonian political principles.

Most of the chapters of this book begin with an analysis of Hamilton's views regarding one of the aforementioned political principles and then turn to Scalia's judicial opinions and scholarly writings to assess how they can be seen to follow these principles. Chapter 1 is an anomaly in that it provides a biographical sketch of Scalia, examining the various academic and governmental positions he has held en route to the Supreme Court. We shall see that Scalia's pro-executivist views were developed during his five and a half years of government service in the Nixon and Ford administrations, which were then reflected in his D.C. Court of Appeals opinions where his colleagues teased him for being a "new monarchist."[54]

Chapters 2 and 3 examine Hamilton's and Scalia's views in the area of separation of powers. Hamilton defended a formalistic interpretation of separation of powers as a way of protecting executive and judicial power, and Scalia has been the Court's consistent (and arguably only) formalist when it comes to interpreting that doctrine. Chapter 2 discusses Scalia's views in the area of legal standing, a constitutional and prudential doctrine that examines whether the parties to a case have the requisite personal stake in a controversy to adjudicate it in federal court. Chapter 3 examines classic interbranch disputes between Congress and the president. Scalia is acutely aware that a formalistic interpretation of separation of powers benefits executive power, and has not been hesitant in voting to strike down federal laws that he believes threaten executive authority.

Chapters 4 and 5 examine Hamilton's and Scalia's views regarding executive power. Pervading all of Hamilton's writings on the executive branch was the need for energy. "Energy in the executive," he wrote in *Federalist* 70, "is a leading character in the definition of good government."[55] Hamilton believed that an energetic executive was essential when the nation was faced with a foreign or domestic threat, but he also regarded it as important for an effective administration of the nation's laws. While Hamilton's contributions to the modern theory of executive power were many, two themes are emphasized in these chapters: Hamilton's defense of presidential inherent powers and his distinct theory of public administration. Justice Scalia's interpretation of executive power most conspicuously identifies him as a Hamiltonian. Like Hamilton, he has defined executive power as including everything that is not expressly forbidden by the Constitution and which would not be patently incompatible with republican principles.[56] In keeping with this view, he has defended various inherent powers of the president, including a broad discretionary authority in the area of foreign affairs, the authority of the executive branch to enter into executive agreements without senatorial approval, executive privilege, and presidential immunity from certain forms of judicial process. A former administrative law professor, Justice Scalia has also defended a theory of public administration strikingly similar to Hamilton's, that is, a theory of administration based on the concepts of unity, discretion, and policy making.

Chapters 6 and 7 examine Hamilton's and Scalia's attitudes about judicial power. Hamilton regarded the judicial branch as by far the "weakest" of the three departments of government. As he put it in *Federalist* 78, having "neither FORCE nor WILL but merely judgment," the judiciary presented the least danger to the basic liberties of the people.[57] But Hamilton did not regard the judiciary's role in the U.S. republic as insignificant. If properly constituted, he believed that the judiciary would have a conservative influence on republican government by checking against congressional usurpations of power and popular forms of democracy. At the same time, Hamilton regarded judges as interpreters of law, not policy makers. The judiciary can be regarded as the least dangerous branch of government if its authority does not encroach upon the prerogatives of the other branches of government. Hamilton thus proposed certain rules of construction to "avoid an arbitrary discretion in the courts."[58] The true test of a just interpretation, he maintained, was the "natural and obvious" sense of a provision.[59]

Justice Scalia has defended a similar conservative role for the federal judiciary. He is acutely aware of the antidemocratic role played by federal courts in the U.S. system of government and unabashedly tells audiences, "My most important job as a judge is to say no to the people."[60] In following this view, Scalia has not been reluctant to strike down federal or state laws that he believes conflict with the text or structure of the Constitution. By the same token, Scalia (like Hamilton) regards judges as interpreters of law, not policy makers, and has employed the same commonsense rule of construction that Hamilton proposed in *The Federalist*: the "natural and obvious" meaning of words. In statutory cases, he has rejected intentionalist and purposive approaches to construing statutes, and has instead defended a "plain meaning" or textualist approach. In constitutional cases, he has refused to rely upon the Declaration of Independence and international law as sources of constitutional interpretation, and has instead defended the "original meaning" of the Constitution's provisions. It is clear that Scalia believes that Hamilton's warning about an imperial judiciary has come true. "[E]very era raises its own peculiar threat to constitutional democracy," Scalia has written, and judicial activism "represents the distinctive threat of our times."[61] In contrast to Hamilton, who was trying to shore up the authority of the federal judiciary at the time of the nation's founding, Scalia is trying to limit its authority to what he believes is its traditional role in republican government.

Hamilton's and Scalia's views in the area of federalism are examined in chapters 8 and 9. Hamilton was the founding generation's most committed nationalist, who deeply distrusted state power. As a lieutenant colonel in the Continental Army, Hamilton experienced firsthand the weaknesses of the Congress established under the Articles of Confederation, and, as a result of this experience, sought to bolster national authority under the new Constitution. At the Constitutional Convention, Hamilton questioned whether two sovereignties could coexist in the new republic and argued that in order to preserve itself, the national government "must swallow up the State powers."[62] Hamilton would later modify his views in this area, but he never wavered from a strictly utilitarian view of the states. Hamilton's basic position regarding federal-state relations was that because the state governments were closer to the people, they had a distinct advantage over the federal government in attracting their affection. What he sought to do was to divert some of this affection toward the national government by demonstrating how important national power was to the people's safety and welfare. While Hamilton ultimately believed that the states had their own sphere of authority, he regarded questions about the proper division of power between the federal and state governments as a matter of convenience to be decided by Congress, and not a legal issue to be decided by the courts. Hamilton's unique contribution to the framers' science of federalism included (1) an advocacy of a broad construction of the national government's powers; (2) an early formulation of what today is called the "political process" approach to federalism disputes; and (3) the use of the federal government to achieve national policy goals.

Justice Scalia has aligned himself with Hamilton on each of these points. In court opinions and extrajudicial comments, Scalia has supported a broad construction of the national government's powers. He has, for example, supported Hamilton's construction of the Necessary and Proper Clause, the general welfare provision, and the broad grants of authority conferred on the president under Article II. Scalia has also supported the political process approach to resolving federalism disputes and has maintained a favorable view of the use of national power to achieve conservative policy goals, which is reflected in his preemption decisions. Remarkably, since taking his seat on the Supreme Court in 1986, Scalia ranks *first* among his colleagues in voting in favor of the federal government in preemption cases.

In the 1990s, however, Justice Scalia moved in the direction of a more balanced Madisonian approach to federalism issues, to the extent that he now claims that "it was Madison's—not Hamilton's—[view] that prevailed" on the subject.[63] Even though this transformation by Scalia detracts somewhat from the thesis of this book, the evidence still shows that Scalia is a nationalist. Scalia's Hamiltonian instincts were dramatically displayed in the 2005 decision *Gonzales v. Raich*,[64] where he broke with his conservative states' rights colleagues and supported federal power to prohibit the homegrown medicinal use of marijuana. Moreover, Scalia's preemption decisions still indicate an acute awareness that the instruments of national power can be used for conservative purposes. Scalia's conscious movement toward a more moderate Madisonian position in the area of federalism can be seen as strategic. In the early 1990s, when the Court was closely divided over the issue of federalism, Scalia moved in the direction of Madison in order to be a major player in federalism disputes. Now he can choose when to support national power or not. In those cases in which the objectives of the federal government are not necessary or defensible, Scalia will likely join his states' rights colleagues, but in those instances when national power can be used for conservative purposes, he will likely be an important ally for his liberal nationalist-leaning colleagues.

This book concludes by considering the shared temperaments of Hamilton and Scalia. If there is one thing that casts a shadow of doubt over the conservative credentials of these two men, it is their temperaments. For traditional conservatives, if there is any doubt about a certain course of action, the best thing to do is to exercise caution. Alexander Hamilton and Justice Scalia are anything but cautious, however. As a young Revolutionary War officer, Hamilton indicated his penchant for a bold and decisive style of leadership by approvingly quoting from Demosthenes' orations in his military pay book:

> As a general marches at the head of his troops, so ought wise politicians, if I dare use the expression, to march at the head of affairs; insomuch that they ought not to wait the *event*, to know what measures to take; but the measures which they have taken, ought to produce the *event*.[65]

This is a view of leadership that Justice Scalia undoubtedly agrees with. By all accounts, he is a "take charge kind of guy,"[66] who once said that the measure of a great leader is not "in predicting where the men he is leading want to go."[67] In fact, Scalia has been exercising a type of bold statesmanship on the Supreme Court, which is evident in two broad areas of his jurisprudence. First, his *choice* of originalism ("the lesser of two evils") as a method of constitutional interpretation has seen him call for the overturning of more court precedents than any other Supreme Court justice, except Hugo Lafayette Black and Clarence Thomas.[68] Second, his advocacy of a rule-based approach to judicial decision making has called into question the common law approach of deciding cases by attempting to limit the amount of discretion judges have in rendering their opinions.[69] If Hamilton and Scalia can be considered conservative, and of course they can be, it is because their political or judicial programs are designed to bring about conservative ends. For Hamilton, his governmental and financial plans were designed to preserve and stabilize the young American republic. For Justice Scalia, his judicial philosophy—textualism and a rule-based approach to deciding cases—is designed to return the country to a jurisprudence of original principles.

  This book has two basic goals. First, by examining the congruence in thought between Hamilton and Scalia, it is hoped that a better and deeper understanding of Scalia's jurisprudence can be achieved. While an abundance of scholarship has been written on Scalia, no one has systematically examined his political philosophy. In the tradition of Justices Hugo Black and Felix Frankfurter, Scalia is both a participant in and theorizer about the great and enduring debate over the proper role of courts in a democratic system of government. The central paradox of Scalia's jurisprudence, which in many respects shares the same restraintist concerns of Felix Frankfurter, is that in terms of methodology he has more in common with Hugo Black.

  The second major goal of this book is that by examining Justice Scalia's political thought, it is hoped that some of the important differences between his jurisprudence and that of his colleagues on the Court (liberal or conservative) will be illuminated. In the last two decades, the conservatives have been able to establish a stronghold on the federal judiciary and, in particular, the Supreme Court, which makes an analysis along these lines both timely and important. What goes completely unnoticed in the public law literature, for example, is that for a period of twenty years, we had two first-rate *political* theorists sitting on the Supreme Court: Justice O'Connor, who represented the Burkean school of conservative thought, and Justice Scalia, who represents the Hamiltonian school. Moreover, jurisprudential differences that at one time seemed latent between the Court's two most conservative members—Antonin Scalia and Clarence Thomas—have now begun to appear. During his first few years on the Court, Thomas (perhaps unfairly) was referred to as a "clone" or "puppet" of Scalia's. It is now clear, however, that there are important philosophical differences between these two justices. For example, the two have reached different conclusions in their originalist interpretation of particular provisions of the Constitution;[70] they have different views of the commerce[71] and general welfare[72] provisions; and, substantiating speculation about his natural law leanings during his confirmation hearings, Thomas has been more willing than Scalia to rely on natural law arguments in his opinions.[73]

  Finally, an examination of Scalia's views in the area of administrative law points to important differences between his understanding of the administrative process and Justice Stephen G. Breyer's—the other former administrative-law professor on the Court. While both Scalia and Breyer are skeptical of "hard-look" scrutiny when it comes to judicial review of administrative substantive decisions, it is safe to say that Breyer has been less so.[74] Moreover, in cases involving agency constructions of law, Breyer has been more willing to use legislative history to interpret statutes and has been more deferential to administrative constructions of law.[75] In short, while Scalia's views of the administrative process appear to be influenced by a Hamiltonian conception of public administration, Breyer's views of the administrative process show clear signs of a Progressive influence.[76]

If the thesis of this book is correct—that is, that Scalia's jurisprudence is guided by Hamiltonian political principles—then Scalia is not the neutral robot he sometimes portrays himself as. In his concurring opinion in *Tome v. United States*,[77] Scalia observed that he did not regard Hamilton's views as any more authoritative than Jefferson's with regard to the meaning of the Constitution. If the evidence of this book demonstrates otherwise, Scalia's remark in *Tome* must be taken with a grain of salt. Except for his vote in *U.S. Term Limits, Inc. v. Thornton*, which unquestionably supported a Jeffersonian states' rights philosophy, but which can also be explained on other grounds (see chapter 9), Scalia's jurisprudence in no way resembles the political principles of the Sage from Monticello. In contrast to Jefferson, Scalia has a strong distrust of popular democracy and is less enamored with states' rights; he believes that the Tenth Amendment is a constitutional redundancy that does not restrict federal power; and he believes in a strong executive with numerous implied and inherent powers. Moreover, except in the area of federalism, where arguably Scalia has strategically moved from a Hamiltonian to a Madisonian, Scalia's jurisprudence does not resemble a Madisonian philosophy either. Scalia's formalism in separation of powers cases conflicts with a Madisonian functionalist approach; Scalia has rejected Madison's construction of the General Welfare and the Necessary and Proper Clauses; and Scalia's broad construction of executive power sides with Hamilton, not Madison, in the famous debate between "Pacificus" and "Helvidius" over the scope of executive power. While Scalia has exhibited a principled jurisprudence in some areas of the law—that is, he has decided some cases in a way that goes against his own personal views—his jurisprudence is animated by a larger political philosophy and purpose. And a judge who follows a Hamiltonian political philosophy is not devoid of exercising discretion. It is true that Scalia is not expanding individual rights into new frontiers, but he is expanding executive and congressional power in important ways. For example, Scalia is quite willing to expansively interpret common law privileges and immunities for executive officials under Article II, and he has broadly interpreted the Court's implied preemption doctrine. Because these decisions are based on judge-made common law, they do not appear in principle to be any different from a judge expansively interpreting individual rights under the Court's substantive due process doctrine. The only difference, it would seem, is in the liberal or conservative orientation of the judge. All of this only goes to show that Justice Benjamin N. Cardozo was right: "We may try to see things as objectively as we please. None the less, we can never see them with eyes except our own."[78]

## NOTES

1. See, e.g., Alexander Bickel, *The Morality of Consent* (New Haven, CT: Yale University Press, 1975); Bruce Ackerman, "The Common Law Constitution of John Marshall Harlan," *New York Law School Law Review* 36 (1991): 5–32; Lewis F. Powell, "Stare Decisis and Judicial Restraint," *Washington and Lee Law Review* 47 (1990): 281–90; Sandra Day O'Connor, "The Judiciary Act of 1789 and the American Judicial Tradition," *University of Cincinnati Law Review* 59 (1990): 1–13 (criticizing the French Revolution for relying upon abstract reason and describing the American Revolution as "conservative" in nature).

2. The *Lochner* era, dating from approximately 1897 to 1937, was a period when conservative members of the Supreme Court read into the Fifth and Fourteenth Amendments' Due Process Clauses a "liberty of contract" doctrine, and, in the process, struck down nearly two hundred social and economic regulations. The era is named after the most important case of the period, *Lochner v. New York*, 198 U.S. 45 (1905), where the Supreme Court struck down a New York law regulating the number of hours employees could work in bakeries.

3. See, e.g., Richard A. Posner, *Law, Pragmatism, and Democracy* (Cambridge, MA: Harvard University Press, 2003); and *Overcoming Law* (Cambridge, MA: Harvard University Press, 1995).

4. 347 U.S. 483 (1954).

5. Herbert Wechsler, "Toward Neutral Principles of Constitutional Law," *Harvard Law Review*, 1959, 1–35.

6. The casebook for this course was published posthumously. See Henry M. Hart Jr. and Albert M. Sacks, *The Legal Process: Basic Problems in the Making and Application of Law*, ed. William N. Eskridge Jr. and Philip P. Frickey (Westbury, NY: Foundation Press, 1994).

7. *Planned Parenthood of Southeastern Pennsylvania v. Casey*, 505 U.S. 833 (1992) (Kennedy, J., plurality opinion) (describing the Constitution as "a covenant running from the first generation of Americans to us and then to future generations").

8. Francis Canavan, *The Political Reason of Edmund Burke* (Durham, NC: Duke University Press, 1960).

9. See, e.g., *Planned Parenthood of Southeastern Pennsylvania v. Casey*, 505 U.S. 833 (1992) (abortion); *Bd. of County Comm'rs v. Umbehr*, 518 U.S. 668 (1996) and *O'Hare Truck Service Inc. v. City of Northlake*, 518 U.S. 712 (1996) (political

patronage). See also *Roper v. Simmons*, 125 S. Ct. 1183 (2005) (capital punishment for minors).

10. See, e.g., *Lawrence v. Texas*, 539 U.S. 558 (2003) (striking down same-sex sodomy laws); *Roper v. Simmons*, 125 S. Ct. 1183 (2005) (overturning capital punishment statutes for minors).

11. Stephen Macedo, *The New Right v. the Constitution* (Washington, DC: Cato Institute, 1987); Randy E. Barnett, *Restoring the Lost Constitution: The Presumption of Liberty* (Princeton, NJ: Princeton University Press, 2004).

12. Bernard H. Siegan, *Economic Liberties and the Constitution* (Chicago: University of Chicago Press, 1980).

13. Richard A. Epstein, *Takings: Private Property and the Power of Eminent Domain* (Cambridge, MA: Harvard University Press, 1985).

14. *Kelo v. City of New London*, 125 S. Ct. 2655 (2005) (Thomas, J., dissenting) (arguing for a narrow interpretation of the Public Use Clause of the Eminent Domain Provision); Douglas H. Ginsburg, "On Constitutionalism," *Cato Supreme Court Review* (2003) 7–20; Alex Kozinski, "Forward: The Judiciary and the Constitution," in Economic Liberties and the Judiciary, eds., James A. Dorn and Henry G. Manne (Fairfax, Virginia: George Mason University Press, 1987).

15. *44 Liquormart, Inc. v. Rhode Island*, 517 U.S. 484 (1996) (Thomas, J., concurring) (arguing that commercial speech should not be treated differently from political speech); *Printz v. United States*, 521 U.S. 898 (Thomas, J., concurring) (suggesting that the Brady Bill may violate the Second Amendment); Alex Kozinski and Stuart Banner, "Who's Afraid of Commercial Speech," *Virginia Law Review* 76 (1990): 627; *Silveira v. Lockyer*, 320 F.3d 567 (9th Cir. 2003) (Kozinski, J., dissenting from denial of rehearsing en banc) (expressing views on the Second Amendment).

16. *Lawrence v. Texas*, 539 U.S. 558 (2003) (Thomas, J., dissenting) (stating that the state's same-sex sodomy law was "uncommonly silly" and that he would have voted against the law if he had been a member of the Texas legislature); *Gonzales v. Raich*, 125 S. Ct. 2195 (2005) (Thomas, J., dissenting) (criticizing the majority for preventing "States like California from devising drug policies that they have concluded provide much-needed respite to the seriously ill").

17. *United States v. Lopez*, 514 U.S. 549 (1995) (Thomas, J., concurring).

18. Thus, although Thomas says that same-sex sodomy laws are "uncommonly silly," he believes that states can regulate the practice. Similarly, although Thomas believes that states can permit abortions, he does not support a woman's right to choose under the Constitution. *Stenberg v. Carhart*, 530 U.S. 914 (2000) (Thomas, J., dissenting).

19. Dworkin opposes affirmative action but supports abortion rights, the right to die, and homosexual rights. See, e.g., Ronald Dworkin, *Freedom's Law: The Moral Reading of the American Constitution* (Cambridge, MA: Harvard University Press, 1996).

20. Harry V. Jaffa, *Storm over the Constitution* (Lanham, MD: Lexington Books, 1999); *Adarand Constructors, Inc. v. Pena*, 515 U.S. 200 (1995) (Thomas, J., concurring) (arguing that affirmative action programs run afoul of the concept of human dignity embedded in the Declaration of Independence).

21. Hadley Arkes, *Beyond the Constitution* (Princeton, NJ: Princeton University Press, 1990); see also Hadley Arkes, *Natural Rights and the Right to Choose* (Cambridge, UK: Cambridge University Press, 2002).

22. 521 U.S. 507 (1997).

23. John T. Noonan Jr., *The Lustre of Our Country: The American Experience of Religious Freedom* (Berkeley and Los Angeles, CA: University of California Press, 1998), 8, 181–210; Russell Hittinger, *The First Grace: Rediscovering the Natural Law in a Post-Christian World* (Wilmington, DE: ISI Books, 2003), 210–13. See also Noonan, *Narrowing the Nation's Power: The Supreme Court Sides with the States* (Berkeley and Los Angeles, CA: University of California Press, 2002).

24. Justice Thomas is an interesting combination of libertarian conservative and natural law conservative. His libertarianism is reflected in his understanding of property rights, the Second Amendment, commercial speech, the Commerce Clause, and his permissive statements regarding state regulation of abortion, same-sex sodomy, and the medicinal use of marijuana. Meanwhile, his natural law conservatism is seen in his invocation of the Declaration of Independence in affirmative action cases and his support of parental rights regarding the upbringing of their children, even though he rejects a general right of privacy under the Constitution. *Troxel v. Granville*, 530 U.S. 57 (2000) (Thomas, J., concurring in judgment). In short, Thomas is closest to the natural law conservatives when he contends the Constitution should be interpreted in light of the Declaration of Independence, but he has distanced himself from some of these thinkers by not supporting a narrow interpretation of the Free Exercise Clause, and by his tolerant statements regarding abortion, same-sex sodomy, and the medicinal use of marijuana. See Clarence Thomas, "The Higher Law Background of the Privileges or Immunities Clause of the Fourteenth Amendment," *Harvard Journal of Law & Public Policy* 12 (Winter 1989): 63–68.

25. Edwin Meese III, "Toward a Jurisprudence of Original Intention," *Benchmark* 2, no. 1 (1985): 1–10.

26. John Austin, *The Province of Jurisprudence Determined*, ed. Wilfred E. Rumble (Cambridge, UK, and New York: Cambridge University Press, 1995), 157.

27. Ibid., 21.

28. Mark Silverstein, *Constitutional Faiths: Felix Frankfurter, Hugo Black, and the Process of Judicial Decision Making* (Ithaca, NY: Cornell University Press, 1984); H. Jefferson Powell, "The Compleat Jeffersonian: Justice Rehnquist and Federalism," *Yale Law Journal* 91 (1982): 1317–70; *U.S. Term Limits Inc. v. Thornton*, 514 U.S. 779 (1995) (Thomas J., concurring); *United States v. Lopez*, 514 U.S. 549 (1995) (Thomas, J., concurring).

29. Raoul Berger, *Federalism: The Founders' Design* (Norman, OK: University of Oklahoma Press, 1987); Robert Bork, *The Tempting of America: The Political Seduction of the Law* (New York: Free Press, 1990).

30. Harvey C. Mansfield Jr., *Taming the Prince: The Ambivalence of Modern Executive Power* (New York: Free Press, 1989); Walter Berns, "The Meaning of the Tenth Amendment," in *A Nation of States: Essays on the American Federal System*, ed. Robert A. Goldwin (Chicago: Henry Regnery, 1963); Frank H. Easterbrook, "Presidential Review," *Case Western Reserve Law Review* 40 (1989–1990):

905–29; and "Unitary Executive Interpretation: A Comment," *Cardozo Law Review* 15 (1993): 313–21.

31. See, e.g., Mansfield, "Edmund Burke," in *History of Political Philosophy*, ed. Leo Strauss and Joseph Cropsey, 3rd ed. (Chicago: University of Chicago Press, 1987), 688–89.

32. Many have argued that Burke was simply a "conservative liberal." See, e.g., Dante Germino, *Machiavelli to Marx: Modern Western Political Thought* (Chicago: University of Chicago Press, 1972), 219. Nevertheless, there were important differences between Burke and Locke. In particular, Burke was much less sanguine than Locke about a system of politics based on choice and reason.

33. See, e.g., Russell Kirk, *The Conservative Mind: From Burke to Santayana* (Chicago: Henry Regnery Company, 1953); Alexander Bickel, *The Morality of Consent*.

34. See, e.g., Antonin Scalia, "The Limits of the Law," *New Jersey Law Journal* 119 (1987): 4–5, 22–23 ("As Madison observed in No. 51 of the *Federalist*: 'What is government itself but the greatest of all reflections on human nature? If men were angels, no government would be necessary'").

35. See Antonin Scalia, "The Two Faces of Federalism," *Harvard Journal of Law and Public Policy* 6 (1982): 19–22 ("The individual possesses, as the Declaration of Independence points out, a God-given freedom, which rightly counsel an attitude of suspicion if not hostility towards novel impositions of governmental constraint").

36. See, e.g., *Morrison v. Olson*, 487 U.S. 654 (1988) (Scalia, J., dissenting) ("It is the proud boast of our democracy that we have 'a government of laws and not of men.' . . . Without a secure structure of separated powers, our Bill of Rights would be worthless, as are the bill of rights of many nations of the world that have adopted, or even improved upon, the mere words of ours").

37. Ibid., (arguing that the special prosecutor provision of the Ethics in Government Act of 1978 will enfeeble the executive and greatly harm the republic).

38. FP (No. 1), 87.

39. David Hume, *Essays: Moral, Political, Literary*, ed. Eugene F. Miller (Indianapolis, IN: Liberty Press, 1987), 14–31.

40. In "The Farmer Refuted," Hamilton cited "a celebrated author" (i.e., David Hume) who has "established it as a maxim, that, in contriving any system of government, and fixing the several checks and controuls of the constitution, *every man* ought to be supposed a *knave*; and to have no other end in all his actions, but *private interest*." PAH, 1:94–95.

41. "New York Ratifying Convention, First Speech of June 21" (June 21, 1788), PAH, 5:39.

42. "Defence of the Funding System" (July 1795), PAH, 19:59–60.

43. PAH, 4:192. See also "The Farmer Refuted," where Hamilton referred to himself as "a warm advocate for limited monarchy." PAH, 1:164.

44. PAH, 4:193.

45. Ibid., 209.

46. Herbert J. Storing, *Toward a More Perfect Union: Writings of Herbert J. Storing*, ed. Joseph M. Bessette (Washington, DC: American Enterprise Institute, 1995), 25–26; Paul Eidelberg, *The Philosophy of the American Constitution: A Reinterpretation of the Intentions of the Founding Fathers* (New York: Free Press, 1968), 109.

47. "New York Ratifying Convention, First Speech of June 25" (June 25, 1788), PAH, 5:81.

48. "New York Ratifying Convention, Remarks" (June 27, 1788), PAH, 5:97.

49. Ibid., 95.

50. "New York Assembly, First Speech on the Address of the Legislature to Governor George Clinton's Message" (January 19, 1787), PAH, 4:11.

51. Scalia, "The Two Faces of Federalism," 19–22.

52. Antonin Scalia, "Reflections on the Constitution," Speech to the Kennedy Political Union at American University. C-SPAN broadcast, November 17, 1988.

53. According to the political process approach to federalism, the framers of the Constitution protected state sovereignty through the structure of the national government rather than through judicially enforceable limits on the scope of national power.

54. W. John Moore, "Tugging from the Right," *National Journal*, October 20, 1990, 1215.

55. FP (No. 70), 402.

56. Scalia, "Originalism: The Lesser Evil," *University of Cincinnati Law Review* 57 (1989): 849–65, 860.

57. FP, 437.

58. FP, 442.

59. FP, 463.

60. Remarks by Justice Antonin Scalia to Professor Henry J. Abraham's "Seminar in American Constitutional Law and Theory" class from the University of Virginia, Supreme Court Building, Washington, D.C., December 2, 1996.

61. "Economic Affairs as Human Affairs," in *Economic Liberties and the Judiciary*, ed. James A. Dorn and Henry G. Manne (Fairfax, VA: George Mason University Press, 1987), 34.

62. PAH, 4:191.

63. *Printz v. United States*, 521 U.S. 898, 915n9 (1997).

64. 125 S. Ct. 2195 (2005).

65. "Pay Book of the State Company of Artillery" (1777), PAH, 1:390.

66. See M. David Gelfand, "Justice Antonin Scalia," in *Eight Men and a Lady: Profiles of the Justices of the Supreme Court* (Bethesda, MD: National Press, Inc., 1990), 249.

67. See Scalia, "Originalism: The Lesser Evil," 849.

68. See Michael J. Gerhardt, "A Tale of Two Textualists: A Critical Comparison of Justices Black and Scalia," *Boston University Law Review* 74 (1994): 32–35.

69. Antonin Scalia, "The Rule of Law as a Law of Rules," *University of Chicago Law Review* 56 (1989): 1175–88; and *A Matter of Interpretation: Federal Courts and the Law*, ed. Amy Gutmann (Princeton, NJ: Princeton University Press, 1997).

70. See *Saentz v. Roe*, 526 U.S. 489 (1999); *McIntyre v. Ohio Elections Comm'n*, 514 U.S. 334 (1995).

71. See, e.g., *United States v. Lopez*, 514 U.S. 549, 584 (1995) (Thomas, J., concurring); *Printz v. United States*, 521 U.S. 898, 936 (1997) (Thomas, J., concurring). See also *Lopez v. Monterey County*, 525 U.S. 266 (1999) (Thomas, J., dissenting).

72. *Cedar Rapids Community School District v. Garret*, 526 U.S. 66 (1999) (Thomas, J., dissenting).

73. See, e.g., *Adarand Constructors, Inc. v. Pena*, 515 U.S. 200 (1995) (Thomas, J., concurring); *Troxel v. Granville*, 530 U.S. 57 (2000) (the two justices disagreed over whether there was a substantive due process right of parents to direct the upbringing of their children).

74. See Lisa Heinzerling, "Justice Breyer's Hard Look," *Administrative Law Journal* 8 (1995): 767.

75. See, e.g., Stephen Breyer, "On the Uses of Legislative History in Interpreting Statutes," *Southern California Law Review* 65 (1992): 845; Richard J. Pierce Jr., "Justice Breyer: Intentionalist, Pragmatist, and Empiricist," *Administrative Law Journal* 8 (1995): 747; Ernest Gellhorn, "Justice Breyer on Statutory Review and Interpretation," *Administrative Law Journal* 8 (1995): 755; Michael D. Sherman, "The Use of Legislative History: A Debate Between Justice Scalia and Justice Breyer," *Administrative Law News* 16 (Summer 1991): 1.

76. See, e.g., Stephen G. Breyer, *Active Liberty: Interpreting Our Democratic Constitution* (New York: Random House, 2005); Stephen G. Breyer, Richard B. Stewart, Cass R. Sunstein, and Matthew L. Spitzer, *Administrative Law and Regulatory Policy: Problems, Text, and Cases* (New York: Aspen Law & Business, 2002).

77. 513 U.S. 150 (1995).

78. Benjamin N. Cardozo, *The Nature of the Judicial Process* (New Haven, CT: Yale University Press, 1921), 13.

*Chapter One*

# Nothing Is Easy:
# The Road to the Supreme Court

Before examining the shared political principles of Alexander Hamilton and Antonin Scalia, a biographical sketch of Justice Scalia is provided, which will emphasize those background experiences and positions he has held that have influenced his jurisprudence, particularly his affection for executive power.

## GROWING UP "NINO"

Antonin Scalia—or "Nino" to his family and friends—was born March 11, 1936, in Trenton, New Jersey, a city rich in and proud of its Revolutionary War history. Scalia attended kindergarten at Trenton's Grant Elementary School, where his aunt Eva A. Panaro taught and played piano for the weekly songfest auditorium programs. At the age of five, Antonin moved to Queens, New York, where his father began a thirty-year teaching position at Brooklyn College. The Scalias resided in Elmhurst, Queens, in a predominantly Irish and Italian middle-class neighborhood. Antonin was the only child of S. Eugene Scalia and the former Catherine Panaro. Following Sicilian tradition, Antonin was named after his paternal grandfather, Antonio, a mechanic from Sicily. His father, whom Scalia recalls as "stern," migrated to New York from Italy when he was a teenager, and his mother, whom Scalia describes as "doting," was a first-generation Italian-American.[1] As a new immigrant and first-generation Italian-American couple, the Scalias stressed the importance of hard work and individual responsibility, values that are evident in many of their son's career positions. On his Supreme Court office wall, Scalia proudly displays a small-framed quotation that says, "Nothing is

1

easy." Scalia demands a lot from himself as well as from others. "He'd catch a mistake that we had made," observed former law clerk Paul Cassell, and remark: "[I]t's hard to get it right." In 1985, Scalia's law clerks at the D.C. Court of Appeals had this same saying inscribed on a plaque which they then gave to Scalia as a present.[2] Scalia's work ethic and self-made attitude have influenced his jurisprudential philosophy in at least one constitutional area: affirmative action. Scalia has been a consistently sharp critic of race- and gender-conscious affirmative action programs. Reflecting upon his own family heritage, Scalia wrote in a 1979 article published in the *Washington University Law Quarterly*:

> My father came to this country when he was a teenager. Not only had he never profited from the sweat of any black man's brow, I don't think he had ever seen a black man. There are, of course, many white ethnic groups that came to this country in great numbers relatively late in its history—Italians, Jews, Irish, Poles—who not only took no part in, and derived no profit from, the major historic suppression of the currently acknowledged minority groups, but were, in fact, themselves the object of discrimination by the dominant Anglo-Saxon majority.[3]

With two teachers as parents, and as an only child, Antonin grew up in an intellectually stimulating household. His father, an authority on Dante, taught Romance languages at Brooklyn College, and his mother was an elementary school teacher. As law professor George Kannar points out,[4] Scalia's literal (or textualist) approach to interpreting laws was undoubtedly influenced by his father, who translated Italian authors, including Giosue Carducci, the nineteenth-century Italian poet and Nobel Prize recipient for literature. In his translation of Carducci's poems, Eugene Scalia made the case for a "literal" translation of his subject's work as "one of the chief merits of a translation." Taking a rather humble view of the translator's craft, the elder Scalia wrote, "The most that a translation can hope to do . . . is to stimulate an interest" in the work being translated. "[I]t is only by direct communion with [the poet's] page that people can come to fully appreciate" what is unique about the work.[5] By contrast, Scalia's love of law and politics seems to have come from his mother's side of the family. Scalia's maternal grandfather, Pasquele Panaro, was a Trenton tailor who regularly attended local courthouse sessions to watch his lawyer-friend argue cases. And in 1958, one of Scalia's uncles, Vincent R. Panaro, became the first Democrat to be elected mayor of Ewing Township, a small community just outside of Trenton. Eugene Scalia regarded Vincent Panaro, who later served as a state assemblyman and Mercy County prosecutor, as a role model for his son.[6]

Not surprisingly, Antonin's education was in the classical tradition and included six years of Latin and five years of Greek. Both of his parents were devout Roman Catholics, which undoubtedly influenced young Nino's choice of schools. He attended the all-male St. Francis Xavier High School, a well-known Catholic military prep school in Manhattan, New York, where he tied for first in his class. Even in high school, Scalia's intellectual talents and conservative beliefs were easily detected. William Stern, a classmate at Xavier who later served as the campaign manager for Mario Cuomo's 1982 gubernatorial race in New York, remarked: "This kid was a conservative when he was 17 years old. An archconservative Catholic. He could have been a member of the Curia. He was a top student in the class. He was brilliant, way above everybody else."[7]

## GEORGETOWN, HARVARD, AND MAUREEN

After completing his secondary education at Xavier High School, Scalia attended another Jesuit institution, Georgetown University, where he received his A.B. summa cum laude in history in 1957 and was class valedictorian. During his junior year at Georgetown, Scalia studied abroad at the University of Fribourg in Switzerland. Scalia then attended Harvard Law School, where he received his LL.B. magna cum laude in 1960. At Harvard, Scalia served as note editor for the prestigious *Harvard Law Review*, and he took classes from such distinguished professors as Lon Fuller, Paul Freund, Louis Jaffe, and Albert Sacks.[8] One of the classes Scalia took was the popular Legal Process course, the casebook for which is credited with launching a new school of jurisprudence in the United States: the Legal Process School. While the course was usually team taught by Henry Hart and Albert Sacks, at the time of Scalia's enrollment, Professor Sacks taught the class alone. While Justice Scalia's jurisprudence is sometimes described as having been influenced by the Legal Process School,[9] there is little evidence of this. In fact, Scalia has been an acerbic critic of the "reasoned elaboration" decision-making approach associated with the Legal Process School,[10] and in judicial decisions and extrajudicial speeches, has drawn a sharp distinction between law and morality. "There are times," Scalia has written, "when even a bad rule is better than no rule at all," and he has admitted that he has "never been able to isolate obligations of justice, except by defining them as those obligations that the law imposes."[11] Moreover, as we shall see in chapters 5 and 7, Scalia has been equally critical of hard-look scrutiny in administrative-law cases and of the use of legislative history in statutory cases, both of which can be said to have their origins with Legal Process theorists.

While at Harvard, Scalia met and became engaged to Maureen McCarthy, an English major at Radcliffe College and the daughter of a Massachusetts physician. According to former solicitor general Rex E. Lee, a close friend of the Scalias, the couple's parents considered the marriage to be a mixed union: Italian-Catholic and Irish-Catholic.[12] The Scalias married on September 10, 1960, and have nine children, five sons and four daughters: Ann Forrest, Eugene, John Francis, Catherine Elisabeth, Mary Clare, Paul David, Matthew, Christopher James, and Margaret Jane. By all accounts, Antonin and Maureen have enjoyed a strong and mutually supportive relationship. Maureen has been described as "smart and funny." Interestingly, when she was a Radcliffe student, she launched the college's Young Democrats in support of John Kennedy's presidential nomination, but soon thereafter became a supporter of the Republican Party. After marrying Scalia, Maureen became what one writer has described as "a model mid-century mother and homemaker, running a large, happy home with a successful husband."[13] As the mother of nine children, Maureen did not have time to hold a professional job outside the home, but over the years she has played an active role in her community, including teaching in Sunday school, volunteering in local schools, helping with programs for the handicapped, and working at an abortion-alternative center.

Antonin and Maureen's relationship is also enriched by their deep faith in Roman Catholicism. Scalia has been known to leave churches where the religious teachings and practices are perceived as too liberal, and he was particularly critical of the late Pope John Paul II's stance on capital punishment. In his 1995 encyclical letter, *Evangelium Vitae*, the pope contended that capital punishment was inconsistent with the sanctity of life and therefore could not be imposed by the state, "except in cases of absolute necessity: in other words, when it would not be possible to otherwise defend society."[14] At a 2002 conference at the University of Chicago Divinity School, Scalia took issue with what he called this new catechism on capital punishment, arguing that it contradicted Christian teaching dating back to St. Paul, which allowed the state, as "the minister of God," to "execute wrath upon him that doeth evil."[15] Not only this, but Scalia regarded the pope's encyclical letter as "disastrous" in terms of its political consequences for American Catholics who want to run for public office, since they must now suffer the political liability of having to state opposition to the death penalty. At the Chicago conference, which was sponsored by the Pew Forum on Religion and Public Life, Scalia also criticized the Supreme Court's "living Constitution" philosophy that allows capital punishment to be decided on the basis of "evolving standards of decency," and maintained that any judge who could not impose the death penalty, which he believes is clearly permissible under the Constitution, should resign from the bench.

## PRIVATE LEGAL PRACTICE

Scalia began his legal career in 1961 as an associate at the law firm now called Jones, Day, Reavis & Pogue in Cleveland, Ohio. At the time, Jones, Day consisted of only about seventy-five lawyers, but today it ranks as one of the nation's largest and most prestigious law firms. Members of the firm recall Scalia as a "brash, instantly likable guy who lit up the firm with his legal abilities and eager conservatism."[16] Scalia's brashness was on display at his own recruitment party, where, in no attempt to ingratiate the firm's senior partners, the twenty-three-year old Harvard Law School graduate argued with eight of the firm's lawyers until three in the morning over whether Sunday blue laws were a good idea. Consistent with his accommodationist view of the Establishment Clause, Scalia took the position that they were, while eight of his future employers were adamantly opposed to them. Scalia's conservatism was also evident at the firm, where he was an avid reader of William F. Buckley's *National Review* and was an early supporter of Barry Goldwater's 1964 presidential campaign.

Members of the firm also recall Scalia's life-of-the-party gregariousness. At office parties, he could always be counted on to play the piano and belt out show tunes from "Guys and Dolls."[17] Scalia was well liked at the firm, even by those who differed with him politically. Richard W. Pogue, a managing partner of the firm, recalled how Scalia always liked to debate. "But even when you disagreed with him," Pogue noted, "you couldn't help but like him."[18] Scalia was a generalist at Jones, Day who dabbled in a bit of everything, including "real estate, corporate financings, labor, and antitrust discovery." Since he was an "inside lawyer," and the firm had so many more-experienced attorneys, Scalia never did get to experience trial work, which is one of the reasons the American Bar Association rated him only "qualified" when he was nominated for the D.C. Court of Appeals in 1982. James T. Lynn, then a partner at Jones, Day, and the person who recruited Scalia to come to the firm, detected a future in academia for the young associate. Scalia's only weakness at the firm, Lynn observed, was that "perhaps he wanted to spend more time on a problem than you might like in a practice. But that's part of what drove him to teach and later drove him to be judge."[19] Although he left the firm before rising to the level of partner, it was not out of any concern that he would not make it. The senior partners at the firm unanimously agreed that he was on the partnership track during his six years as an associate.

Scalia has always led an active and full life, and at Jones, Day this was no exception. Scalia was an avid jogger, liked to play tennis and softball, played a mean piano, loved to sing, and went to operas and symphonies. Like his reputation as a Supreme Court justice, he was a very social person and enjoyed having a good time. One of the activities Scalia particularly enjoyed was a low-stakes poker game, which some of the members of the firm engaged in on a weekly basis. Scalia occasionally participated in these penny-ante sessions, often sporting a fishing cap. According to Pogue, a participant in the weekly games, Scalia played with a great deal of "zest."[20] Scalia's love of poker continued after he was appointed to the Supreme Court, where he participated in a legendary monthly poker game with such notables as William Rehnquist, the late Chief Justice of Supreme Court; William Bennett, former secretary of education; and Leonard Garment, a former Nixon attorney and partner at Dickstein, Shapiro & Morin. Garment observed that Scalia has a great sense of humor and "deals standing up and sometimes gives off with an aria."[21] Bennett, who no longer participates in the poker games, says that Scalia is a skilled player who doesn't like to fold.[22]

## UNIVERSITY OF VIRGINIA

In 1967, Scalia left a lucrative law practice at Jones, Day to become a law professor at the University of Virginia (UVA), where he taught contracts, conflict of laws, comparative law—including German law—and commercial transactions. At UVA, Scalia authored or coauthored several articles on a range of subjects, including the extent to which sovereign immunity prevents judicial review of administrative action;[23] an examination of the appellate court system in Virginia, where the coauthors made the case for the institution of a permanent intermediate appellate court;[24] and an analysis of the hearing examiner loan program for federal agencies under the Administrative Procedure Act of 1946.[25] Although his full-time status at UVA was a short four years, Scalia continued to teach at the university after he accepted government positions and after his formal resignation in 1974. During academic year 1971–1972, for example, Scalia, who was then general counsel at the Office of Telecommunications Policy (OTP), offered seminars at the law school examining particular issues involving U.S. communications policy. Moreover, from 1983 to 1986, he was the John A. Ewald Jr. distinguished visiting professor of law, where, in conjunction with his judgeship on the D.C. Court of Appeals, he occasionally taught a course titled "Regulated Industries." During his reassociation with UVA in the 1980s, Scalia was instrumental in helping to start the *Journal of Law & Politics*, whose members still meet annually with the justice at the Supreme Court building in Washington, D.C.

## THE NIXON AND FORD ADMINISTRATIONS

Scalia took leave from UVA from 1971 to 1974 to serve in the Nixon administration. From 1971 to 1972, he was the first general counsel for the Office of Telecommunications Policy, which was created in April 1970 and placed in the Executive Office of the President (EOP). The purpose of OTP was to formulate and coordinate telecommunications policy in the United States.[26] While the agency was supposed to work with the Federal Communications Commission (FCC) in developing the government's telecommunications policy, the fact that OTP's responsibilities overlapped substantially with the FCC's gave the unmistakable impression that the president wanted to develop his *own* communications policy. Relations between the media and the president were at an all-time low during the Nixon administration. Independent reporting of news was threatened by trumped-up investigations of individual broadcasters, and the Nixon White House vetoed the appropriations bill for the Corporation for Public Broadcasting. The general attitude of the administration was that the media had a liberal bias and was hostile toward the administration. While Scalia almost certainly agreed with this general attitude, he is given credit for walking a fine line between exercising independent judgment and not antagonizing his Republican bosses. One example came when Clay T. Whitehead, the director of OTP, received a memo from the president mandating that a certain TV program be eliminated. Scalia responded, "Hell, write back a memo that says it's illegal." Later, after acknowledging that the measure was not clearly illegal, Scalia added, "Hell, they don't know that."[27] Scalia's advice was ultimately accepted, and the White House let the matter die, preferring instead to further study the issue. As general counsel for OTP, Scalia is also given credit for brokering an important compromise between television networks, the cable industry, and the motion picture industry over retransmission rights of copyrighted programs on cable, which ended the FCC's 1966 "freeze" on the development of cable programming.[28] Another controversy during Scalia's tenure with the OTP was the "fairness doctrine." This doctrine, which was promulgated by the FCC in 1949, required broadcasters to present contrasting viewpoints on controversial issues. Because of the limited availability of broadcast licenses and the pervasive nature of radio and television, the fairness doctrine was designed to reduce biased

reporting and increase a free flow of public discussion on controversial issues. The Nixon administration and the OTP opposed the fairness doctrine
and sought to eliminate or at least curtail it. In a 1972 speech before the Federal Communications Bar Association, Scalia argued that while the fairness
doctrine might have good intentions, it came at too high a cost in terms of
First Amendment values. While acknowledging the possibility of maintaining
the fairness doctrine for specific categories of issues (e.g., candidacies for political office), Scalia contended that the best and least intrusive way of ensuring that a "fairness" obligation is enforced is through an overall inquiry into
the licensee's journalistic responsibility at the time a license is renewed.[29]
Later, Scalia joined a D.C. Court of Appeals panel decision by his colleague
Robert Bork finding that the fairness doctrine was not statutorily required,
which opened the door for the FCC to abandon the doctrine in 1987 on both
constitutional and policy grounds.[30]

In September 1972, President Nixon appointed the thirty-six-year-old
Scalia to be the third chair of the Administrative Conference of the United
States, an independent federal agency staffed by cabinet members, agency
heads, and administrative-law experts. The purpose of the Administrative
Conference was to conduct studies and make recommendations to administrative agencies and the three branches of government on the efficiency, ade-
quacy, and fairness of administrative procedure. During its twenty-eight-year
existence,[31] the conference made over two hundred recommendations, many
of which were later codified into law.[32] During Scalia's tenure as chair of the
conference, the agency held seminars for one or several agencies on administrative procedure; conducted comprehensive statistical analyses of how the
different agencies were operating, including the commencement of an ex-
haustive study of the Internal Revenue Service; and published the first manual for administrative-law judges. As the head of the conference, Scalia also
served as the agency's mouthpiece and appeared before Congress on numerous occasions to testify about issues important to the conference, including
the formation of the new Consumer Protection Agency (which Scalia had
mixed views about[33]), the opening of the administrative process to the public,
the procedures for the U.S. Board of Parole, and proposed amendments to the
Freedom of Information Act. Scalia was heartened by an increase in funding
for the agency during his tenure, which would allow the conference to conduct more long-range projects. In the chairman's foreword for the conference's 1973–1974 report, Scalia wrote, "While the capacity of the Conference
is increasing, the need for its efforts is increasing as well. Improvement of administrative procedure in the past was sometimes impeded by the fact that the
subject did not attract enough attention; there was insufficient awareness of

its importance to sound government."[34] Scalia's appointment to chair the conference was further recognition of his expertise in the arcane and complex area of administrative law. In 1995, when the Administrative Conference was being reviewed for reauthorization, which it did not receive, Justice Scalia wrote a prepared statement supporting the continued existence of the conference,[35] and in May 2004 he testified before Congress (along with Justice Stephen Breyer) arguing in favor of congressional reauthorization of the conference, which Congress ultimately did grant with passage of the Federal Regulatory Improvement Act of 2004.[36]

In August 1974, Scalia resigned his law professorship at the University of Virginia in order to become assistant attorney general for the Justice Department's Office of Legal Counsel. Scalia arrived at his new post at a most inopportune time. On July 30, 1974, Scalia was nominated for the position by President Nixon, but due to the Watergate scandal and Nixon's eventual resignation from office on August 9, 1974, he was not confirmed until thirteen days after Gerald Ford was sworn into office. One of Scalia's first opinions as assistant attorney general was the delicate and sensitive matter of whether President Nixon's papers and tapes were his personal property. Over the course of his six years in the White House, President Nixon accumulated over 40 million pages of documents and 880 tape recordings, which he claimed were his personal belongings when he left office. President Ford asked his attorney general, William B. Saxbe, for his legal opinion on the issue, and Saxbe then delegated the task to his new assistant. Scalia, who likely did not even have time to unpack his office boxes, researched and drafted an opinion that reportedly was only slightly tinkered with by Justice Department officials before being signed by Saxbe. Scalia's opinion, dated September 6, 1974, argued that except for a few limited exceptions,[37] President Nixon's papers and tapes were his personal property. For evidence of this, Scalia cited historical understanding and practices since the time of George Washington's administration, the assumption that the president's papers were his personal property when Congress passed the Presidential Libraries Act of 1955, and the absence of any modern statutory language that stated anything to the contrary.[38] The day after this opinion was issued, President Nixon entered into a contract with the general services administrator, Arthur F. Sampson, detailing the procedures for how the president's papers and tapes were to be held. Under the terms of the agreement, Nixon would have control over the materials and, in a set number of years, the authority to destroy them. Congress responded quickly with the Presidential Recordings and Materials Preservation Act of 1974, which rebuked the president's claim of private ownership of the papers and tapes and contained a provision allowing for the safe deposit of the materials. When the law was challenged by President Nixon as a violation of separation of powers, executive privilege, privacy rights, and Article I's bill of attainder provision, the Supreme Court upheld the law.[39] Thus, Scalia's opinion, which was unpopular at the time, and yet did have substantial historical support, was firmly repudiated by Congress and the Court.

It was as assistant attorney general for the Office of Legal Counsel that Scalia began to show an appreciation for the presidency as an institution — a respect that would later mark his judicial writings. During his tenure at the Justice Department, Scalia testified before Congress on a wide array of issues, including congressional oversight of agency rule making, the Arab economic boycott against Israel, and proposals dealing with New York City's financial problems. His most controversial testimony, however, involved classic interbranch disputes over the scope of executive privilege and congressional limitations on the president's ability to enter into executive agreements. As discussed more extensively in chapter 4, one year after the conclusion of the Watergate scandal, Scalia defended an expansive view of executive privilege, and on two separate occasions broadly defended the president's authority to enter into executive agreements without congressional authorization. In February 1975, Scalia testified against a proposed change to the Twenty-fifth Amendment, ratified in 1967, which would have required a special presidential election if the vice president succeeded to the presidency with more than a year remaining in the presidential term. Congress held hearings to examine the issue after President Ford, the first president in the nation's history not to be elected as vice president or as president, came into office with two and a half years remaining in President Nixon's term. On behalf of the administration, Scalia argued against the constitutional change to the Twenty-fifth Amendment on both theoretical and practical grounds. On a theoretical level, the proposed constitutional change, in Scalia's view, would disrupt "the presumption of our system that major changes of direction in the executive branch of Government are to be made no more frequently than every 4 years." And, on a practical level, a special election would likely shorten the nomination and general election campaigns, which would increase the prospect of a more extreme candidate winning the special election and/or of having such contests thrown into the House of Representatives. Moreover, Scalia contended that during the "caretaker" transition between the vice president's occupying the office and the new president's inauguration, "the executive branch and the Government [would be] enfeebled." According to Scalia, the Constitution should not be amended without careful consideration: "To propose a change in the existing provision on vacancies less than a decade after its last revision, is to contribute to an appearance of impermanence that is inconsistent with the very concept and purpose of a constitution. Of course, a change must be made if it is needed, but the reasons should be weighty and clear."[40]

In April 1975, Scalia also testified against a national "newsmen's privilege"— or a right of the press to withhold information or the identity of sources from state and federal investigators when subpoenaed to appear before a grand jury or a court. The institutional press has long sought such a protection on the grounds that if it is forced to divulge the identity of its sources, it will lose many of them, thereby resulting in an indirect prior restraint. In *Branzburg v. Hayes*,[41] the Supreme Court rejected this argument, but noted that the states or the federal government could legislate such a privilege if they wanted to. With its proposed 1975 bill, Congress was attempting to achieve statutorily what the Court held was not a constitutional right. The proposed bill granted "newsmen" a privilege in state or federal proceedings against disclosing information or the identity of sources of information, unless by clear and convincing evidence such disclosure "is indispensable to the establishment of the offense charged" and "cannot be obtained by alternative means," and "there is a compelling and overriding public interest in requiring disclosure of the identity or the information." Representing the Justice Department, Scalia argued against a federal newsmen's privilege. Although Scalia conceded that such a bill did not violate the letter of the Constitution, he testified that it conflicted with "the spirit of federalism" because Congress would be intruding upon the criminal law practices of the fifty states. As a matter of policy, Scalia noted that twenty-six states already had some sort of newsmen's privilege, and therefore Congress would be acting prematurely in nationalizing such a right. He also testified that such a privilege would dramatically impede law enforcement's ability to combat crime and would have the consequence of citizens taking laws and their enforcement less seriously. Scalia informed the members of the committee that the Justice Department already had rules in place that adequately balance the interests in domestic tranquility and constitutional freedoms. In Scalia's view, this balance "can best be achieved by wise exercise of administrative discretion under constant guidance and prodding, if necessary, of legislative inquiries such as this."[42]

A common theme running through Scalia's testimony before Congress in the mid-1970s was that Congress should place more confidence and trust in the executive branch. As he explained at a 1976 conference on congressional oversight and review of administrative-agency decision making,

> While I question neither the legitimacy nor the desirability of the congressional oversight function, both in its purpose and in its importance, it should, in my view, be subordinate to the function of legislating. You might ask yourselves when you read the daily newspapers how many of the congressional activities which are reported pertain to the difficult and politically risky process

of hammering out specific and detailed legislative proposals, and how many consist of much more scintillating inquiries into alleged executive malfeasance or inefficiency, with no particular legislative purpose in mind.

As I say, I believe the latter function is necessary and useful, but in this role the Congress is merely backstopping the President, who has the primary responsibility for, in the words of the Constitution, "taking care that the laws be faithfully executed."[43]

During his time in the Justice Department, Scalia was also instrumental in working on and initiating legislative proposals for the executive branch. For example, he worked extensively on Executive Order (EO) 11905, promulgated on February 18, 1976, which dealt with the functions and coordination of intelligence organizations. The administration was worried about a competing congressional intelligence policy that would have curtailed domestic spying and covert international operations. In order to derail this more restrictive legislation, the Ford administration issued EO 11905 to give the intelligence community more latitude in countering domestic and international terrorism. Scalia reportedly took a very active role in formulating the executive order, "attending top-level White House meetings, and working on drafts."[44] The EO established a Committee on Foreign Intelligence, which reported directly to the National Security Council; the Operations Advisory Group, which considered and developed policy recommendations for the president prior to any decision of special activity in support of national foreign policy objectives; and an Intelligence Oversight Board, comprising three members from outside the government, which was authorized to make reports on any intelligence activities that raise legal or ethical issues. In order to improve the protection of sources of and methods of intelligence, the order also authorized appropriate disciplinary action against any executive branch member found to have made unauthorized disclosure of information.

Scalia also initiated a law passed by Congress in October 1976 that abandoned the federal government's sovereign immunity in equity cases challenging agency action.[45] Historically, the federal government had eliminated large areas of its sovereign immunity in cases involving contracts and torts, but it retained absolute immunity in certain areas, such as in cases against a federal agency or an officer or employee thereof in which the plaintiff was seeking nonmonetary relief. Scalia's interest in this issue dated back to his 1970 law review on the subject,[46] and it was also a policy change examined during his chairmanship of the Administrative Conference. Scalia allegedly convinced his colleagues in the Justice Department that this was the right thing to do, and he lobbied members of Congress for the bill's passage.[47] Even though Scalia is a pro-executivist, his support for this piece of legislation is consistent with a Hamiltonian rule of law approach, according to which each branch of government is held accountable. Scalia's role in the passage of this legislation should also be balanced against his restrictive interpretation of legal standing, which is discussed in chapter 2.

As assistant attorney general in the Ford administration, Scalia also actively campaigned against the legislative veto, the procedure by which Congress could disapprove of executive action by a one-house or two-house vote. Beginning in the early 1930s, Congress used this device as a way of holding the executive branch accountable. As the Justice Department's spokesperson on this issue, Scalia testified against the legislative veto on six different occasions. His involvement with the legislative veto did not stop with his service in the Justice Department, however. Scalia later wrote an article on the subject, arguing that the legislative veto was an unconstitutional and impractical device to rein in the federal bureaucracy;[48] he coauthored the brief for the American Bar Association in the case in which the Court struck down the legislative veto, *Immigration and Naturalization Service v. Chadha*;[49] and in 1984 he testified before Congress, this time as a member of the D.C. Court of Appeals, against a proposed constitutional amendment that would have restored the legislative veto as a form of congressional oversight of executive action.[50] Scalia's basic constitutional argument, briefly stated here, was that the legislative veto violated separation of powers, since it allowed Congress to bypass the president's legislative function, and Article I's Presentment Clause, because all bills passed by Congress must be presented to the president for his approval. We shall see in chapter 3 that Scalia's formalistic interpretation of the Presentment Clause in analyzing the constitutionality of the legislative veto is hard to reconcile with his approval of the Line Item Veto Act of 1996 in *Clinton v. City of New York*[51]—unless, of course, the two legal issues are examined from a Hamiltonian perspective.

## AMERICAN ENTERPRISE INSTITUTE

After President Ford lost the 1976 presidential election to Jimmy Carter, a Democrat, Scalia left public office and accepted a position as a scholar in residence at the American Enterprise Institute (AEI), a conservative think tank located in Washington, D.C. Scalia must have been in his element at AEI. The organization sponsors research, conducts seminars and conferences, and publishes books and periodicals "dedicated to preserving and strengthening the foundations of freedom—limited government, private enterprise, vital cultural and political institutions, and a strong foreign policy and national defense."[52] At the time of Scalia's affiliation with AEI, he participated in "brown-bag" lunches with several prominent academicians and former public officials, many of whom went on to accept political or judicial appointments during the Reagan administration, including Robert Bork and Laurence Silberman, both of whom were appointed by Reagan to the D.C. Court of Appeals; James C. Miller III, Reagan's director of the Office of Management and Budget; Jeane J. Kirkpatrick, U.N. ambassador during the Reagan administration; Rudolph G. Penner, director of the Congressional Budget Office from 1983–1987; Irving Kristol, one of the founders of the neoconservative movement; the late Jude Wanniski, founder of Polyconomics and influential editorial writer for the *Wall Street Journal*; and Herbert Stein, former chairman of the Council of Economic Advisers under the Nixon and Ford administrations.[53] The members of the group engaged in free-flowing and lively discussions across a wide array of issues, including the popular subject of supply-side economics. Wanniski, the author of the "supply-side bible," *The Way the World Works*,[54] often held forth and gave his views on the free market system. According to Wanniski, Scalia was a "serious participant" in the discussions and "was quite intrigued by the impact that economic growth would have on social mores." During these open forums, Scalia often discussed his views about separation of powers and, in particular, his opposition to the legislative veto. While at AEI, Scalia found time to testify before Congress and served as a visiting law professor at Georgetown University. After leaving AEI in the summer of 1977, Scalia maintained contacts with the organization. In 1978, he participated in an AEI roundtable on the topic "An Imperial Judiciary: Fact or Myth?,"[55] during which Scalia criticized the Court's decisions in the areas of abortion rights and school busing. In 1989, Scalia presented the Francis Boyer Lecture to the organization on the subject "The Courts and the Press."[56]

## UNIVERSITY OF CHICAGO

In fall 1977, Scalia left AEI to join the University of Chicago law faculty— a logical choice for Scalia for two major reasons. First, on a professional level, Chicago was a bastion of conservatism. The law school was at the forefront of the law-and-economics movement, and the political science department was steeped in the "Straussian" methodology of "content analysis," or a careful reading of original texts. Ironically, it is the latter tradition that has had the more obvious influence on Justice Scalia's jurisprudence. While he is a strong supporter of a free market system, Scalia has distanced himself from the libertarian streak of the law-and-economics school that seeks to reinvent the "liberty of contract" doctrine under the Due Process Clauses of the Fifth and Fourteenth Amendments.[57] Meanwhile, Scalia's textualist approach to interpreting laws, as well as his support for a strong executive, are quintessentially "Straussian."

On a more personal level, the University of Chicago was a logical choice for the Scalias because the school gave its faculty the fringe benefit of paying their children's tuition to any college in the country up to the level of Chicago's—which was a significant benefit for the Scalias, who had seven children at the time.[58] To house their large and growing family, the Scalias bought an old fraternity house three blocks from the campus. Scalia's teaching repertoire at Chicago included Contracts; Administrative Law; Constitutional Law I: Structures and Powers; Constitutional Law II: Freedom of Expression; Federal Communications Law; Regulated Industries; and Federal Regulatory Reform. Aside from the previously mentioned affirmative action and legislative veto articles, Scalia authored a number of other articles at the University of Chicago, including a follow-up piece on administrative-law judges,[59] which is discussed in chapter 3, and a lengthy, laudatory, and carefully-researched examination of the Supreme Court's 1978 decision in *Vermont Yankee Nuclear Power Corp. v. Natural Resources Defense Council,*[60] which is discussed in chapter 5.

During his time at Chicago, Scalia also served as the editor of *Regulation*, a bimonthly magazine published by AEI, which is devoted to analyzing the implications of government regulatory policy. As the editor of this magazine, Scalia's views became decidedly political. He was troubled by proposed congressional legislation that he regarded as anti-executive and detrimental to "genuine regulatory reform." More generally, he criticized those within the Republican Party whose limited-government philosophy opposed the use of the federal government and, in particular, the executive branch to achieve the objectives of deregulation. "Regulatory reformers who do not recognize [that the rules of the game have changed]," Scalia wrote in a 1981 issue of *Regulation*, "and who continue to support the unmodified proposals of the past as though the fundamental game had not been altered, will be scoring points for the other team."[61] Scalia also wrote an article supportive of President Reagan's plan to have "central clearance" of all government regulations, believing that "big-brother" central clearance by the Office of Management and Budget (OMB) would prevent individual agencies from imposing excessive costs on private industry and would allow for a more uniform and comprehensive regulatory program.

As editor of *Regulation*, Scalia also wrote an important article criticizing the 1974 amendments to the Freedom of Information Act (FOIA), referring to them as "the Taj Mahal of the Doctrine of Unanticipated Consequences, the Sistine Chapel of Cost/Benefit Analysis Ignored." Scalia did not quarrel with the basic purpose of the original 1966 FOIA, which for the first time gave the public access to government documents, but he strenuously objected to the 1974 amendments. In Scalia's view, those amendments, adopted at a time of heightened distrust of government activity, contained numerous unintended consequences and lacked the necessary balance between the need for public information and other competing interests. In terms of the unintended consequences, Scalia said that the FOIA amendments had been used more to obtain data in the government's hands concerning private institutions than about the operations of the government itself. He also argued that corporate lawyers, as opposed to the "the press, the public interest group, [and] the little guy," have been the chief beneficiaries of the FOIA amendments, and that rather than being a minor imposition on the operations of government, the FOIA amendments "have greatly burdened investigative agencies and the courts." In terms of the lack of balance and the costs associated with the FOIA amendments, Scalia cited many: (1) the expense of administering the numerous (and, in his view, often frivolous) FOIA requests in terms of both real dollars and the time it takes for staff to work on requests; (2) the unreasonable time frame (ten days) in which to fulfill requests; (3) the possibility of disciplinary action against agency officials for noncompliance; (4) the imposition of attorney fees and litigation costs on the government if it loses FOIA suits in courts; (5) de novo judicial review of agency determinations denying a request; (6) and the heightened chance of court involvement in national security and foreign affairs when determining the propriety of documents designated classified. In direct opposition to James Madison, who said that "a people who mean to be their own Governors, must arm themselves with the power knowledge gives,"[62] Scalia wrote in his tour de force against the FOIA, "The defects of the Freedom of Information Act cannot be cured as long as we are dominated by the obsession that gave them birth—that the first line of defense against an arbitrary executive is do it yourself oversight by the public and its surrogate, the press."[63]

From 1981 to 1982, Scalia was chair of the American Bar Association's (ABA) Administrative Law Section. In that capacity, he wrote four chairman's messages about the administrative process. In one of his messages, titled "Rulemaking as Politics," Scalia challenged the Progressive view of the administrative process, where "neutral technocrats" are assumed to make rules based not on political calculation but on what is in the public interest. In contrast to this "enlightened" conception of the administrative process, Scalia embraced the Hamiltonian conception of agency decision making, according to which agencies exercise political discretion, and there are no demonstrably right or wrong answers to administrative problems. As chairman of the ABA's Administrative Law Section, Scalia urged that more needs to be done to bring "the political, accommodationist, value-judgment aspect of rulemaking out of the closet," for "what an agency wishes to do and not to do, within a broad range of alternatives available under its charter—is up to the agency itself. It is a large and important area of political discretion."[64] We will see that Scalia's belief that agency action is often a value choice informs his view of judicial review of those decisions. As chapter 5 points out, Scalia is a strenuous defender of judicial deference toward agency decisions.

While at Chicago, Scalia also became the first faculty adviser for the law school's chapter of the Federalist Society, which has grown into one of the most influential legal organizations in the United States. Starting out as a small student organization at a few law schools in 1982, the Federalist Society now boasts 145 law school chapters, 25,000 members, and lawyer divisions in over sixty cities. The organization includes law students, practicing attorneys, and high-ranking public officials and judges, and comprises an eclectic group of libertarians and conservatives. Well organized and financially secure, the Federalist Society has established fifteen "practice groups," modeled after the ABA's sections, which actively engage in litigation and proposed legislation. It also serves as an important network for placing its members into judicial clerkships, government positions (particularly in the Justice Department), and onto federal courts. There was a running joke during the Reagan administration that all a person had to do was to become a faculty adviser for the organization, and he or she got nominated for a federal judgeship. Due to the perception that the ABA's screening system for federal judges had become too politicized, particularly after Robert Bork's defeat in 1987, President George W. Bush abandoned the ABA's fifty-year historical role of screening nominees for federal judgeships in 2001. Many speculated that the Federalist Society, many of whose members have served in the Bush administration, would assume this role. However, when asked about this possibility, Steven G. Calabresi, the national cofounder of the organization, said that the Bush administration had not asked the Federalist Society to perform this function, and, even if it had, the Federalist Society would not undertake such a role.[65]

Scalia has maintained close ties with the Federalist Society over the years. Several of his law clerks have been founding members of the organization, including Calabresi, a former special assistant to Attorney General Edwin Meese III; Lee Liberman-Otis, who served as a deputy associate attorney general in the Reagan Justice Department; and Gary Lawson, a former aide to Charles Cooper, head of the Office of Legal Counsel during the Reagan administration.[66] Scalia has also participated in a number of the society's annual conferences. During its inaugural conference at Yale in April 1982, Scalia undoubtedly surprised many of its members when he invoked Hamilton, not Madison or Jefferson, on the subject of federalism, and asserted that "the federal government is not bad but good. The trick is to use it wisely."[67]

In 2003 and 2005, Scalia co-taught (along with law professor John Baker of Louisiana State University) a ten-hour course on separation of powers exclusively to members of the Federalist Society.

Scalia's second-to-last year as a professor at Chicago (1980–1981) was spent at Stanford Law School, where he served as a visiting professor. During his time at Stanford, Scalia testified before Congress in support of a federal tuition tax credit for individuals to attend a private elementary or secondary school, or a public or private college or vocational school. Foreshadowing his Establishment Clause jurisprudence on the Supreme Court, Scalia described the Court's decisions in church-state matters as inconsistent and irrational. He also regarded the Court's "neutrality" doctrine as "incompatible with the existence of the free exercise clause in the first amendment."[68] In early 1981, Scalia was a finalist for the solicitor general position in President Reagan's first administration. He was one of two finalists interviewed for the position by Attorney General William French Smith, but ultimately Rex E. Lee received the position. At the time, Scalia confided to friends that he was very disappointed about not getting the position, but it might have been a blessing in disguise for him since the solicitor general has to author a large number of legal opinions on a wide array of controversial subjects (including abortion), and a "paper trail" on those sorts of issues could have been damaging to Scalia in a confirmation battle.[69]

## COURT OF APPEALS

On July 15, 1982, President Ronald Reagan nominated Scalia to the U.S. Court of Appeals for the District of Columbia, widely regarded as the second-most influential court in the land and as a stepping-stone for future Supreme Court justices. After a brief appearance before the Senate Judiciary Committee, where Scalia defended his FOIA article and expressed his view that the Tenth Amendment was a constitutional redundancy, the full Senate confirmed him on August 17, 1982. Scalia wrote 135 published opinions during his time on the Court of Appeals: 105 majority opinions (77.8 percent), 5 concurring opinions (3.7 percent), 7 concurring-in-part-and-dissenting-in-part opinions (5.2 percent), and 18 dissenting opinions (13.3 percent). His jurisprudence on the D.C. Circuit was marked by a formalistic interpretation of separation of powers, a deferential view of executive power in the area of foreign affairs, broad immunity for executive branch officials, an expansive interpretation of the "state secrets" privilege, a strict interpretation of legal standing, and judicial deference toward administrative-agency action—all of which are consistent with a Hamiltonian philosophy.

Judge Scalia's most important decision on the subject of separation of powers came in *Synar v. United States*,[70] which is discussed more extensively in chapter 3. For a special three-judge panel of the D.C. District Court, Scalia held that the Balanced Budget and Emergency Deficit Control Act of 1985 violated separation of powers because it gave Congress the authority to remove the comptroller general—the official responsible for making the budget cuts under the act—whose functions were regarded as executive in nature. Scalia also took the occasion in *Synar* to criticize the creation of independent regulatory agencies as irreconcilable with the text and structure of the Constitution which establishes three branches of government. Demonstrating his Hamiltonian leanings, Scalia also sided with the executive branch in two other cases challenging the president's authority in foreign affairs. In *Ramirez de Arellano v. Weinberger*,[71] Scalia dissented from a decision allowing a case to be brought in federal court disputing the establishment of a military base in Honduras, and in *Sanchez-Espinoza v. Reagan*,[72] he wrote the majority opinion dismissing an action challenging the Reagan administration's financial and military support of the "Contra" rebels in Nicaragua. In both cases, which are discussed more specifically in chapter 4, Scalia contended that the courts should stay out of foreign affairs, a province uniquely suited for the executive branch and a subject about which "judges know little."

Scalia also wrote three important opinions broadening the scope of qualified immunity for high-level executive branch officials in the national security context. The qualified immunity doctrine is derived from common law and attempts to balance the need to vindicate public officials' violations of law with their ability to carry out their official responsibilities without fear of being sued. In *Harlow v. Fitzgerald*, the Supreme Court held that "government officials performing discretionary functions . . . are shielded from liability for civil damages insofar as their conduct does not violate clearly established statutory or constitutional rights of which a reasonable person would have known."[73] According to this ruling, the subjective motivations of government officials are not dispositive on whether the qualified immunity applies, but the critical question is whether the officials' acts are objectively reasonable as measured by reference to clearly established law. The *Harlow* Court adopted this objective test on the grounds that discovery into the subjective motivations of government officials does not prevent insubstantial claims from proceeding to trial. But what if the substantive law upon which a plaintiff seeks relief makes the conduct legal or illegal depending upon the intent with which it is performed? For example, malicious intent on the part of government officials can be used to rebut a qualified immunity defense in civil rights cases, and certain government actions (otherwise unlawful) might be validated if the purpose was to protect national security information. The latter was the novel legal issue presented in three companion cases decided by the D.C. Circuit Court in 1986.

The three suits grew out of a Nixon administration program launched in May 1969 to identify the sources of government secrets disclosed to the press. Under this program, Morton H. Halperin, a National Security Council staff member, had four private telephones tapped for twenty-one months from 1969 to 1971 because he was suspected as the source of a leak to the *New York Times* of the secret U.S. bombing raids on Cambodia.[74] Hedrick Smith, a *New York Times* reporter, had his home phone tapped for eighty-nine days in 1969 after he reported details of the U.S. negotiating stance on the return of Okinawa to Japan.[75] H. Peter Young, an attorney in the "Pentagon Papers" criminal prosecution, had four of his conversations overheard between September 17, 1970 and June 23, 1971, during wiretap surveillance of the Los Angeles chapter of the Black Panthers.[76] In all three cases, there was no question that the wiretaps were illegal under federal law and the Fourth Amendment, unless an argument could be made that they were used for the purpose of preventing national security information from being disclosed to foreign intelligence operatives. Scalia, who authored the three opinions after he had already been appointed to the Supreme Court,[77] held that the defendants were immune in the Smith and Young cases, and that they were partially immune in the Halperin case.[78] Even though Scalia acknowledged that the court was broadening the qualified immunity doctrine established in *Harlow*, he noted that separation of powers concerns are prominent in national security matters, and thus "if the facts establish that the purported national security motivation would have been reasonable, the immunity defense will prevail." On this basis, Scalia wrote in *Halperin* that while a reasonable jury might not agree with the decision to tap the plaintiff's phones, "no reasonable jury could fail to find that there were reasonable national security grounds for such a wiretap."[79]

As a member of the D.C. Court of Appeals, Judge Scalia also broadly interpreted the state secrets privilege, a common law evidentiary privilege that allows the government to resist discovery of information that would injure the national defense or foreign policy. In 1979, Daniel Molerio applied to be an FBI special agent. Even though he ranked fifth out of 785 applicants in the Special Agent Selection System and was included in a list of agents tentatively scheduled for the new class of special agents, he did not get the position. Molerio alleged that the reason he was denied the position was because of his father's political beliefs, a onetime member of the "26th of July" group, a Cuban political organization that supported the Castro revolution. Molerio brought suit against the FBI, its director, and its personnel officer, claiming that the reason he was not hired violated Title VII of the Civil Rights Act, the First Amendment, the Due Process Clause, and the Privacy Act. The bureau complied with some of Molerio's discovery requests, but it refused to turn over any document that would jeopardize national security and moved to dismiss the case. In *Molerio v. F.B.I.*,[80] the D.C. Court of Appeals, in an opinion by Judge Scalia, granted summary judgment to the defendants on all counts. After examining a sworn affidavit by an assistant director in charge of the bureau's intelligence division, which provided the bureau's reasons for not hiring Molerio, Scalia ruled that the bureau properly invoked the state secrets privilege. According to Scalia, where "the whole object of the suit and of the discovery is to establish a fact that is a state secret, we are of the view that it suffices for the cabinet secretary to determine on personal consideration that disclosure of that fact would impair national security, whereupon compliance with the discovery request is excused in gross, without the necessity of examining individual documents."[81]

As a court of appeals judge, Scalia also maintained a restrictive view of legal standing, a subject discussed in more detail in chapter 2. Scalia wrote eighteen opinions in the area of standing,[82] and he ruled in favor of a challenge to standing in every case where the parties could not show a concrete and particularized injury. For example, Scalia dissented from two court rulings finding that consumer organizations had standing to challenge a National Highway Traffic Safety Administration (NHTSA) final rule reducing 1985 and 1986 fuel economy standards for light trucks from 21 miles per gallon to 19.5 and 20 miles per gallon, respectively.[83] The consumer groups argued that the lower standards conflicted with the Energy Policy and Conservation Act of 1975 and adversely affected energy conservation. The majority granted standing on the basis that the organizations' purposes included the promotion of energy conservation and the availability of fuel-efficient vehicles, and regarded it as "irrelevant" that the injury was widespread or general, so long as the organizations' members suffered a distinct injury. In his dissent filed for both cases, Scalia challenged that reasoning: "If the injuries hypothesized by the interest groups suing in the present cases are sufficient, it is difficult to imagine a contemplated public benefit under any law which cannot—simply by believing in it ardently enough—be made the basis for judicial intrusion into the business of the political branches."[84] Scalia also filed a partial dissent in a case in which the majority allowed three individual consumers to challenge Department of Agriculture market orders that assured producers uniform prices for raw milk. The consumers objected to the orders as applied to reconstituted milk, because it precluded them from purchasing "a nutritious dairy beverage at a lower price than fresh drinking milk." In dissent, Scalia complained that the consumers did not allege a concrete and particularized injury different from a generalized grievance shared by the public at large. "Government mischief whose effects are widely distributed is more readily remedied through the political process," wrote Scalia, "and does not call into play the distinctive function of the courts as guardians against oppression of the few by the many. Thus, for such matters it is less likely that Congress intended the creation of private attorneys general to supplement, through the courts, the President's primary responsibility to 'take care that the laws be faithfully executed.'"[85]

On the Court of Appeals, Scalia also defended a deferential view of judicial oversight of substantive agency decisions. Over the years, Scalia has been a sharp critic of "hard-look" scrutiny by courts in reviewing the factual and policy determinations of administrative agencies. An example of this came in his majority opinion in *Center for Auto Safety v. Peck*,[86] where the court examined whether a new automobile-safety standard established during the Reagan administration was "arbitrary and capricious" under the Administrative Procedure Act (APA) of 1946. In 1982, the National Highway Traffic Safety Administration adopted a new minimum performance standard for automobile bumpers, "which reduce[d] the primary test impact speed from 5.0 mph to 2.5 mph, with the effect that lighter, less protective, and less costly bumpers [would] now satisfy the standard." The Center for Auto Safety and two automobile insurance companies sued NHTSA, contending that the new standard jeopardized automobile safety and was arbitrary and capricious under the APA. They also claimed that because the new rule replaced a thirteen-year-old rule, which set the primary test impact speed for bumpers at 5.0 mph, the court should exercise a "more heightened and exacting scrutiny" in reviewing the new policy. Scalia rejected both of these arguments. As for the first argument, he reasoned that the change in the standard was supported by numerous studies showing that the safety benefits of the 5.0 system were exaggerated. And Scalia rejected petitioners' request for the court to apply hard-look scrutiny, because in his view there was no difference in the scope of judicial review when the agency action involved the rescission or modification of a rule. Scalia also took strong exception to the petitioners' suggestion that the agency's new rule was somehow improper because it came as a result of a change in presidential administrations. When he came into office, President Reagan sought to have the old rule reexamined because it was regarded as hurting the automobile industry. According to Scalia, "There is nothing either extraordinary or unlawful in the fact that a federal agency opens an inquiry into a matter which the President believes should be inquired into. Indeed, we thought the system was supposed to work that way."[87]

## HAMILTONIAN INFLUENCE

Judge Scalia's opinions in each of the aforementioned areas reveal a Hamiltonian philosophy. Like Hamilton, Scalia supports a unitary and energetic executive. For Scalia, the fatal defect of the Balanced Budget and Emergency Deficit Control Act was that it gave power to Congress to remove the comptroller general, thereby threatening the president's ability to control officials within the government who perform executive functions. Prior to John Marshall, Hamilton regarded the president as the "sole organ" in foreign affairs, and Scalia's opinions in *Ramirez de Arellano* and *Sanchez-Espinoza* lend strong support to such a conception of the presidency. In both cases, Scalia questioned the role of the judiciary in overseeing the functions of the executive branch in the area of foreign affairs. Hamilton was the founding father who made the case for the president to exercise certain inherent or implied powers under Article II of the Constitution. Scalia's expansive interpretation of qualified immunity for high-level executive officials in the national security context, and of executive branch authority to deny discovery requests under the state secrets privilege, supports a broad construction of the president's inherent powers under Article II. Scalia's decisions in the area of legal standing are also consistent with a Hamiltonian philosophy. Both Hamilton and Scalia share an elitist conception of the democratic process, whereby elected officials have considerable authority to make decisions on behalf of the people. Part of Scalia's defense of a strict interpretation of legal standing is that it prevents private citizens from exercising enforcement power properly belonging to the executive branch. And Scalia's *Center for Auto Safety* opinion, which rejects hard-look scrutiny in judicial review of agency substantive policies, supports Hamilton's theory of public administration, whereby administrators are supposed to exercise discretion and should not be second-guessed by courts. In short, Scalia's strong executivist views were already on display as a member of the court of appeals and only became more pronounced after he was appointed to the Supreme Court. According to Abner Mikva, a liberal colleague of Scalia's on the D.C. Court of Appeals, Scalia was teased by his colleagues for being a "new monarchist."[88] And, at the time of Scalia's nomination to the Supreme Court, Mikva aptly observed, "Scalia is a conservative but [he is] not antigovernment."[89]

As in previous positions he has held, Judge Scalia was well liked by his colleagues on the D.C. Court of Appeals, whether liberal or conservative. It was during this time that Scalia formed a lasting friendship with his liberal colleague Ruth Bader Ginsburg. The Scalias and the Ginsburgs socialize together, including a New Year's Eve celebration each year. In her Supreme Court chambers, Ginsburg proudly displays two pictures of her and Scalia together: one as extras on the stage production of the opera *Ariadne auf Naxos*,[90] where the two are dressed in eighteenth-century costume, and the other of the two justices riding an elephant together in Jaipur, India.[91] Ginsburg says that she and Scalia are old and dear friends, and she credits him with having a great sense of humor. In a 2002 speech, Ginsburg jokingly said that she hoped they could maintain their friendship, but admitted "there are a couple of times each year when I wonder."[92] Judge Mikva regarded Scalia as collegial, open-minded, and easy to talk to about a case. Even though the two were often on the opposite sides of court decisions, Mikva described Scalia as "a delightful colleague."[93] In 1988, then chief judge Patricia Wald, another liberal colleague of Scalia's on the D.C. Court of Appeals, said of her former colleague, "[His] vibrancy, genuine warmth, irrepressible humor, paired with his formidable intellectual gifts, in truth, endeared him to me and to our colleagues for four years. Even his consistent reversals of our opinions now cannot entirely erase those fond memories."[94] Scalia's colleagues did note, however, that he was less flexible on issues where he had strong beliefs. Once he made up his mind in a case, Mikva explained, "He'll plant his flag and go down in flames with it if he needs to."[95] This quality of giving no quarter on certain legal issues earned Scalia the nickname "Ninopath" on the Court of Appeals.

## APPOINTMENT TO THE SUPREME COURT

In May 1986, when Chief Justice Warren E. Burger unexpectedly informed President Ronald Reagan that he would retire at the end of the 1985–1986 term, he gave the president a golden opportunity of appointing the nation's sixteenth chief justice to the Supreme Court. For only the fourth time in the country's history, Reagan nominated a sitting justice, William H. Rehnquist, to be the new chief justice, which meant that a vacancy on the Court still had to be filled. The two leading contenders for the associate position were Antonin Scalia and Robert Bork, both of whom were then serving on the D.C. Court of Appeals and had impeccable legal credentials. The Reagan administration likely gave Scalia the nod for several reasons. At fifty, Scalia was nine years younger than Bork, and Scalia did not have the controversial paper trail that Bork did. Scalia's ethnicity, however, was also a major consideration. No Italian-American had ever been appointed to the Supreme Court, and this reportedly was *the* decisive factor for Reagan. Having appointed Sandra Day O'Connor to the Supreme Court in 1981 as the first woman to sit on the nation's highest tribunal, Reagan liked the idea of being the "first" at doing something.[96]

In light of the controversy that has surrounded him since, Judge Scalia's confirmation hearings were not what one might expect. Senator Joseph R. Biden (D-DE), one of eighteen members of the Senate Judiciary Committee, described the hearings as dull, at one point prodding Scalia, "[L]et yourself go. Because it is pretty boring so far."[97] But Scalia did not bite at the bait, refusing to testify about any legal issue that could possibly come before him as a Supreme Court justice. Instead, members of the committee lavishly praised

Scalia. He was described as a man of integrity, a man possessed with an uncommon legal mind, and a person who in all likelihood would bring consensus to the Supreme Court. Edward Kennedy (D-MA), for example, compared the Rehnquist and Scalia confirmation hearings in this manner: "[T]he nomination of Judge Scalia presents none of the troubling issues with respect to truthfulness, the candor, judicial ethics, and full disclosure that have marked the nomination of Justice Rehnquist." On most issues, he added, "it is difficult to maintain that Judge Scalia is outside the mainstream."[98] About the only controversial issue that surfaced during Scalia's hearings was that from 1971–1985 he had been a member of the all-male Cosmos Club in Washington, D.C. Scalia testified that he did not believe that single-sex clubs, like racially segregated clubs, represented a form of "invidious discrimination."[99] Some interest groups, such as the National Organization of Women, the AFL-CIO, Americans for Democratic Action, the National Abortion Rights Action League, and Americans United for the Separation of Church and State, opposed Scalia's nomination, but the civil rights groups that actively campaigned against Rehnquist's nomination took no stand on the nominee. Scalia assured the members of the Judiciary Committee that he did not have an agenda as a prospective justice on the Supreme Court. "My only agenda," he said, "is to be a good judge."[100] He also testified that while he finds certain practices to be morally wrong, such as abortion, he would not base his judicial opinions on his personal beliefs. After only one day of testimony, Scalia was unanimously approved by the Senate Judiciary Committee, and on September 17, 1986 was confirmed by the full Senate by a vote of ninety-eight to zero.

As a member of the Supreme Court, Scalia has authored numerous opinions across a wide array of issues, some of which have brought about major doctrinal changes to the law. In the area of religious freedom, for example, Scalia wrote the 1990 ruling that neutral, generally applicable laws, which only incidentally burden religion, do not have to be supported by a compelling state interest. In that case, two individuals, one of whom was a full-blooded Native American, were fired from their jobs as counselors at a private drug rehabilitation clinic in Douglas County, Oregon, for using peyote during Native American Church ceremonies. When they were denied unemployment compensation because they had been discharged from their jobs for work-related "misconduct," the two individuals challenged this administrative ruling under the Free Exercise Clause of the First Amendment. Essentially, they sought an exemption from the state's criminal laws when peyote was used for sacramental purposes. In *Employment Division, Department of Human Resources of Oregon v. Smith*,[101] Scalia held that there was no religious exemption from a state's criminal laws prohibiting the use of the peyote and that neutral, generally applicable laws do not have to survive the Court's strict scrutiny analysis. "It may fairly be said that leaving accommodation to the political process will place at a relative disadvantage those religious practices that are not widely engaged in," wrote Scalia. "[B]ut that unavoidable consequence of democratic government must be preferred to a system in which each conscience is a law unto itself or in which judges weigh the social importance of all laws against the centrality of all religious beliefs."[102] The Court's decision sparked a national outcry from religious groups across the political spectrum, and Congress attempted to overturn the decision by passing the Religious Freedom Restoration Act of 1993 (RFRA), which required strict scrutiny analysis in cases in which a law indirectly burdens religious practices. Nonetheless, the Court would have the last say in 1997 when it struck down the RFRA as going beyond Congress's enforcement authority under the Fourteenth Amendment, thereby restoring Scalia's analysis in *Smith*.[103]

Justice Scalia has also written two significant opinions broadening property rights under the Takings Clause. In *Nollan v. California Coastal Commission*,[104] the Court held that property owners must be compensated for being required to provide a public easement in front of their beachfront property as a condition of receiving a building permit. After closely examining the zoning regulation, Scalia rejected the state's purpose as illegitimate, referring to the building restriction as "an out-and-out plan of extortion." Similarly in *Lucas v. South Carolina Coastal Council*,[105] Scalia authored the majority opinion finding that a property owner must be compensated when a regulation deprives him of all economic use of his property. In that case, South Carolina enacted the Beachfront Management Act of 1988 to protect additional coastal areas from erosion and other dangers. Two years before the enactment of this law, David Lucas had purchased two vacant lots on a South Carolina barrier island that he sought to develop. The South Carolina Coastal Council, however, interpreted the 1988 law to include Lucas's lots as a "critical area" and banned construction of permanent habitable structures. For the Court, Scalia held that "when the owner of real property has been called upon to sacrifice all economically beneficial uses in the name of the common good, that is, to leave his property economically idle, he has suffered a taking."

At the same time, it is fair to say that Scalia has been on the losing side of most of the contentious issues decided by the Rehnquist Court, including those involving separation of powers, abortion, homosexual rights, church-state issues, affirmative action, criminal procedure, capital punishment, and political patronage. Even his initial victories in the area of legal standing have been tempered by subsequent decisions. Although things can certainly change with more appointments to the Court, at this point in Scalia's career, he has not had a major impact on the overall jurisprudence of the Supreme Court. His influence in particular areas of the law has been marginalized by the formation of a majority bloc, typically consisting of the Court's four liberal justices and the vote of one of the moderate conservatives: Sandra Day O'Connor, Anthony Kennedy, or sometimes both.

Scalia's style of leadership on the Court can only be described as energetic. During his first year on the Court, he showed no signs of a "freshman effect," authoring the same number of opinions as his colleagues.[106] Scalia has also been an active and tenacious questioner during the Court's oral arguments, striking fear into any attorney who is not well prepared for his or her case, and adeptly using the occasions to make points with his colleagues over particular legal issues. Scalia fully recognizes the importance of selling his jurisprudence both on and off the Court. He is the Court's most visible justice, and each year travels around the country delivering speeches on law and democracy. In terms of the Court's internal processes, Scalia is known for his legendary "Ninograms," memoranda sent to his colleagues attempting to persuade them to incorporate his views into their opinions. During his time on the Court, Scalia has written more concurring opinions than any of his colleagues, has authored the third most dissenting opinions,[107] and has been very active in signaling lawyers through the use of dissents from denials of certiorari.[108] Another area in which Scalia has been quite active is in voting to overturn court precedents. In Supreme Court history, only Justices Hugo Black and Clarence Thomas have sought to alter as many of the Court's precedents.[109] In short, Scalia's idea of judicial restraint is not modeled after what Alexander Bickel called the Court's "passive virtues."[110] As Scalia put it, "By judicial activism I do not mean judges actively doing what they are *supposed* to be doing; and by judicial restraint I do not mean judicial indolence."[111]

One prediction about Scalia that has proven wide of the mark is that he is someone who is willing to compromise. Like Hamilton, Scalia is not someone who attempts to accommodate the views of others. In his Francis Boyer speech before the American Enterprise Institute, Scalia quoted one of his favorite passages from T. S. Eliot's *Murder in the Cathedral*: "To do the right deed for the wrong reason" is the highest form of treason.[112] On this basis, Scalia has strongly criticized pragmatic approaches to deciding cases and has instead defended a decision-making approach based on the rule of law.[113] Scalia relishes maintaining his pure vision of law and is willing to challenge his colleagues when they make decisions in a manner with which he disagrees. Across a wide range of issues, including abortion, homosexual rights, church-state issues, and the death penalty, Scalia charges his colleagues with imposing their "elite" values on the majority of the people. He has, for example, sharply criticized his colleagues for inventing rights through abstract legal tests, such as the "undue-burden" test in the area of abortion rights. For Scalia, these sorts of judicially created tests erode traditional moral values and allow the Court to engage in policy making. In its 1992 abortion decision, Scalia accused the majority of "leading a Volk" in defense of a constitutional right that he did not believe existed under the Constitution.[114] Scalia has also been willing to criticize the analysis used by his colleagues in particular cases and often uses words like "irrational," "absurd," or "ludicrous" in describing their opinions. In *Romer v. Evans*,[115] for example, where the Court struck down a Colorado constitutional amendment removing homosexuals from the protection of antidiscrimination laws, Scalia referred to Justice Kennedy's majority opinion as "terminal silliness." In *Webster v. Reproductive Services*,[116] where the Court upheld several restrictions on a woman's right to obtain an abortion, Scalia called Justice O'Connor's concurring opinion "indecisive" and one that "cannot be taken seriously." And, in *United States v. Virginia*,[117] where the Court struck down Virginia Military Institute's male-only admissions policy, Scalia skewered Chief Justice William Rehnquist's concurring opinion by saying, "Any lawyer who gave that advice to the Commonwealth ought to have been either disbarred or committed." In short, Scalia is not the consensus builder he was billed as. Hamilton was the undisputed "controversial genius" during his lifetime, and Scalia can lay claim to that title today.

## NOTES

1. Antonin Scalia, "The Limits of the Law," *New Jersey Law Journal* 119 (1987): 4.

2. Ruth Marcus and Susan Schmidt, "Scalia Tenacious after Staking out a Position," *Washington Post*, June 22, 1986, A1.

3. "The Disease as Cure: 'In Order to Get beyond Racism We Must First Take Account of Race,'" *Washington University Law Quarterly* (1979): 152.

4. George Kannar, "The Constitutional Catechism of Antonin Scalia," *Yale Law Journal* 99 (1990): 1297–1357.

5. S. Eugene Scalia, *Carducci: His Critics and His Translators in England and America, 1881–1932* (1937), 90, 95.

6. Marcus and Schmidt, "Scalia Tenacious after Staking out a Position," A1.

7. Irvin Molotsky, "Judge with Tenacity and Charm: Antonin Scalia," *New York Times*, June 18, 1986, A31.

8. Richard A. Brisbin Jr., *Justice Antonin Scalia and the Conservative Revival* (Baltimore, MD: Johns Hopkins University Press, 1997), 15.

9. See, e.g., Brisbin, *Justice Antonin Scalia and the Conservative Revival*; Peter B. Edelman, "Justice Scalia's Jurisprudence and the Good Society: Shades of Felix Frankfurter and the Harvard Hit Parade of the 1950s," *Cardozo Law Review* 12 (1991): 1799–1815.

10. See, e.g., *Planned Parenthood of Southeastern Pennsylvania v. Casey*, 505 U.S. 833 (1992) (Scalia, J., concurring in the judgment in part and dissenting in part); *Bd. of County Comm'rs v. Umberhr*, 518 U.S. 668 (1996) (Scalia, J., dissenting); *O'Hare*

*Truck Service, Inc. v. City of Northlake*, 518 U.S. 712 (1996) (Scalia, J., dissenting); *Roper v. Simmons*, 125 S. Ct. 1183 (2005) (Scalia, J., dissenting).

11. Antonin Scalia, "The Rule of Law as a Law of Rules," *University of Chicago Law Review* 56 (1989): 1179; and "Morality, Pragmatism, and the Legal Order," *Harvard Journal of Law & Public Policy* 9 (1986): 125.

12. Marcus and Schmidt, "Scalia Tenacious after Staking out a Position," A1.

13. Ethan Bronner, "Bulldog Justice," *The Washingtonian*, December 1990, 247.

14. Pope John Paul II, *The Gospel of Life* [*Evangelium Vitae*] (New York: Random House, 1995), 100.

15. Antonin Scalia, "God's Justice and Ours," *First Things: A Monthly Journal of Religion and Public Life* 123 (May 2002): 18–19 (quoting Holy Bible, King James Version, Romans 13:1–5).

16. Stephen J. Adler, "Live Wire on the DC Circuit," *American Lawyer*, March 1985, 86–93, 86.

17. Paul Marcotte, "New Kid on the Block: Scalia Seen as a Charming Conservative with Ability to Effect Compromises," *American Bar Association Journal* 72 (1986): 20.

18. Robert L. Jackson and Ronald J. Ostrow, "He Has His Own Style of Conservatism: Scalia's Independent Past Suggests Future Surprises," *Los Angeles Times*, July 6, 1986, 1.

19. Adler, "Live Wire on the DC Circuit," 89.

20. E. R. Shipp, "Scalia's Midwest Colleagues Cite His Love of Debate, Poker and Piano," *New York Times*, July 26, 1986, A7.

21. Aaron Epstein, "Well, That's Your Opinion!" *Philadelphia Inquirer Magazine*, October 5, 1997, 27.

22. Debra Rosenberg, "It's Hard to Get It Right," *Newsweek*, May 3, 2004, 40.

23. Antonin Scalia, "Sovereign Immunity and Nonstatutory Review of Federal Administrative Action: Some Conclusions from the Public-Lands Cases," *Michigan Law Review* 68 (1970): 867–924.

24. Graham C. Lilly and Antonin Scalia, "Appellate Justice: A Crisis in Virginia?" *Virginia Law Review* 57 (1971): 3–64.

25. Antonin Scalia, "The Hearing Examiner Loan Program," *Duke Law Journal* (1971): 319–66.

26. Under the Carter administration, the OTP was eliminated, and a new agency, the National Telecommunications and Information Administration, was created and placed in the Department of Commerce.

27. Adler, "Live Wire on the DC Circuit," 89. See also Ronald J. Ostrow, "Style and Personality Called Contagious: Scalia Described as Persuasive, Affable," *Los Angeles Times*, June 18, 1986, 1; Jackson and Ostrow, "He Has His Own Style of Conservatism," 1.

28. Adler, "Live Wire on the DC Circuit," 89. See also Honorable Charles S. Gubser, "Appointment of Antonin Scalia to Be Chairman of the Administrative Conference of the United States," *Congressional Record* 36547 (October 14, 1972).

29. Antonin Scalia, "Don't Go Near the Water," *Federal Communications Bar Journal* (1972): 111–20.

30. *Telecommunications Research & Action Center v. FCC*, 801 F.2d 501 (D.C. Cir. 1986); *Telecommunications Research & Action Center v. FCC*, 806 F.2d 1115 (1986) (petition for rehearing en banc denied).

31. The conference was established by the Administrative Conference Act of 1964 and was activated by the appointment of its first chairperson in January 1968. The agency was discontinued in November 1996 when it failed to get reauthorization from Congress, but received reauthorization for an additional three years in 2004 under the Federal Regulatory Improvement Act.

32. See, e.g., the Administrative Dispute Resolution Act of 1990, the Negotiated Rulemaking Act of 1996, the Equal Access to Justice Act of 1980, the Magnuson-Moss Warranty Act of 1975, and the Government Performance and Results Act of 1993.

33. See U.S. Senate, *To Establish an Independent Consumer Protection Agency: Joint Hearings before the Subcommittee on Reorganization, Research and International Organizations of the Committee on Government Operations and the Subcommittee on Consumers of the Committee on Commerce*, 93rd Cong., 1st sess., April 5, 1973, 578 ("On the basic issue of desirability of a consumer advocate, if you will, I am not an unrestricted enthusiast of the concept"); U.S. House of Representatives, *To Establish a Consumer Protection Agency: Hearings before a Subcommittee on Government Operations*, 93rd Cong., 1st sess., October 11, 1973, 516 ("In short, I think the Federal consumer advocate is an idea whose time has come; at least, its time for a trial has come. It seems to be the most likely solution to the problem of important but voiceless interests. It may prove a failure, but, if so, I suspect the solution must then be sought in a much more drastic alteration of our traditional processes, away from the adversary system"). See also Antonin Scalia and Frank Goodman, "Procedural Aspects of the Consumer Product Safety Act," *UCLA Law Review* 20 (1973): 899–953.

34. "Chairman's Foreword," *1973–74 Report, Administrative Conference of the United States, September 1974* (Washington, DC: U.S. Government Printing Office, 1974), 1.

35. Prepared Statement of Antonin Scalia, Supreme Court Justice, before the Subcommittee on Administrative Oversight of the Senate Judiciary Committee, August 2, 1995.

36. Prepared Statement and Testimony before the House Judiciary Subcommittee on Commercial and Administrative Law on the Reauthorization of the Administrative Conference, May 20, 2004.

37. These exceptions were national security documents and information allowing for the smooth functioning of the executive office.

38. 43 Op. Atty. Gen. 1 (1974).

39. *Nixon v. Administrator of General Services*, 433 U.S. 425 (1977).

40. U.S. Senate, *Examination of the First Implementation of Section Two of the Twenty-Fifth Amendment: Hearing before the Subcommittee on Constitutional Amendments of the Committee on the Judiciary*, 94th Cong., 1st sess., February 26, 1975, 47–67.

41. 408 U.S. 665 (1972).

42. U.S. House of Representatives, *Newsmen's Privilege: Hearings before the Subcommittee on Courts, Civil Liberties, and the Administration of Justice of the Committee on the Judiciary*, 94th Cong., 1st sess., April 23, 1975, 2–36. Representative Robert F. Drinan (D-MA) challenged Scalia's claim that the current Justice Department practices sufficiently protect freedom of the press. In fact, Scalia had to admit in a follow-up letter that some of the Justice Department's procedures were not initially followed, and that "subpoenas were sought without explicit Attorney General approval." At one point, Drinan remarked to Scalia, "Your first norm seems to be whatever is good for law enforcement is good for the country. That is the way it comes out to me."

43. "1976 Bicentennial Institute—Oversight and Review of Agency Decisionmaking," *Administrative Law Review* 28, no. 4 (1976): 695.

44. Adler, "Live Wire on the DC Circuit," 90.

45. Pub. L. 94-574.

46. Scalia, "Sovereign Immunity and Nonstatutory Review of Federal Administrative Action."

47. Adler, "Live Wire on the DC Circuit," 91.

48. Antonin Scalia, "The Legislative Veto: A False Remedy for System Overload," *Regulation* 3 (1979): 19–26.

49. 462 U.S. 919 (1983).

50. U.S. Senate, *Constitutional Amendment to Restore Legislative Veto: Hearing before the Subcommittee on the Constitution of the Committee on the Judiciary*, 98th Cong., 2nd sess., March 2, 1984, 245–52.

51. 524 U.S. 417 (1998).

52. www.aei.org/aboutaei.htm.

53. Sidney Blumenthal, "A Well-Connected Conservative," *Washington Post*, June 22, 1986, A16.

54. Jude Wanniski, *The Way the World Works: How Economies Fail—and Succeed* (New York: Basic Books, 1978).

55. *An Imperial Judiciary: Fact or Myth?*, roundtable held on December 12, 1978, and sponsored by the American Enterprise Institute for Public Policy Research (Washington, DC: American Enterprise Institute, 1979).

56. Francis Boyer Lecture, delivered at the American Enterprise Institute, December 6, 1989. C-SPAN video.

57. See, e.g., Richard A. Epstein, "Needed: Activist Judges for Economic Rights," *Wall Street Journal*, November 14, 1985, 32; Bernard H. Seigan, *Economic Liberties and the Constitution* (Chicago: University of Chicago Press, 1980); Stephen Macedo, *The New Right v. the Constitution* (Washington, DC: Cato Institute, 1987). In extrajudicial writings, Scalia has argued that there is not a constitutional ethos for reinventing the liberty of contract doctrine, and that judicial re-creation of such a doctrine is ill advised since it would provide an important precedent for judicial activism in other constitutional areas. Antonin Scalia, "Economic Affairs as Human Affairs," in *Economic Liberties and the Judiciary*, ed. James A. Dorn and Henry G. Manne (Fairfax,

VA: George Mason University Press, 1987), 31–37. On this basis, Scalia has consistently ruled against substantive due process rights in judicial opinions. See, e.g., *BMW of North America v. Gore*, 517 U.S. 559 (1996) (Scalia, J., dissenting).

58. See "Text of Scalia's Letter on Reinstating Honoraria," *The Recorder*, 3 October 2000, p.3; and Jackson and Ostrow, "He Has His Own Style of Conservatism."

59. Antonin Scalia, "The ALJ Fiasco—A Reprise," *University of Chicago Law Review* 47 (1979): 57–80.

60. Antonin Scalia, "*Vermont Yankee*: The APA, the D.C. Circuit, and the Supreme Court," *Supreme Court Review* (1978): 345–409.

61. Antonin Scalia, "Regulatory Reform—The Game Has Changed," *Regulation* 5, no. 1 (January–February 1981): 13–15.

62. Letter to William T. Barry (August 4, 1822), WJM, 9:103.

63. Antonin Scalia, "The Freedom of Information Act Has No Clothes," *Regulation* 6, no. 2 (March–April 1982): 15–19.

64. Antonin Scalia, "Rulemaking as Politics," *Administrative Law Review* 34 (1982): v–xi.

65. Adrienne Drell, "Group Dismisses Judicial Screening Role," *Chicago Sun-Times*, April 19, 2001, 30.

66. Al Kamen, "Scalia's Federalists from Justice," *Washington Post*, December 22, 1986, A23.

67. Antonin Scalia, "The Two Faces of Federalism," *Harvard Journal of Law and Public Policy* 6 (1982): 19–22.

68. U.S. Senate, *Tuition Tax Credits: Hearings before the Subcommittee on Taxation and Debt Management of the Committee on Finance*, 97th Cong., 1st sess., June 3–4, 1981, 243–51.

69. Bronner, "Bulldog Justice," 245.

70. 626 F. Supp. 1374 (D. D.C. 1986).

71. 745 F.2d 1500 (D.C. Cir. 1984) (Scalia, J., dissenting).

72. 770 F.2d. 202 (D.C. Cir. 1985).

73. 457 U.S. 800, 818 (1982).

74. *Halperin v. Kissinger*, 807 F.2d 180 (D.C. Cir. 1986).

75. *Smith v. Nixon*, 807 F.2d 197 (D.C. Cir. 1986).

76. *Ellsberg v. Mitchell*, 807 F.2d 204 (D.C. Cir. 1986).

77. After hearing the cases as a member of the court of appeals, Scalia was allowed to decide the three cases under a special procedure allowing Supreme Court justices to sit as designated circuit judges on the date the opinion is issued. See 28 U.S.C. secs. 42, 43(b) (1982).

78. The Court did find that a substantial issue of material fact existed as to the reasonableness of continuing the Halperin wiretaps after one year when no evidence bearing upon national security concerns was discovered.

79. *Halperin*, 807 F.2d at 191.

80. 749 F.2d 815 (D.C. Cir. 1984).

81. Ibid., at 821.

82. Michael A. Perino, "Justice Scalia: Standing, Environmental Law, and the Supreme Court," *Boston College Environmental Affairs Law Review* 15 (1987): 135n173.

83. *Center for Auto Safety v. N.H.T.S.A.*, 793 F.2d 1322 (D.C. Cir. 1986); *In re Center for Auto Safety*, 793 F.2d 1346 (D.C. Cir. 1986).

84. 793 F.2d at 1342.

85. *Community Nutrition Institute v. Block*, 698 F.2d 1239, 1256–57 (1983) (quoting Article II, Section 3) (Scalia, J., concurring in part and dissenting in part).

86. 751 F.2d 1336 (D.C. Cir. 1985).

87. Ibid., 1368.

88. W. John Moore, "Tugging from the Right," *National Journal*, October 20, 1990, 1215.

89. Molotsky, "Judge with Tenacity and Charm: Antonin Scalia," A31.

90. www.oyez.org/oyez/tour/p-opera-from-ginsburgchamber.

91. www.oyez.org/oyez/tour/rbg_chambers/elephant.jpg.

92. "Fast Friends," *Kansas City Star*, June 24, 2002, 2.

93. Robert P. Hey, "Judge Scalia Seen as a Major Force on Supreme Court," *Christian Science Monitor*, June 19, 1986, 3.

94. "Proceedings of the Forty-Ninth Judicial Conference of the District of Columbia," *Federal Rules Decisions* 124 (1988): 283.

95. Ruth Marcus, "Judge a Favorite with Conservative Lawyers, Activists," *Washington Post*, June 18, 1986, A1.

96. See David G. Savage, *Turning Right: The Making of the Rehnquist Supreme Court* (New York: John Wiley & Sons, 1993), 17–18.

97. U.S. Senate, *The Nomination of Judge Antonin Scalia: Hearings before the Committee on the Judiciary of the United States Senate*, 99th Cong., 2nd. sess., August 5, 1986, 47.

98. Ibid., 12.

99. Ibid., 90–91.

100. Ibid., 38.

101. 494 U.S. 872 (1990).

102. Ibid., 890.

103. *City of Boerne v. Flores*, 521 U.S. 507 (1997).

104. 483 U.S. 825 (1987).

105. 505 U.S. 1003 (1992).

106. Thea F. Rubin and Albert P. Melone, "Justice Antonin Scalia: A First Year Freshman Effect?" *Judicature* 72, no. 2 (August–September, 1988), 98–102.

107. Lee Epstein, Jeffrey A. Segal, Harold J. Spaeth, Thomas G. Walker, *The Supreme Court Compendium: Data, Decisions & Developments*, 3rd ed. (Washington, DC: Congressional Quarterly, 2003), 594–96.

108. See, e.g., *Virginia Military Institute v. United States*, 508 U.S. 946 (1993) (Scalia, J., opinion respecting the denial of certiorari) (while agreeing that the petition for certiorari should be denied, Scalia advised the litigants that they can refile their case after a final judgment is entered by the court below); *Callins v. Collins*, 510 U.S. 1141 (1994) (Scalia, J., concurring in denial of certiorari) (arguing that capital punishment is permissible under the text and tradition of the Constitution); *Bush v. Gore*, 531 U.S. 1046 (2000) (Scalia J., concurring in the grant of certiorari) (expressing that "[t]he counting of votes that are of questionable legality does in my view threaten

irreparable harm to petitioner, and to the country, by casting a cloud upon what he claims to be the legitimacy of his election"); *Tangipahoa Parish Bd. of Educ. v. Freiler*, 530 U.S. 1251 (2000) (Scalia, J., dissenting from denial of certiorari) (expressing that the Court should review the Fifth Circuit's decision striking down a state-mandated requirement that whenever evolution theory is taught in public schools [either by oral or written presentation] the teacher must state that it is "not intended to influence or dissuade the Biblical version of Creation or any other concept"); *City of Elkhart v. Books*, 532 U.S. 1058 (2001) (Rehnquist, C.J., dissenting from denial of certiorari) (Scalia joined Rehnquist's opinion that a six-foot monument of the Ten Commandments placed in front of a municipal building did not violate the Establishment Clause); *Concrete Works of Colorado, Inc. v. City and County of Denver*, 540 U.S. 1027 (2003) (Scalia, J., dissenting from denial of certiorari) (arguing that the Court should hear a challenge to a municipality's affirmative action program in public contracting); *Bunting v. Mellen*, 541 U.S. 1019 (2004) (Scalia, J., dissenting from denial of certiorari) (stating that the Court should hear a challenge to VMI's supper prayer); *Cox v. Larios*, 124 S. Ct. 2806 (2004) (Scalia, J., dissenting from denial of certiorari) (arguing that the Court should hear a political gerrymander case).

109. Michael J. Gerhardt, "A Tale of Two Textualists: A Critical Comparison of Justice Black and Scalia," *Boston University Law Review* 74 (1994): 25–66.

110. Alexander M. Bickel, "The Supreme Court, 1960 Term—Forward: The Passive Virtues," *Harvard Law Review* 75 (1961): 40. See also Bickel, *The Least Dangerous Branch: The Supreme Court at the Bar of Politics*, 2nd ed. (New Haven, CT: Yale University Press, 1986).

111. Antonin Scalia, "Use of Legislative History: Judicial Abdication to Fictitious Legislative Intent" (unpublished article on file with the author).

112. Francis Boyer Lecture, delivered at the American Enterprise Institute, December 6, 1989. C-SPAN video (quoting T. S. Eliot's *Murder in the Cathedral* [New York: Harcourt, Brace and Co., 1935], 44).

113. Scalia, "The Rule of Law as a Law of Rules."

114. *Planned Parenthood of Southeastern Pennsylvania v. Casey*, 505 U.S. 833 (1992).

115. 517 U.S. 620 (1996).

116. 492 U.S. 490 (1989).

117. 518 U.S. 515 (1996).

*Chapter Two*

# Separation of Powers and Access to Justice

James Madison described the doctrine of separation of powers as one of the principal "auxiliary precautions" against tyrannical government.[1] Referring to Montesquieu, whom he called the great "oracle" of this modern invention in political science, he wrote,

> No political truth is certainly of greater intrinsic value, or is stamped with the authority of more enlightened patrons of liberty. . . . The accumulation of all powers, legislative, executive, and judiciary, in the same hands . . . may justly be pronounced the very definition of tyranny.[2]

Many of the framers, including Alexander Hamilton and James Madison, were so convinced that a system of divided and balanced powers would protect against violations of individual liberty that they did not think a bill of rights was necessary. In *Federalist* 84, for example, Hamilton boldly argued that a bill of rights was both unnecessary and dangerous. It would be unnecessary, according to Hamilton, because it was assumed under the proposed Constitution that all powers not delegated to the national government were to be retained by the people. On this reasoning, it would be illogical to provide a bill of rights defining the rights of the people since the preamble to the Constitution already proclaims, "WE THE PEOPLE . . . ordain and establish this Constitution."[3] Moreover, a bill of rights would be dangerous, Hamilton argued, because a fixed set of rights would provide "a colorable pretext" for tyranny. As Hamilton saw it, since a bill of rights would likely contain various protections against powers *not* granted to the national government, it would "furnish, to men disposed to usurp, a plausible pretense for claiming" powers they did not have.[4] What Hamilton and many of the framers believed would secure rights was a carefully designed *structure* of government, including a separate and balanced system of national powers, a bicameral legislature, and a division of authority between the national and state governments. This is primarily what Hamilton had in mind when he said "the Constitution is itself, in every rational sense, and to every useful purpose, A BILL OF RIGHTS."[5]

This and the next chapter examine Justice Antonin Scalia's views in the area of separation of powers. It would not be an exaggeration to say that separation of powers is Scalia's strongest doctrinal commitment. He once referred to the doctrine as "the cornerstone of our Constitution and the North Star of our founding fathers' constellation."[6] Like Hamilton, Scalia has defended separation of powers as the chief bulwark of individual liberties in the American political system, and he often shocks audiences by telling them that the Bill of Rights would be meaningless without it:

> The public generally, law students, and, I am sorry to say, most lawyers, regard separation of powers issues as dealing with a hyper-technical picky-picky portion of the Constitution. Of concern to politicians, perhaps, but of no real interest to the people. What the people care about, what affects them, is the Bill of Rights. . . . That is a *profoundly* mistaken view. . . . For the fact is, that it is the structure of government, its constitution, in the real sense of that word, that ultimately preserves or destroys freedom. The Bill of Rights is no more than ink on paper unless . . . it is addressed to a government which is so constituted that no part of it can obtain excessive power.[7]

Moreover, Justice Scalia has been the Supreme Court's staunchest defender of a formalistic interpretation of separation of powers. As he put it in a 1995 case, "Separation of powers, a distinctly American political doctrine, profits from the advice authored by a distinctly American poet: Good fences make good neighbors."[8] Accordingly, other than the few instances in which a sharing of powers is contemplated under the Constitution, Justice Scalia has argued that the three branches of government should be kept strictly separate:

> Today's decision follows the regrettable tendency of our recent separation-of-powers jurisprudence . . . to treat the Constitution as though it were no more than a generalized prescription that the functions of the Branches should not be commingled too much—how much is too much to be determined, case-by-case, by this Court. The Constitution is not that. Rather, as its name suggests, it is a prescribed structure, a framework, for the conduct of government. In designing that structure, the Framers themselves considered how much commingling was, in the generality of things, acceptable, and set forth their conclusions in the document.[9]

Justice Scalia has defended a formalistic interpretation of separation of powers primarily on the ground that it will make government officials more accountable and thereby better protect liberty.[10] But there appears to be another reason for Scalia's formalism: to protect the powers of the executive branch. A central purpose of the framers' system of separation of powers was to guard against legislative tyranny. It was against this branch of government, Madison warned, that "the people ought to indulge all their jealousy and exhaust all their precautions."[11] This concern about legislative tyranny has not been lost on Justice Scalia, who has said that the doctrine of separation of powers "not only protects, but pre-eminently protects, the Executive obligation to 'take care that the Laws be faithfully executed.'"[12] He has also warned that if government officials (particularly the members of Congress) do not begin giving "more than lip service" to the doctrine, "[W]e will soon find ourselves living not under the Constitution but under a parliamentary democracy."[13]

Equally important, a double standard is apparent in Justice Scalia's separation of powers jurisprudence. He has been much less concerned about making fine distinctions about the powers of the executive branch when its authority is called into question. Consider, for example, then Assistant Attorney General Antonin Scalia's testimony before Congress on the subject of executive privilege—a power he fully supported and expansively defined:

> Senator, I sympathize with the search for a neat, packaged procedure to resolve this highly political dispute between two branches of the Government. Unfortunately, the very concept of separation of powers and checks and balances makes it impossible that all disputes of this nature can be susceptible of a neat answer—let's let the Supreme Court decide it or do it thus-and-so. What you are suggesting is indeed a very neat answer, but one that is entirely destructive of the necessary independence of the executive branch, leaving it for the Congress—in each case for the Congress—to decide whether it will receive the information or not.[14]

Moreover, Justice Scalia is less "picky-picky" about congressional conferrals of *core* legislative power on the executive branch than he is about congressional usurpation of *core* executive functions. This was most apparent in his dissenting opinion in *Clinton v. City of New York*,[15] where he supported (against Presentment Clause objections) the conferral of line-item veto authority on the president. Whether Justice Scalia's separation of powers jurisprudence "masks [an] underlying vision of a preeminent Executive," as one Court observer has argued,[16] his opinions clearly promote the Hamiltonian goal of a strong and independent executive. Justice Scalia's opinions in the area of separation of powers will be examined in order to illuminate his pro-executive position. Before this can be done, however, a brief description of the framers' understanding of separation of powers will be provided, paying particular attention to the different interpretations of that doctrine by James Madison and Alexander Hamilton.

## THE FRAMERS' CONCEPTION OF SEPARATION OF POWERS

In *Federalist* 9, Alexander Hamilton listed the separation of powers as one of the modern inventions in political science, "either not known at all, or imperfectly known to the ancients."[17] Ironically, most of the discussion in *The Federalist Papers* is devoted to defending the Constitution's provisions for shared powers—a seeming violation of the separation of powers maxim. The framers were put on the defensive by Anti-Federalist charges that the proposed Constitution violated a strict (or pure) theory of separation of powers. According to this view, the liberties of the people could only be protected by completely separating the three branches of government. In *Federalist* 47–51, James Madison made two responses to these charges. First, Madison consulted the great "oracle" of the doctrine of separation of powers: Charles Louis de Secondat Montesquieu. The Anti-Federalists claimed that this eighteenth-century French philosopher and author of *The Spirit of the Laws* supported a pure form of the separation of powers. Madison, however, rejected this interpretation of Montesquieu. In discussing the doctrine of separation of powers, Montesquieu relied on the British Constitution, which he praised as "the mirror of political liberty" in the modern world.[18] Madison pointed out, however, that the British Constitution contained many examples of an intermixture of powers. For example, the English monarch had "the prerogative of making treaties with foreign nations," which under certain circumstances had "the force of legislative acts"; the House of Lords was "the sole depositary [*sic*] of judicial power in cases of impeachment," and was "invested with the supreme appellate jurisdiction in all other cases"; and judges were "so far connected with the legislative department as often to attend and participate in its deliberations."[19] These examples, Madison contended, furnish ample evidence that Montesquieu did not support a strict theory of separation of powers. Instead, what Montesquieu meant by the doctrine was not that the "departments ought to have no *partial agency* in, or no *control* over, the acts of each other," but rather "that where the *whole* power of one department is exercised by the same hands which possess the *whole* power of another department, the fundamental principles of a free constitution are subverted."[20]

   Second, Madison challenged the Anti-Federalist defense of a pure theory of separation of powers on its own terms. Reflecting his realistic view of politics, Madison maintained that if there were no intermixture of powers among the three branches of government, "[T]he degree of separation which the maxim requires, as essential to a free government, can never in practice be duly maintained," because "power is of an encroaching nature."[21] Officeholders, being ambitious and self-interested by nature, will attempt to usurp the powers belonging to the other branches of government. The solution to this problem is to provide the constitutional means for each department to protect itself from attack:

> [T]he great security against a gradual concentration of the several powers in the same department consists in giving to those who administer each department the necessary constitutional means and personal motives to resist encroachments of the others. The provision for defense must . . . be made commensurate to the danger of attack. Ambition must be made to counteract ambition.[22]

The framers intended the doctrine of separation of powers to serve primarily as a check on legislative power. In monarchical systems, the branch of government to be guarded against the most is the executive. But in republican systems, Madison contended that "the legislative authority necessarily predominates" and "is everywhere extending the sphere of its activity and drawing all power into its impetuous vortex."[23] Congress, with its more extensive and ill-defined powers, "can, with the greater facility, mask, under complicated and indirect measures, the encroachments which it makes on the co-ordinate departments."[24] Since the legislative branch has both the means and ambition to usurp authority, Madison claimed that the shared powers provided in the Constitution (e.g., treaties, appointments, and the making of laws) were necessary in order for the more feeble branches (the executive and judicial departments) to defend themselves from attack.

## MADISON VERSUS HAMILTON

James Madison is rightly credited as the primary theorist of separation of powers in *The Federalist Papers*, but he was not alone in the importance he placed on the doctrine. One of Hamilton's main objections to the Articles of Confederation was the absence of separation of powers. During the Revolutionary War, Lieutenant Colonel Hamilton complained that "Congress have kept the power too much into their own hands and have meddled too much with the details of every sort." In Hamilton's view, "Congress is properly a deliberative corps and it forgets itself when it attempts to play the executive."[25] Twenty-two years later, when Hamilton perceived that the independence of the federal judiciary was under attack, he described separation of powers as "the fundamental maxim of free government" and confessed that he would give "a drop of [his] heart's blood" to preserve the independence of the federal judiciary.[26] But Madison and Hamilton were not of one mind in how to interpret the doctrine. Madison defended a functionalist approach to the doctrine, while Hamilton defended a formalistic view. The modern debate over these two approaches to separation of powers can thus be traced back to the writings of these two men.

Not unlike Madison, Hamilton regarded the doctrine of separation of powers as primarily a check on the legislative branch. As he put it in *Federalist* 71:

> The representatives of the people, in a popular assembly, seem sometimes to fancy that they are the people themselves, and betray strong symptoms of impatience and disgust at the least sign of opposition from any other quarter; as if the exercise of its rights, by either the executive or judiciary, were a breach of their privilege and an outrage to their dignity. They often appear disposed to exert an imperious control over the other departments; and as they commonly have the people on their side, they always act with such momentum as to make it very difficult for the other members of the government to maintain the balance of the Constitution.[27]

With the legislature's extensive powers and close ties to the people, Hamilton argued that the more feeble branches must have the "constitutional arms" to defend themselves from attack. "To what purpose separate the executive or the judiciary from the legislative," admonished Hamilton, "if both the executive and the judiciary are so constituted as to be at the absolute devotion of the legislative? Such a separation must be merely nominal, and incapable of producing the ends for which it was established."[28] Where Madison and Hamilton differed was over how strictly to interpret the doctrine of separation of powers. Of the two men, Hamilton was (or at least became) the formalist.

Hamilton's early statements about separation of powers did not foreshadow his later formalistic views. In fact, at the New York State Ratifying Convention, Hamilton seemed to care less about forms of government:

> I have found, that Constitutions are more or less excellent, as they are more or less agreeable to the natural operation of things: I am therefore disposed not to dwell long on curious speculations, or pay much attention to modes and forms; but to adopt a system whose principles have been sanctioned by experience; adapt it to the real state of our country; and depend on probable reasonings for its operation and result.[29]

Then, in *Federalist* 68, Hamilton cited the poet Alexander Pope for the following proposition: "For forms of government let fools contest—That which is best administered is best."[30] While Hamilton said that "we cannot acquiesce in the political heresy" of this poet's statement,[31] his mere mention of it seems to indicate a less than full commitment to a formalistic interpretation of separation of powers. These early statements by Hamilton, however, have to be read in context. At the time of the founding, Hamilton's main object was to build a strong national government that would have the necessary power to hold together the union and accomplish its chief purposes.

Moreover, Hamilton was less scrupulous about separation of powers when it came to the powers of the executive branch—although never denying that there were such limits.[32] Hamilton subscribed to John Locke's right of prerogative (or the doctrine of necessity), where the president has the authority to act without law or even against it for the public good. In defending the Washington administration's Proclamation of Neutrality in 1793, Hamilton defined executive power as including everything not prohibited by the Constitution nor patently incompatible with principles of free government.[33] In Hamilton's view, the executive branch would be primarily responsible for promoting the welfare of the people. The legislative branch, he believed, was too attached to the people who often "*intend* the PUBLIC GOOD, but do not always *reason right* about the *means* of promoting it."[34] For this reason, Hamilton defended the president's veto power not only as a check against usurpations by Congress, but also as a device to prevent "the enaction of improper laws."[35] As Hamilton saw it, a properly balanced system of separation of powers must allow the president "to dare to act his own opinion with vigor and decision" in the interest of the public good.[36]

What is more, when the occasion arose, Hamilton defended a formalistic interpretation of separation of powers. In his draft of President George Washington's Farewell Address, for example, Hamilton cautioned against one department of government encroaching upon another and urged those officials serving within the respective departments to confine themselves within their respective constitutional spheres. With the House's constitutional challenge to the Jay Treaty still fresh on his mind, Hamilton noted that "[t]he spirit of encroachment tends to absorb & consolidate the powers of the several branches and departments into one, and thus to establish under whatever forms a despotism."[37] If a change to the structure or distribution of powers was necessary, Hamilton counseled that the people could amend the Constitution, but he warned against any change by mere usurpation. Hamilton's draft of the Farewell Address also reveals a chief aim of a formalistic interpretation of separation of powers: to fortify the executive branch. "One method of assault [upon the Constitution]," wrote Hamilton, "may be to effect alterations in the forms of the constitution tending to impair the energy of the system and so to undermine what cannot be directly overthrown."[38]

Another important example of Hamilton's formalistic interpretation of separation of powers came in response to President Thomas Jefferson's attempt to structurally modify the federal courts, which the president regarded as the last stronghold of the Federalist Party. In his First Annual Message to Congress, Jefferson mentioned that the judiciary, "and especially that portion of it recently erected," will undoubtedly be given some attention by Congress.[39] In response to this suggestion, Congress passed the Judiciary Act of 1802, which eliminated the new tier of federal circuit courts created under the Judiciary Act of 1801. Prior to the act's adoption, Hamilton wrote eighteen essays appearing in the *New-York Evening Post*, arguing that the abolition of the federal courts violated the "Good Behaviour" provision of the Constitution, and would prove "absolutely fatal to the independence of the Judiciary department."[40] In discussing the doctrine of separation of powers, Hamilton's formalism was apparent: "To prevent a concentration of powers it is essential that the departments among which [the powers of government] shall be distributed, should be effectually independent of each other."[41] To support Congress's right to "annihilate at discretion the organs" of another branch, he added, would affirm that there "are *no constitutional limits to the legislative Authority*," which Hamilton called the "AARON'S ROD" in republican government, "most likely to swallow up the rest, and therefore to be guarded against with particular care and caution."[42] In order for Congress to work such a fundamental change to the basic structure of government, Hamilton argued that an explicit power must be conferred in the Constitution:

> It would require a most express provision, susceptible of no other interpretation, to confer on that branch of the government an authority, so dangerous to the others, in opposition to the strong presumptions, which in conformity with the fundamental maxims of free government, arise from *the care taken in the Constitution, to establish and preserve the reciprocal and complete independence of the respective branches, first by a separate organization of the departments, next by a precise definition of the powers of each, lastly by precautions to secure to each a permanent support.*[43]

James Madison, by contrast, was a pragmatist when it came to separation of powers issues—and has been interpreted as such.[44] His interpretation of Montesquieu, for example—that the doctrine of separation of powers does not forbid the departments a *"partial agency"* and *"control"* over the acts of each other, so long as "the *whole* power of one department is [not] exercised by the same hands which possess the *whole* power of another department"—would seemingly allow for a sharing of powers beyond those specified in the Constitution. What seemed to concern Madison the most was a complete or overruling influence by one department over another.[45] Madison's pragmatic view of separation of powers was particularly evident in *Federalist* 37, perhaps his most philosophical essay, in which he states that there is an "unavoidable inaccuracy" in all laws and in language in general:

> All new laws, though penned with the greatest technical skill and passed on the fullest and most mature deliberation, are considered as more or less obscure and equivocal, until their meaning be liquidated and ascertained by a series of particular discussions and adjudications. Besides the obscurity arising from the complexity of objects and the imperfection of the human faculties, the medium through which the conceptions of men are conveyed to each other adds a fresh embarrassment. The use of words to express ideas. . . . [N]o language is so copious as to supply words or phrases for every complex idea, or so correct as not to include many equivocally denoting different ideas. Hence it must happen that however accurately objects may be discriminated in themselves, and however accurately the discrimination may be considered, the definition of them may be rendered inaccurate by the inaccuracy of the terms in which it was delivered. And this unavoidable inaccuracy must be greater or less, according to the complexity and novelty of the objects defined.[46]

These are not the words of a formalist. In referring to the difficulties that the delegates faced in dividing powers among the two levels of government, Madison mentioned similar linguistic difficulties concerning separation of powers:

> Experience has instructed us that no skill in the science of government has yet been able to discriminate and define, with sufficient certainty, its three great provinces—legislative, executive, and judiciary; or even the privileges and powers of the different legislative branches. Questions daily occur in the course of practice which prove the obscurity which reigns in these subjects, and which puzzle the greatest adepts in political science.[47]

And in a letter to Thomas Jefferson, written immediately after the close of the Constitutional Convention, Madison raised the same concern: "Even the boundaries between Executive, Legislative, and judiciary powers, though in general so strongly marked in themselves, consist, in many instances, of mere shades of difference."[48]

Consistent with Madison's nonliteral conception of separation of powers was the flexible approach he used to resolve some of the major interbranch conflicts of his life. While Madison did occasionally make formalistic separation of powers arguments,[49] he more often sounded like a functionalist. For example, in his legislative campaign against the Jay Treaty, Madison argued (in contrast to the plain language of the Constitution) that treaties dealing with

the lawmaking powers of Congress required the "sanction of the House before they could take effect."[50] Moreover, in the dispute during the First Congress over the president's power to remove executive branch officials—sometimes referred to as the Decision of 1789—Madison embraced a functionalist
approach to separation of powers. The initial bill creating the Department of
Foreign Affairs provided that the Secretary of Foreign Affairs was "[t]o be removable from office by the President."[51] An acrimonious debate ensued over
whether this language meant the president did not have the inherent authority
to remove executive officials. Madison took the position (ultimately the prevailing one) that the president did have such authority, because he believed
the functions performed by the Secretary of Foreign Affairs were purely executive in nature and that the president had the right to require the obedience
of those who serve under him. One month later, however, Madison qualified
his position regarding the president's removal power. In discussing the Office
of Comptroller General, Madison argued that the president's removal authority could be limited since this particular official performs functions not purely
executive in nature:

> It will be necessary . . . to consider the nature of this office, to enable us to
> come to a right decision on the subject; in analyzing its properties, we shall
> easily discover they are not purely of an executive nature. It seems to me that
> they partake of a judiciary quality as well as executive; perhaps the latter ob-
> tains in the greatest degree. . . . [T]here may be strong reasons why an officer
> of this kind should not hold his office at the pleasure of the executive branch
> of Government.[52]

Madison's analysis of the comptroller general's responsibilities was relied
upon by the Supreme Court in *Humphrey's Executor v. United States*,[53] where
the justices limited the president's ability to remove "quasi-legislative" and
"quasi-judicial" officers, thereby constitutionalizing what some call our
"headless" fourth branch of government: the independent regulatory agencies.
      In sum, while Hamilton and Madison both defended the doctrine of sepa-
ration of powers, they interpreted it differently. Hamilton was a formalist
while Madison was a functionalist. This interpretation of these two men is
also supported by their different political philosophies. A strict or formalistic
interpretation of separation of powers was congenial to Hamilton because he
supported a strong and energetic executive. Meanwhile, Madison placed the
foundation of republican government on the legislative branch, and while he
was concerned about legislative overreaching of power (as were most of the
founders[54]), he regarded the legislative branch as the most important institution for national policy making. Their differences in political philosophy was
the principal reason cited by Madison for their falling out as friends:

I deserted Colonel Hamilton, or rather Colonel H. deserted me; in a word, the divergence between us took place—from his wishing to *administration*, or rather to administer the Government . . . into what he thought it ought to be; while, on my part, I endeavored to make it conform to the Constitution as understood by the Convention that produced and recommended it, and particularly by the State conventions that *adopted* it.[55]

Even though Justice Scalia has argued that Madison would be "aghast" at the Court's functionalist approach to separation of powers,[56] it is clear that Madison was not a formalist. Rather, it was Hamilton who vigorously defended a formalistic interpretation of separation of powers at the time of the nation's founding. Justice Scalia's opinions on the subject of separation of powers will now be examined in order to reveal his Hamiltonian, pro-executive slant.

## JUSTICE SCALIA AND SEPARATION OF POWERS

### Legal Standing

Standing is an important doctrine dealing with access to federal courts, and asks, in particular, whether the *parties* to a case have the requisite personal interest in the controversy to adjudicate it in court. The doctrine serves separation of powers goals by preventing courts from using generalized claims to impede the policy decisions of the elected branches of government, and it serves judicial management and efficiency goals by ensuring that all litigants who come before a court have "such a personal stake in the outcome of the controversy as to assure that concrete adverseness which sharpens the presentation of issues upon which the court so largely depends for illumination."[57] The Court has held that standing is derived from two distinct sources. Some aspects of the doctrine are derived from the "Cases" and "Controversies" provision of Article III, Section 2, while others—the so-called "prudential" aspects of the doctrine—go beyond the constitutional requirements and have been developed and imposed by the Court itself.[58] Not surprisingly, Justice Scalia has questioned the Court's authority to establish the prudential standing limitations,[59] but has been the Court's most strenuous enforcer of the constitutional impediments of the doctrine. While standing is a technical procedural requirement, its importance cannot be underestimated. If a person aggrieved by governmental action (or inaction) cannot claim an actual and particularized injury, then relief will not be granted, and the underlying issue will not likely get resolved.

In a 1983 law review article, Scalia discussed several of the major themes of his standing doctrine that would later resurface in judicial opinions. In that article, Scalia contended that the doctrine of standing "is a crucial and inseparable element" of separation of powers, which if interpreted correctly prevents "an overjudicialization of the processes of self-governance."[60] He also said that enforcement of standing limits relegates courts to performing their traditional function of protecting minority rights and not the more undemocratic function of protecting majority rights. And, most importantly, he claimed that Article III's "Cases" and "Controversies" provision limits Congress's ability to extend standing to individuals who do not satisfy the "core" requirements of standing—that is, Congress cannot convert a generalized grievance into a legal right. Although not discussed in this particular article, another major theme of Justice Scalia's standing doctrine is that citizen lawsuits impede the president's ability to faithfully execute the laws under Article II. Many lawsuits, we shall see, challenge the actions (or inactions) of administrative agencies. Under Scalia's conception of standing, there is an intimate connection between Articles II and III of the Constitution. As courts provide liberal interpretations of standing, they impede the president's authority to "take Care" that the laws are faithfully executed under Article II. By contrast, as they strictly enforce the doctrine, they stay within their traditional role of adjudicating "legal" rights and allow the executive branch to enforce the laws as it sees fit. Scalia ridiculed the charge that "important legislative purposes, heralded in the halls of Congress, [can be] lost or misdirected in the vast hallways of the federal bureaucracy." That is a good thing, wrote Scalia, and he added, "Yesterday's herald is today's bore."[61] Since he began serving as a federal judge in 1982, Scalia has spilled much ink on the subject of standing. As noted in chapter 1, Scalia wrote eighteen opinions involving legal standing as a court of appeals judge,[62] and since his appointment to the Supreme Court in 1986, he has authored a number of important decisions in that area as well. In fact, for over a decade the Supreme Court's standing doctrine had an unmistakable Scalian stamp. More recently, however, Scalia has suffered a couple of major defeats.

In *Lujan v. National Wildlife Federation*,[63] the Court ruled that the National Wildlife Federation (NWF) did not have standing to challenge the Bureau of Land Management's (BLM) "land withdrawal review program," on the grounds that NWF did not allege specific facts showing how BLM's actions "adversely affected" its interests. Under the Federal Land Policy and Management Act (FLPMA) of 1976, BLM, an executive branch agency located in the Department of Interior, was delegated various responsibilities with respect to the management of pubic lands in the United States. As a general matter, NWF objected to BLM's reclassification of large tracts of federal land in such a way as to open them to various forms of development, including mining. In its complaint, NWF specifically alleged that BLM had failed to fulfill its responsibilities under the act by not revising land use plans in proper fashion, by not considering multiple uses for the lands, by focusing inordinately upon mineral exploitation and development, and by not providing public notice of its decisions. The NWF also claimed that BLM did not complete the requisite environmental impact statements under the National Environmental Policy Act (NEPA). NWF sued under section 702 of the Administrative Procedure Act of 1946 (APA), which allows judicial review of cases in which an individual suffers a "legal wrong" because of a challenged agency action, or is "adversely affected or aggrieved by agency action within the meaning of a relevant statute."[64] The NWF submitted two affidavits by its members to show that BLM's actions "adversely affected" its interests by negatively impacting its members' "recreational use and aesthetic enjoyment" of federal lands. For example, Peggy Kay Peterson claimed that she used land "within the vicinity" of Green Mountain, Wyoming, which is located in a 4,500-acre area now opened to mining because of a BLM order.

The secretary of interior moved for summary judgment, arguing that the NWF members' affidavits did not set forth specific facts showing there was a general issue for trial, which the district court granted. The district court held that Peterson's claim of using lands "within the vicinity" of the lands covered by BLM's decisions was inadequate, because it was unclear whether her recreational use and enjoyment extended to the particular 4,500 acres covered by those decisions. The court of appeals reversed, contending that the district court's ruling made Peterson's affidavit "a meaningless document" unless it could be interpreted to refer to the lands covered by the program. In a closely divided opinion the Supreme Court then reversed. In his opinion for the Court, Scalia held that the NWF members' affidavits were not specific enough to survive a summary judgment challenge. As a case progresses from the time a complaint is filed to the time of trial, Scalia maintained that the pleadings must be held to a higher standard of particularity. While he conceded that the members of NWF alleged harms—recreational use and aesthetics—that were within the zone of interests of the FLPMA and NEPA, he said that they were deficient in alleging specific facts that showed how BLM's actions affected those interests. A motion for summary judgment is "not satisfied by averments which state only that one of respondent's members uses unspecified portions of an immense tract of territory, on some portions of which mining activity has occurred or probably will occur by virtue of the governmental action."[65] While noting that piecemeal change can be frustrating to an organization like NWF, Scalia said that it "cannot seek wholesale improvement of this program by court decree"; rather, it should bring its grievances to "the offices of the Department [of Interior] or the halls of Congress, where programmatic improvements are normally made."[66]

Following *National Wildlife Federation*, Scalia authored what is probably his most important standing decision in the 1992 case *Lujan v. Defenders of Wildlife*.[67] There a majority denied standing to a wildlife conservation group challenging a revised joint ruling by the Secretary of the Interior and the Secretary of Commerce that the "consultation" requirement of the Endangered Species Act of 1973 (ESA) no longer applies to government activities outside of the United States. ESA's consultation requirement mandates that federal agencies consult with the Secretary of Interior to ensure that any federally funded program does not jeopardize endangered or threatened species.[68] Defenders of Wildlife (DoW) claimed that it was injured by this revised interpretation of ESA, because the lack of consultation with respect to certain funded activities abroad will increase the rate of extinction of threatened and endangered species. It sought an injunction requiring the Secretary of Interior to promulgate a new regulation restoring the initial interpretation.

Scalia rejected standing to the DoW members on two separate grounds, only the first of which was supported by a majority of the Court. According to Scalia, the Court had previously established "the irreducible constitutional minimum of standing" to contain three elements: the plaintiff must allege (1) "injury in fact" that is (a) concrete and particularized, and (b) actual or imminent, not conjectural or hypothetical; (2) causation, or a "causal connection between the injury and the conduct complained of"; and (3) redressability, or that it is likely that the injury will be redressed by a favorable court decision.[69] Scalia held that the plaintiffs did not satisfy the injury-in-fact requirement, because they did not show how injury to the animals would "imminently" injure the plaintiffs. The "some day" intentions of DoW members to return to places where they had previously visited did not "support a finding of the 'actual or imminent' injury" required by prior case law.[70] A plurality of the Court also held that, even if the plaintiffs were injured by the revised consultation provision, the injuries were not likely redressable by a favorable court ruling. On this point, Scalia argued that there was no evidence that the agencies involved in the overseas projects would follow a new ruling by the Secretary of Interior that ESA's consultation provision applies in foreign countries, and he reasoned that since the amount of federal agency spending on these projects was negligible, there was no assurance that the projects would be suspended or that animals would not be harmed if the Secretary of Interior issued a new order restoring the initial interpretation. Perhaps the most important aspect of Scalia's opinion was his interpretation of ESA's citizen suit provision, which was relied upon by the lower court to grant DoW standing. ESA, like most other environmental statutes, contains a citizen suit provision allowing "any person [to] commence a civil suit on his own behalf . . . to enjoin any person, including the United States and any other governmental instrumentality or agency . . . who is alleged to be in violation of any provision of this chapter."[71] Scalia ruled that this provision was unconstitutional as applied, on the grounds that if the constitutional limitations of standing are intended to preserve separation of powers principles, then Congress cannot confer standing on parties the Court traditionally has not granted standing to:

> To permit Congress to convert the undifferentiated public interest in executive officers' compliance with the law into an "individual right" vindicable in the courts is to permit Congress to transfer from the President to the courts the Chief Executive's most important constitutional duty, to "take Care that the Laws be faithfully executed."[72]

Justice Scalia's last major victory in a standing case came in *Steel Co. v. Citizens for a Better Environment*.[73] Citizens for a Better Environment (CBE), an association of individuals interested in environmental issues, brought suit against Steel Company, a small manufacturing company based in Chicago, for past violations of the Emergency Planning and Community Right-to-Know Act of 1986 (EPCRA). EPCRA requires users of specified toxic and hazardous chemicals to file annual forms containing such information as "the name and location of the facility, the name and quantity of the chemical on hand, and, in the case of toxic chemicals, the waste-disposal method employed and the annual quantity released into each environmental medium."[74] EPCRA allows citizens to bring suits to enforce compliance with the reporting requirements, provided they give sixty days' notice to the administrator of the EPA, the state in which the alleged violation occurs, and the alleged violator. If EPA's administrator chooses to bring suit, then the citizen suit cannot go forward. In 1995, CBE gave notice to Steel Company that since 1988 (the first year of EPCRA's filing deadlines) it had failed to submit its mandated annual reports. Upon receipt of this notice, Steel Company filed all overdue annual reports, and EPA chose not to bring further action. After the sixty-day notice period expired, CBE brought suit against Steel Company for (among other things) a declaratory judgment that the company violated EPCRA and civil penalties of $25,000 per day for each violation of the act.

At the Supreme Court, all of the justices agreed that CBE lacked standing to sue in this case, but they did so on different grounds. For five of his colleagues, Justice Scalia ruled that petitioners did not satisfy the redressability requirement under Article III. According to Scalia, there was no basis for declaratory or injunctive relief, because "there were no allegations of ongoing or imminent injuries," and civil penalties would not remediate any injury to CBE, because, under EPCRA, any imposed civil penalty must be paid into the United States Treasury. "[A]lthough a suitor may derive great comfort and joy

from the fact that the United States Treasury is not cheated, that a wrongdoer
gets his just deserts, or that the nation's laws are faithfully enforced, that 'psy-
chic satisfaction is not an acceptable Article III remedy.'"[75]

Only one month after *Steel Company*, however, a majority of the Rehnquist
Court distanced themselves from Scalia's formalism and harsh criticism of
federal citizen suit provisions in the area of standing. In *Federal Election
Commission v. Akins*,[76] the Court ruled that a group of voters had standing to
challenge the Federal Election Commission's (FEC) determination that the
American Israel Public Affairs Committee (AIPAC) is not a "political committee" under the Federal Election Campaign Act (FECA), thereby exempting it from disclosure requirements regarding membership, contributions, and
expenditures. Respondents, a group of voters with views opposed to AIPAC,
filed a complaint with the FEC, contending that AIPAC was a "political committee" under FECA and thus was in violation of the act's disclosure requirements. FEC ruled that AIPAC was not a political committee for purposes of
the act, but rather was an issue-oriented lobbying organization. Respondents
then sought relief under a FECA provision allowing "any party aggrieved by
an order of the Commission dismissing a complaint filed by such party" to
bring a case in federal court to review that dismissal.[77] When the case was
filed, FEC argued that the voters did not have standing. On appeal, the
Supreme Court, in an opinion by Justice Stephen Breyer, disagreed. According to Breyer, Congress can confer standing on citizens as long as all three
constitutional requirements of Article III are satisfied, which he believed they
were in this case. The Court found that the alleged injury—inability to obtain
information about campaign-related activities—to be sufficiently concrete
and specific; that the FEC's ruling against respondents to have caused their
injury; and that a favorable ruling by a court would likely redress their injury.
The Court acknowledged that the injury suffered here was a "generalized
grievance"—that is, one shared alike by a large number of people—but nevertheless determined that the mere fact that the harm is widely shared does not
deprive Congress of the power to authorize its vindication in federal courts.

Justice Scalia filed a sharp dissent arguing that respondents lacked standing for two separate reasons. First, the FEC's decision not to prosecute
AIPAC for the alleged FECA violations was not challengeable under the Administrative Procedure Act, because it was "enforcement action traditionally
deemed 'committed to agency discretion by law.'"[78] Second, Scalia claimed
that the citizen provision of the FECA was unconstitutional as applied. In
light of the "extraordinary" nature of FECA's citizen suit provision, Scalia
said that it should not be interpreted more broadly than its fair meaning. For
Scalia, petitioners were not an "aggrieved" party under the act, because they
were seeking information that was not currently available to the FEC. "What

the respondents complain of in this suit . . . is not the refusal to provide information, but the refusal (for an allegedly improper reason) to commence agency enforcement action against a third party," which would make such information available. Scalia reasoned that the majority's interpretation of the citizen suit provision, which would allow any person to sue to compel the agency to require registration of any entity as a political committee, would expand the meaning of the statute beyond what the Constitution permits and severely disrupt the separation of powers. Since respondents did not allege a concrete and particular injury from the citizenry at large, Scalia contended that standing should be denied:

> When the Executive can be directed by the courts, at the instance of any voter, to remedy a deprivation which affects the entire electorate in precisely the same way—and particularly when that deprivation (here, the unavailability of information) is one inseverable part of a larger enforcement scheme—there has occurred a shift of political responsibility to a branch designed not to protect the public at large but to protect individual rights . . . This is not the system we have had, and it is not the system we should desire.[79]

Another major defeat for Scalia came in the 2000 decision *Friends of the Earth v. Laidlaw Environmental Services*,[80] where the majority provided an expansive interpretation both to the injury-in-fact and redressability prongs of standing. Under the Clean Water Act of 1972 (CWA), a number of environmental groups, including Friends of the Earth (FOE), challenged a wastewater treatment plant's compliance with a National Pollutant Discharge Elimination System (NPDES) permit. Laidlaw Environmental Services (Laidlaw), a hazardous waste incinerator facility located in South Carolina, was found to be in violation of the mercury limits of its permit on 489 separate occasions between 1987 and 1995. The environmental plaintiffs claimed that Laidlaw's discharges of pollutants into the North Tyger River injured them by resulting in diminished enjoyment of the river and decreased property values. Not unlike the federal statute in *Steel Company*, the Clean Water Act allows for citizen suits to enforce compliance with the law, but only after the citizen plaintiff gives sixty days' notice to the administrator of the EPA, the affected state, and the alleged violator. Upon receiving notice, Laidlaw's lawyer asked the South Carolina Department of Health and Environmental Control (DHEC) to file suit against Laidlaw, which it did. On the last day before FOE's sixty-day notice period expired, "DHEC and Laidlaw reached a settlement requiring Laidlaw to pay $100,000 in civil penalties and to make 'every effort' to comply with its permit obligations."[81] Subsequently, FOE filed a citizen suit against Laidlaw in federal court seeking injunctive relief and an award of civil penalties because of Laidlaw's ongoing violations of the pollutant discharge requirements under its permit. The district court, while conceding that the issue was "awfully close," ruled that FOE had standing. The court of appeals, however, reversed. Following the precedent established in *Steel Company*, it found that FOE did not have standing because any civil penalty paid into the U.S. treasury did not redress its injuries.

The Supreme Court reversed. For the majority, Justice Ruth Bader Ginsburg determined that FOE had satisfied all three elements of standing: injury in fact, causation, and redressability. Ginsburg held that the sworn affidavits by the environmental plaintiffs adequately demonstrated injury in fact, and distinguished this case from both *National Wildlife Federation* and *Defenders of Wildlife*. In contrast to *National Wildlife Federation*, the petitioners here lived by or used the affected river, and, unlike *Defenders of Wildlife*, the injuries were not speculative or conjectural. "[W]e see nothing improbable about the proposition that a company's continuous and pervasive illegal discharges of pollutants into a river would cause nearby residents to curtail their recreational use of that waterway and would subject them to other economic and aesthetic harms."[82] As for redressability, Ginsburg maintained that *Steel Company* was not controlling, because Laidlaw, unlike the company in that case, was still in violation of its permit responsibilities, and civil penalties against the company, even if payable to the U.S. treasury, are a form of punishment that can deter future violations and thus amount to a form of redress for petitioners.

In an impassioned dissent, Scalia argued that the Court's opinion represented "a revolutionary new doctrine of standing." In Scalia's view, the majority's injury-in-fact analysis was a "sham," and he maintained that the petitioners' "subjective apprehensions" about pollution in the North Tyger River were not sufficient to qualify as concrete and particularized injury under Article III. For evidence of this, Scalia cited the district court's finding that there was "no demonstrated proof of harm to the environment" by Laidlaw's unlawful discharges into the river.[83] The majority's analysis of the redressability prong of standing was "equally cavalier," according to Scalia. Civil penalties payable to the U.S. Treasury, he claimed, can in no way redress alleged injuries suffered by citizen plaintiffs. "[I]t is entirely speculative whether [fear of future penalties] will make a difference between these plaintiffs' suffering injury in the future and these plaintiffs' going unharmed."[84] Scalia went on to argue that the Court's new, revolutionary standing doctrine will do great harm to the structure of government and, in particular, to the president's ability to faithfully execute the laws. By permitting citizens to pursue civil penalties payable to the U.S. Treasury, the Court (and Congress) "turns over to private citizens the function of enforcing the law."[85]

According to Scalia, a large private-interest group—or what he called a "self-appointed mini-EPA"—will now be in the position of deciding what companies to prosecute under federal law, and with the ability to obtain large civil penalties, will have "massive bargaining power" to "achieve settlements requiring the defendant to support environmental projects of the plaintiff's choosing."[86] While the Clean Water Act allows the EPA to take over a suit once notice of a violation has taken place, Scalia still maintained that citizen suits force the hand of the executive branch in deciding *when* enforcement should be undertaken. In his view, "Elected officials are entirely deprived of their discretion to decide that a given violation should not be the object of suit at all, or that the enforcement decision should be postponed."[87] Scalia concluded his opinion by noting that "[t]he undesirable and unconstitutional consequence of today's decision is to place the immense power of suing to enforce the public laws in private hands."[88]

## CONCLUSION

Justice Scalia's record of success in the area of standing has been mixed. His major victory came when he convinced his colleagues that there are constitutional limits on Congress's authority to extend standing beyond the core requirements of Article III. Article III contains no explicit constitutional requirements for standing and, as law professor Cass Sunstein has shown, "[t]here is absolutely no affirmative evidence that Article III was intended to limit congressional power to create standing." Rather, according to Sunstein, history shows that "people have standing if the law has granted them a right to bring suit."[89] The novelty of Scalia's decision in *Defenders of Wildlife* is that none of the cases he relied on for support of his position involved congressional grants of standing; the petitioners in the cases he cites relied upon constitutional provisions to confer standing. Interestingly, Justice Scalia backs up his interpretative theory of Article III with an argument based on republican principles of government. Citizen suits, in his view, would convert the U.S. political system into something akin to "an Athenian democracy or a New England town meeting," where every individual is a private attorney general who "can oversee the conduct of the National government by means of lawsuits in federal courts."[90]

At the same time, *Akins* and *Friends of the Earth* represent major setbacks for Scalia, because they rehabilitate congressional authority to allow citizen suits. The two decisions stand for the proposition that if plaintiffs can satisfy the "core" constitutional requirements of Article III, then Congress has the authority to confer standing, and, just as importantly, that a majority of justices

will give a fairly lenient view to the proof needed to satisfy the threefold constitutional requirements. The problem for the majority in *Defenders of
Wildlife* was that the injuries suffered by the members of DoW (although perhaps real) were too speculative, which probably means that Justice Harry
Blackmun's observation in dissent was correct: If the DoW members bought
airline tickets to the overseas sites they had previously visited, the Court
would likely have found standing under ESA's citizen suit provision.

Justice Scalia's standing decisions are strong evidence of his Hamiltonian
conception of democracy and the conservative role of the federal judiciary in
the United States. The application of Scalia's rule of law approach in standing cases reveals an authoritarian top-down approach to democracy whereby
citizens are regarded as passive subjects, not major policy makers.[91] While
"[w]e the people" in theory own the government, we have limited authority
to hold public or private actors accountable for their actions. Justice Scalia's
basic attitude about the national government and, in particular, the executive
branch, is that the people should, in Hamilton's words, "place confidence"
in their national officials. Executive branch agencies should have the discretion to enforce (or not enforce) laws as they please, and the people should not
second-guess these decisions except at election time. Scalia's formalistic
view of standing fulfills his separation of powers goals of preventing Congress and the courts from depriving the president of his ability to enforce the
laws and from turning citizens into private attorneys general.

# NOTES

1. FP, 320. The primary safeguard of individual liberties was a "dependence on the
people" through a system of elections. Ibid.
2. Ibid., 303.
3. Ibid., 475 (quoting the preamble to the Constitution). Hamilton argued that the
preamble "is a better recognition of popular rights than volumes of those aphorisms
which make the principal figure in several of our State bills of rights and which would
sound much better in a treatise of ethics than in a constitution of government." Ibid.,
475–76.
4. Ibid., 476.
5. Ibid., 477. Interestingly, Justice Scalia would leave the content and protection
of many rights to the political process as well. In *Employment Division, Department
of Human Resources of Oregon v. Smith*, 494 U.S. 872 (1990), he wrote, "Values that
are protected against government interference through enshrinement in the Bill of
Rights are not thereby banished from the political process." On another occasion, he
said that Congress is the "first line of constitutional defense" against the invasion of
rights, and that "congressional interpretations [of the Constitution] are of enormous

importance—of greater importance, ultimately, than those of the Supreme Court." Scalia, "The Legislative Veto: A False Remedy for System Overload," *Regulation* 3 (1979): 20.

6. "1976 Bicentennial Institute—Oversight and Review of Agency Decisionmaking," *Administrative Law Review* 28, no. 4 (1976): 569–742, 693.

7. Remarks by Justice Antonin Scalia at roundtable discussion of "Separation of Powers in the Constitution," sponsored by the U.S. Court of Appeals, Washington, D.C. C-SPAN audiotape broadcast, November 15, 1988.

8. *Plaut v. Spendthrift Farm, Inc.*, 514 U.S. 211, 240 (1995). The American poet was Robert Frost.

9. *Mistretta v. United States*, 488 U.S. 361, 426 (1989) (Scalia, J., dissenting).

10. See, e.g., *Morrison v. Olson*, 487 U.S. 654, 697 (1988) (Scalia, J., dissenting).

11. FP, 310.

12. David Ryrie Brink, Antonin Scalia, and Richard B. Smith, Brief for American Bar Association as *Amicus Curiae* in *INS v. Chadha*.

13. "1976 Bicentennial Institute—Oversight and Review of Agency Decisionmaking," 694. Scalia is thus no fan of the Progressive critique of the separation of powers system, which would allow for greater cooperation among the political branches of government modeled after the British parliamentary system. See, e.g., Woodrow Wilson, *Congressional Government* (Boston: Houghton Mifflin Co., 1885).

14. U.S. Senate, *Executive Privilege—Secrecy in Government: Hearings before the Subcommittee on Intergovernmental Relations of the Committee on Government Operations*, 94th Cong., 2nd. sess., October 23, 1975, 67–128, 92.

15. 524 U.S. 417 (1998).

16. David N. Reisman, "Deconstructing Justice Scalia's Separation of Powers Jurisprudence: The Preeminent Executive," *Albany Law Review* 53 (1988): 52.

17. FP, 119.

18. Ibid., 303.

19. Ibid., 303–4.

20. Ibid., 304.

21. Ibid., 308–9.

22. Ibid., 319.

23. Ibid., 308, 320.

24. Ibid., 310.

25. Letter to James Duane (September 3, 1780), PAH, 2:404.

26. PAH, 25:526, 549.

27. FP, 410–11.

28. Ibid., 410, 418.

29. PAH, 5:36.

30. FP, 395.

31. Ibid.

32. Hamilton, for example, spoke positively about the checks placed on the president under the new constitution, including the Senate's role in both the ratification of treaties and in confirming presidential appointments. He also commended the writ of habeas corpus as an important right that individuals have against tyrannical government.

33. PAH, 15:39 ("The general doctrine then of our constitution is, that the EXECU-TIVE POWER of the Nation is vested in the President; subject only to the *exceptions* and *qualifications* which are expressed in the instrument").

34. FP, 410.

35. Ibid., 418 (The veto "establishes a salutary check upon the legislative body, calculated to guard the community against the effects of faction, precipitancy, or of any impulse unfriendly to the public good, which may happen to influence a majority of that body").

36. Ibid., 410.

37. PAH, 20:279.

38. Ibid., 276.

39. PAH, 25:448.

40. Ibid., 535.

41. Ibid., 551.

42. Ibid., 534, 551, 554.

43. Ibid., 551–52 (emphasis added).

44. See, e.g., *Mistretta v. United States*, 488 U.S. 361, 381 (1989) (Madison recognized that our constitutional system imposes upon the branches a degree of interdependence as well as independence the absence of which 'would preclude the establishment of a Nation capable of governing itself effectively.'").

45. See, e.g., FP (No. 48), 308 ("It is agreed on all sides that the powers properly belonging to one of the departments ought not to be directly and completely administered by either of the other departments").

46. FP, 245.

47. FP, 244.

48. Letter to Thomas Jefferson, October 24, 1787, L&OWJM, 1:349.

49. Writing as "Helvidius," Madison argued that the Proclamation of Neutrality of 1793, issued in response to armed conflict between France and Britain, encroached upon Congress's right to declare war and make treaties. PJM, 15:66–73, 80–87, 95–103, 106–11, 113–20.

50. *Annals of Congress*, 4th Cong., 1st sess., 5:487–95.

51. *Annals of Congress*, 1st Cong., 1st sess., 1:473.

52. Ibid., 635–36.

53. 295 U.S. 602 (1935).

54. See, e.g., Thomas Jefferson, "Notes on the State of Virginia," in *The Portable Thomas Jefferson*, ed. Merrill D. Peterson (New York: Penguin Books, 1975), 164 ("All the powers of government, legislative, executive, and judiciary, result to the legislative body. The concentrating of these in the same hands is precisely the definition of despotic government. It will be no alleviation that these powers will be exercised by a plurality of hands, and not a single one. 173 despots would surely be as oppressive as one").

55. "N. P. Trist Memoranda" (September 27, 1834), Records 3:534.

56. *Mistretta v. United States*, 488 U.S. at 426.

57. *Baker v. Carr*, 369 U.S. 186, 204 (1962).

58. See *Valley Forge Christian College v. Americans United for Separation of Church and State*, 454 U.S. 464, 472–75 (1982).

59. Scalia, "The Doctrine of Standing as an Essential Element of the Separation of Powers," *Suffolk University Law Review* 17 (1983): 885 ("Personally, I find this bifurcation [between constitutional and prudential limitations] unsatisfying—not least because it leaves unexplained the Court's source of authority for simply granting or denying standing as its prudence might dictate. As I would prefer the matter, the Court must always hear the case of a litigant who asserts the violation of a legal right").

60. Ibid., 881.

61. Ibid., 897.

62. Michael A. Perino, "Justice Scalia: Standing, Environmental Law, and the Supreme Court," *Boston College Environmental Affairs Law Review* 15 (1987): 135n173.

63. 497 U.S. 871 (1990).

64. 5 U.S.C. sec. 702.

65. 497 U.S. at 889.

66. Ibid., 891.

67. 504 U.S. 555 (1992).

68. 16 U.S.C. sec. 1536(a)(2).

69. 504 U.S. 560–61.

70. Ibid., 564.

71. 16 U.S.C. sec. 1540(g).

72. 504 U.S. 577 (quoting U.S. Const. art. II, sec. 3).

73. 523 U.S. 83 (1998).

74. Ibid., 87 (citing 42 U.S.C. secs. 11022 and 11023).

75. Ibid., 107.

76. 524 U.S. 11 (1998).

77. Ibid., 19 (citing 2 U.S.C. sec. 437g[8][A]).

78. Ibid., 30 (citing 5 U.S.C. sec. 701[a][2]).

79. Ibid., 36–37.

80. 528 U.S. 167 (2000).

81. Ibid., 177.

82. Ibid., 184.

83. Ibid., 199.

84. Ibid., 208.

85. Ibid., 209.

86. Ibid., 209–10.

87. Ibid., 210.

88. Ibid., 215.

89. Cass R. Sunstein, "What's Standing after Lujan? Of Citizen Suits, 'Injuries,' and Article III," *Michigan Law Review* 91 (1992): 163, 177–78.

90. *Federal Election Commission v. Akins*, 524 U.S. 33 (citing *United States v. Richardson*, 418 U.S. 166, 179 [1974]).

91. Steven L. Winter, "Citizen Suits and the Future of Standing in the 21st Century: From *Lujan* to *Laidlaw* and Beyond: What If Justice Scalia Took History and the Rule of Law Seriously?" *Duke Environmental Law & Public Policy Forum* 12 (2001): 155.

## Chapter Three

# Interbranch Conflicts between Congress and the President

This chapter analyzes classic interbranch disputes between Congress and the president. Scalia's formalistic approach to separation of powers is clearly evident in cases where Congress encroaches upon or erodes executive power, but it disappears when the president is the beneficiary of additional "legislative" power. This was most conspicuous in Scalia's dissenting opinion in the 1998 decision *Clinton v. City of New York*,[1] where he voted to uphold the Line Item Veto Act of 1996. The parties in that case challenged the conferral of line-item veto authority on the president as a violation of Article I's Presentment Clause and the doctrine of separation of powers. Scalia disagreed. While his opinion in that case is hard to reconcile with his opposition to the legislative veto, which dates back to the mid 1970s, it is understandable from a Hamiltonian perspective.

### THE BALANCED BUDGET ACT

Antonin Scalia's first decision in a separation of powers conflict between the political branches of government came in *Synar v. United States*,[2] and he would make the most of it. As a result of mounting federal budget deficits, Congress passed the Balanced Budget and Emergency Deficit Control Act, popularly known as the Gramm-Rudman-Hollings bill, in 1985. The law set annual maximum budget-deficit levels, which if exceeded required across-the-board budget cuts. Beginning in fiscal year 1986, the size of the deficit was gradually to decrease until it reached zero in 1991. The act required the director of the Office of Management and Budget (OMB), an executive branch official, and the director of the Congressional Budget Office (CBO), a legislative official, to independently estimate the projected deficit and file a joint report with the comptroller general of the United States. The comptroller general, who heads the General Accountability Office (GAO), an agency created by Congress in 1921, must then review the reports and issue his own report with recommendations to the president, who then must issue a "sequestration" order mandating the spending reductions. Representative Mike Synar (D-OK), who had voted against the bill, filed suit against Comptroller General Charles Bowsher, contending that the act violated the separation of powers for two reasons. First, the act unconstitutionally delegated legislative power to the comptroller general and, second, the act conferred executive power on the comptroller general, who, while appointed by the president, is removable from office by a joint resolution of Congress. Judge Antonin Scalia decided this case as part of a three-judge panel for the D.C. District Court, and the opinion was issued per curiam—although Judge Scalia is widely reported to have authored it,[3] which is amply borne out by both the substance and style of the decision.

   In light of how the court would ultimately resolve the removal issue, Judge Scalia noted that the judges did not have to address the excessive delegation issue, but he boldly declared, "[W]e depart from normal prudential practice and provide our view *obiter dicta.*"[4] The nondelegation doctrine, which was discussed by John Locke in his *Second Treatise of Government*, is derived from the age-old Latin maxim "A power once delegated cannot be redelegated." In the United States, this has come to mean, in particular, that Congress cannot confer core lawmaking authority on the executive branch. The Court, however, has not been particularly aggressive in enforcing the doctrine. In its 225-year history, only two congressional laws have been struck down as violative of the nondelegation doctrine, leading some to wonder if the doctrine is not dead. The classic test used in excessive delegation cases was provided by Chief Justice William H. Taft in *J. W. Hampton, Jr. & Co. v. United States*:

> [T]he separation-of-powers principle does not prevent the legislative branch from seeking the "assistance" of coordinate branches; "the extent and character of that assistance must be fixed according to common sense and the inherent necessities of the governmental coordination"; and so long as Congress "lay[s] down by legislative act an intelligible principle to which the person or body authorized to [exercise the delegated authority] is directed to conform, such legislative action is not a forbidden delegation of legislative power."[5]

Applying that test to the facts of this case, Judge Scalia found that Congress provided an "intelligible principle" to the officials who make the budget calculations under the act. For example, the act assumes "the continuation of current law in the case of revenues and spending authority," and defines such terms as "real economic growth," "budget outlays," "budget authority," and "deficit."[6] Moreover, Scalia contended that "the required assumptions and definitions are given additional meaning by reference to years of administrative and congressional experience in making similar economic projections and calculations under the Congressional Budget Act of 1974."[7] For these reasons, the court held that the act did not violate the nondelegation doctrine. While Scalia admitted that the authority conferred by Congress on the comptroller general involved "a good deal of judgment," he insisted that Congress made the "hard political choices":

> What is significant about this case, and what distinguishes it from many other cases in which delegation has been upheld, is that the *only* discretion conferred is in the ascertainment of facts and prediction of facts. The Comptroller General is not made responsible for a single *policy* judgment as to, for example, what is a "fair price," or when it would be "appropriate" to freeze wages and prices, or wherein lies the "public interest." . . . Compared with the cases upholding administrative resolution of such issues, the present delegation is remote from legislative abdication.[8]

Notably absent in Judge Scalia's opinion regarding the excessive delegation question is the formalism that appears in his other separation of powers decisions. For example, the court rejected petitioners' argument that the act violated the nondelegation doctrine by assigning *core* legislative powers to administrative officials. According to Scalia, the Constitution does not make a distinction between *core* and *noncore* legislative functions. Without such textual guidance, he argued, any such line drawing would have to be done "on the basis of the court's own perceptions of the relative importance of various legislative functions," which was a role for the courts he did not want to support.[9] For Scalia, "the doctrine of unconstitutional delegation . . . is preeminently *not* a doctrine of technicalities":[10]

> [T]he Court's decisions display a much greater deference to Congress' power to delegate, motivated in part by concerns, that "[i]n an increasingly complex society, Congress obviously could not perform its functions if it were obliged to find all the facts subsidiary to the basic conclusions which support the defined legislative policy."[11]

The petitioners, however, also claimed that the act violated the doctrine of separation of powers by conferring executive authority on an official who is removable from office by Congress.[12] On this point, Scalia was in agreement. The Constitution does not explicitly confer the removal power on either the president or the Congress, except in cases of impeachment. The Appointments Clause, however, does provide some guidance:

> The President . . . shall nominate, and by and with the Advice and Consent of the Senate, shall appoint . . . all other Officers of the United States, whose Appointments are not herein otherwise provided for, and which shall be established by Law; but the Congress may by Law vest the Appointment of such inferior Officers, as they think proper, in the President alone, in the Courts of Law, or in the Heads of Departments.[13]

In *Myers v. United States*,[14] the Supreme Court's first major removal decision, the justices struck down a federal statute that required the advice and consent of the Senate before the president could remove first-, second-, and third-class postmasters. In a broad and sweeping opinion, Chief Justice (and ex-President) William Taft held that "the power of removal . . . was incident to the power of appointment."[15] For support of this view, Taft cited several sources, including the Appointments Clause, the doctrine of separation of powers, and Hamilton's "Pacificus" papers, in which Hamilton made the case for inherent presidential powers. Taft also argued that in order for the president to faithfully execute the laws, he must have confidence in those who serve under him. For Congress to reserve the removal power to itself, Taft concluded, would upset the delicate balance of powers and substantially diminish the independence and authority of the executive branch.

Nine years later, however, the Hughes Court substantially restricted the president's removal power in *Humphrey's Executor v. United States*.[16] In that case, the Court considered whether Congress had the power to limit the president's removal power under the Federal Trade Commission Act. Placing reliance upon James Madison's arguments during the so-called "Decision of 1789," the Court held unanimously that it could and made a fundamental distinction between administrative officials who perform "purely executive" functions and those who perform "quasi-legislative" and "quasi-judicial" functions. For those agency officials who perform "purely executive" functions, such as the postmasters in *Myers*, the Court held that the president has an absolute or illimitable power of removal. But for those officials who perform "quasi-legislative" and "quasi-judicial" functions, such as the commissioner of the Federal Trade Commission, the Court held that the president's removal power could be limited by Congress. In the process, the Court gave constitutional legitimacy to our headless fourth branch of government: the "independent" regulatory agencies.

Justice Scalia has long been a critic of *Humphrey's Executor*. He has objected to the decision on several grounds: that the "nature-of-the-functions" test announced by the Court does not make any sense, that the decision may have been the result of political opposition to FDR's New Deal program, and that the precise holding of the case has been expanded beyond its original meaning to prevent any influence by the president over the independent agencies. On several occasions, Justice Scalia also has gone out of his way to praise Chief Justice Taft's opinion in *Myers*—and, on one occasion, even took the unusual step of suggesting some ways of bolstering its historical analysis.[17] In *Synar*, Scalia's hostility toward *Humphrey's Executor* was particularly apparent:

> It has in any event always been difficult to reconcile *Humphrey's Executor*'s "headless fourth branch" with a constitutional text and tradition establishing three branches of government—assuming, as the rationale though not the narrow holding of *Humphrey's Executor* requires, that the presidential removal for cause permitted under the statute upheld there did not include removal because of the appointee's failure to accept presidential instructions regarding matters of policy or statutory application delegated to him by Congress.[18]

In the end, though, Judge Scalia had to concede that *Humphrey's Executor* was still the law of the land and therefore had to be followed in making the court's decision.

In following the reasoning of *Humphrey's Executor*, a determinative question for the Court was whether the comptroller general was an executive or legislative official. Judge Scalia was at a loss in making this determination. According to him, the functions performed by the comptroller general "[fall] neatly between the two stools of *Myers* and *Humphrey's Executor*. The Comptroller General is neither a 'purely executive [officer],' whom *Myers* . . . requires to be subject to discretionary presidential removal; nor an officer such as that said to be involved in *Humphrey's Executor*, who 'occupies no place in the executive department and who exercises no part of executive power vested by the Constitution in the President.'"[19] But while, as a general matter, the functions of the comptroller general were not easy to classify, Judge Scalia had no question that the functions performed by the comptroller general under the Balanced Budget and Emergency Deficit Control Act were executive in nature. According to Scalia, the act requires "the exercise of substantial judgment concerning present and past facts that affect the application of the law—the sort of power normally conferred upon the executive officer charged with implementing a statute."[20] Moreover, Scalia noted that another distinguishing factor between this case and *Humphrey's Executor* is that Congress reserved the removal power to itself, which is impermissible under the reasoning of *Myers*. Thus, the court struck down the act insofar as it lodged executive power in the comptroller general who is subject to removal by Congress.

Judge Scalia's discussion of the removal power in *Synar* places great importance on preserving the balance of power between Congress and the president. As he put it, "What has been at issue in the congressional-executive dispute over the power of removal that began in the First Congress is not control over the officer but, ultimately, control over the governmental functions that he performs."[21] "Once an officer is appointed," Scalia added, "it is only the authority that can remove him, and not the authority that appointed him, that he must fear and, in the performance of his functions, obey."[22] For this reason, Scalia doubted whether the act would have passed had the comptroller general been subject to removal by the president. In contrast to the president's removal power, Scalia contended that a congressional power to remove can have a devastating effect on the balance of powers:

> [I]nsofar as effect upon balance of powers is concerned, congressional power to remove is much more potent, since the Executive has no means of retaliation that may dissuade Congress from exercising it—other than leaving the office vacant, thereby impairing the Executive's own functions. Congress, on the other hand, has many ways to make the President think long and hard before he makes a "for cause" removal that Congress disapproves, ranging from budget constriction to refusal to confirm a successor.[23]

Based on these various considerations, Scalia concluded that "the Constitution grants only a subordinate role to the Congress" in making appointments and removals.[24]

## THE POLITICS OF *SYNAR*

Since the first sequestration order by the president was to take place in March 1986, Scalia completed the panel's opinion in *Synar* at a very rapid pace. The case was filed on December 12, 1985, just hours after it was signed by President Ronald Reagan; oral argument took place on December 31, 1985; and the three-judge panel's thirty-page comprehensive and detailed opinion was handed down on February 7, 1986. The decision was likely a major factor in Judge Scalia's being selected to fill the Supreme Court vacancy left after the retirement of Chief Justice Warren E. Burger in June 1986, since, even though President Reagan signed the bill into law, the Justice Department adamantly opposed the role played by the comptroller general under the act. On appeal, the Supreme Court handed down its decision in *Bowsher v. Synar*[25] after Judge Scalia had already been nominated to the high court but before he was confirmed. During the Court's conference and opinion-writing process, several of the justices expressed concern about the far-reaching implications of the lower court's opinion. Justice William J. Brennan, in particular, was alarmed that "[t]he District Court opinion includes a lot of dictum that questions the continuing validity of *Humphrey's Executors* [*sic*]." "This dictum," in his view, "is simply wrong."[26] The Court ultimately affirmed Scalia's lower-court opinion, but not before pointing out explicitly that *Humphrey's Executor* was still good law.[27]

## THE TAX COURT AND THE UNITARY EXECUTIVE

In the U.S. separation of powers system, there are really three types of judges: Article I legislative judges, Article II administrative judges, and Article III "independent judiciary" judges—only the last of which enjoy the safeguards of life tenure and an undiminished salary. In 1979, University of Chicago law professor Antonin Scalia called for a major restructuring of the appointment-and-promotion process for Article II administrative law judges (ALJs), the approximately 1,000 in-house agency adjudicators who decide cases within the federal government's bureaucracy. Instead of continuing with a merit system for these judges, Scalia argued that appointments and promotions of ALJs should be handled by the individual agencies themselves. In Scalia's view, this would make the ALJ system more efficient and would allow for the recruitment and retention of better-quality judges. The present merit system, according to Scalia, "violates a fundamental tenet of sound administration: he who decides should know. It also violates another tenet: he who decides should reap the grief or benefit of his decision."[28] Scalia largely dismissed as "exaggerated" the fears that making these judges political appointees would lead to undue influence and to decisions favoring the employing agency. Interestingly, under the U.S. tripartite system of government, Scalia saw no conflict with the agency serving as accuser, prosecutor, and judge in particular cases. The important thing was that ALJs be responsible to the affected agency and that a unitary executive be preserved. In an oft-overlooked separation of powers decision, Justice Scalia examined the appointment process for Article I *legislative* judges in *Freytag v. Commissioner of Internal Revenue*.[29] Not surprisingly, Scalia made the case for executive appointment and responsibility.

*Freytag* involved the appointment authority of the chief judge of the United States Tax Court. Under the Tax Reform Act of 1986, Congress authorized the chief judge of that court to appoint special trial judges to hear certain specially designated proceedings and "any other proceeding which the chief judge may designate."[30] Petitioners, who were allegedly deficient in reporting taxable income, challenged the ruling of the special trial judge appointed in their case by contesting the method of appointing these judges under the Appointments Clause. The Excepting Clause of Article II, Section 2 allows Congress to "vest the Appointment of . . . inferior Officers" in "the President alone, in the Courts of Law, or in the Heads of Departments."[31] Petitioners claimed that the chief judge of the Tax Court does not fall within one of these three constitutionally designated repositories of appointment power, and therefore the appointment of the special trial judge in their case was unconstitutional.

The Supreme Court's decision was unanimous,[32] but there was wide disagreement among its members over how the Tax Court should be designated under Article II's Excepting Clause. The majority, in an opinion by Justice Harry Blackmun, ruled that the Tax Court was one of the "Courts of Law" under the clause. For support of this view, Blackmun relied on the political theory of the Appointments Clause, the text of the Constitution, and "the clear intent of Congress to transform the Tax Court into an Article I legislative court."[33] According to Justice Blackmun, the primary purpose of the Appointments Clause was to protect against executive despotism: "The 'manipulation of official appointments' had long been one of the American revolutionary generation's greatest grievances against executive power."[34] Consequently, Blackmun maintained that the framers "carefully husband[ed] the appointment power to limit its diffusion."[35]

In a vigorous concurring opinion, Justice Scalia took strong exception to the majority's analysis, concluding that it was "wrong and full of danger for the future of our system of separate and coequal powers."[36] While he agreed that petitioners' Appointments Clause claim was not supportable, he disagreed with the majority's designation of the Tax Court as a court of law. Rather, Scalia determined that the Tax Court was a department with the chief judge as its head. This conclusion, reasoned Scalia, is borne out by "[a] careful reading of the Constitution and attention to the apparent purpose of the Appointments Clause." The Appointments Clause, Scalia pointed out, does not refer generally to "Bodies exercising judicial Functions," or to "Courts" generally, or even to "Courts of Law." Rather, it refers to "*the* Courts of Law." Scalia argued that the definite article *the* narrows the class of eligible "Courts of Law" to those envisioned by the Constitution.[37] The only courts of law referred to in the Constitution, he argued, are Article III courts, whose judges serve during good behavior and have irreducible salaries, which the Tax Court is not.

This understanding of the Appointments Clause, Scalia contended, is buttressed by the framers' "considered political theory for the appointment of officers."[38] In contrast to the majority, Scalia claimed that the Appointments Clause was designed as a limitation on Congress. "The Framers' experience with postrevolutionary self-government had taught them that combining the power to create offices with the power to appoint officers was a recipe for legislative corruption. The foremost danger was that legislators would create offices with the expectancy of occupying them themselves."[39] As a result of these concerns, Scalia argued that the federal appointment power was purposefully removed from Congress. The power of appointment, coupled with the other powers and protections of the executive branch under the Constitution, was a powerful means to ward off intermeddling by Congress:

> A power of appointment lodged in a President surrounded by such structural fortifications [a separate political constituency, the veto power, and permanent salary] could be expected to be exercised independently, and not pursuant to the manipulations of Congress. The same is true, to almost the same degree, of the appointment power lodged in the heads of departments. Like the President, these individuals possess a reputational stake in the quality of the individuals they appoint; and though they are not themselves able to resist congressional encroachment, they are directly answerable to the President, who is responsible to *his* constituency for their appointments and has the motives and means to assure faithful actions by his direct lieutenants.[40]

Scalia claimed that the majority's interpretation of the Appointments Clause "utterly destroys" the framers' "carefully constructed scheme" for appointments, because it allows Congress to confer appointment authority on legislative courts "without regard to whether their personnel are either Article III judges *or* 'Heads of Departments.'"[41] The fact that the Tax Court had been conferred adjudicatory functions by Congress made no difference to Justice Scalia. Many executive agencies, he contended, possess adjudicatory powers: "Today the Federal Government has a corps of administrative law judges numbering more than 1,000 whose principal statutory function is the conduct of adjudication under the Administrative Procedure Act. . . . They are all *executive* officers."[42] Adjudication, in Scalia's view, is a necessary but not a sufficient condition for the exercise of federal judicial power. What separates Article III courts from executive agencies, whose officials exercise adjudicative functions, is that Article III judges possess life tenure with an undiminishable salary. "Where adjudicative decisionmakers do not possess" these qualities, "they are 'incapable of exercising any portion of the judicial power.'"[43] For this reason, while the Tax Court may exercise adjudicatory functions, it is not a court of law, and in reality is not constitutionally distinct from other independent or executive agencies, such as the Internal Revenue Service, the Federal Communications Commission, and the National Labor Relations Board, which all exercise adjudicatory functions.

Instead of classifying the Tax Court as a court of law, Scalia argued that it should be designated as a department. Scalia strongly disagreed with the majority's ruling that "Heads of Departments" are confined to cabinet-level officials. As Scalia saw it, the text of the Constitution makes no such distinction, and the founders rejected proposals to create a cabinet-like entity. For Scalia, the term "Heads of Departments" should be given its ordinary meaning and should be read to include "the heads of all agencies immediately below the President in the organizational structure of the Executive Branch."[44] Under such a conception, the Tax Court would be regarded as "a freestanding, self-contained entity in the Executive Branch, whose Chief Judge is removable by the President (and, save impeachment, no one else)."[45]

Interestingly, due to the Court's removal decision in *Humphrey's Executor*, Scalia conceded that the *"raison d'etre"* for permitting the appointment power to be lodged in "Heads of Departments" does not exist today with the same force that it did at the founding. Nevertheless, he was of the view that "adjusting the remainder of the Constitution to compensate for *Humphrey's Executor* is a fruitless endeavor."[46] Moreover, Scalia argued that it was important to place the appointment power with the right institution in order to preserve the balance of powers. While in this case Congress did not attempt to reserve the appointment power to itself, as it has done in other cases, Scalia maintained that it will be easier for Congress to exert more influence over a court of law (especially as defined by the majority) than it would be to influence an independent agency, subject (at least to some extent) to the control and influence of the president.

The importance of Justice Scalia's concurring opinion in *Freytag* cannot be overestimated. Under his interpretation of the Excepting Clause of Article II, only Article III courts can be considered courts of law; therefore, all non–Article III courts must be considered departments whose members must be appointed by either the president or the head of a department, which presumably would include such Article I courts as the Court of Federal Claims, the Court of Veterans Appeals, and the U.S. Court of Appeals for the Armed Forces. If Scalia's views were to be accepted, and he did come close to obtaining a majority, Congress's ability to place appointment authority in judicial bodies not subject to presidential influence would be sharply limited. Scalia's opinion in *Freytag* (as well as his views concerning the appointment and promotion of ALJs) can be criticized for putting too much weight on accountability and clear lines of authority, and not enough on judicial independence. Although the Tax Court and other legislative courts are not Article III judicial bodies, there is a concern that if these judges are kept too much under the control and influence of the executive branch, they will not be able to render impartial decisions. Arthur L. Nims III, who was the chief judge of the U.S. Tax Court at the time *Freytag* was decided, observed that if Scalia's opinion had prevailed, it would have been "disastrous" to any credible independence from the executive branch. If the Tax Court was classified as a "department," Nims believed it "would have to follow policies and procedures adopted by the administration, just like any other department," and he added, "I don't think the executive branch should be allowed to control what judges do."[47] Nevertheless, Scalia's *Freytag* opinion represents classic Hamiltonian political philosophy, defending, as he does, the need for a unitary executive and political responsibility through clear lines of responsibility.

## THE SPECIAL PROSECUTOR

A central concern in a democratic system of government is political accountability. If government officials commit crimes, they violate the people's trust and should be removed from office. But how, and by what means, should this accountability be accomplished? State courts appoint special prosecutors when government attorneys have to disqualify themselves because of conflicts of interest, and on the federal level, special prosecutors have been appointed by the executive branch on an ad hoc basis to investigate official misconduct.[48] This ad hoc approach, however, ran into problems during the Watergate crisis, when President Richard Nixon ordered the firing of Special Prosecutor Archibald Cox, who was appointed to investigate the president's involvement in the break-in of the Watergate Office Building and the subsequent cover-up. In response to President Nixon's actions, Congress passed the Ethics in Government Act in 1978,[49] Title VI of which allows for the appointment of independent counsels by a panel of judges to investigate federal crimes by high-ranking officers of the executive branch. Under the act, the attorney general, upon receipt of information that discloses that there may have been a violation of federal criminal law, is required to conduct a preliminary investigation. After the attorney general has completed this investigation, she is required to report to a special three-judge court—called the Special Division—which was created by the act for the purpose of appointing independent counsels. If the attorney general determines that there are "reasonable" grounds to believe that further investigation is warranted, then she shall apply to the Special Division for the appointment of an independent counsel. The selection of the independent counsel and the description of his or her jurisdiction are the Special Division's only functions. Once appointed, special prosecutors are granted the "full power and independent authority to exercise all investigative and prosecutorial functions of the Department of Justice," and they can be removed from office by the attorney general only for "good cause."

Theodore Olson, then an assistant attorney general in the Office of Legal Counsel under the Reagan administration, was accused of giving false testimony during a congressional hearing involving the Justice Department's enforcement of, and subsequent refusal to provide documents about, the "Superfund" law. The House Judiciary Committee, after conducting its own investigation of the matter, requested that the attorney general initiate actions for the appointment of an independent counsel, and the Justice Department, upon completing its own investigation, recommended the appointment of a special prosecutor for the sole purpose of determining whether Olson had lied before Congress. The Special Division appointed James McKay as independent counsel, but when he resigned a month later, the judges selected Alexia Morrison. Olson, however, refused to cooperate with Morrison's orders to produce evidence in the case, contending that the special prosecutor law violated the Appointments Clause of Article II by vesting the appointment of a "principal" officer in a court of law, and violated the doctrine of separation of powers by (among other things) impeding the president's ability to "take Care that the Laws be faithfully executed."[50] The D.C. District Court found Olson in contempt for failing to answer subpoenas, but the D.C. Court of Appeals reversed. Morrison then appealed to the Supreme Court.

In an opinion by Chief Justice William Rehnquist, the Court rejected Olson's claims. According to Rehnquist, the special prosecutor is an "inferior" officer of the United States who, pursuant to the Appointments Clause, may be appointed by a court of law.[51] For support of this view, Rehnquist pointed out that the special prosecutor can be removed from office by the attorney general, and is granted responsibilities under the act that are limited in scope, jurisdiction, and duration. The majority also rejected Olson's separation of powers claim. Even though "it is undeniable that the Act reduces the amount of control that the Attorney General and, through him, the President exercise over the investigation and prosecution of a certain class of alleged criminal activity," the limitations on the president's ability to prosecute federal crimes are not so severe as to impede his ability to perform his constitutional duties.[52] The principle of separation of powers, Rehnquist concluded, does not require that "the three Branches of Government 'operate with absolute independence.'"[53]

Matching the length of the majority opinion, Justice Scalia wrote a thirty-eight-page solo dissent, major portions of which he read from the bench. In contrast to the majority, Scalia argued that the special prosecutor was a "principal" officer of the United States who must be nominated by the president and confirmed by the Senate in order to be in compliance with the Appointments Clause. Rather than spend much time on this relatively "technical" point, however, Scalia devoted most of his opinion to showing how the act violated "the absolutely central guarantee of just Government": separation of powers. Scalia portrayed this case as about power. Usually separation of powers questions come to this Court "clad . . . in sheep's clothing," but here "this wolf comes as a wolf."[54] Scalia described the criminal investigation of Assistant Attorney General Olson as a "bitter power dispute between the President and the Legislative Branch."[55] The investigation by the House Judiciary Committee, which culminated in the appointment of the special prosecutor, lasted a substantial amount of time and produced an enormous report, with the result that the attorney general no longer had a choice about whether or not to appoint an independent counsel. "How could it not be, the public would ask, that a 3,000-page indictment drawn by our representatives over 2½ years does not even establish 'reasonable grounds to believe' that further investigation or prosecution is warranted?"[56] As Scalia saw it, the pressure put on the attorney general to appoint an independent counsel under the act was "acrid with the smell of threatened impeachment."[57]

On the merits, Justice Scalia regarded the case as an easy one. Article II provides that "[t]he executive Power shall be vested in the President of the United States,"[58] which "does not mean some of the executive power, but all of the executive power."[59] If, according to Scalia's reasoning: (1) the conduct of a criminal prosecution is purely executive power, and (2) the act deprives the president of exclusive control over the exercise of that power, then the act must be struck down. In Scalia's view, there is no other way to answer these two questions than in the affirmative. As for the former, the independent counsel's functions are clearly executive in nature. The investigation and prosecution of crime is a "quintessentially executive function" and "the virtual embodiment of the power to 'take care that the laws be faithfully executed.'"[60] In terms of the latter, the attorney general and the president are unquestionably deprived of exclusive control of prosecution. In fact, the whole purpose of the act, Scalia argued, is to protect the special prosecutor's ability to act independently of the president's control. Scalia also strongly objected to the Court's functionalist balancing test of determining "how much of the purely executive powers of government must be within the full control of the President." For Scalia, "The Constitution prescribes they all are."[61] As Scalia saw it, the independent counsel statute constitutes a serious deprivation of executive power and will substantially affect the balance of power between the two political branches of government.

Most interestingly, Justice Scalia mentioned several ways in which the act would "enfeeble" the institution of the presidency. First, he argued that the act would weaken the executive branch "by reducing the zeal of [the president's] staff" in giving advice to the president and advocating his interests and policies before the Congress. Prior to the adoption of the act, government officials who were suspected of doing something wrong were at least afforded a "sympathetic forum" in the executive branch as to whether a criminal investigation should be pursued. Under the Ethics in Government Act, however, that forum is replaced by the Office of Special Prosecutor, which, in making the decision whether or not to prosecute, is not subject to the control of the president. Under these circumstances, Scalia questioned whether the president's high-level assistants could be expected to advise him effectively without feeling intimidated, and whether they could defend the administration's policies and interests strenuously before Congress, since the law "deeply wounds the President, by substantially reducing the President's ability to protect himself and his staff."[62]

Second, Justice Scalia argued that the independent counsel statute would hurt the presidency even more directly "by eroding his public support." The ability of Congress to seek appointments of independent counsels, as well as the lenient standard for obtaining such appointments—whether there are reasonable grounds to believe that further investigation is warranted—will make appointments of special prosecutors all too common. "Nothing is so politically effective," observed Scalia, "as the ability to charge that one's opponent and his associates are not merely wrongheaded, naive, ineffective, but, in all probability, 'crooks.' And nothing so effectively gives an appearance of validity to such charges as a Justice Department investigation, and, even better, prosecution."[63]

Finally, Justice Scalia cited several potential misuses of the law by the judges who serve on the Special Division as well as by the special prosecutors who carry out the investigations. Justice Scalia maintained that "[u]nder our system of government, the primary check against prosecutorial abuse is a political one."[64] If crime is not investigated and prosecuted fairly, the people can place the blame (via the ballot box) on the president and his staff. But under this act, Scalia argued, the judges who serve on the Special Division, and the independent counsels who are appointed by those judges, are not accountable to anyone. For example, the Special Division might choose a special prosecutor for partisan reasons: "What if [the judges on the Special Division] are politically partisan, as judges have been known to be, and select a prosecutor antagonistic to the administration, or even to the particular individual who has been selected for this special treatment? There is no remedy for that, not even a political one. Judges, after all, have life tenure, and appointing a surefire enthusiastic prosecutor could hardly be considered an impeachable offense."[65] With respect to the potential abuses of authority by independent counsels themselves, Scalia noted several concerns about the method by which criminal investigations could be conducted under the act. Because criminal investigations usually concentrate on only one or a few individuals, this could result in an improper allocation of money, time, and energy in carrying out investigations: "What would normally be regarded as a technical violation . . . may in [the special prosecutor's] small world assume the proportions of an indictable offense. What would normally be regarded as an investigation that has reached the level of pursuing such picayune matter that it should be concluded, may to him or her be an investigation that ought to go on for another year."[66] Scalia concluded his tour de force against the independent prosecutor law by expressing grave concerns about what it would do to the institution of the presidency as well as the nation:

> How frightening it must be to have your own independent counsel and staff appointed, with nothing else to do but investigate you until investigation is no longer worthwhile—with whether it is worthwhile not depending upon what such judgments usually hinge on, competing responsibilities. . . . By its shortsighted action today, I fear the Court has permanently encumbered the Republic with an institution that will do it great harm.[67]

## THE FATE OF THE INDEPENDENT COUNSEL STATUTE

In June 1999, Congress allowed the independent counsel statute to expire. Over the course of its checkered two-decade existence, twenty special prosecutors were appointed to investigate executive branch officials.[68] The most memorable examples came in the 1980s with the investigation of the Iran-Contra scandal, and then in the 1990s with the investigation of President William Jefferson Clinton. During and after the Clinton investigation, supporters of the president assailed the independent counsel statute and lauded Scalia's prescient views in his *Morrison* dissent. While the Ethics in Government Act was enacted with good intentions (the need for independence in conducting criminal investigations of executive branch officials), the act spawned numerous unintended consequences, not the least of which was the lack of any political control over the scope and length of independent counsels' investigations. By not reauthorizing the law, Congress evidently came to the conclusion that the political checks supplied by the Constitution's traditional separation of powers system, while not perfect, adequately protect the "independence" of special prosecutors in conducting criminal investigations of official misconduct. Whether or not Justice Scalia was right in 1988, his *Morrison* dissent is a ringing endorsement of Hamiltonian political principles. Throughout his opinion, Scalia reminded his colleagues that the legislature was the institution that the framers feared the most, and therefore counseled that all necessary precautions be taken to counteract its influence, including fortifying the more feeble branches with "the necessary constitutional means and personal motives to resist encroachments."[69] Congress, the realist Scalia observed, will try to extend its authority as far as it will be permitted, and the Court's functionalist approach to such interbranch disputes will not adequately defend the executive branch from such attacks. One of the major fortifications that the executive branch has against Congress is the veto power, but Scalia also made the case for a unitary executive, one that will allow the president to take decisive action and maintain responsibility within the department. "[T]he Founders," wrote Scalia, "conspicuously and very consciously declined to sap the Executive's strength in the same way they had weakened the Legislature: by dividing the executive power."[70] The basic problem with the independent counsel statute for Scalia was that Congress placed executive power in an institution not subject to control by the president. To do this, in Scalia's view, not only impedes the president's ability to faithfully execute the laws under Article II, but also weakens the institution when criminal investigations are carried out for political purposes.


## SENTENCING REFORM

In the interest of reducing arbitrariness in federal sentencing, Congress passed the Sentencing Reform Act of 1984, which (among other things) created the United States Sentencing Commission as an independent body located within the judicial branch.[71] The primary duty of this commission is to promulgate determinate sentencing guidelines across a wide range of federal offenses. The act provides that three of the seven members of the commission must be federal judges, who are nominated by the Judicial Conference of the United States and who may serve without resigning from the bench. All seven members of the commission are appointed by the president, by and with the advice and consent of the Senate, and are removable by the president only for "good cause."[72]

John Mistretta, who was sentenced to eighteen months in prison for selling drugs under the new federal sentencing guidelines, challenged his sentence on the grounds that the act conferred excessive rule-making authority on the commission in violation of the nondelegation doctrine, and that the establishment of the commission in the judicial branch violated the doctrine of separation of powers by vesting the judges who sit on the commission with rule-making (or legislative) authority. He also argued that the act compromised the integrity of the judiciary by allowing the federal judges who sit on the commission to work closely with other public officials in establishing policy-laden sentencing guidelines and by allowing them to be removed from their posts by the president.

In *Mistretta v. United States*,[73] the Court rejected each of these arguments and embraced a pragmatic approach to separation of powers conflicts. In terms of the excessive delegation argument, Justice Harry Blackmun, the author of the majority opinion, noted that the Court's precedents require only that Congress "lay down by legislative act an intelligible principle to which the person or body authorized to [exercise the delegated authority] is directed to conform."[74] In his view, Congress did that here. For example, Congress directed the commission to develop a system of "sentencing ranges" applicable "for each category of offense," and directed it to use current average sentences "as a starting point" for structuring the sentencing guidelines.[75] Moreover, Congress required the commission to consider several factors in formulating "offense" and "defendants" categories, including the grade of a crime, aggravating and mitigating circumstances, and the age of the defendant.[76] While Blackmun conceded that the delegation of rule-making authority in this case was broad, he did not believe it violated the nondelegation doctrine. As he saw it, "Congress simply cannot do its job absent an ability to delegate power under broad general directives."[77]

The majority also rejected Mistretta's separation of powers claims. According to Blackmun, the Court had previously upheld delegations of rule-making authority to the judicial branch. He cited, for example, the Rules Enabling Act of 1934, which conferred upon the judiciary the power to promulgate federal rules of civil procedure. The Court had also recognized Congress's authority to create within the judicial branch various auxiliary agencies to assist judges in the fair and efficient administration of the courts, including the creation of the Judicial Conference of the United States in 1922. These examples, Blackmun argued, provide ample proof that judges can perform rule-making functions without running afoul of the separation of powers principle. While he acknowledged that the rule-making authority granted under the act involved more policy-laden judgment than under previous statutes, Blackmun held that this authority did not violate Montesquieu's warning against joining the legislative and judicial branches of government. Blackmun also rejected Mistretta's argument that requiring service of federal judges on the commission compromised the impartiality and integrity of the federal judiciary. Blackmun noted that historically there have been many precedents where federal judges have assumed extrajudicial responsibilities while still serving on the bench. He also argued that judicial service on the commission would not compromise the integrity of the judiciary, because (1) service by any particular judge is voluntary; (2) service on the commission will not likely result in many judicial recusals; (3) "judicial participation on the Commission ensures that judicial experience and expertise will inform the promulgation of rules for the exercise of the Judicial Branch's own business—that of passing sentence on every criminal defendant";[78] and (4) the president's appointment and removal of the commission's judges will not lead to undue presidential influence over the federal judiciary, because the judges who serve on the commission are serving in a nonadjudicatory capacity.

Justice Scalia again filed a lone dissent. He agreed with the majority that the act did not break any new ground in terms of the *scope* of authority given to the commission. Prior Court decisions had broadly interpreted Congress's ability to delegate rule-making authority. What could be more broad, asked Scalia, than a "public interest" standard that the Court has upheld in various contexts? For Scalia, what makes this case different from other nondelegation cases is that Congress conferred rule-making authority on the commission without making it subject to executive or judicial control. "The power to make law," reasoned Scalia, "cannot be exercised by anyone other than the Congress, except in conjunction with the lawful exercise of executive or judicial power."[79] Yet that is precisely what happened here:

> The lawmaking function of the Sentencing Commission is completely divorced from any responsibility for execution of the law or adjudication of private rights under the law. It is divorced from responsibility for execution of the law not only because the Commission is not said to be "located in the Executive Branch" . . . but, more importantly, because the Commission neither exercises any executive power on its own, nor is subject to the control of the President who does. . . . And the Commission's lawmaking is completely divorced from the exercise of judicial powers since, not being a court, it has no judicial powers itself, nor is it subject to the control of any other body with judicial powers. The power to make law at issue here, in other words, is not ancillary but quite naked. The situation is no different in principle from what would exist if Congress gave the same power of writing sentencing laws to a congressional agency such as the General Accounting Office, or to members of its staff.[80]

In contrast to the majority, Justice Scalia did not see this as a commingling-of-powers problem either. Rather, Congress, in his view, created "a new Branch [of government] altogether, a sort of junior-varsity Congress."[81] According to Scalia, the establishment of this new branch of government, whose only function is the making of laws, violates the nondelegation doctrine: "In the present case . . . a pure delegation of legislative power is precisely what we have before us. It is irrelevant whether the standards are adequate, because they are not standards related to the exercise of executive or judicial powers; they are, plainly and simply, standards for further legislation."[82]

## ANALYSIS

The Court's opinion in *Mistretta* was a clear victory for a Madisonian pragmatic approach to separation of powers. Justice Blackmun received several letters from academics complimenting him on his opinion and his flexible approach to the issues presented in the case. For example, Stephen G. Breyer, then a judge on the First Circuit Court of Appeals and a leading defender of the U.S. sentencing guidelines, regarded Blackmun's analysis as "ironclad," and predicted that it will be "the key to Separation of Powers analysis for many years to come."[83] Former solicitor general Erwin N. Griswold also wrote Blackmun to express his view that *Mistretta* was "a truly great opinion." He also regretted that his "brother Scalia speaks in such strong terms" in dissent. He had hoped that Scalia "might mellow after a while on the Court."[84] Scalia's opinion in *Mistretta* has been interpreted as an attempt to reinvigorate the nondelegation doctrine,[85] but that is not likely. In fact, Scalia said in *Mistretta* that "we have almost never felt qualified to second-guess Congress regarding the permissible degree of policy judgment that can be left to those executing or applying the law."[86] Scalia's record in excessive delegation cases bears this out. In all of the nondelegation decisions in which he has participated, only once (i.e., *Mistretta*) did he rule that an excessive delegation of power had occurred, and that was for a particular reason. To be sure, Scalia's rule of law judicial philosophy has led him to express concerns about the Court's lenient scrutiny in nondelegation cases,[87] but those concerns are never strenuously made and (more importantly) are not reflected in his judicial opinions.[88] Scalia's approach to the nondelegation doctrine is ultimately political. In the modern era, in which the business of government is increasingly complex, Scalia realizes that Congress is going to have to delegate considerable authority to the executive branch. And, as a Hamiltonian conservative, he is not going to raise a stink about it. What really irked Scalia about the act was Congress's attempt to insulate the commission from presidential control.[89] For him, the fatal flaw of the act was not an *excessive* delegation of power but rather the placement of the commission in the judicial branch, where it was not accountable either to the president or to Article III judges:

> Until our decision last Term in *Morrison v. Olson* . . . it could have been said that Congress could delegate lawmaking authority only at the expense of increasing the power of either the President or the courts. Most often, as a practical matter, it would be the President, since the judicial process is unable to conduct the investigations and make the political assessments essential for most policymaking. Thus, the need for delegation would have to be important enough to induce Congress to aggrandize its primary competitor for political power, and the recipient of the policymaking authority, while not Congress itself, would at least be politically accountable. But even after it has been accepted, pursuant to *Morrison*, that those exercising executive power need not be subject to the control of the President, Congress would still be more reluctant to augment the

power of even an independent executive agency than to create an otherwise powerless repository for its delegation. . . . By reason of today's decision I anticipate that Congress will find the delegation of lawmaking powers much more attractive in the future. If rulemaking can be entirely unrelated to the exercise of judicial or executive powers, I foresee all manner of "expert" bodies, insulated from the political process, to which Congress will delegate various portions of its lawmaking responsibility. How tempting to create an expert Medical Commission (mostly M.D.'s, with perhaps a few Ph.D.'s in moral philosophy) to dispose of such thorny, "no-win" political issues as the withholding of life-support systems in federally funded hospitals.[90]

## THE LINE-ITEM VETO

In the interest of curtailing "pork-barrel" politics, U.S. presidents, at least since the time of Ulysses S. Grant, have sought line-item veto authority—or the ability to strike out particular provisions from tax and spending bills. Ironically, in 1996, a Republican-led Congress gave President William Jefferson Clinton such authority when it passed the Line Item Veto Act. Pursuant to this act, the president could "cancel in whole" three kinds of provisions already signed into law: "(1) any dollar amount of discretionary budget authority; (2) any item of new direct spending; or (3) any limited tax benefit."[91] The president may exercise this authority only after determining that doing so will "(i) reduce the Federal budget deficit; (ii) not impair any essential Government functions; and (iii) not harm the national interest."[92] To exercise this cancellation authority, the president must transmit a special message to Congress within five calendar days after enactment of the canceled provision. A cancellation takes effect upon Congress's receipt of this special message, and the act provides a process by which Congress can "disapprove" of the president's cancellation. With respect to both an item of new direct spending and a limited tax benefit, the cancellation prevents the item from having "legal force or effect." Prior to the law being challenged, President Clinton used his line-item veto authority on eighty-two separate occasions.

Controversy developed when, on August 11, 1997, President Clinton canceled one provision of the Balanced Budget Act of 1997 involving an item of new direct spending, and two provisions of the Taxpayer Relief Act of 1997 involving limited tax benefits. Petitioners, including the City of New York and Snake River Potato Growers Inc. brought suit, claiming that the president's cancellation of these provisions injured them financially. They sought a declaratory judgment that the cancellation authority conferred under the Line Item Veto Act violated the Presentment Clause of Article I and the doctrine of separation of powers. In *Clinton v. City of New York*,[93] the Supreme

Court sided with the petitioners and struck down the Line Item Veto Act as
violative of the Presentment Clause.

In an opinion by Justice John Paul Stevens, the Court held that the cancellation authority provided under the act did not conform to constitutionally
mandated procedures for both the enactment and repeal of laws. According to
the Presentment Clause, after a bill is passed by both houses of Congress, it
must be presented to the president, who then has three options: (1) the president can approve the bill by signing it; (2) he can veto it by noting his objections and returning it to the House in which it originated; or (3) he can do
nothing, which will result in the bill's becoming law after ten days, unless
Congress adjourns during the ten-day period. According to Justice Stevens,
the ability to veto a bill differs from the authority conferred under the act in
two fundamental ways: "The constitutional return takes place *before* the bill
becomes a law; the statutory cancellation occurs *after* the bill becomes law.
The constitutional return is of the entire bill; the statutory cancellation is of
only a part."[94] While Stevens admitted that the Constitution is silent with respect to presidential authority to repeal or amend only parts of duly enacted
statutes, he maintained that "constitutional silence on this profoundly important issue" was "equivalent to an express prohibition":[95]

> The procedures governing the enactment of statutes set forth in the text of Arti-
> cle I were the product of the great debates and compromises that produced the
> Constitution itself. Familiar historical materials provided abundant support for
> the conclusion that the power to enact statutes may only "be exercised in accord
> with a single, finely wrought and exhaustively considered, procedure." . . . Our
> first President understood the text of the Presentment Clause as requiring that he
> either "approve all the parts of a Bill, or reject it in toto."[96]

The majority also rejected the government's arguments that the act did not
really amend or repeal properly enacted statutes in violation of the Presentment Clause, because "the cancellations were merely exercises of discretionary authority granted to the President by the Balanced Budget Act and the
Taxpayer Relief Act read in light of the previously enacted Line Item Veto
Act," and because "the substance of the authority to cancel tax and spending
items" is the same as the discretionary power given to the president "to 'decline to spend' specified sums of money, or to 'decline to implement' specified tax measures" under other statutes.[97] In terms of the former, the majority
argued that "[i]n both legal and practical effect, the President has amended
two Acts of Congress by repealing a portion of each."[98] With respect to the
latter, the majority held that there is a substantial difference between the discretion that the president has received under many tax and spending statutes
and the authority given to him under this act.

Justice Scalia dissented. From the standpoint of his rule of law, formalistic approach to separation of powers, his opinion should be seen as a surprise, but not when one factors into the equation his Hamiltonian political philosophy. Scalia argued that the title of the act "succeeded in faking out the Supreme Court."[99] In spite of its title, Justice Scalia argued, the act does not really confer veto authority on the president. According to Scalia, when the president exercises his cancellation authority, the laws do not change; they stay exactly the same. Since the laws involved in this case were passed in compliance with the Presentment Clause, Scalia saw no constitutional problem:

> The short of the matter is this: Had the Line Item Veto Act authorized the President to "decline to spend" any item of spending contained in the Balanced Budget Act of 1997, there is not the slightest doubt that authorization would have been constitutional. What the Line Item Veto Act does instead—authorizing the President to "cancel" an item of spending—is technically different. But the technical difference does not relate to the technicalities of the Presentment Clause, which have been fully complied with.[100]

For Scalia, the real issue in this case was not the Presentment Clause but the nondelegation doctrine—that is, whether Congress has "transferr[ed] to the Executive a degree of political, lawmaking power that our traditions demand be retained by the Legislative Branch."[101] On this point, Scalia argued that the authority granted to the president under the act was no broader than the discretion traditionally granted presidents in executing spending laws. "Insofar as the degree of political, 'law-making' power conferred upon the Executive is concerned," wrote Scalia, "there is not a dime's worth of difference between Congress's authorizing the President to *cancel* a spending item, and Congress's authorizing money to be spent on a particular item at the President's discretion."[102]

Justice Scalia's decision in *Clinton v. City of New York* is remarkable in several respects. First and foremost, there is no mention of the doctrine of separation of powers. One would have expected to see Scalia map out, as he normally does, the basic outline of governmental powers: Article I provides that "[a]ll legislative Powers herein granted shall be vested in a Congress of the United States"; Article II provides that "[t]he executive Power shall be vested in a President of the United States of America"; and Article III provides that "[t]he judicial Power of the United States, shall be vested in one supreme Court, and in such inferior Courts as the Congress may from time to time ordain and establish." But Scalia's opinion contained none of this. While Scalia joined certain parts of Justice Anthony Kennedy's concurring opinion, which embraced a formalistic analysis of the doctrine of separation of powers, he did not join the result of that opinion. According to Justice Kennedy, the fatal flaw of the Line Item Veto Act was that it "enhance[d] the President's powers beyond what the Framers would have endorsed."[103] Evidently, Scalia did not think so.

Second, Justice Scalia's claim that there is only a "technical difference" between the president's ability to "decline to spend" a particular authorization and his authority under the act to "cancel" an item of spending is not very convincing. Under the former, the president is exercising discretionary authority conferred under a particular statute agreed to by both the president and the Congress; meanwhile, the latter allows the president to alter the substance of previously enacted statutes in contravention of Article I's Presentment Clause and, in some cases potentially, the majoritarian view of one or both houses of Congress that passed the law. Moreover, the authority given to the president under the Line Item Veto Act is a clear violation of the nondelegation doctrine. As Justice Stevens observed, "[W]henever the President cancels an item of new direct spending or a limited tax benefit he is rejecting the policy judgment made by the Congress and relying on his own policy judgment."[104] Could one imagine a more "naked" conferral of legislative power than what was attempted under the Line Item Veto Act? Did Congress make the "hard political choices" that Scalia spoke of in *Synar*? The authority conferred on the president under certain tax and spending statutes and the power given to the executive branch under the Line Item Veto Act represent the difference between a permissible delegation of discretionary tax and spending authority and an impermissible delegation of lawmaking authority.

Finally, Justice Scalia's decision conflicts with his strenuous criticism of the legislative veto dating back to the 1970s. The legislative veto was a procedure by which Congress could cancel a rule or regulation issued by an executive agency by mere resolution (thus avoiding the president's veto power) and by one house of Congress (thereby circumventing the bicameral provision of the Constitution).[105] As assistant attorney general under the Ford administration, Scalia argued before Congress on numerous occasions that the legislative veto violated the Presentment Clause, because congressional resolutions that defeat executive policy must be reviewed by the president.[106] The Presentment Clause, Scalia maintained, requires that all bills or resolutions be presented to the president. The provision was meant "to ensure presidential participation in *all* lawmaking, under whatever form it might disguise itself."[107] In response to those who claimed that a legislative veto was not new legislation but only the exercise of a right previously reserved in the statute creating the agency, Scalia disagreed. Once a bill is enacted into law, Scalia contended Congress can only retract a delegated authority through the normal process of amendment or repeal. Scalia's opposition to the legislative veto raises an important question: Should not the same logic apply to the president's ability to cancel provisions from duly enacted laws? Constitutionally speaking, can a principled distinction be made between a legislative veto and the line-item veto? As the lower-court judge in *City of New York v. Clinton* observed,

> Unilateral action by any single participant in the law-making process is precisely what the Bicameralism and Presentment Clauses were designed to prevent. Once a bill becomes law, it can only be repealed or amended through another, independent legislative enactment, which itself must conform with the requirements of Article I. Any rescissions must be agreed upon by a majority of both Houses of Congress. The President cannot single-handedly revise the work of the other two participants in the lawmaking process, as he did here when he vetoed certain provisions of these statutes.[108]

Justice Scalia's dissent in *Clinton v. City of New York* reveals an apparent double standard in his separation of powers jurisprudence. For Scalia, it is permissible for Congress to confer extraconstitutional authority on the president, but it is not permissible for it to usurp what he considers to be *core* executive powers. While Scalia's different perspectives on the legislative and line-item vetoes are irreconcilable as a matter of constitutional interpretation, they can be reconciled if one takes into account his Hamiltonian political philosophy. For the Hamiltonian Scalia, legislative vetoes violate the Presentment Clause because they attempt to negate previously conferred authority on the executive branch by circumventing the president's role in the lawmaking process. At the same time, the Line Item Veto Act simply represents an effort by Congress to confer discretionary tax and spending authority on the president that does not conflict with Article I's requirements for making laws or with a broad interpretation of the nondelegation doctrine.

## CONCLUSION

Justice Scalia has remarked that "if there is anyone who, over the years, [has] had a greater interest in the subject of separation of powers [than I], he does not come readily to mind."[109] This is certainly true. Separation of powers is the unifying theme in Justice Scalia's jurisprudence. Like Hamilton and the Federalists, Scalia has defended Montesquieu's conception of separation of powers as the best safeguard of liberty, and there are hints of this in some of his opinions discussed in this chapter. In *Morrison*, Scalia emphasized the potential political misuses of the special prosecutor law, as well as concerns about the broad prosecutorial discretion of the independent counsel once appointed. In *Mistretta*, Scalia expressed concerns about the broad discretionary authority of the U.S. Sentencing Commission in establishing sentencing guidelines across a wide range of crimes, including conceivably the death penalty. For Scalia, the structure of balanced and separated powers is the most important safeguard to liberty, and he stressed this at the outset of his confirmation hearings for the Supreme Court:

> I think most of the questions today will probably be about that portion of the Constitution that is called the Bill of Rights, which is a very important part of it, of course. But if you had to put your finger on what has made our Constitution so enduring, I think it is the original document before the amendments were added.
>
> Because the amendments, by themselves, do not do anything. The Russian constitution probably has better, or at least as good guarantees of personal freedom as our document does. What makes it work, what assures that those words [in the Bill of Rights] are not just hollow promises, is the structure of government that the original Constitution established, the checks and balances among the three branches, in particular, so that no one of them is able to "run roughshod" over the liberties of the people as those liberties are described in the Bill of Rights.[110]

Justice Scalia's interpretation of separation of powers, however, is shaped by a Hamiltonian vision of a strong and unitary executive. His opinions in this area are designed to limit encroachments on executive power so as to allow the president the necessary flexibility and discretion to create a legislative program that can compete with Congress's. In *Synar*, he supported a broad interpretation of the nondelegation doctrine and sought to severely restrict Congress's ability to remove government officials who perform executive functions. In *Freytag*, he sought to limit Congress's ability to place appointment power in judicial bodies not subject to the control of the president. In *Morrison*, he argued that Congress could not consign "purely" executive functions to an official (the independent counsel) who is not subject to the supervision and control of the president. In *Mistretta*, he argued that Congress could not confer lawmaking authority on a government agency (the U.S. Sentencing Commission) that is not subject to presidential control. Finally, and perhaps most importantly, Scalia revealed a double standard in his separation of powers jurisprudence by supporting the conferral of line-item veto authority on the president in *Clinton v. City of New York*. For Justice Scalia, the other important purpose of a properly balanced system of separation of powers is the Hamiltonian goal of allowing the president "to dare to act his own opinion with vigor and decision."[111]

## NOTES

1. 524 U.S. 417 (1998).
2. 626 F. Supp. 1374 (D. D.C. 1986).

3. See, e.g., Anthony Lewis, "The Court: Scalia," *New York Times*, June 26, 1986, 23, col. 1; James G. Wilson, "Constraints of Power: The Constitutional Opinions of Judges Scalia, Bork, Posner, Easterbrook and Winter," *University of Miami Law Review* 40 (1986): 1201.

4. 626 F. Supp. at 1382–83.

5. Ibid., 1383 (quoting *J. W. Hampton* 276 U.S. 394, 406, 409 [1928]).

6. Ibid., 1388.

7. Ibid., 1388–89.

8. Ibid., 1389.

9. Ibid., 1385.

10. *Clinton v. City of New York*, 524 U.S. 417, 469 (1998).

11. 626 F. Supp. at 1384 (quoting *Opp Cotton Mills, Inc. v. Administrator*, 312 U.S. 126, 145 [1941]).

12. 31 U.S.C. sec. 703(e)(1)(B) (1982).

13. U.S. Const. art. II, sec. 2, cl. 2.

14. 272 U.S. 52 (1926).

15. Ibid., 119.

16. 295 U.S. 602 (1935).

17. Scalia, "Originalism: The Lesser Evil," *Cincinnati Law Review* 57 (1989): 849–65.

18. 626 F. Supp. at 1398.

19. Ibid., 1399.

20. Ibid., 1400.

21. Ibid.

22. Ibid., 1401.

23. Ibid., 1404.

24. Ibid.

25. 478 U.S. 714 (1986).

26. "*Bowsher v. Synar*," memo from William J. Brennan to Chief Justice Warren E. Burger, June 3, 1986, HABP, box 456, folder 6. See also Bernard Schwartz, "'Shooting the Piano Player'? Justice Scalia and Administrative Law," *Administrative Law Review* 47 (1995): 4–5.

27. "Appellants . . . are wide of the mark in arguing that an affirmance in this case requires casting doubt on the status of the 'independent' agencies because no issues involving such agencies are presented here." *Bowsher v. Synar*, 478 U.S. 714, 725n4 (1986).

28. Scalia, "The ALJ Fiasco—A Reprise," *University of Chicago Law Review* 47 (1979): 57–80, 77.

29. 501 U.S. 868 (1991).

30. 26 U.S.C. sec. 7443A(b)(4).

31. U.S. Const. art. II, sec. 2, cl. 2.

32. All of the justices agreed that a special trial judge was an "inferior officer" within the meaning of the Appointments Clause, and that the Tax Court was *one* of the constitutionally designated repositories of appointment authority under Article II. Thus, they unanimously rejected petitioners' Appointments Clause challenge.

33. 501 U.S. at 888.

34. Ibid., 883 (quoting G. Wood, *The Creation of The American Republic 1776–1787* [Chapel Hill: University of North Carolina Press, 1969], 79).

35. Ibid.

36. Ibid., 901.

37. Ibid., 901–2.

38. Ibid., 904.

39. Ibid.

40. Ibid., 907.

41. Ibid., 907–8.

42. Ibid., 910.

43. Ibid., 911 (quoting *Ex parte Randolph*, 20 F. Cas. 242, 254 [No. 11, 558] [CC Va. 1833] [Marshall, C.J.]).

44. Ibid., 918.

45. Ibid., 915.

46. Ibid., 921.

47. Richard C. Reuben, "High Court Affirms 'Special' Tax Judges," *Los Angeles Times Journal*, July 9, 1991; see also letter from Arthur L. Nims III to Harry A. Blackmun, July 19, 1991, HABP, box 579, folder 1, commending Justice Blackmun for his decision and expressing that he did not "think anyone has truly reckoned how much the concurring view would have harmed the Tax Court had that view prevailed—at least in the short term."

48. See, generally, Katy J. Harriger, *The Special Prosecutor in American Politics*, 2nd ed. (Lawrence, KS: University Press of Kansas, 2000).

49. 28 U.S.C. secs. 49, 591, et seq. (1982).

50. U.S. Const. art. II, sec. 3.

51. The excepting provision of the Appointments Clause provides that Congress may "vest the Appointment of . . . inferior Officers, as they think proper, in the President alone, in the Courts of Law, or in the Heads of Departments." U.S. Const. art. II, sec. 2, cl. 2.

52. 487 U.S. 654, 695–96 (1988).

53. Ibid., 693–94 (quoting *United States v. Nixon*, 418 U.S. 683, 707 [1974]).

54. Ibid., 699.

55. Ibid., 703.

56. Ibid., 702.

57. Ibid.

58. U.S. Const. art. II, sec. 1, cl. 1.

59. 487 U.S. at 705.

60. Ibid., 706, 726.

61. Ibid., 709.

62. Ibid., 712–13.

63. Ibid., 713.

64. Ibid., 728.

65. Ibid., 730.

66. Ibid., 732.

67. Ibid., 732–33.

68. Harriger, *The Special Prosecutor in American Politics*, 1–14.

69. 487 U.S. at 698 (quoting *Federalist* No. 51).

70. Ibid., 698–99.

71. 18 U.S.C. sec. 3551 et seq. (1982), and 28 U.S.C. secs. 991–98 (1982).

72. 488 U.S. 361, 368 (1989) (quoting 28 U.S.C. sec. 991[a]).

73. 488 U.S. 361 (1989).

74. Ibid., 372 (quoting *J.W. Hampton, Jr., & Co. v. United States*, 276 U.S. 394, 409 [1928]).

75. Ibid., 374–75.

76. Ibid., 375–76.

77. Ibid., 372.

78. Ibid., 408.

79. Ibid., 417.

80. Ibid., 420–21.

81. Ibid., 427.

82. Ibid., 420.

83. Letter from Stephen Breyer to Harry A. Blackmun, January 19, 1989, HABP, box 531, folder 8.

84. Letter from Erwin N. Griswold to Harry A. Blackmun, January 23, 1989, HABP, box 531, folder 8.

85. See, e.g., David A. Schultz and Christopher E. Smith, *The Jurisprudential Vision of Justice Antonin Scalia* (Lanham, MD: Rowman & Littlefield, 1996), xxii.

86. 488 U.S. at 416.

87. Scalia, "A Note on the Benzene Case," *Regulation* (July–August 1980): 25–28 ("Even with all its Frankenstein warts, knobs and (conceded) dangers, the unconstitutional delegation doctrine is worth hewing from the ice"); see also Scalia, "Rulemaking as Politics," *Administrative Law Review* 34 (1982): x (expressing disbelief at the FCC's mandate to regulate in the interest of the public good).

88. *Whitman v. American Trucking Association*, 531 U.S. 457 (2001).

89. As a historical note, the U.S. Sentencing Commission consolidated the power that had previously been exercised by the sentencing judge and the Parole Commission, an executive branch agency.

90. 488 U.S. at 421–22.

91. 524 U.S. 417, 436 (1998) (quoting 2 U.S.C. sec. 691[a]).

92. Ibid. (citing 2 U.S.C. sec. 691[a][A]).

93. 524 U.S. 417 (1998).

94. Ibid., 439.

95. Ibid.

96. Ibid., 439–40.

97. Ibid., 442 (citing Brief for Appellants, 40).

98. Ibid., 438.

99. Ibid., 469.

100. Ibid., 468–69.

101. Ibid., 465.

102. Ibid., 466.

103. Ibid., 451.

104. Ibid., 444.

105. Scalia, "The Legislative Veto: A False Remedy for System Overload," *Regulation* (November–December 1979): 19–25.

106. See, e.g., U.S. Senate, *Congressional Oversight of Executive Agreements— 1975: Hearings before the Subcommittee on Separation of Powers of the Committee on the Judiciary*, 94th Cong., 1st sess., May 15, 1975, 167–203; U.S. House of Representatives, *Congressional Review of International Agreements: Hearings before the Subcommittee on International Security and Scientific Affairs of the Committee on International Relations*, 94th Cong., 2nd sess., July 22, 1976. See also Judge Scalia's congressional testimony as a member of the D.C. Circuit Court opposing a constitutional amendment allowing for legislative vetoes. U.S. Senate, *Constitutional Amendment to Restore Legislative Veto: Hearing before the Subcommittee on the Constitution of the Committee on the Judiciary*, 98th Cong., 2nd sess., March 2, 1984, 245–52.

107. "The Legislative Veto: A False Remedy for System Overload," 20.

108. *City of New York v. Clinton*, 985 F. Supp. 168, 179 (D. D.C. 1998).

109. Remarks by Justice Antonin Scalia at roundtable discussion of "Separation of Powers in the Constitution," sponsored by the U.S. Court of Appeals, Washington, DC. C-SPAN audiotape broadcast, November 15, 1988.

110. U.S. Senate, *The Nomination of Judge Antonin Scalia: Hearings before the Committee on the Judiciary of the United States Senate*, 99th Cong., 2nd sess., August 5, 1986, 32.

111. FP, 410.

*Chapter Four*

# Executive Power

One of Alexander Hamilton's most important legacies as a framer of the federal Constitution was the case he made for a strong executive. As Richard Loss has pointed out, two of the foremost authorities on the American presidency, Edward S. Corwin and Clinton Rossiter, both "concurred that the 'modern theory of presidential power' is 'the contribution primarily of Alexander Hamilton.'"[1] While Hamilton was not at the Constitutional Convention when many of the powers of the executive branch were hammered out, he became that branch's primary defender in the fight to get the Constitution ratified and in subsequent battles over the scope of executive power under Article II. For this reason, James MacGregor Burns has observed that "[i]f [Hamilton] had a limited influence on the Constitution of 1787, he had a substantial influence on the Constitution of 1789 and 1792 and 1795 and hence all the later ones."[2]

A crucial theme in Hamilton's writings on the executive branch was the need for energy. "Energy in the executive," he declared in *Federalist* 70, "is a leading character in the definition of good government" (FP, 402). Republican government, particularly one spread out over a large and diverse territory, required energy. Unlike Congress, where slow and deliberate action was regarded as desirable, Hamilton viewed the presidency as the one institution of government capable of acting with dispatch. Energy was essential when the nation was confronted with a foreign or domestic threat, but it was also necessary for a steady and upright administration of the laws. In contrast to Jeffersonian Republicans, who regarded the executive as merely a "clerk" to the more dominant Congress, Hamilton believed that the president would compete with Congress in establishing the national policies of the country. In a representative system of government, Hamilton stressed that the president, too, had an independent claim of authority to pursue the interests of the people. As conceived by Hamilton, the president would lead the country in times of war and, under the right type of leader, be out in front of the Congress in setting the policy agenda of the nation.

Hamilton, however, did not believe executive power was unlimited. The claims that he was a monarchist (at least of the hereditary sort) have been exaggerated,[3] and after his controversial convention speech in which he defended a life term for the president,[4] Hamilton never again publicly supported such an idea, making him a less than committed defender of an elective monarchy. Moreover, as political scientist Karl-Friedrich Walling has observed, Hamilton was not a disciple of Machiavelli's omnipotent Prince who acts out of necessity and not from what is legitimate or consensual.[5] Hamilton's candid and principled nature, Christian faith, desire for virtuous leadership in elected officials, advocacy of natural rights, and the case he made for executive accountability all counsel against any such comparisons. Rather, and as others have ably demonstrated,[6] Hamilton was the founding generation's great reconciler of executive energy with republican principles. Hamilton thus fully supported the constitutional limits placed on executive power, including the Senate's role in confirming presidential appointments and ratifying treaties; the Congress's ability to impeach executive officials (including the president) for official misconduct; and one of the most important protections afforded the individual against tyrannical government: the writ of habeas corpus.[7]

At the same time, it is equally true that during the formative years of the republic, no one defended executive power more aggressively than Hamilton. A constant worry of Hamilton's throughout his life was that if the national government did not have sufficient authority, it could lead to rebellion, and from rebellion to a state of tyranny. This was reflected in how he reacted to the various domestic rebellions that took place during his life, such as the Shays' (1786), Whiskey (1794), and Fries' (1799) rebellions, and in how he feared that the French Revolution could be replicated in the United States. While Hamilton always held doubts about whether the U.S. experiment in republican government would be successful, he placed the primary responsibility for harmonizing the two chief ends of government—safety and liberty—on the executive branch. "The success of every government," observed Hamilton, "its capacity to combine the exertion of public strength with the preservation of personal right and private security, qualities which define the perfection of a government, must always naturally depend on the energy of the executive department."[8] And in order for the executive branch to perform this balancing act competently, Hamilton construed the Constitution and, in particular, Article II in such a way that the executive could act with energy. In this way, the president could, in Teddy Roosevelt's words, be "a steward of the people bound actively and affirmatively to do all he could for the people, and not to content himself with keeping his talents undamaged in a napkin."[9]

In court opinions and extrajudicial writings, Justice Scalia has defended Hamilton's theory of executive power. No less a defender of authority in republican government than Hamilton, Scalia once remarked that "it's not a good argument against the existence of power that it be abused; every power can be abused. The question is how it will be used or exercised."[10] In order to allow executive officials the discretion to exercise power successfully, Scalia has interpreted Article II in the same way that Hamilton did. He has, for example, defended the "sole organ" theory of the presidency in foreign affairs, the authority of the executive branch to make treaties and executive agreements, the president's power as commander in chief, the authority of executive officials to withhold sensitive national security documents from Congress and the public, and civil immunity from lawsuits for executive officials. At the same time, Scalia has drawn limits on executive power where the Constitution and tradition clearly prescribe such limits, as was evident in the majority opinion he joined in *Clinton v. Jones* (1997),[11] which rejected a broad executive immunity claim protecting the president from civil actions that challenge his unofficial actions, and his dissenting opinion in *Hamdi v. Rumsfeld* (2004),[12] where Scalia ruled against the George W. Bush administration's indefinite detention of U.S. citizens during the war on terror. In fact, in the post–New deal era (and arguably in the history of the Supreme Court), no one on the nation's highest court has surpassed Scalia as a consistent defender of a Hamiltonian conception of the presidency.[13]

## THE SCOPE OF EXECUTIVE POWER

### Pacificus versus Helvidius

Alexander Hamilton's most extensive analysis of the scope of executive power came in a famous debate with James Madison over the so-called Proclamation of Neutrality of 1793. The Washington administration issued the proclamation in order to make clear to the world that the United States was "impartial" in the war between France and Great Britain, and to caution U.S. citizens not to take actions that would jeopardize that position. In taking this stance, the administration interpreted the Franco-American Treaty of Alliance of 1778 not to require the United States to defend France, because it was regarded as the aggressor in the European conflict. The Jeffersonian Republicans opposed the proclamation because they believed it went beyond the executive's authority under Article II and encroached upon the powers of Congress to declare war and make treaties. None of the specific grants of power under Article II, they claimed, allowed the president to issue a proclamation that judges whether a cause of war exists under international treaties.

Writing under the pseudonym "Pacificus," Hamilton defended the president's authority to issue the proclamation and relied on two separate provisions of Article II for support. The first is the Vesting Clause of Article II, which provides that "the executive Power shall be vested in a President."[14] Hamilton interpreted this clause to provide a broad general grant of authority to the president. Because of the difficulty of listing all of the powers that belong to the executive branch under Article II, Hamilton argued that it would violate "rules of sound construction" to interpret the enumeration of particular authorities [under Article II] as derogating from the more comprehensive grant contained in the general clause."[15] For support of this interpretation, Hamilton relied upon a "joker," as Charles Thach called it, that Gouverneur Morris put into the final version of the Constitution. As the chief drafter of the convention's Committee of Style—a committee that Hamilton sat on as well—Morris (a strong executivist from Pennsylvania) is credited with changing the Vesting Clause of Article I to state, "All legislative Powers herein granted shall be vested in a Congress of the United States."[16] Since the Vesting Clause of Article II contained no similar limitation, this language change allowed distinctions to be drawn between the Vesting Clauses of Articles I and II, which is exactly what Hamilton did in his Pacificus essays. According to Hamilton, since the Vesting Clause of Article II does not contain the qualifier "herein granted," executive power is not limited to the enumerated powers under Article II. Based on the comprehensive nature of executive power and the semantic differences between the Vesting Clauses of Articles I and II, Hamilton derived the following principle: "[T]he EXECUTIVE POWER of the Nation is vested in the President; subject only to the *exceptions* and *qualifications* which are expressed in the instrument."[17] Importantly, in construing the exceptions and qualifications to executive authority under the Constitution, Hamilton maintained that they should be construed strictly so as not to extend any "further than is essential to their execution."[18]

So what about the constitutionality of the proclamation of neutrality? By a process of elimination, Hamilton determined that the issuance of the proclamation was executive in nature. The judicial branch, in his view, was not competent to issue such a proclamation, and Congress was not the institution charged with making or interpreting treaties. Meanwhile, the executive branch was the proper and lawful institution to issue the proclamation "as the *organ* of intercourse between the Nation and foreign Nations—as the interpreter of National Treaties in those cases in which the Judiciary is not competent, that is in the cases between Government and Government—as that Power, which is charged with the Execution of the Laws, of which Treaties form a part—as that Power which is charged with the command and application of the Public Force."[19] By vesting the executive power in the president, Hamilton argued that the Constitution gave the president the concurrent authority to interpret national treaties and to declare neutrality. Thus, while Congress has the constitutional authority to declare war, and can judge for itself whether or not the country should go to war, the president can supply the legislature with information for it to consider prior to committing us to war. As Hamilton put it, "The Legislature is free to perform its own duties according to its own sense of them—though the Executive in the exercise of its constitutional powers, may establish an antecedent state of things which ought to weigh in the legislative decisions. From the division of the Executive Power there results, in reference to it, a *concurrent* authority, in the distributed cases."[20]

The other provision of Article II relied on by Hamilton was the Take Care Clause. The president has the duty to "take Care that the Laws be faithfully executed."[21] This clause, Hamilton argued, gives the president broad authority and discretion in executing the laws. Since the president is the chief executive of the United States, and since treaties are part of the law of the land, Hamilton reasoned that the president had the authority "to judge for himself whether there was any thing in our treaties incompatible with an adherence to neutrality."[22] According to Hamilton's interpretation of the Franco-American treaties, since France was the aggressive party in the European conflict, the U.S. was not obligated to come to its defense. The Republicans maintained that the administration acted too precipitously and perhaps unnecessarily in issuing the proclamation, since Citizen Genet,[23] the French foreign minister, had recently arrived in the United States and had plans to visit the nation's capital. Hamilton responded that if the proclamation was in the United State's best interest, then the executive branch did not have to wait to discuss the matter with the French foreign minister before declaring its neutrality. Sounding every bit the realist in foreign affairs, Hamilton sized up the situation and argued that U.S. involvement in the British-Franco war would jeopardize the nation's "[s]elf preservation," which is "the first duty of a Nation."[24] The United States, which was still a nascent republic with potential enemies on all of its borders, and with no standing army or navy to speak of, would be reckless in aiding France in this contest, reasoned Hamilton, and he added "*[I]f France is not in some way or other wanting to herself she will not stand in need of our assistance and if she is our assistance cannot save her.*"[25] While Hamilton knew there was sympathy for the French among the Republican Party, he counseled against U.S. entanglement in foreign conflicts that are not in its own interest: "RULERS are only TRUSTEES for the happiness and interest of their nation, and cannot, consistently with their trust, follow the suggestions of kindness or humanity towards others, to the prejudice of their constituents."[26] Over the years, Hamilton's construction of Article II has formed the basis of various claims of implied or inherent presidential authority, including the right to issue executive orders, to remove executive branch officials from office, to withhold national security documents from the Congress and the public, to enter into international agreements without the approval of the Senate, and to immunize executive officials from civil liability.

## JUSTICE SCALIA

One of the central issues in the debate between Alexander Hamilton and James Madison over the Washington administration's issuance of the neutrality proclamation concerned the meaning and scope of Article II's Vesting Clause. Hamilton claimed that the clause constituted a broad grant of discretionary authority to the president, "subject only to the *exceptions* and *qualifications* . . . expressed in the instrument," as well as "principles of free government."[27] Madison, meanwhile, claimed that the clause did not confer independent authority on the president, but rather was declaratory of the more specific grants of authority enumerated under Article II. In extrajudicial speeches and court opinions, Justice Scalia has adopted Hamilton's view.

Justice Scalia once defined "executive power" as including everything that is not expressly forbidden by the Constitution and which would not be patently incompatible with republican principles.[28] The occasion was a speech he gave commemorating the legal and judicial career of Chief Justice William Howard Taft. In prior judicial opinions, Scalia lavishly praised Taft's opinion in *Myers v. United States*[29] as one that "exhaustively examin[ed] the historical record bearing upon the meaning of the applicable constitutional texts."[30] But in this speech Scalia noted one shortcoming of the opinion: In determining whether Article II's Vesting Clause gave the president the authority to remove executive branch officials appointed by and with the advice and consent of the Senate, Taft placed some reliance on English history. In particular, he wrote,

> In the British system, the Crown, which was the executive, had the power of appointment and removal of executive officers, and it was natural, therefore, for those who framed our Constitution to regard the words "executive power" as including both. . . . Unlike the power of conquest of the British Crown, considered and rejected as a precedent for us in *Fleming v. Page* . . . the association of removal with appointment . . . is not incompatible with our republican form of Government.[31]

Not so fast, said Justice Scalia. The framers were put on the defensive by Anti-Federalist charges that the proposed Constitution would establish a tyrannical monarchy in America, and thus they took great pains to emphasize "the important differences between British royal prerogatives and the powers of the presidency."[32] Consequently, Chief Justice Taft's unconditional reliance on British royal prerogatives was not persuasive to Scalia. Nevertheless, he contended that the opinion was still salvageable and took pains to show just how.

According to Scalia, research conducted since the *Myers* decision has shown that the framers were fully aware of British royal prerogatives and took measures to prevent their abuses.[33] For example, about one-half of the powers given to Congress under the Constitution were considered traditional royal prerogatives of the king. Moreover, some of the powers formerly exercised solely by the king are now shared by the president and Congress under the Constitution—those being the veto and treaty powers. Thus, Scalia argued, one could reasonably infer that the term "executive power" under Article II was "a reference to the traditional powers of the English King," and that "what was not expressly reassigned [under the Constitution] would—at least absent patent incompatibility with republican principles—remain with the executive."[34] For a justice who has single-mindedly sought to keep a tight lid on congressional and judicial power, this interpretation of Article II is extraordinary. It was, of course, the same interpretation of Article II's Vesting Clause given by Alexander Hamilton in his "Pacificus" essays. Scalia has employed his broad interpretation of executive power in many substantive areas,[35] five of which will be examined here: (1) the president's authority to conduct foreign relations as the "sole organ" of the United States; (2) the president's authority to make treaties and executive agreements; (3) the president's authority as commander in chief; (4) the president's ability to withhold sensitive national security information from the public (i.e., executive privilege); and (5) presidential immunity from court-ordered injunctive and declaratory relief as well as civil liability in private actions.

## THE PRESIDENT AS THE SOLE ORGAN IN FOREIGN AFFAIRS

Alexander Hamilton was an early defender of what John Marshall would later call the "sole organ" theory of the presidency. On this view, "The President is the sole organ of the nation in its external relations, and its sole representative with foreign nations."[36] Hamilton defended this vision of the presidency on two grounds: First, in comparison to the other branches of government, the executive branch was better equipped to deal with foreign affairs. "The qualities elsewhere detailed indispensable in the management of foreign negotiations"—those being decision, activity, secrecy, and dispatch—"point out the Executive as the most fit agent in those transactions," wrote Hamilton (FP, 425). Second, unlike members of Congress who are often concerned with parochial interests, the president is the main channel of communication between this country and foreign nations. Hamilton thus concluded his "Pacificus" essays by stating that the president is the "constitutional organ of intercourse between the Ustates & foreign Nations—whenever he speaks to them, it is in that capacity; it is the name of and on behalf of the Ustates."[37]

In *United States v. Curtiss-Wright Export Corp.*,[38] the Supreme Court constitutionalized the sole organ theory of the presidency. Just one year after striking down major portions of President Franklin Delano Roosevelt's National Industrial Recovery Act as an unconstitutional delegation of legislative authority to the executive branch,[39] the Court recognized "the very delicate, plenary and exclusive power of the President . . . in the field of international relations."[40] Writing for the Court, Justice George Sutherland maintained that the president,

> not the Congress, has the better opportunity of knowing the conditions which prevail in foreign countries. . . . He has his confidential sources of information. He has his agents in the form of diplomatic, consular and other officials. Secrecy in respect of information gathered in them may be highly necessary, and the premature disclosure of it productive of harmful results.[41]

In court opinions and extrajudicial speeches, Justice Scalia has supported the sole organ theory of the presidency in foreign affairs. As a member of the D.C. Court of Appeals, Scalia participated in two decisions involving presidential authority in the conduct of foreign policy, and in both cases wrote an opinion calling for considerable judicial deference toward the executive branch. In *Ramirez de Arellano v. Weinberger*,[42] for example, the D.C. Circuit Court had before it a challenge to the establishment of a Regional Military Training Center (RMTC) on a private cattle ranch in the northern region of Honduras for training Salvadoran soldiers. Temistocles Ramirez de Arellano, a U.S. citizen, was the sole owner and general manager of a large agricultural-industrial complex in Honduras. In March 1983, the U.S. Department of Defense decided to establish an RMTC in Honduras to train soldiers from the army of El Salvador. The chosen site was Ramirez de Arellano's cattle ranch. Ramirez de Arellano brought suit seeking injunctive and declaratory relief in federal district court, claiming that the occupation and destruction of his property was not authorized by any federal statute or provision of the Constitution, and that the RMTC deprived him of the use and enjoyment of his property without due process of law.[43] The D.C. District Court dismissed the complaint on the ground that the controversy involved a nonjusticiable political question.[44] The D.C. Court of Appeals, sitting en banc, reversed.

The majority, in an opinion by Judge Malcolm R. Wilkey, ruled that the case did not present a nonjusticiable political question. According to Wilkey, not every case involving foreign relations lies outside the scope of judicial cognizance.[45] The case before the court, in Wilkey's view, was distinguishable from other foreign affairs cases that have been dismissed for raising political questions, since it did not involve a sweeping challenge to the executive branch's authority in that area, but rather sought "adjudication of the narrow issue whether the United States defendants may run military exercises throughout the plaintiff's private pastures when [his] land has not been lawfully appropriated."[46] This, according to Judge Wilkey, "is a paradigmatic issue for resolution by the Judiciary."[47]

Without expressing a view on the merits of the controversy, the majority ruled that additional evidence must be gathered to determine whether equitable relief should be granted in this case. As Judge Wilkey saw it, the authority of the executive branch to manage the nation's foreign affairs is not absolute; it must be balanced with the rights of the individual. "The Executive's power to conduct foreign relations free from the unwarranted supervision of the Judiciary cannot give the Executive *carte blanche* to trample the most fundamental liberty and property rights of this country's citizenry. The Executive's foreign relations prerogatives are subject to constitutional limitation; no agreement with a foreign country can confer upon the Executive Branch any power greater than those bounded by the Constitution."[48]

In a sharply worded dissent, Judge Scalia blasted the majority for getting involved in a controversy about which "judges know little."[49] Unlike the federal district court, however, Scalia did not argue that the suit should be dismissed on political question grounds. Rather, he contended that the case should be dismissed for lack of jurisdiction, since, under the Tucker Act of 1982, the U.S. Court of Claims had jurisdiction to hear monetary claims against the federal government. Moreover, even though the case was being heard on the pleadings, Scalia objected to further testimony being heard on the alleged claims for two separate reasons. First, in his view, the case involved questions "preeminently the business of another Branch":

> The majority's apparent belief that the trial court should hold a hearing on exactly how harmful to our foreign and defense policies an injunction would be . . . is absurd. Even assuming that we are competent judges of such matters, which we are not . . . we cannot expect or require the Commander-in-Chief to take us (much

less the plaintiffs) into his confidence regarding activities now in hand. . . . And
without such knowledge we have no idea what damage to our national interests
the discretionary and extraordinary relief sought here might produce.[50]

Second, Scalia argued that injunctive relief would likely tarnish diplomatic
relations with the Honduras government, because the Reagan administration
and the Honduras government had already approved of the site for the training facility and were in the process of expropriating the property. An injunction under these circumstances would have devastating and unintended consequences. "We need no additional fact finding to know that [an injunction]
will undermine Honduran confidence in the ability of the United States to
speak and act with a single voice in the region, cast doubt upon the stead-
fastness of our commitment to our policies, and delegitimize the Honduran
authorities' participation in the training activities in the eyes of the Honduran
people."[51] Finally, Judge Scalia sharply criticized the majority for what he
perceived as its unwarranted judicial activism:

> In Old Testament days, when judges ruled the people of Israel and led them into
> battle, a court professing the belief that it could order a halt to a military opera-
> tion in foreign lands might not have been a startling phenomenon. But in mod-
> ern times, and in a country where such governmental functions have been com-
> mitted to elected delegates of the people, such an assertion of jurisdiction is
> extraordinary. The court's decision today reflects a willingness to extend judi-
> cial power into areas where we do not know, and have no way finding out, what
> serious harm we may be doing.[52]

Judge Scalia wrote another significant U.S. foreign policy opinion as a
member of the D.C. Court of Appeals, this time involving Nicaragua. In the
1980s, the Reagan administration gave financial and military support to the
so-called "Contra" forces that were attempting to overthrow the ruling Communist Sandinista regime in Nicaragua. This support was challenged in
*Sanchez-Espinoza v. Reagan*[53] by twelve Nicaraguan citizens who claimed
that they or their families were tortured at the hands of the Contras, resulting
in "summary execution, murder, abduction, torture, rape, wounding, and the
destruction of private property and public facilities."[54] The government's foreign policy in Nicaragua was also challenged by twelve members of the
House who claimed that military and financial support of the Contras violated
Congress's authority to declare war under Article I, Section 8, clause 11 of the
Constitution, the War Powers Resolution of 1973, and the Boland Amendment, which prohibited financial assistance "to any group or individual, not
part of the country's armed forces, for the purpose of overthrowing the Government of Nicaragua."[55]

Petitioners brought suit in federal district court, seeking monetary damages and injunctive and declaratory relief. The D.C. District Court dismissed the suit on the ground that the case presented a nonjusticiable political question,[56] which was then appealed to the D.C. Court of Appeals. In an opinion by Judge Scalia, the lower-court decision was affirmed. Interestingly, Scalia again did not think the Nicaraguan petitioners' complaint should be dismissed as presenting a nonjusticiable political question; rather, he contended that their case should be dismissed for two other reasons. First, for purposes of monetary damages, Scalia could find no statute that specifically authorized compensatory damages against government officials in suits brought by citizens of foreign countries. Without such specific authorization, Scalia maintained that the Court should not get involved in the dispute. Second, in terms of the request for injunctive relief by the Nicaraguan petitioners, Scalia determined that discretionary relief would not be appropriate in this case. As he saw it, particularly in the areas of military and foreign affairs, "[I]t would be an abuse of our discretion to provide [the] discretionary relief" requested by the petitioners since this was a foreign policy matter clearly committed to another branch of government:

> The support for military operations that we are asked to terminate has, if the allegations in the complaint are accepted as true, received the attention and approval of the President, the Secretary of State, the Secretary of Defense, and the Director of the CIA, and involves the conduct of our diplomatic relations with at least four foreign states—Nicaragua, Costa Rica, Honduras, and Argentina. Whether or not this is, as the District Court thought, a matter so entirely committed to the care of the political branches as to preclude our considering the issue at all, we think it at least requires the withholding of discretionary relief.[57]

Judge Scalia also ruled against the congressional petitioners in *Sanchez-Espinoza* for two separate reasons. Following precedent established by the D.C. Court of Appeals,[58] Scalia said that the constitutional issues surrounding the war power raise a nonjusticiable political question, and he also dismissed the congressional parties' suit because the Boland Amendment had expired in 1983.[59]

Judge Scalia's opinions in *Ramirez de Arellano* and *Sanchez-Espinoza* provide strong evidence of a Hamiltonian "sole organ" conception of the executive branch in foreign affairs. While he did not regard these cases as raising purely political questions (except for the congressional parties in *Sanchez-Espinoza*), Scalia was not willing to grant the injunctive relief requested because it could have jeopardized the foreign policy decisions of the executive branch—even where, as in *Ramirez de Arellano*, a constitutional violation was alleged by a U.S. citizen. While this is an area where courts have traditionally exhibited considerable deference toward the executive branch, Scalia's opinions in these two cases illustrate that he will almost always deny equitable relief in cases challenging the foreign policy decisions of the executive branch. For the same reasons cited by Hamilton—that the executive is better equipped to deal with foreign policy and military matters, and is the nation's main communicator with other countries—Scalia believes that foreign policy concerns are preeminently the business of the executive branch and that judges should defer to those decisions.

## TREATIES AND EXECUTIVE AGREEMENTS

One of the primary ways presidents engage in foreign relations is through the use of treaties and executive agreements. The authority to make treaties is shared by the president and the Senate. Although the Constitution does not specify the functions to be performed by each of the parties responsible for making treaties, it has been customary that the executive negotiates a treaty with a foreign power and then presents the draft to the Senate for its advice and consent.[60] In order to ratify a treaty, two-thirds of the senators present for the vote must approve it. By contrast, executive agreements concluded between heads of state or their representatives have the force of law and are entered into without the advice and consent of the Senate. There are three kinds of executive agreements: (1) "those made pursuant to, or in accordance with, an existing treaty"; (2) "those made subject to congressional approval or implementation ('congressional-executive agreements')"; and (3) "those made under, and in accordance with, the president's constitutional powers ('the sole executive agreements')."[61] While many executive agreements are routine and uncontroversial, others have had great significance and have produced contentious debate. The sole executive agreement is the most controversial, because the president or other top executive official is acting alone without any explicit (or implicit) congressional authorization. Throughout history, there have been far more executive agreements than treaties,[62] and numerous constitutional issues have arisen regarding both, including whether presidents can unilaterally abrogate a treaty,[63] whether the Senate can condition its assent to a treaty on the executive's adherence to explicit conditions, whether presidents can reinterpret a treaty in such a way that it conflicts with the original understanding of the treaty consented to by the Senate, and whether presidents have the constitutional authority to enter into sole executive agreements. Since Justice Scalia has addressed the last three issues in court opinions and congressional testimony, we will concentrate on them.

Alexander Hamilton vigorously defended the president's treaty making power. Whether or not he believed that treaties were executive in nature, as alleged by Madison in the famous debate between the two men over the neutrality proclamation of 1793,[64] Hamilton was quick to rebuff any sort of encroachment upon the president's constitutional authority to make treaties.[65] For example, he was the "undisputed champion" of the unpopular Jay Treaty of 1795, and on one occasion suffered the humiliation of being struck on the forehead by a stone hurled by an angry protester during a New York speech in which he defended the treaty.[66] After Republicans strongly criticized the Jay Treaty for conceding too many American commercial interests to the British, Hamilton published a remarkable twenty-eight essays over a six-month period in which he meticulously defended the treaty on both policy and constitutional grounds, earning him the accolade from Ron Chernow, his superb biographer, of being "arguably the foremost political pamphleteer in American history."[67] Writing under the pseudonym "Camillus," Hamilton acknowledged that while he did not like some of the provisions of the treaty, particularly the restrictions concerning American trade in the British West Indies, he believed that overall the treaty was beneficial to U.S. commercial interests. When the House, led by Albert Gallatin and James Madison, claimed that if the objects of a treaty embrace powers exclusively and specially granted to the House, it requires the "sanction" of that branch,[68] Hamilton disagreed with that interpretation and argued that it conflicted with the express language of Article II's treaty provision. In typical dramatic flair, Hamilton concluded his "Camillus" essays by remarking that if the House could unilaterally abrogate treaties, "There would be no security at home, no respectability abroad. Our Constitutional Charter would become a dead letter & The Organ of our Government for foreign Affairs would be treated with derision whenever he should hereafter talk of negotiation or Treaty. May the Great Ruler of Nations avert from our Country so grievous a calamity!"[69]

Justice Scalia has also been a strenuous defender of the president's constitutional authority to make treaties. Prior to ratifying a treaty with a foreign nation, the Senate has the authority to condition its assent on the executive's acceptance of explicit conditions. But how formalized do these conditions have to be in order to be accepted as a condition placed on the approval of a treaty? Put another way, to what extent can presidents interpret a treaty in such a way that it conflicts with the original meaning of the treaty, as understood by the Senate in preratification debates and as represented to it by executive officials? These questions were at issue in the mid-1980s when the Reagan administration interpreted the Anti-Ballistic Missile (ABM) Treaty with the Soviet Union, ratified in 1972 during the Nixon administration, not to prohibit the development, testing, and deployment of the administration's Strategic Defense

Initiative. In the view of many senators, this "unilateral" interpretation of the ABM Treaty conflicted with the original understanding of that agreement by the senators who approved it, and with the representations of executive officials who explained its provisions in preratification hearings before the Senate. In taking a broad interpretation of the ABM Treaty, the Reagan administration placed reliance upon the treaty negotiation record that was classified and not shared with the Senate, and contended that the Senate gives advice and consent to a treaty, not to the explanations of the treaty offered by executive officials. In reaction to this controversy, the Senate added an amendment to the Intermediate-Range Nuclear Forces (INF) Treaty of 1988, commonly called the "Biden Condition." Named after its chief sponsor in the Senate, Joseph R. Biden Jr. (D-DE), this amendment states that treaties shall be interpreted "in accordance with the common understanding of the Treaty shared by the President and the Senate at the time the Senate gave its advice and consent to ratification." The term "common understanding" was defined to include "the text of the treaty" and "the authoritative representations which were provided by the President and his representatives to the Senate and its Committees, in seeking Senate consent to ratification."[70] In a letter sent to the Senate by White House Counsel Arthur Culvahouse, the Reagan administration expressed concern about this amendment and maintained that it was bound by a particular interpretation of a treaty only when three criteria are met: "[W]hen consent was given, the interpretation must have been (1) 'generally understood' by the Senate, (2) 'clearly intended' by the Senate, and (3) 'relied upon' by the Senate."[71] For many senators, this meant that "the Executive would almost never be bound by its own presentation [of the meaning of a treaty] to the Senate."[72]

The Supreme Court heard a case implicating the reinterpretation controversy over the ABM Treaty in the context of interpreting another treaty—the Convention Respecting Double Taxation—entered into by the United States and Canada in 1942. In *United States v. Stuart*,[73] the Supreme Court unanimously held that the plain meaning of the treaty did not impose a restriction on the issuance of Internal Revenue Service (IRS) summonses pursuant to treaty requests parallel to the restriction it expressly imposes on summonses issued by the IRS in connection with domestic tax investigations. The justices split sharply, however, over whether the Senate's preratification debates and reports could be used as an interpretative guide in gleaning the meaning of unambiguous treaties. Justice William Brennan, for the majority, ruled that these sources could be relied upon and suggested they might be a better guide to the treaty's actual meaning than the negotiating record kept by the executive branch, which is usually not a matter of public record.[74]

Justice Scalia filed a solo concurring opinion in which he strongly objected to the majority's reliance on the Senate's preratification debates and reports to interpret the intent of the parties to the convention. Scalia objected to such legislative background, not only for the normal reasons he cites when interpreting domestic laws (i.e., congressional intent should not override the clear language of a statute), but also because he believed reliance upon senatorial understanding alone might not reflect the mutual understanding of the signatories of the treaty. If any extratextual sources were to be relied upon, Scalia maintained that they should be the negotiating history of the treaty conducted by the executive branch, not the "unilateral understanding" by the Senate represented in preratification debates, hearings, and reports. Reliance upon such materials, in Scalia's view, "significantly reduces what has hitherto been the President's role in the interpretation of treaties, and commits the United States to a form of interpretation plainly out of step with international practice."[75] According to Scalia, the majority's use of preratification reports and debates went against court precedent and historical understanding, because he could only find two federal district court decisions (both involving the same controversy) in which binding authority was given to executive representations to the Senate concerning the meaning of an unambiguous treaty.[76] Interestingly, in making this argument, Scalia took notice of the reinterpretation controversy over the ABM Treaty and cited three articles that had recently appeared in the *Washington Post*.[77] Other than the Senate's role in placing explicit conditions on the formation of treaties, Scalia strongly objected to courts relying upon Senate preratification debates and reports in gleaning the meaning of treaties, which in his view diminishes the president's authority as the sole interpreter of treaties.

Justice Scalia has also been a strong defender of the president's authority to enter into sole executive agreements. During his years in the Justice Department, Assistant Attorney General Scalia vigorously defended the president's authority to enter into international agreements without congressional authorization. Due to a sharp rise in the use of executive agreements in the 1960s and 1970s, particularly those involving the commitment of U.S. forces, military training, and equipment overseas, Congress attempted to reassert its authority in foreign affairs by proposing several bills that would effectively limit the president's ability to enter into unilateral executive agreements. Most of the bills involved various kinds of reporting requirements and allowed Congress to disapprove of any unilateral agreement within sixty days by a one-house or two-house vote.[78] On two separate occasions in the mid-1970s,[79] Assistant Attorney General Scalia testified before Congress in opposition to such measures. According to Scalia, the Constitution strongly implies that international executive agreements are lawful. For example, Article I, Section 10 of the Constitution, which deals with the foreign policy powers of the states, makes a distinction between treaties on the one hand and agreements or compacts with foreign countries on the other—entirely forbidding the former (Clause 1), but permitting the latter with the consent of Congress (Clause 3).[80] As Scalia saw it, this provision is "ample recognition that there are such animals in the international field as agreements that are not treaties."[81] This, however, does not answer the question of where the authority resides for entering into such agreements. Scalia found presidential authority for making international agreements in case law and under specific provisions of the Constitution. In terms of the former, Scalia cited several cases upholding executive agreements that were not authorized by a prior statute or treaty.[82] And as for the latter, he found support for executive agreements under at least two clauses of the Constitution. According to Scalia, the principal constitutional basis for allowing the president to enter into executive agrements is the Vesting Clause of Article II.[83] "Authorities since Alexander Hamilton," Scalia testified before Congress, "have found within this [clause] the power to conduct foreign relations."[84] In addition to that clause, the source of authority for the president to enter into international agreements, Scalia maintained, is the power conferred on the president as commander in chief. Interestingly, Scalia defended a broad presidential authority to enter into executive agreements, contending at various points during his testimony that there are certain types of agreements (e.g., the conduct of military operations) that are exclusively presidential in nature and cannot be limited by an act of Congress.[85]

## THE PRESIDENT'S WAR POWER AS COMMANDER IN CHIEF

Under the Constitution, the war power is shared between the Congress and the president. The Congress declares war, while the president, as commander in chief, is responsible for military strategy and supervision of troops in conducting the war. As predicted by Madison in the debate with Hamilton over the scope of executive power, the history of war has been "the true nurse of executive aggrandizement."[86] Despite the numerous "police actions" in which the United States has been involved, Congress has formally declared war on only five occasions. Ironically, in the early 1790s, Hamilton advocated a non-interventionist philosophy toward international conflicts, believing that the United States was not militarily prepared to risk entanglement in wars that could imperil its existence. This should not be meant to suggest that Hamilton was a pacifist, however. At the tender age of twelve, the seeds of a military mindset were already planted in the young Hamilton. Unhappy about the clerkship position he held in St. Croix, the Caribbean island where Hamilton spent much of his childhood, he confessed in a letter to a friend that he desired a war so that he could "willingly risk [his] life tho' not [his] Character to exalt [his] Station."[87] In fact, Hamilton's military experience as a lieutenant colonel in the Revolutionary Army was an important influence on how he viewed politics and the structure of government. In contrast to Jeffersonian Republicans, Hamilton was an early defender of a standing army and, out of frustration with the lack of assistance from the states during the war, firmly believed that military matters must be handled exclusively at the national level. Hamilton's rather dark view of human nature led him to believe that war was a fact of life and that perpetual peace was not a realistic possibility. When the time was appropriate, then, Hamilton clearly believed that the country had to be ready to protect its interests, and there was no doubt in whom he placed this great trust. "Of all the cares or concerns of government," Hamilton wrote in *Federalist* 74, "the direction of war most peculiarly demands those qualities which distinguish the exercise of power by a single head."[88]

Following the September 11, 2001 terrorist attacks against the United States, the Bush administration took a number of actions to combat terrorism. Signed into law on October 26, 2001, the Congress and president passed the Uniting and Strengthening America by Providing Appropriate Tools Required to Intercept and Obstruct Terrorism (USA PATRIOT) Act, which made a number of changes to the current legal environment, most notably by loosening search warrant and wiretap requirements, and by fostering greater cooperation and information gathering between the intelligence and law enforcement communities.[89] By executive order promulgated on November 13, 2001, the administration authorized, for the first time since World War II, the use of military commissions to try noncitizen enemy combatants who are either members of al Qaeda, have engaged in international terrorism adversely affecting the United States, or have knowingly harbored such terrorists.[90] And the administration challenged the right of habeas corpus by asserting the authority to detain indefinitely foreign nationals associated with al Qaeda, as well as U.S. enemy combatants purportedly fighting for the Taliban government in Afghanistan, while armed hostilities in the fight against terrorism continue. In two major decisions during its 2003–2004 term, the Supreme Court reviewed the administration's authority to detain foreign nationals without any judicial process whatsoever, and U.S. enemy combatants on the basis of unilateral government interrogations and declarations.

## Detention of Noncitizens

One case decided by the Supreme Court involved the Bush administration's detention of some 640 noncitizens, representing approximately forty-three countries, who had been held in Guantanamo Bay, Cuba, since being captured in Afghanistan early in 2002—a period of two and a half years by the time the Court handed down its decision. The petitioner detainees, two Australian and twelve Kuwaiti citizens, claimed that they were not enemy combatants or terrorists against the United States, and that they had not been charged with any crime, afforded counsel, or given access to any court or other tribunal. They challenged the legality of their detention under the Constitution, international law, and various treaties of the United States, and alleged causes of action under a number of federal statutes, including the habeas statute, which grants federal district courts "'within their respective jurisdictions' the authority to hear applications for habeas corpus by any person who claims to be held 'in custody in violation of the Constitution or laws or treaties of the United States.'"[91] The Bush administration, relying primarily on the Supreme Court's decision in *Johnson v. Eisentrager*,[92] maintained that the federal courts did not have jurisdiction over noncitizen enemy combatants who were captured and held outside of the territorial jurisdiction of the United States. *Eisentrager*, which was decided in 1950, denied habeas jurisdiction to twenty-one German nationals who had continued to aid the Japanese after Germany had unconditionally surrendered to the United States, on the grounds that they were not U.S. citizens and were captured and tried by military commission outside the territorial boundaries of the United States.

In *Rasul v. Bush*,[93] the Supreme Court held that the federal habeas statute does provide district courts with jurisdiction to hear the foreign national detainees' claims. In an opinion by Justice John Paul Stevens, the Court pointed out that statutory federal habeas had dramatically changed since *Eisentrager*. In denying habeas relief in *Eisentrager*, the justices made only "passing reference" to the statutory claim, because Court precedent at that time denied relief unless petitioners were actually being held in the territorial jurisdiction of the particular federal court.[94] But since *Eisentrager*, Stevens argued that the Court filled the "statutory gap" in federal habeas law with its decision in *Braden v. 30th Judicial Circuit of Kentucky*,[95] where the Court held "that the prisoner's presence within the territorial jurisdiction of the district court is not an 'invariable prerequisite' to the exercise of district court jurisdiction under the federal habeas statute."[96] Instead, the Court ruled that "because 'the writ of habeas corpus does not act upon the prisoner who seeks relief, but upon the person who holds him in what is alleged to be unlawful custody,' a district court acts 'within [its] respective jurisdiction' within the meaning of [the habeas statute] as long as 'the custodian can be reached by service of process.'"[97] Since no one denied that in this case the district court had territorial authority over the detainees' custodians, Stevens held that petitioners' claims could be heard in federal court. The Court also maintained that the unique status of the Guantanamo Bay naval base militated against the presumption that federal statutes should not have extraterritorial application. Unlike in *Eisentrager*, where the German nationals were tried by a military commission in Nanking, China, the U.S. exercises complete jurisdiction and control over the Guantanamo naval base under a lease agreement entered into by the United States and Cuba dating back to 1903.

Justice Scalia filed a bitter dissent in which he accused the majority of "judicial adventurism of the worst sort." For Scalia, the plain meaning of the habeas statute denied federal district courts jurisdiction in this case. Under the statute, federal judges may grant habeas corpus petitions "within their respective jurisdictions," and the Guantanamo Bay detainees were not located within the territorial jurisdiction of any federal district court. Scalia viewed the Court's reading of *Braden* as "implausible in the extreme." That case, he argued, involved a detention issue between two U.S. states, which had no affect on custody issues taking place outside of the United States. Understood in this way, "*Braden* stands for the proposition, and only the proposition, that where a petitioner is in custody in multiple jurisdictions within the United States, he may seek a writ of habeas corpus in a jurisdiction in which he suffers legal confinement, though not physical confinement, if his challenge is to that legal confinement."[98] Any suggestion that *Braden* overturned what the majority called "the statutory predicate" of *Eisentrager* "would not pass the laugh test," wrote Scalia. As Scalia saw it, the reality of the Court's decision was that it overturned *Eisentrager*, and he predicted dire consequences as a result: "From this point forward, federal courts will entertain petitions from these prisoners, and others like them around the world, challenging actions and events far away, and forcing the courts to oversee one aspect of the Executive's conduct of a foreign war."[99] Like Justice Robert Jackson, who wrote the majority opinion in *Eisentrager*, Scalia argued that habeas corpus relief for foreign nationals "would hamper the war effort," because it would require the transportation of the trial's participants to the United States, and would diminish the prestige of military commanders by requiring them to appear before civilian courts to defend their actions, thereby diverting their "efforts and attention from the military offensive abroad to the legal defensive at home."[100] Moreover, since petitioners could file their cases in any of the ninety-four federal district courts, Scalia predicted that they would forum shop for the most lenient judge. Scalia accused the majority of "spring[ing] a trap" on the Executive and making it look "foolish," because the administration had every reason to believe, based on the Court's decision in *Eisentrager*, that it could place the detainees at Guantanamo Bay without having to litigate controversies in federal courts. "Departure from our rule of *stare decisis* in statutory cases is always extraordinary," wrote Scalia; "it ought to be unthinkable when the departure has a potentially harmful effect upon the Nation's conduct of war."[101]

## Detention of U.S. Citizens

The other major decision handed down by the Supreme Court on the same day as *Rasul* was *Hamdi v. Rumsfeld*,[102] which involved whether the executive branch could indefinitely detain U.S. enemy combatants held after 9/11, without formal charges or proceedings, while the war on terror continues. Yaser Esam Hamdi, a U.S. citizen, was captured in Afghanistan in November 2001 by the Northern Alliance, a coalition of military groups opposed to the Taliban government. Hamdi was turned over to the U.S. government, which initially detained and interrogated him in Afghanistan, before sending him in January 2002 to the U.S. naval base at Guantanamo Bay. In April 2002, after his American captors learned that he was a U.S. citizen, Hamdi was transferred to a navy brig in Norfolk, Virginia, and then later to one located in Charleston, South Carolina. The Bush administration, relying upon the commander in chief provision of Article II, as well as on the Authorization for Use of Military Force (AUMF) passed by Congress one week after the 9/11 attacks, claimed that Hamdi was an enemy combatant and could be detained by the United States "indefinitely—without formal charges or proceedings—unless and until it makes the determination that access to counsel or further process is warranted."[103] The sole evidence of Hamdi's enemy combatant status was his initial and subsequent interrogations by military personnel, and the Mobbs Declaration, an affidavit by Michael Mobbs, a special adviser to the under secretary of defense for policy. According to this declaration, Hamdi had trained with the Taliban before 9/11, had remained with his Taliban unit after the 9/11 attacks, and upon being captured had surrendered his Kalashnikov assault rifle to the Northern Alliance.[104] Hamdi's father filed a petition for habeas corpus on behalf of his son, denying that his son was an enemy combatant. According to the elder Hamdi, his son had not trained with or fought for the Taliban, but rather was a relief worker who had arrived in Afghanistan only two months before the 9/11 attacks. He requested that counsel be appointed for his son, that incommunicado interrogations of his son cease, that a declaration be issued that his son was being held in violation of the Due Process Clauses of the Fifth and Fourteenth Amendments, that an evidentiary hearing be held on his son's enemy combatant status, and that his son be released from custody.[105]

The district court determined that the Mobbs Declaration fell "far short" of supporting Hamdi's detention. Considering the declaration as "little more than the government's 'say-so,'" the district court called for more evidence to be produced to support Hamdi's detention, "including copies of all of Hamdi's statements and notes taken from interviews with him that related to his reasons for going to Afghanistan and his activities therein; a list of all interrogators who had questioned Hamdi and their names and addresses; statements by members of the Northern Alliance regarding Hamdi's surrender and capture; a list of all the dates and locations of his capture and subsequent detentions; and the names and titles of the United States Government officials who made the determinations that Hamdi was an enemy combatant and that he should be moved to a naval brig."[106] On appeal, the Fourth Circuit reversed and dismissed the habeas petition. According to the Fourth Circuit, the Mobbs Declaration, as well as the fact that Hamdi was captured in a zone of active combat in a foreign theater of conflict, amply support the president's authority to detain Hamdi as an enemy combatant. It also held that no further factual inquiry or evidentiary hearing was necessary or appropriate, because the detention of enemy combatants is an essential incident to war and is constitutionally committed to the political branches of government. Any additional fact-findings by the judiciary, in the Fourth Circuit's judgment, would violate separation of powers principles.

The Supreme Court vacated and remanded, but was sharply divided over its reasoning. The plurality, in an opinion by Justice Sandra Day O'Connor, and joined by Chief Justice William Rehnquist and Justices Anthony Kennedy and Stephen Breyer, avoided the constitutional issue of whether the president's commander in chief authority allowed for Hamdi's detention, but held that the AUMF authorized the detention. The AUMF, passed by Congress on September 18, 2001, authorized the president "to use all necessary and appropriate force against those nations, organizations, or persons he determines planned, authorized, committed, or aided the terrorist attacks" or "harbored such organizations or persons."[107] According to the plurality, the detention of enemy combatants during war so that they are unable to return to the battlefield is the type of war measure Congress authorized the president to undertake under the AUMF. Even though the plurality acknowledged that Hamdi's concern about "the substantial prospect of endless detention" was "not far-fetched," it noted that since the war in Afghanistan was still being waged, he could continue to be held pursuant to the AUMF. In reaching its decision, the plurality relied upon the Court's decision in *Ex parte Quirin*,[108] the Nazi saboteur case, where the justices upheld the detention of eight enemy combatants (one of whom was a U.S. citizen) and their subsequent trial by military commission during World War II. Although siding with the administration with respect to the lawfulness of Hamdi's detention, the plurality ruled against the administration's assertion that the evidence gleaned from Hamdi's interrogations and the Mobbs Declaration was sufficient due process protection to hold him indefinitely during the war on terror. Balancing the weighty concern of national security against Hamdi's substantial interest in not being deprived of liberty by his own government, the plurality ruled that some meaningful judicial process must be afforded him, which it defined as "notice of the factual basis for [the enemy combatant] classification, and a fair opportunity to rebut the Government's factual assertions before a neutral decisionmaker."[109] At the same time, the plurality noted that under "the exigencies of the circumstances," normal criminal process rights are not required, the government could use hearsay evidence, the defendant could be required to carry the burden of proof, and military officers (not Article III judges or juries) could be the "neutral" decision makers.

A crucial concurring opinion was filed by Justice David Souter and joined by Justice Ruth Bader Ginsburg. According to Justice Souter, the clear and unqualified language of the Non-Detention Act of 1971 required that Hamdi be released. That act, which was passed in order to prohibit the type of Japanese internment camps seen during World War II, bars imprisonment or detention of a citizen except pursuant to an act of Congress.[110] The AUMF, in Souter's view, cannot fairly be read to allow detention of enemy combatants in contravention of the clear language of this act. The focus of the AUMF, according to Souter, is on the use of military power, whether against other armies or individual terrorists, and says nothing at all about detentions. On this basis, Souter concluded that Hamdi must be set free unless either criminal charges are brought, the government can show that his detention conforms to the laws of war, or it is demonstrated that the Non-Detention Act is unconstitutional. Recognizing that a majority did not support his interpretation of the AUMF, however, Souter joined the plurality's judgment in order to obtain a result that most closely approximated his own. On remand, and according to the votes of the plurality and Justices Souter and Ginsburg, Hamdi would at least be afforded the opportunity to contest his enemy combatant status.

Perhaps somewhat surprisingly, Justice Scalia filed a dissenting opinion. For Scalia, under U.S. law and tradition, Hamdi had to be released unless criminal charges were brought against him or Congress suspended the writ of habeas corpus. Scalia began his opinion by noting the significance of the Constitution's Due Process Clause and the writ of habeas corpus as crucial safeguards against unlawful detentions. Scalia approvingly cited a long passage from William Blackstone's *Commentaries on the Laws of England*, where the English jurist stated that "confinement of the person, by secretly hurrying him to gaol, where his sufferings are unknown or forgotten; is a less public, a less striking, and therefore a more dangerous engine of arbitrary government."[111] Scalia also cited Hamilton's discussion and elaboration of that passage in *Federalist* 84, where the principled defender of executive power noted that the writ was an important check against "the practice of arbitrary imprisonment . . . in all ages, [one of] the favourite and most formidable instruments of tyranny."[112] In fact, Scalia pointed out that one of the reasons Hamilton gave for opposing a bill of rights was that the Constitution already guaranteed the writ of habeas corpus and the right to a jury trial. Scalia maintained that throughout history, American citizens who have been accused of waging war against the United States were treated as traitors and were subject to criminal process unless, due to the exigencies of war, Congress suspended the writ of habeas corpus. In Scalia's view, if Congress has not suspended the writ, and the courts are open, then the suspected traitor must be criminally charged or released. Scalia also criticized the government's reliance on *Ex parte Quirin*, in which the Court upheld the trial of eight Nazi saboteurs by military commission. Reminiscent of an observation made by Justice Felix Frankfurter about that case,[113] Scalia referred to *Quirin* as "not the Court's finest hour." The *Quirin* justices, in Scalia's view, unfaithfully revised the Court's opinion in *Ex parte Milligan*,[114] which held that during wartime, and absent a suspension of habeas corpus, there is "no exception to the right to trial by jury for citizens who could be called 'belligerents' or 'prisoners of war.'"[115] For Scalia, the *Milligan* Court was quite clear that U.S. citizens could not be tried by military commission under the law of war if the civilian courts were open. Thus, as Scalia saw it, the general principle of *Milligan* still governed, and anything to the contrary in *Quirin* should not be given precedential weight. Even if his interpretation of *Milligan* was wrong, however, and the *Quirin* Court's interpretation was right, Scalia noted that *Quirin* is still distinguishable because the defendants in that case were known enemy combatants. In this case Hamdi is challenging that classification. Since no one argues that the AUMF suspended the writ of habeas corpus, and since no criminal charges had been brought against Hamdi, Scalia concluded that he must be released or turned over to law enforcement to be criminally charged.

Justice Scalia also took the plurality to task for its "Mr. Fix-It Mentality" and for "transmogrifying the Great Writ." Since Congress is the only institution capable of suspending the writ of habeas corpus—and no one claims that it has done so here—the Court, in Scalia's view, cannot effectively suspend the writ for Hamdi and then devise the due process procedures that the executive should have created. "The problem with this approach," according to Scalia, "is not only that it steps out of the courts' modest and limited role in a democratic system; but that by repeatedly doing what it thinks the political branches ought to do it encourages their lassitude and saps the vitality of government by the people."[116] Scalia was not sure if the circumstances were such that Congress could have suspended the writ of habeas corpus after the attacks on 9/11, or whether it could still do so several years later, but one thing he knew for sure was that it was the responsibility of Congress to make that decision, not the courts.

As a way of lessening the blow of his opinion, Scalia noted that the number of American enemy combatants detained in the United States was not likely to be high, and at the time he was aware of only two, Hamdi and Jose Padilla. He also said that American enemy combatants who are captured and held outside of the territorial jurisdiction of the United States are not entitled to habeas relief and should be treated the same way that he argued foreign nationals should be treated in *Rasul*: with no process at all. And, of course, as a matter of policy, Scalia was not claiming that Hamdi should be set free; he would have almost certainly preferred to see him criminally charged and convicted for any wrongdoing he may have committed. Interestingly, three months after the Court handed down its decision, Hamdi was set free.

Scalia's dissent is not a departure from Hamiltonian political principles; in fact, he clearly affirms them. Hamilton is mentioned throughout Scalia's opinion: He is cited for the importance of the writ of habeas corpus as a check against executive tyranny; for the founders' distrust and concern about military establishments; and for the differences between the powers of the president under Article II and those of the British king at the time that the Constitution was adopted. Hamilton is also cited dramatically at the end of Scalia's dissent for the proposition that "[s]afety from external danger is the most powerful director of national conduct. Even the ardent love of liberty will, after a time, give way to its dictates."[117] But Scalia rejected the proposition that the laws and, in particular, the Constitution are silent during times of war, which was a viewpoint shared by Hamilton. Although a defender of the right of prerogative, Hamilton believed that in a republic founded on the principle of consent, there were limits to what the executive could do. Scalia clearly believes, as did Hamilton, that one of those limits was the writ of habeas corpus. In fact, Hamilton made this point abundantly clear in his "Phocion" letters, where he argued that New York laws passed in 1783, which were designed to punish British loyalists after the Revolutionary War, violated the Treaty of Paris and the republican principle that no U.S. citizen who is not specifically charged with a crime (i.e., treason) can be punished without due process of law.[118]

While we have seen in cases like *Ramirez de Arellano* and *Sanchez-Espinoza* that Justice Scalia is willing to give substantial deference to the executive as the sole organ in foreign affairs, this is not the case when a U.S. citizen raises a clear constitutional violation of habeas corpus and is being detained within the territorial boundaries of the United States. It is also important to emphasize that Scalia's bright-line ruling in *Hamdi* serves to delimit the judicial role in foreign affairs. According to his *Rasul* and *Hamdi* opinions, suspected foreign national enemy combatants who are detained outside of the United States do not have to be afforded habeas corpus relief, nor do American-citizen belligerents held outside of the territorial jurisdiction of the United States have this right. But suspected American enemy combatants who are being held within the United States do have the habeas corpus right, as long as Congress has not suspended it. Almost apologetically, Scalia said at the end of his opinion that, as a result of his understanding of the habeas corpus provision and court precedent, he did not know if the executive would have the tools it needed to meet the security needs of the country during the war on terrorism, particularly "the need to obtain intelligence through inter-rogation." But he viewed the administration's position as a clear violation of the right to habeas corpus and rejected the motto *inter arma silent leges* (amidst war laws are silent).

## EXECUTIVE PRIVILEGE

Executive privilege is "the right of the president and important executive branch officials to withhold information from Congress, the courts, and, ulti-mately, the public."[119] While no textual provision speaks directly to the issue, there is historical support for the privilege. The Washington administration, for example, refused the House's request to turn over the negotiating docu-ments for the Jay Treaty, many of which were prepared by Alexander Hamil-ton. The House requested these documents in March 1796 to judge whether or not the treaty should receive its sanction. Aside from the constitutional concern that the House was overstepping its authority with respect to the making of treaties, President Washington asked Hamilton, who by that time had resigned his position as treasury secretary, for his views on whether the documents were privileged. Hamilton responded that they were and argued that if the administration turned over the documents it would set a bad prece-dent that "will be fatal to the negotiating power of the government, if it is to be a matter of course for a call of either House of Congress to bring forth all the communications, however confidential."[120] Hamilton's concerns were later reflected in Washington's letter responding to the House's request for the documents: "The nature of foreign negotiations requires caution, and their success must often depend on secrecy; and even when brought to a conclu-sion a full disclosure of all the measures, demands, or eventual concessions which may have been proposed or contemplated would be extremely im-politic; for this might have a pernicious influence on future negotiations, or produce immediate inconveniences, perhaps danger and mischief, in relation to others."[121] Similarly, in *Federalist* 64, John Jay defended the importance of executive secrecy to the process of negotiating treaties with foreign countries:

> It seldom happens in the negotiation of treaties, of whatever nature, but that per-fect *secrecy* [is] requisite . . . ; and there doubtless are many [apprehensive agents] who would rely on the secrecy of the President, but who would not con-fide in that of the Senate, and still less in that of a large popular assembly. The convention have done well, therefore, in so disposing of the power of making treaties that although the President must, in forming them, act by the advice and consent of the Senate, yet he will be able to manage the business of intelligence in such a manner as prudence may suggest.[122]

Nevertheless, assertions of executive privilege do not sit well in a system of government based on popular consent. Many constitutional scholars have questioned this presidential prerogative, which does not have explicit textual authorization. The late legal historian Raoul Berger, for example, argued that executive privilege is "a constitutional myth."[123] According to Berger, any implied power that the president may have to withhold information must give way to Congress's superior authority to investigate wrongdoing by executive branch officials. In *United States v. Nixon*,[124] the Court recognized a qualified right of executive privilege. There, while ruling against President Richard Nixon's claim of executive privilege in a criminal proceeding in which he was named as an unindicted co-conspirator, the Court held that "a presumptive privilege for Presidential communications . . . is fundamental to the operations of Government and inextricably rooted in the separation of powers of the Constitution."[125]

As assistant attorney general under the Ford administration, Antonin Scalia boldly defended the concept of executive privilege before Congress just one year after President Nixon resigned from office because of the Watergate Scandal.[126] The bill on which Scalia testified sought to limit the assertion of executive privilege to the president; allowed Congress to seek a subpoena from a federal district court when it is denied information from the executive branch; and required that every federal agency keep Congress "fully and currently informed with respect to all matters relating to that agency."[127] Scalia objected to the bill on both theoretical and practical grounds.

On a theoretical level, Scalia testified that while Congress has the undoubted power under the Constitution to oversee the activities of the executive branch—for example, to ascertain that funds appropriated are being properly and efficiently spent—this authority is not absolute. As Scalia saw it, the president has an implicit right, indeed a duty, to withhold certain information from the Congress. For support of this claim, Scalia relied on the historical example of President Washington withholding sensitive documents from the House related to the Jay Treaty, as well as the Supreme Court's decision in *Nixon*. Scalia contended that "the congressional power [to receive information] is restricted to the extent necessary to preserve the constitutionally established functions and independence of the second branch of government," and that "the constitutional basis of executive privilege means that the President may exercise it without congressional leave and in spite of congressional disapproval."[128]

On a more practical level, Scalia reasoned that executive compliance with congressional demands "to be fully and currently informed" would lead to a shadow bureaucracy in one or both houses of Congress. "To be 'fully and currently informed,'" Scalia testified, "in any meaningful sense . . . would require a staff of considerable size—perhaps almost as large as the policy level staff of the executive agency itself."[129] This, according to Scalia, will be "positively destructive of fair and efficient operation of the government."[130] Rather than impose "a wholesale approach to oversight," Scalia contended that Congress should place more trust in the executive branch:

> Senator, I think what it comes back to in some degree is the requirement of trust that Senator Fulbright's testimony, which I quoted, referred to. I think what you are saying is quite true if you have a President who is not trustworthy. But that is certainly a rare occurrence—and when it does happen it does not last for long, it appears.[131]

Scalia's testimony angered at least one expert witness and several of the senators before whom he sat. At one point during his testimony, Scalia described Raoul Berger's earlier statements in support of the bill as "wrong," provoking the latter to write a sharp letter in response criticizing Scalia's view as "departmental boilerplate."[132] Senator Edmund Muskie (D-ME), who chaired the subcommittee investigating whether it would be appropriate to place limits on the scope of executive privilege, repeatedly interrupted Scalia during his testimony. On one occasion, he remarked:

> The whole thrust of the issue is that we get information from the executive branch, in your view, only as a matter of grace. The notion that the Congress has as a matter of constitutional right the power to inquire into anything that happens in the executive branch is challenged by your logic. . . . I will listen to the rest of your statement, but I have listened for 10 pages here to this logic that is the most incredible exposition of this point of view that I have been exposed to in all the time I have been in the Senate. . . . With that why don't you proceed and give your argument whatever credibility you can.[133]

Scalia's testimony on executive privilege can be considered far-reaching for several reasons. First, he argued that the right to invoke the privilege extended not only to the president but to cabinet-level secretaries and agency heads as well—an interpretation that broadened the scope of the privilege beyond that recognized in *Nixon*.[134] Second, Scalia argued that under certain circumstances, a blanket claim of executive privilege could be invoked by the president, which would protect all employees of a particular department from testifying before Congress or producing any documents, as was done by the Eisenhower administration during the Army-McCarthy hearings of 1954.[135] Third, Scalia did not believe that all aspects of the privilege must yield to legitimate demands of the judicial branch. *Nixon* involved a claim of executive privilege in a pending criminal investigation. The opinion suggested, and Scalia expressed support for the idea, that a criminal prosecution would not override the president's right to withhold information pertaining to military and diplomatic secrets.[136] For Scalia, congressional requests for information are quintessential nonjusticiable political questions that should be worked out in "the hurly burly" of the political process, not in the courts.[137] Scalia concluded his remarks by saying,

> I realize that anyone saying a few kind words about executive privilege after the events of the last few years is in a position somewhat akin to the man preaching the virtues of water after the Johnstown flood, or the utility of fire after the burning of Chicago. But fire and water are, for all that, essential elements of human existence. And executive privilege is indispensable to the functioning of our system of checks and balances and separation of powers. I hope that . . . you will not seek to eliminate a vital element of our system merely because it may sometimes have been abused.[138]

## THE NATIONAL ENERGY POLICY
## DEVELOPMENT GROUP OF 2000

Since *Nixon*, the Supreme Court had not decided many executive privilege controversies. During the Clinton administration, the justices declined to review two lower-court opinions rejecting a "protective function" privilege for Secret Service agents,[139] and a "government attorney" privilege for lawyers working in the Office of the President.[140] In granting certiorari in *Cheney v. United States Dist. Court*,[141] however, the justices had the opportunity to make a major ruling involving an executive privilege claim by the George W. Bush administration. The controversy began a few days after President Bush assumed office, when he issued a memorandum establishing the National Energy Policy Development Group (NEPDG), whose purpose was "to develo[p] . . . a national energy policy designed to help the private sector, and government at all levels, promote dependable, affordable, and environmentally sound production and distribution of energy for the future."[142] Located within the Executive Office of the President, members of the NEPDG included Vice President Dick Cheney, who served as the group's chair; various cabinet and agency heads; and other assistants to the president—all of whom were federal government employees. Five months after its creation, NEPDG made its final report, which was approved by the president,[143] and the group disbanded. Environmental groups criticized the Bush administration's energy policy for being too lenient on polluters and friendly toward energy companies. Rumors also circulated that various private individuals and lobbyists participated in the group's policy development sessions, including, most prominently, Kenneth Lay, the former chief executive officer of Enron, which raised the legal issue of whether the group complied with the open-meeting and disclosure requirements of the Federal Advisory Committee Act (FACA) of 1972. FACA, a Nixon-era federal statute designed to eliminate the wasteful expenditure of public funds by the proliferation of private advisory groups for the executive branch, imposes a variety of public disclosure obligations on groups that have been established to advise officers and agencies in the executive branch of the federal government.[144] Exempted from the act's requirements, however, "is any committee that is composed wholly of full-time, or permanent part-time, officers or employees of the Federal Government."[145]

In two separate lawsuits that were subsequently consolidated, Sierra Club, an environmental group seeking to promote the responsible use of the earth's resources, and Judicial Watch, a nonprofit watchdog organization, sued the government employee members of NEPDG—that is, Vice President Dick Cheney, the cabinet and agency heads who served on the group, and the president's assistants—as well as private individuals and lobbyists who they claimed were instrumental in the formation of NEPDG's energy policy recommendations. The two organizations argued that NEPDG should not be exempt from the public disclosure requirements under FACA, because the private individuals and lobbyists were, in essence, de facto members of the group. Sierra Club and Judicial Watch also brought claims under the Administrative Procedure Act (APA) and sought relief under the Mandamus Act, which authorizes district courts "to compel an officer or employee of the United States or any agency thereof to perform a duty owed to the plaintiff."[146] The consolidated suit sought declaratory relief and an injunction requiring defendants to produce all materials allegedly subject to FACA's requirements.

The government filed a motion to dismiss, asking the district court to remove the vice president from the suit under APA, because he is not an executive branch agency, and to dismiss the FACA claims against the federal employees and nongovernmental defendants, because the statute does not allow for private causes of action. The government also argued that application of FACA to the NEPDG's operations would directly interfere with the president's constitutional authority under Article II, including his responsibility to recommend legislation to Congress and his power to require opinions from his department heads. "An expansive reading of FACA," the government argued, "would encroach upon the President's constitutionally protected interest in receiving confidential advice from his chosen advisors, an interest that is also rooted in the principle of separation of powers."[147] Accordingly, the government sought summary judgment based on the administrative record, which included "the President's memorandum creating the NEPDG, the NEPDG's final report, and an affidavit by Karen Knutson, Deputy Assistant to the Vice President for Domestic Policy," declaring that "'[t]o the best of

[her] knowledge, no one other than the officers of the Federal Government who constituted the NEPDG . . . attended any of the [NEPDG] meetings.'"[148] The district court granted the motion to dismiss in part and denied it in part. While it agreed that APA does not apply to the vice president, and that FACA does not allow for private causes of action against any of the defendants,[149] the court held that FACA's substantive requirements could be enforced against the vice president and other governmental participants on the NEPDG under the Mandamus Act, and against agency defendants under the APA. The district court deferred ruling on the government's constitutional issues until specific privilege claims were made by the administration, and in anticipation of such claims, ordered the defendants to produce nonprivileged documents related to the group's work and a privilege log. The government appealed the district court's ruling by requesting a writ of mandamus of its own, asking the court of appeals to find that the lower court had abused its discretion and to require it to vacate its discovery orders, dismiss the vice president from the suit, and grant summary judgment based on the administrative record alone. The court of appeals upheld the district court's ruling. While acknowledging that respondents' discovery requests were quite broad, the court of appeals held that the district court did not abuse its discretion and, when specific privilege claims are made by the government, it could narrow its discovery order so as not to interfere with the president's constitutional authority.

In an opinion by Justice Anthony Kennedy, the Supreme Court vacated the court of appeals' ruling and remanded the case back to that court to reconsider the mandamus request in light of the administration's constitutional concerns. Because of the unique nature of the Office of the Vice President, the majority contended that the two lower courts did not adequately address the administration's concerns that specific claims of executive privilege would impede the executive's constitutional prerogatives and unnecessarily cause strain between the executive and judicial branches of government. The Court distinguished its decision in *Nixon* on several grounds: First, that case involved a subpoena in a criminal case, while the request for discovery in this case comes in a civil action. Unlike in criminal cases, privilege claims in civil cases do not impair the criminal justice system's search for the truth and do not impair the judiciary's essential function "to do justice in criminal prosecutions." Moreover, in criminal cases there are various institutional checks that prevent the abuse of the discovery process from taking place, whereas in civil cases these same checks are not present, and discovery requests can often be meritless. Second, the breadth of the discovery requests in this case, Kennedy contended, distinguishes it from *Nixon*. In *Nixon*, and in light of the fact that the president was named as an unindicted co-conspirator, the subpoena orders were quite narrow. Here, respondents are asking "for everything under the sky." Based on these differences, the majority held that the executive does not have the burden of invoking specific executive privilege claims in response to respondents' broad discovery requests. Citing a district court precedent, *United States v. Poindexter*,[150] in which the court took it upon itself to narrow the scope of subpoena orders in a criminal case where the executive raised constitutional concerns, Justice Kennedy strongly suggested that before the executive is forced to invoke executive privilege, the scope of the discovery requests should be narrowed. Significantly, however, the Court declined to order the court of appeals to issue a writ of mandamus against the district court, finding that it did not abuse its discretion in not ordering the lower court to dismiss the case. Thus, while the Court believed that the court of appeals should reconsider its mandamus ruling in light of separation of powers concerns, it left it up to that court to make the decision.

Justice Thomas filed an opinion concurring in part and dissenting in part, which Scalia joined. If not for the controversy surrounding his involvement in the case, Scalia would have almost certainly written his own opinion. As discussed in the conclusion of this book, just three weeks after the Court granted certiorari in *Cheney*, Scalia went on a duck-hunting trip with Vice President Cheney and, despite a formal request for him to do so, refused to recuse himself from sitting in the case. By joining Justice Thomas's opinion, however, Scalia was at least able to join an opinion that strongly protected the NEPDG's proceedings and deliberations prior to a formal privilege claim ever having to be made. According to Justice Thomas, there were two mandamus requests in the *Cheney* case, one by the Sierra Club and Judicial Watch, which sought discovery of materials that would determine if FACA's government employees exception applied, and the other by the government, which requested the court of appeals to find that the district court abused its discretion in ordering the discovery. In both instances, a writ of mandamus carries a high burden of proof. Unlike the majority, Thomas chose to concentrate on the Sierra Club and Judicial Watch's mandamus request and concluded that their right to the materials was not "clear and indisputable," as required by the mandamus act. For Justice Thomas, FACA's requirement that records related to an advisory committee be made public raised both constitutional and statutory issues when applied to the NEPDG. The constitutional issue related to the president's ability to receive confidential advice from his advisers, and the statutory issue related to whether, after discovery takes place, respondents would get the relief they sought under FACA. Thomas pointed out that the district court left open the possibility that the government might prevail on summary judgment because the de facto member doctrine might not apply to NEPDG. According to Justice Thomas, "application of the *de facto* member doctrine to authorize broad discovery into the inner-workings of the NEPDG has the same potential to offend the Constitution's separation of powers as the actual application of FACA to the NEPDG itself."[151] Even though he acknowledged that "the District Court might later conclude that FACA applies to the NEPDG as a statutory matter and that such application is constitutional," he did not believe that "the mere fact that the District Court *might* rule in respondents' favor [could] establish the clear right to relief necessary for mandamus."[152] Accordingly, Thomas (joined in silence by Scalia) voted to reverse the court of appeals and remand the case with instructions to issue the government's writ, meaning that no discovery would be permitted, the vice president would be dropped from the case, and there would be a summary judgment ruling based on only the bare-bones administrative record. On remand, the D.C. Court of Appeals issued a writ of mandamus directing the district court to dismiss the complaints filed by Sierra Club and Judicial Watch.[153]

Justice Scalia's testimony before Congress in the mid-1970s and his vote in *Cheney* demonstrate that he is a tenacious and willing defender of executive privilege. Edmund Muskie, who served in the Senate for twenty-one years, described Scalia's interpretation of executive privilege as "the most incredible exposition" of the subject that he had been exposed to in all of his years in the Senate. In addition to Scalia's congressional testimony and vote in *Cheney*, he has also defended an expansive view of the state secrets doctrine,[154] and has been sharply critical of the 1974 amendments to the Freedom of Information Act,[155] which were intended to give citizens greater access to government documents.

## PRESIDENTIAL IMMUNITY FROM
## CERTAIN FORMS OF JUDICIAL PROCESS

### Court-Ordered Injunctive and Declaratory Relief

Another important area in which Justice Scalia has defended inherent authority under Article II is presidential immunity from certain forms of judicial process. For example, Scalia argued in a separate opinion in *Franklin v. Massachusetts* (1992)[156] that the president was absolutely immune from court-ordered injunctive or declaratory relief concerning his official responsibilities. In that case, the Court was faced with a statutory and constitutional challenge to the calculation of the decennial census, which (among other things) is used to apportion the number of congressional representatives for each state. In the 1920s, Congress authorized the secretary of commerce and the president to calculate the census. For the 1990 census, Secretary of Commerce Robert Mosbacher included (for only the second time since 1900) overseas federal employees in the census. As a direct result of this decision, the state of Massachusetts lost one of its congressional seats, while the state of Washington gained one. Massachusetts sued, claiming that the inclusion of the overseas federal employees in the census violated the Administrative Procedure Act (APA) and Article I, Section 2, Clause 3 of the Constitution, which (as amended by Section 2 of the Fourteenth Amendment) provides that members of the House "shall be apportioned among the several states according to their respective numbers, counting the whole number of persons in each State."[157]

The U.S. federal district court ruled in favor of Massachusetts, holding that the decision to allocate military personnel serving overseas to their "homes of record" was arbitrary and capricious under the APA, and ordered the secretary of commerce to eliminate the overseas federal employees from the apportionment enumeration. As part of its order, the court also "directed the President to recalculate the number of representatives per state and transmit the new calculation to Congress."[158] On appeal, the Supreme Court reversed. In a badly fractured opinion by Justice Sandra Day O'Connor, five of the justices (including Scalia, who apparently was the "mastermind" behind this part of the court's decision[159]) rejected the APA claim on the grounds that, under the act, the ultimate authority for determining how the census is to be calculated belongs to the president, and the president's discretionary decisions cannot be considered administrative agency action for which the courts can exercise judicial review. As for the constitutional claim, the same five justices held that an injunction could not be issued against the president of the United States, which, in O'Connor's words, is an "extraordinary" form of relief and "should have raised judicial eyebrows."[160] Nevertheless, eight of Scalia's colleagues ruled that the secretary of commerce's method of calculating the census could be challenged under the Constitution or the APA, but rejected the challenge on the merits.

In his solo opinion concurring in part and concurring in judgment, Scalia took issue with the plurality's finding that the constitutional claim could proceed against the secretary of commerce on the merits. For Scalia, Massachusetts lacked standing to challenge the method of calculating the census, because it did not satisfy one of the three basic elements of standing under Article III: redressability. As Scalia saw it, since the ultimate responsibility for conducting the census belonged to the president (who may or may not adopt the recommendations of the secretary of commerce), Massachusetts could not be certain that its injuries would be redressed by a court order running against the secretary of commerce. As he explained, "I do not think that for purposes of the Article III redressability requirement we are *ever* entitled to assume, no matter how objectively reasonable the assumption may be, that the President (or, for that matter, any official of the Executive or Legislative Branches), in performing a function that is not wholly ministerial, will follow the advice of a subordinate official. The decision is by Constitution or law conferred upon him, and I think we are precluded from saying that it is, in practical effect, the decision of someone else."[161] Scalia also sharply rebuked the district court for ordering the president to recalculate the census and resubmit his findings to Congress. "It is a commentary upon the level to which judicial understanding—indeed, even judicial awareness—of the doctrine of separation of powers has fallen, that the District Court entered this order against the President without blinking an eye."[162] Finally, Scalia underscored the plurality's finding that an injunction could never be issued by a court against the president of the United States concerning his official responsibilities:

> I am aware of only one instance in which we were specifically asked to issue an injunction requiring the President to take specified executive acts: to enjoin President Andrew Johnson from enforcing the Reconstruction Acts. As the plurality notes . . . we emphatically disclaimed the authority to do so. . . . The apparently unbroken historical tradition supports the view, which I think implicit in the separation of powers established by the Constitution, that the principals in whom the executive and legislative powers are ultimately vested—viz., the President and the Congress (as opposed to their agents)—may not be ordered to perform particular executive or legislative acts at the behest of the Judiciary.[163]

Scalia's separate concurring opinion in *Franklin* strongly supports presidential immunity from court-imposed injunctive and declaratory relief. Unlike his eight colleagues, Scalia was not willing to allow a declaratory judgment to be issued against the secretary of commerce, because the president ultimately has the authority over whether to follow a subordinate's recommendations. Except for injunctions against the executive officers who attempt to enforce the president's orders, Scalia regarded the president's official policy decisions to be unreviewable.

## Presidential Immunity from Civil Liability

Justice Scalia has also supported presidential immunity from civil liability. Recall that as a member of the D.C. Court of Appeals, Scalia wrote three companion decisions substantially immunizing high-level executive branch officials from civil liability for unlawfully wiretapping the phones of individuals suspected of leaking national security information to the press.[164] In *Nixon v. Fitzgerald* (1982),[165] the Court held that presidents are absolutely immune from civil suits challenging their *official* actions. Even though the Constitution does not explicitly mention presidential immunity from civil suits, the Court based its decision on the unique status of the president in the U.S. constitutional system, the doctrine of separation of powers, and various policy arguments.

*Clinton v. Jones*, which was decided in 1997,[166] raised the novel issue of whether a president's absolute immunity from civil liability extends to private conduct or *unofficial* actions. On the afternoon of May 8, 1991, Paula Corbin

Jones, then an employee of the Arkansas Industrial Development Commission (AIDC), was working at a registration desk for a management conference at the Excelsior Hotel in Little Rock, Arkansas, where then Governor William Jefferson Clinton gave a speech. She claimed that a state trooper, Danny Ferguson, who was assigned to Governor Clinton's security detail, persuaded her to go to the governor's business suite at the hotel, where the governor made "abhorrent" sexual advances that she emphatically rebuffed. She also claimed that after she returned to her AIDC job, her superiors dealt with her "very rudely" and changed her responsibilities and ultimately her position to punish her for not engaging in sexual relations with the governor. Finally, she claimed that after Governor Clinton was elected president, Officer Ferguson defamed her by making a statement to a reporter implying that she had accepted Clinton's alleged overtures, and that various administration spokespersons branded her a liar by denying that the incident had occurred.

On May 6, 1994, just two days before the three-year statute of limitations had expired, and after Clinton had assumed the Office of the President, Paula Jones brought suit against him and Officer Ferguson, alleging two federal claims (sexual harassment and conspiracy) and two state common law claims (intentional infliction of emotional distress and defamation). She sought $75,000 in actual damages and $100,000 in punitive damages. The president, asserting a claim of immunity from civil suit, filed a motion to dismiss the complaint without prejudice to its refiling when he was no longer president or, in the alternative, for a stay of the proceedings for so long as he was president. Jones's lawyers claimed that the president's immunity from civil suit did not extend to his private personal behavior, and argued further that any delay in the proceedings would prejudice her case because of the potential loss of evidence and the advantages the president would have in the public relations arena.

The district court found no support for the president's broad immunity claim and thus rejected the motion to dismiss and allowed discovery in the case to go forward. Nevertheless, due to concerns about the president's busy schedule and the possibility that other lawsuits could be filed against him, District Court Judge Susan Webber Wright granted a temporary immunity from immediate trial until the end of Clinton's presidency. The court of appeals affirmed the denial of the motion to dismiss but reversed the postponement order on the ground that concerns about judicial interference with the president's schedule could be avoided by sensitive case management of the legal proceedings.

The Supreme Court, in an opinion by Justice John Paul Stevens, affirmed. The Court examined two issues, one constitutional and the other prudential: (1) whether litigation of a private civil damages action against an incumbent president must in all but the most exceptional circumstances be deferred until the president leaves office, and (2) whether the district court abused its discretion in postponing the trial under the circumstances of the case. The Court answered no to question one and yes to question two. According to Justice Stevens, the *Fitzgerald* case held that presidents are immune from civil litigation where suits challenge their official actions; it did not, however, extend such immunity to their unofficial actions, which were the issue here since the alleged conduct happened while Clinton was governor of the state of Arkansas. In making a distinction between the president's official and unofficial duties, the *Jones* Court rejected Clinton's argument that the immunity should be based on the nature of the presidential office, which, as the *Fitzgerald* Court recognized, assigns the president singularly important duties in the U.S. constitutional system. On this view, any sort of civil suit (whether challenging the official or unofficial actions of the president) must be delayed because it would impede the president's ability to carry out the functions of the office. Instead, the Court limited the scope of presidential immunity to official, public responsibilities on the ground that no official, even the president, is above the law when it comes to his or her private conduct. With respect to the prudential issue—whether a postponement should have been allowed under the circumstances of this case—the court ruled that the district court abused its discretion by delaying the trial (except for the taking of depositions) until after the president left office. While the Court acknowledged that in some situations civil suits against presidents involving their unofficial behavior might be postponed, it did not find support for such a delay in this case because President Clinton had not established a specific need to delay the proceedings; moreover, the Court did not believe that the district court had adequately considered Paula Jones's concerns that such postponement would prejudice her case. Barring such a specific need shown by the president, the Court ordered the case to go forward.

In light of his strong executivist views and previous support for civil immunity for executive branch officials (including the president[167]), it is surprising that Justice Scalia did not write an opinion in the *Jones* case. The only justice to write separately was Stephen Breyer (also a strong executivist), who, while not supportive of an automatic temporary immunity for the personal conduct of the president, argued that if the president could show a specific need to postpone the trial, then *constitutional* principles forbid a federal judge from interfering with the president's discharge of his public duties. Even though Scalia did not write a separate opinion in *Jones*, he was far from silent during the case's oral argument. While Scalia did not support the president's claim of an automatic temporary constitutional immunity, presumably for the same reasons discussed in Justice Stevens's majority opinion (i.e., there is no automatic immunity for the president's unofficial actions), he was quite supportive of a presidential claim that his official responsibilities prevented him from complying with a court order requiring a deposition or court appearance. In contrast to Justice Breyer, however, Scalia did not cast this immunity claim in *constitutional* terms, but rather viewed it as a political question with which the courts should not get involved. In fact, according to Scalia, once the president has the fortitude to make such a claim, the courts should then recognize an "absolute immunity." In a question to Gilbert K. Davis, Paula Jones's attorney, Scalia made precisely this point:

> I am unlikely to favor a disposition that allows any judge, Federal or State, to sit in judgment of the President's assertion of whether his executive duties are too important or not.
>
> What about an alternative to your proposal that would draw a distinction between the person of the President being hauled before the court and depositions of other people, and say the latter, and the worry about the trial, and all of that, is just like worry about his personal health or his financial affairs, or marital problems at home, or whatever. It's just something you've got to live with, even when you're President.
>
> However, to be hauled personally before a judge is something else, and so give the President absolute immunity. If he makes the claim, I'm too busy to come, you cannot enter judgment against him simply because he refuses to appear, but the rest of the trial can proceed.[168]

What troubled Scalia during the *Jones* oral argument was the idea that federal judges would assess the president's "too-busy" claim, which he did not believe they had the authority to do. Scalia instead wanted a bright-line test that whenever presidents make such claims, then they are absolutely immune from civil process. In Scalia's view, courts should not be allowed to second-guess the judgment of the president concerning the responsibilities of the office, and, not unlike contests between the president and Congress over executive privilege, Scalia maintained that the president does not have to comply with a subpoena request from a court. In a question to Acting Solicitor General Walter Dellinger, Scalia queried:

> But let's say [the Office of the President] is singular. Now, it seems to me you're talking about intrusion of the judiciary upon the executive's time. You also have, sometimes, intrusion by the legislature upon the executive's time. Now, the way we've chosen to handle that with respect, in particular, to claims of presidential privilege—not to testify, not turn over documents, not to give information to Congress—is we haven't adopted an absolute rule that, because it would be so intrusive upon the President, you can't make any such demands. We wait for the case to arise.

And if and when the President has the intestinal fortitude to say, as, for instance, Dwight Eisenhower did with respect to the Army-McCarthy hearings, I am not going to give any testimony: I am not going to allow any of my people to give testimony. If and when that comes up, I'm willing to allow a total executive privilege at that point. Why can't we adopt the same rule here? If and when the President says, I just don't have the time to come when you subpoena me, I'll give him an absolute immunity in that situation.[169]

Justice Scalia's vote in *Jones*, therefore, should not be read as a deviation from his support of presidential immunity from civil suits. Since Scalia holds the record on the Rehnquist Court for filing concurring opinions,[170] it is curious that he did not write a separate opinion in the case.[171] Nevertheless, Scalia fully supports complete civil immunity for the president's official actions and would generously view any "too-busy" claim by the president in civil actions challenging his unofficial conduct. The *Jones* Court was quite explicit in noting the narrow nature of its ruling. It did not rule on whether a civil suit filed in state court against the president would violate federalism principles, nor did it rule on whether a court could compel the president to comply with a court order at a specific time or place. The *Jones* Court simply ruled that the president had no blanket constitutional immunity from civil suit involving his unofficial actions, and that Paula Jones's suit against President Clinton should not be postponed until the end of his presidency, unless the president could provide specific reasons for doing so. Scalia rejected the president's broad constitutional immunity claim, but that can be attributed to the fact that *Fitzgerald* and *Jones* are readily distinguishable cases. Neither the lower courts that heard the case, nor the many academics who had written on the subject, defended complete presidential immunity from civil suit, irrespective of the date of the alleged acts or with whether they related to the official duties of the president. That would, in effect, put the president above the law with respect to his private conduct. Scalia was quite receptive, however, to the president's concerns about being too busy to attend court proceedings or to sit for depositions, and stated during the oral argument that if the president claims that his responsibilities prevent him from complying with a court order, he would support an "absolute immunity" from proceeding against the president.

## CONCLUSION

Justice Scalia's interpretation of executive power most conspicuously identifies him as a Hamiltonian. Like Hamilton, he has defined "executive power" as including everything that is not expressly forbidden by the Constitution and that would not be patently incompatible with republican principles. In keeping with this view, Scalia has defended various inherent powers of the president, including a broad discretionary authority in the area of foreign affairs, the authority of the president to enter into executive agreements without senatorial approval, executive privilege, and presidential immunity from certain forms of judicial process. What is most interesting about Scalia's interpretation of the president's inherent powers is that he has defended them against congressional attempts to limit or restrict such authority.[172]

The president's authority in the area of foreign affairs and national security is particularly sacrosanct to Scalia. His decisions in *Ramirez de Arellano* and *Sanchez-Espinoza* demonstrate that he will deny equitable relief in cases challenging the foreign policy decisions of the executive branch in all but the rarest of circumstances. For Scalia, military and foreign policy concerns are preeminently the business of the executive branch, and judges (who "know little" about these issues) should stay out of them. It is true that Scalia's dissenting opinion in *Hamdi* represents an important exception to his broad deference to presidential authority, but the limitations of that opinion should be kept in mind as well. While Scalia reaffirmed the basic holding of *Ex parte Milligan*—that is, that U.S. citizens cannot be tried by military commission when civilian courts are open and Congress has not suspended the writ of habeas corpus—he qualified this ruling by finding that federal courts could not hear habeas cases by American "enemy combatants" who are detained outside the territorial jurisdiction of the United States. Thus, if Hamdi were kept at Guantanamo Bay, where he was originally sent after his capture in Afghanistan, Scalia would have had little difficulty denying him the right of habeas corpus and would have deferred to the executive's classification of him as an enemy combatant.

One detects from Scalia's reading of Article II a strong hint of John Locke's right of prerogative. According to Locke, the executive has the "power to act according to discretion for the public good, without the prescription of law *and sometimes even against it.*"[173] In *Ramirez de Arellano* and *Sanchez-Espinoza*, for example, Scalia defended a broad presidential authority in the area of foreign affairs, and in *Franklin* he argued that the president's statutory responsibilities were not reviewable by Court-mandated injunctive or declaratory relief. We shall see in the next chapter that Scalia will argue that there are certain agency decisions that are not reviewable by courts, even when they raise significant constitutional issues. Scalia's dissent in *Hamdi*, which at first blush seems inconsistent with the right of prerogative, can also be squared with that doctrine. As Scalia saw it, the detention of an American citizen detained within U.S. territorial borders, who had not been charged with any crime, did not allow the executive to rely upon the doctrine of necessity, because Congress had not suspended the writ of habeas corpus.

Justice Scalia's opinions regarding executive power also reveal a strong conviction that republican government needs energy. It is interesting to note the difference in how Scalia treats executive power on the one hand, and legislative and judicial power on the other. Scalia has not been particularly interested in harnessing the political power of the executive branch. By contrast, in separation of powers and federalism cases, Scalia has sought to place at least some restrictions on congressional power, and in numerous ways has attempted to rein in judicial power. In fact, Scalia boldly and audaciously defines executive power in the same way that "Pacificus" did, where the president is prevented from taking a certain action only when the Constitution clearly prohibits the president from acting, or the executive action violates republican principles. Recall from the discussion in chapter 3 that Scalia has a much less formalistic attitude about separation of powers when the powers of the executive branch are called into question. At the same time, Scalia has supported broad delegations of power to the executive branch and has been a sharp critic of the legislative veto. Scalia's desire for an energetic executive can be seen in other areas of his jurisprudence as well. His removal decisions and scathing criticism of independent regulatory agencies evince a desire for a unitary executive; his concerns about "judicial adventurism" in foreign affairs are directed against courts' unnecessarily hamstringing the president's authority in military and national security matters; he has strongly defended the president's treaty power and ability to enter into sole executive agreements without congressional authorization; and his broad interpretations of executive privilege and presidential immunity from judicial process prevent the executive from getting bogged down with what he believes are unnecessary disclosure requests and frivolous lawsuits. Like Hamilton, Scalia wants to grant the executive branch as much authority as necessary to engage in foreign affairs, to protect the nation from international threats, and to effectively administer the nation's laws. In short, he wants the executive branch to have the capacity to lead. Overall, Scalia's opinions regarding executive power reveal that he believes national safety (or self-preservation) is a more important political end than individual liberty. Echoing Hamilton, Scalia has written, "All government represents a balance between individual freedom and social order, and it is not true that every alteration of that balance in the direction of greater individual freedom is necessarily good."[174]

## NOTES

1. Richard Loss, *The Letters of Pacificus and Helvidius* (1845) (Delmar, NY: Scholars' Facsimiles & Reprints, 1976), v (quoting Edward S. Corwin, ed., *The Con-*

*stitution of the United States of America: Analysis and Interpretation* [Washington, DC: Government Printing Office, 1953], 381). See also Clinton Rossiter, *Alexander Hamilton and the Constitution* (New York: Harcourt, Brace & World, Inc., 1964), 248 ("the 'Stewardship Theory' of Theodore Roosevelt . . . may be traced back in unbroken line to Hamilton's teachings").

2. *Presidential Government: The Crucible of Leadership* (Boston: Houghton Mifflin Co., 1965), 17.

3. In *Federalist* 69, Hamilton approvingly described the fundamental distinctions between the powers possessed by the president under the proposed Constitution and those that then belonged to the British King. As further evidence that Hamilton did not support a British-style hereditary monarchy, he criticized Republicans in 1802 for suggesting that the standard of good behavior for federal judges only applied against removal attempts by the president, not the legislature, since, in their view, "ALL OFFICES ARE HOLDEN OF THE PRESIDENT." For Hamilton, this was an antirepublican principle because, unlike in England, the U.S. president "is not the Sovereign; the sovereignty is vested in the Government, collectively; and it is of the sovereignty, strictly and technically speaking, that a public officer holds his office." PAH, 25:569–76, 570, 571.

4. PAH, 4:207–11.

5. Karl-Friedrich Walling, *Republican Empire: Alexander Hamilton on War and Free Government* (Lawrence, KS: University Press of Kansas, 1999), 15–16. See also Harvey C. Mansfield Jr., *Taming the Prince: The Ambivalence of Modern Executive Power* (New York: Free Press, 1989).

6. See, e.g., Walling, *Republican Empire*; Mansfield, *Taming the Prince*; David F. Epstein, *The Political Theory of the Federalist* (Chicago: University of Chicago Press, 1984); Harvey Flaumenhaft, *The Effective Republic: Administration and Constitution in the Thought of Alexander Hamilton* (Durham, NC: Duke University Press, 1992); Morton J. Frisch, ed., *Selected Writings and Speeches of Alexander Hamilton* (Washington, DC: American Enterprise Institute, 1985).

7. See FP, Nos. 69, 75, 76, and 84.

8. PAH, 12:615.

9. Theodore Roosevelt, *The Autobiography of Theodore Roosevelt*, ed. Wayne Andrews (New York: Octagon Books, 1975), 197.

10. Scalia, "Reflections on the Constitution," address to the Kennedy Political Union at American University, November 17, 1988. C-SPAN broadcast.

11. 520 U.S. 681 (1997).

12. 124 S. Ct. 2633 (2004).

13. The only justices who can be put in the same category with Justice Scalia as defenders of presidential power are Chief Justices John Marshall, a Federalist and disciple of Hamilton's; William Howard Taft, a former president; and Warren Burger, an anglophile and consistent defender of executive power. There have been other strong executivists that have served on the Supreme Court (e.g., George Sutherland, Robert Jackson, and Fred Vinson), but they did not amass the same number of executive-type opinions and/or were not as consistent in their defense of the presidency as Scalia and the other justices mentioned above. Justice Stephen Breyer is also a notable defender of a strong executive, but he has not written enough separation of powers decisions to

assess his overall view of the presidency. In contrast to Scalia, Breyer's pro-executivist views are based on a Progressive conception of the administrative state.

14. U.S. Const. art. II, sec. 1. Interestingly, this is the first time that Hamilton provides an interpretation of the Vesting Clause, because in *The Federalist* he never mentions it.

15. PAH, 15:39.

16. Charles C. Thach Jr., *The Creation of the Presidency* (Baltimore, MD: Johns Hopkins University Press, 1922), 138–39. See also Milkis and Nelson, *The American Presidency*, 41–42.

17. PAH, 15:39.

18. Ibid., 42.

19. Ibid., 38.

20. Ibid., 42.

21. U.S. Const. art. II, sec. 3.

22. PAH, 15:43.

23. His full name was Edmond Charles Genet.

24. PAH, 15:66.

25. Ibid., 678, "Americanus," No. 1 (emphasis in original).

26. PAH, 15:85n.

27. PAH, 15:39.

28. Antonin Scalia, "Originalism: The Lesser Evil," *University of Cincinnati Law Review* 57 (1989): 860.

29. 272 U.S. 52 (1926).

30. *Synar v. United States*, 626 F. Supp. 1374, 1396 (D. D.C. 1986).

31. Scalia, "Originalism: The Lesser Evil," 857 (quoting *Myers*, 272 U.S. at 118).

32. Ibid., 859. Hamilton, for example, devoted an entire essay of *The Federalist* to making these sorts of distinctions. See FP (No. 69), 396–402.

33. W. Crosskey, *Politics and the Constitution in the History of the United States*, vol. 1 (Chicago: University of Chicago Press, 1953), 428–29.

34. Scalia, "Originalism: The Lesser Evil," 860.

35. The president's removal power is also regarded as an implied power, but it is discussed in chapters 3 and 5.

36. *Annals of Congress*, 6th Cong., 1st sess., 10:613 (Marshall's "sole organ" description of the presidency came in a speech in the House on March 7, 1800).

37. PAH, 15:135.

38. 299 U.S. 304 (1936).

39. See *Panama Refining Co. v. Ryan*, 293 U.S. 388 (1935); *Schechter Poultry Corp. v. United States*, 295 U.S. 495 (1935).

40. 299 U.S. 304, 320 (1936).

41. Ibid.

42. 745 F.2d 1500 (D.C. Cir. 1984).

43. By the time the pleadings were filed in court, over half of the ranch's 14,000 acres and nearly 90 percent of the grazing land had already been seized by soldiers of the RMTC. Ibid., 1508.

44. *Ramirez de Arellano v. Weinberger*, 568 F. Supp. 1236 (D. D.C. 1983).

45. 745 F.2d. at 1512 (citing *Baker v. Carr*, 369 U.S. 189 [1962] and *Youngstown Sheet & Tube Co. v. Sawyer*, 343 U.S. 579 [1952]).

46. Ibid.

47. Ibid.

48. Ibid., 1515.

49. Ibid., 1562.

50. Ibid., 1561. Along these lines, Scalia expressed concern about the unforeseen consequences such an injunction might have:

> While it is acknowledged that the land in question is being used for a training base, we do not know what other military purposes it may be designed to serve. If, for example, it had been the staging area for our recent military operations in Grenada, the injunction sought here could have caused incalculable harm. (Ibid.)

51. 745 F.2d. at 1562. On this point, Scalia joined Judge Kenneth Starr's dissent, which held that the act of state doctrine bars plaintiffs' actions. The act of state doctrine prevents judicial relief for certain claims that would require the court to pass on the validity of the laws of a foreign state. Ibid., 1566–74.

52. Ibid., 1551. Interestingly, after deriding the idea of judicial tyranny, Scalia approvingly quotes the following passage from the Bible:

> Now appoint for us a king to govern us like all nations. . . . [W]e will have a king over us; that we also may be like all the nations, and that our king may govern us, and go out before us, and fight our battles. (Ibid., 1551n1)

53. 770 F.2d. 202 (D.C. Cir. 1985).

54. Ibid., 205.

55. Pub. L. No. 97-377, Sec. 793, 96 Stat. 1865 (1982).

56. *Sanchez-Espinoza v. Reagan*, 568 F. Supp. 596 (D. D.C. 1983).

57. 770 F.2d at 208.

58. *Crockett v. Reagan*, 720 F.2d 1355 (D.C. Cir. 1983).

59. 770 F.2d at 210.

60. U.S. Const. art. II, sec. 2, cl. 2.

61. Burns H. Weston, "Executive Agreement," in *Encyclopedia of the American Constitution*, ed. Leonard W. Levy, Kenneth L. Karst, Dennis J. Mahoney (New York: MacMillan Publishing Co., 1986), 2:666.

62. From 1981 to 1996, only 5 percent of international agreements took the form of treaties. Kiki Caruson, "International Agreement-Making and the Executive-Legislative Relationship: A Review of the Exercise of Formal Diplomacy under the Reagan, Bush and Clinton Administrations (1981–1996)," paper presented at the 2004 American Political Science Meeting. See also David M. O'Brien, *Constitutional Law and Politics: Struggles for Power and Governmental Accountability*, 6th ed. (New York: W. W. Norton, 2005), 1:241; Lawrence Margolis, *Executive Agreements and Presidential Power in Foreign Policy* (New York: Praeger Publishers, 1986).

63. See *Goldwater v. Carter*, 444 U.S. 996 (1979).

64. In *Federalist* 75, Hamilton clearly referred to treaties as a shared power and explained that the responsibility of conducting foreign relations was too important to

place in one institution. But in his "Camillus" essays defending the Jay Treaty, Hamilton seemed to suggest that the treaty power resided mostly with the president and cited for evidence of this the fact that it is enumerated under Article II.

65. See e.g., PAH, vol. 3, pp. 483–97, 530–58 (writing as "Phocion," Hamilton defended the authority of U.S. treaties against state attempts to disregard their provisions).

66. Ron Chernow, *Alexander Hamilton* (New York: Penguin Press, 2004), 488–500.

67. Ibid., 493.

68. *Annals of Congress*, 4th Cong., 1st sess., 5:464–74 (Gallatin's views); ibid., 487–95 (Madison's views). See also Madison, "The Jay Treaty. Speech in the 4th Congress, April 6," WJM, 6:263–95; and Madison's Letter to Thomas Jefferson, WJM, 6:296–302.

69. PAH, 20:33–34.

70. Joseph Biden Jr. and John B. Ritch III, "The Treaty Power: Upholding a Constitutional Partnership," *University of Pennsylvania Law Review* 137 (1989): 1529n16 (quoting *Congressional Record*, 134 [1988]:S6937).

71. Ibid., 1537–38.

72. Ibid., 1538.

73. 489 U.S. 353 (1989).

74. Ibid., 367n7.

75. Ibid., at 376.

76. See *Rainbow Navigation, Inc. v. Department of Navy*, 686 F. Supp. 354 (D.C. Dist. 1988); *Rainbow Navigation, Inc. v. Department of Navy*, 699 F. Supp. 339 (D.C. Dist. 1988). Both of these decisions were subsequently overturned in *Rainbow Navigation, Inc. v. Department of Navy*, 911 F.2d. 797 (D.C. Cir. 1990).

77. "White House Opposes Condition Democrats Seeking for the INF Treaty," *Washington Post*, March 19, 1988, A11, col. 1; "When Treaty Interpretations Differ, Who Has the Last Word?" *Washington Post*, February 17, 1988, A17, col. 1; "Dispute Threatens INF Treaty; Democrats at Odds with White House on Senate's Legal Role," *Washington Post*, February 6, 1988, A1, col. 6.

78. The impetus for congressional hearings on the subject was the discovery that the Nixon administration entered into two executive agreements in 1972–1973 without reporting them to Congress as required by the Case Act of 1972. One of these agreements involved a letter by President Nixon to the former South Vietnamese president Nguyen Van Thieu, pledging a U.S. response to any Communist violation of the 1973 Vietnam peace accords.

79. U.S. Senate, *Congressional Oversight of Executive Agreements—1975: Hearings before the Subcommittee on Separation of Powers of the Committee on the Judiciary*, 94th Cong., 1st sess., May 15, 1975, 167–203, 302–5; U.S. House of Representatives, *Congressional Review of International Agreements: Hearings before the Subcommittee on International Security and Scientific Affairs of the Committee on International Relations*, 94th Cong., 2nd sess., July 22, 1976, 182–200.

80. Ibid., *Congressional Oversight of Executive Agreements—1975*, 302.

81. Ibid., 192.

82. See, e.g., *United States v. Belmont*, 301 U.S. 324 (1937).

83. U.S. Const. art. II, sec. 1 ("the executive Power shall be vested in a President").

84. *Congressional Oversight of Executive Agreements—1975*, 303.

85. Scalia also mentioned the recognition of foreign governments, the conclusion of operational arrangements on the battlefield, and the evacuation of citizens who are under attack abroad as areas of exclusive executive authority under the Constitution. Ibid., 176–77. He explained his view as follows:

> I don't think you could, without violating international law, undo after the fact—even though [*sic*] legislation enacted by a two-thirds vote overriding a Presidential veto—a valid executive agreement already entered into. That is, entered into under the President's exclusive authority or entered into under some unconditional authority which the Congress had given. . . . [T]here are certain areas where I don't even think an act of Congress can stop the President from entering into an executive agreement. However few or however many there may be, there are some. (Ibid., 200)

86. PJM, 15:108.

87. PAH, 1: 4–5.

88. FP, 422.

89. Pub. L. No. 107-56, 115 Stat. 272 (2001).

90. Military Order of November 13, 2001, "Detention, Treatment, and Trial of Certain Non-Citizens in the War against Terrorism," 66 F.R. 57833 (November 16, 2001).

91. *Rasul v. Bush*, 124 S. Ct. 2686, 2692 (2004) (quoting 28 U.S.C. secs. 2241[a], [c][3]).

92. 339 U.S. 763 (1950).

93. 124 S. Ct. 2686 (2004).

94. *Ahrens v. Clark*, 335 U.S. 188 (1948).

95. 410 U.S. 484 (1973).

96. 124 S. Ct. 2695 (quoting *Braden*, 410 U.S. at 495).

97. Ibid. (quoting *Braden*, 410 U.S. at 494–95).

98. Ibid., 2704.

99. Ibid., 2707.

100. Ibid. (citing *Johnson v. Eisentrager*, 339 U.S. at 778–79).

101. Ibid., 2710.

102. 124 S. Ct. 2633 (2004).

103. Ibid., 2636.

104. Ibid., 2636–37.

105. Ibid., 2636.

106. Ibid., 2637.

107. Pub. L. No. 107-40, 115 Stat. 224.

108. 317 U.S. 1 (1942).

109. 124 S. Ct. at 2648.

110. 18 U.S.C. sec. 4001(a).

111. 124 S. Ct. at 2661 (quoting W. Blackstone, *Commentaries on the Laws of England* 1:132–33 [1765]).

112. Ibid., 2662–63 (quoting *Federalist* 84).

113. Justice Frankfurter, who participated in the Court's decision in *Quirin*, said years later that it "[is] not a happy precedent." David J. Danelski, "The Saboteur's Case," *Journal of Supreme Court History* 1 (1996): 61–82, 80.

114. 71 U.S. 2 (1866).
115. 124 S. Ct. at 2670.
116. Ibid., 2673.
117. Ibid., 2674 (quoting *Federalist* No. 8).
118. PAH, 3:483–97, 530–58.
119. Mark J. Rozell, *Executive Privilege: The Dilemma of Secrecy and Democratic Accountability* (Baltimore: Johns Hopkins University Press, 1994), xi.
120. Chernow, *Alexander Hamilton*, 498 (citing PAH, 20:68).
121. *Messages and Papers of the Presidents*, ed. James D. Richardson (New York: Bureau of National Literature and Art, 1910), 1:186–87.
122. FP, 377.
123. Raoul Berger, *Executive Privilege: A Constitutional Myth* (Cambridge, MA: Harvard University Press, 1974).
124. 418 U.S. 683 (1974).
125. Ibid., 708.
126. U.S. Senate, *Executive Privilege—Secrecy in Government: Hearings before the Subcommittee on Intergovernmental Relations of the Committee on Government Operations*, 94th Cong., 1st sess., 1975, 67–128.
127. Ibid., 164.
128. Ibid.
129. Ibid., 70.
130. Ibid.
131. Ibid., 94.
132. Ibid., 67–68, 126–28.
133. Ibid., 72.
134. Scalia argued that the president could delegate the authority of executive privilege to his cabinet secretaries and agency heads, and that the delegation did not have to be in writing. Ibid., 75–82.
135. Ibid., 81–84.
136. Ibid., 78–79.
137. See e.g. *Morrison v. Olson*, 487 U.S. 654, 697 (Scalia, J., dissenting) ("The District Court declined (in my view correctly) to get involved in the [executive privilege] controversy, and urged the other two branches to try '[c]ompromise and cooperation, rather than confrontation'"); *Webster v. Doe*, 486 U.S. 592, 606 (1988) (Scalia, J., dissenting) ("Of course the [Central Intelligence Agency] can seek to protect itself, ultimately, by an authorized assertion of executive privilege. . . .but that is a power to be invoked only *in extremis*, and any scheme of judicial review of which it is a central feature is extreme. I would, in any event, not like to be the agent who has to explain to the intelligence services of other nations, with which we sometimes cooperate, that they need have no worry that the secret information they give us will be subjected to the notoriously broad discovery powers of our courts, because, although we have to litigate the dismissal of our spies, we have available a protection of somewhat uncertain scope known as executive privilege, which the President can invoke if he is willing to take the political damage that it often entails").
138. *Executive Privilege—Secrecy in Government*, 86.

139. *Rubin v. United States*, 525 U.S. 990 (1998) (denying review of whether the president's Secret Service agents could refuse to testify against the president in non-felonious criminal cases).

140. *Office of the President v. Office of the Independent Counsel*, 525 U.S. 996 (1998) (not granting review in a case requiring the president's government attorney to testify in a criminal proceeding about nonpersonal legal advice given to the administration).

141. 124 S. Ct. 2576 (2004).

142. Ibid., 2582.

143. whitehouse.gov/energy/National-Energy-Policy.pdf.

144. 5 U.S.C. App. sec. 2(a).

145. 5 U.S.C. App. sec. 3(2).

146. 28 U.S.C. sec. 1361.

147. *In re Cheney*, 334 F.3d 1096, 1100 (D.C. Cir. 2003).

148. Ibid., 1100–1101.

149. On this basis, the district court dismissed respondents' claims against the nongovernmental defendants.

150. 727 F. Supp. 1501 (D.C. Dist. 1989).

151. 124 S. Ct. at 2595.

152. Ibid.

153. *In re Cheney*, 406 F.3d 723 (2005).

154. See *Molerio v. F.B.I.*, 749 F.2d 815 (D.C. Cir. 1984) (prohibiting the discovery of sensitive documents involving national security interests).

155. Antonin Scalia, "The Freedom of Information Act Has No Clothes," *Regulation* 6, no. 2 (March–April 1982), 15–19 (describing the Freedom of Information Act as "the Taj Mahal of the Doctrine of Unanticipated Consequences, the Sistine Chapel of Cost/Benefit Analysis Ignored").

156. 505 U.S. 788 (1992).

157. See U.S. Const. art I, sec. 2, cl. 3 and Section 2 of the Fourteenth Amendment.

158. 505 U.S. at 791.

159. Besides Scalia, the other three justices who joined this part of O'Connor's opinion were Chief Justice William Rehnquist and Justices Byron White and Clarence Thomas. The theory of the court's opinion was not argued by the Solicitor General and was developed for the first time at conference. One of Justice Harry Blackmun's law clerks described Scalia as the "mastermind" behind that part of the Court's decision and cited a four-page, single-spaced, "Ninogram" that Scalia sent to O'Connor while she was drafting the opinion. HABP, box 603, folder 8.

160. 505 U.S. at 802.

161. Ibid., 824–25.

162. Ibid., 826.

163. Ibid., 827.

164. *Halperin v. Kissinger*, 807 F.2d 180 (D.C. Cir. 1986); *Smith v. Nixon*, 807 F.2d. 197 (D.C. Cir. 1986); and *Ellsberg v. Mitchell*, 807 F.2d 204 (D.C. Cir. 1986).

165. 457 U.S. 731 (1982).

166. 520 U.S. 681 (1997).

167. In his separate opinion in *Franklin*, Scalia approvingly cited *Fitzgerald* as support for absolute presidential immunity from injunctive and declaratory relief. See 505 U.S. at 827–28.

168. *Clinton v. Jones*, no. 95-1853. U.S. Supreme Court Official Transcript, January 13, 1997, 44–45.

169. Ibid., 27.

170. Lee Epstein, Jeffrey A. Segal, Harold J. Spaeth, and Thomas G. Walker, *The Supreme Court Compendium: Data, Decisions & Developments*, 3rd ed. (Washington, DC: Congressional Quarterly, 2003), 594–96.

171. This might be explained on purely political grounds, since it is unimaginable that Scalia (with the strong views he has on the subject) would not have gone on record if the president happened to be Ronald Reagan, George H. W. Bush, or George W. Bush.

172. In one case, for example, Scalia suggested that the president's authority as commander-in-chief can override contrary congressional laws. In *Rainbow Navigation, Inc. v. Department of Navy*, 783 F.2d. 1072, 1078 (D.C. Cir. 1986), then Judge Scalia wrote:

> It may well be that the president has certain constitutionally conferred powers as commander-in-chief that this essentially domestic statute, intended to subsidize the United States merchant marine, was not intended to, or could not constitutionally, displace. We doubt, for example, whether a decision that the Navy should use a foreign ship, faster or less vulnerable than any American ship available, to deliver urgently needed supplies to troops in wartime would (even if it did not fall within the proviso at issue here) be prohibited. We need not decide, however, whether the statute is subject to an implied exception in deference to such presidential powers, enabling foreign ships to be used when the Executive concludes that military-foreign policy considerations so require. The Secretary of the Navy did not assert the exercise of any independent presidential authority here. . . .

173. *The Second Treatise of Government*, ed. Thomas P. Peardon (Indianapolis, IN: Bobbs-Merrill Co., 1952), 92 (emphasis added).

174. *A Matter of Interpretation: Federal Courts and the Law* (Princeton, NJ: Princeton University Press, 1997), 42.

# Chapter Five

# The "Politics" of Administration

The late political scientist Leonard D. White, a pioneer himself in the field of public administration, regarded Alexander Hamilton as "the greatest administrative genius of his generation in America, and one of the great administrators of all time."[1] Hamilton defined good government as "its aptitude and tendency to produce a good administration."[2] While all of the departments of government participated in the administration of law, Hamilton believed that "in its most precise signification, it is limited to executive details, and falls peculiarly within the province of the executive department."[3]

Hamilton advanced a distinct theory of public administration,[4] which differed in significant ways from the early Republican and later Progressive theories of administration, and contained three central ingredients. First, Hamilton stressed that the administrative branch should be under the direct control of the president. All executive officials, wrote Hamilton, "ought to be considered as the assistants or deputies of the Chief Magistrate, and on this account they ought . . . to be subject to his superintendence."[5] Organizing administration in this way allows for two things. Most importantly, it enables the president to exercise leadership. "Decision, activity, secrecy and dispatch will generally characterize the proceedings of one man in a much more eminent degree than the proceedings of any greater number, wrote Hamilton."[6] And a unified executive has the added benefit of making the officials who exercise political power more accountable. "One of the weightiest objections to a plurality in the executive," observed Hamilton, "is that it tends to conceal faults and destroy responsibility."[7]

The second ingredient of Hamilton's administrative theory stressed administration as a distinct and important aspect of governance, not merely (as Progressive theorists would later argue) a mechanical or technical function. No statute can foresee all contingencies and circumstances. Laws, by their very nature, are concerned with generalities. Thus, the administration of laws requires that someone make important and often politically sensitive judgments. Hamilton believed that an effective system of administration should allow the heads of departments, acting under the supervision of the president, to exercise a reasonable degree of discretion.

Finally, Hamilton's administrative theory emphasized the interrelationship of administration and policy formulation. The administration of laws does not simply involve detail work. Administration in "its largest sense comprehends all the operations of the body politic,"[8] including the making of laws. Unlike the Jeffersonian Republicans, who regarded Congress as the dominant policy-making institution, Hamilton envisioned a large legislative role for the president. As Hamilton saw it, the officials who are largely responsible for directing or carrying out certain executive functions should not be shy about proposing new programs and legislation to the president, which he himself demonstrated by formulating and defending a whole program of domestic and foreign policy initiatives during the Washington administration. These three elements of Hamilton's administrative theory—unity, discretion, and policy formulation— were designed to promote what political scientist Harvey Flaumenhaft has called an "effective republic."[9] In a very real sense, Hamilton believed that the executive branch would do the actual business of governing in the United States. In his view, the members of Congress, with their short terms and close ties to the people, would not be able to perform this function very well.

## JUSTICE SCALIA'S HAMILTONIAN CONCEPTION OF THE ADMINISTRATIVE PROCESS

Justice Scalia's appointment to the Supreme Court in 1986 made him the first administrative law professor to sit on the high court since Felix Frankfurter's retirement in 1962. Not surprisingly, the two justices' administrative law views have been compared and contrasted. What's surprising are the conclusions that have been drawn. Several commentators have argued that Scalia's understanding of the administrative process was influenced by Felix Frankfurter, James Landis, and the Legal Process School.[10] The Legal Process School, which reached its high-water mark in the 1950s as a reaction to the nihilistic tendencies of Legal Realism, developed two major ideas about the law: (1) institutional competence, and (2) a form of judging referred to as "reasoned elaboration."[11] In the area of administrative law, Legal Process theorists defended the Progressive theory of administration whereby agency heads are regarded as neutral scientific experts whose decisions are insulated from an undesirable political process. What animated the Progressive theory of administration was a strong dissatisfaction with the corrupt machine politics of the late nineteenth century. Favorably disposed toward government regulation of "Big Trusts," and heavily influenced by the scientific rationalism of German administrative theory, the Progressives viewed administrators as technocrats who could transcend the parochial partisan interest in order to regulate for the public good. Importantly, judges participate in the Progressive understanding of the administrative process by ensuring that agency decisions comport with reason. Accordingly, while the Legal Process School had its conservative tendencies (e.g., the idea of institutional competence, and that each institution of government had its proper role and sphere of authority), its emphasis on reason as the linchpin of both administrative and judicial decisions made process jurisprudents, such as Felix Frankfurter, James Landis, Louis Jaffe, Lon Fuller, Henry Hart, and Albert Sacks, early defenders of what is now called "hard-look" review of administrative action.[12] Justice Scalia, who studied law under Fuller, Jaffe, and Sacks at Harvard in the late 1950s, and whose views of the administrative process are often mistakenly associated with the Legal Process School, could not disagree more with the school's two central beliefs about the administrative process: (1) administrators are neutral, scientific experts, and (2) judges should apply hard-look scrutiny in reviewing agency decisions. Justice Scalia's views on the administrative process will now be examined by comparing them with the three central ingredients of Hamilton's administrative theory: unity, discretion, and policy making.

## SCALIAS'S HAMILTONIAN ADMINISTRATIVE THEORY

With his usual sharp wit and sense of humor, Justice Scalia began a speech at Duke University Law School in 1989 by telling his audience, "Administrative law is not for sissies." He also warned the members of the audience to "lean back, clutch the sides of your chairs, and steel yourselves for a pretty dull lecture."[13] In making these statements, Scalia was acknowledging the common perception about administrative law: it is complex and boring. But one should not assume from this that Scalia regards it as unimportant. The German sociologist Max Weber predicted that bureaucrats would play a substantial role in "who governs" modern democracies. Due to the increasing complexity of governmental affairs, Weber believed that legislators would be required to delegate considerable authority to administrative agencies, which in fact happened in the United States in the 1930s when the Progressive vision of the administrative state came into fruition under Franklin

Delano Roosevelt's New Deal program. Justice Scalia, who has extensive experience in administrative law,[14] clearly recognizes the importance of public administration to the question of who governs.

## Unity

Justice Scalia's support for Hamilton's theory of unity is apparent in several different areas of his jurisprudence. As discussed in chapter 4, Scalia has argued that the president must "speak and act with a single voice" in the area of foreign policy.[15] But Scalia has also supported a unified executive in the area of domestic relations. In *Printz v. United States* (1997),[16] the Court struck down the interim provisions of the Brady Handgun Violence Prevention Act of 1993 (the Brady Bill) for violating the so-called anticommandeer principle. Under the temporary provisions of the act, local sheriffs were required to perform background checks on gun purchasers. Justice Scalia, for the majority, held that that the Brady Bill violated constitutional principles of federalism, because local sheriffs, not federal agents, were mandated to perform the checks. Interestingly, however, Scalia made the additional argument (only briefly commented upon by Justice John Paul Stevens in dissent) that the federal law violated the doctrine of separation of powers and, in particular, the framers' concept of a unitary executive. For Scalia, the other fatal defect of the Brady Bill was the placement of federal law enforcement authority (supervision of federal gun restrictions) in the hands of state and local sheriffs who were not subject to presidential control. As Scalia put it, "The insistence of the Framers upon unity in the Federal Executive—to insure both vigor and accountability—is well known. . . . That unity would be shattered, and the power of the President would be subject to reduction, if Congress could act as effectively without the President as with him, by simply requiring state officers to execute its laws."[17]

Moreover, as editor of the journal *Regulation* in the early 1980s, Scalia avidly supported the Reagan administration's attempt to impose central-clearance authority over administrative rule making.[18] One month after his inauguration in 1981, President Ronald Reagan issued Executive Order 12991, which required executive branch agencies (1) to conduct cost-benefit analysis with respect to the issuance of any new rule, and (2) to submit proposed rules to the Office of Management and Budget (OMB) for "advice." Scalia regarded the cost-benefit requirement as "nothing new," but had high hopes that the central-clearance component would bring about lasting structural regulatory reform. Scalia reasoned that instead of looking at the regulatory costs exacted on private industry by just one executive agency, such as the Environmental Protection Agency, the administration, through the OMB, could now conduct a cost-benefit analysis of the entire regulatory program. Furthermore, even though he doubted that it could happen without some sort of statutory authorization, Scalia supported the application of EO 12991 to the independent agencies. With such authority, Scalia believed the OMB would have the means "to take the agency to the mat in the Oval Office if it refuses to heed the advice, with final decision to be made by the President."[19]

But perhaps the most important evidence of Justice Scalia's support of a unified executive has been his decisions regarding the president's right to remove executive branch officials. As discussed in chapter 3, Scalia has been a vociferous critic of *Humphrey's Executor v. United States*,[20] where the Supreme Court limited the president's ability to remove independent agency heads. Scalia's disdain for *Humphrey's Executor* was also shown in his dissenting opinion in *Morrison v. Olson*,[21] where the majority upheld the independent counsel provision of the Ethics in Government Act. Under the act, the president was only able to remove an independent counsel for "good cause." In an opinion by Chief Justice William Rehnquist, the majority held that even though prosecution is a purely executive function, the president still retains enough authority over the independent counsel to assure that the laws are faithfully executed. In the process, the Court announced a new standard for analyzing removal cases:

> We undoubtedly did rely on the terms "quasi-legislative" and "quasi-judicial" to distinguish the officials involved in *Humphrey's Executor* . . . from those in *Myers*, but our present considered view is that the determination of whether the Constitution allows Congress to impose a "good cause"-type restriction on the President's power to remove an official cannot be made to turn on whether or not that official is classified as "purely executive." . . . We do not mean to suggest that an analysis of the functions served by the officials at issue is irrelevant. But the real question is whether the removal restrictions are of such a nature that they impede the President's ability to perform his constitutional duty, and the functions of the officials in question must be analyzed in that light.[22]

Justice Scalia was flabbergasted. In his opinion, *Humphrey's Executor* required the Court to strike down the law if prosecution is a "purely executive" function, which the Court admitted it was. Far be it from him to defend *Humphrey's Executor*, Scalia reasoned, "[b]ut at least it permitted the identification of certain officers, and certain agencies, whose functions were entirely within the control of the President."[23] In *Mistretta v. United States*,[24] decided one year after *Morrison*, Scalia observed that as a result of the *Morrison* decision, the term "independent agency" no longer means "an agency independent of all three Branches" but an "agency within the Executive Branch (and thus authorized to exercise executive powers) independent of the control of the executive."[25] Scalia argued in his scathing dissent in *Morrison* that the Court's new test in removal decisions was an open invitation for Congress to further restrict the president's removal power:

> What about a special Assistant Secretary of State, with responsibility for one very narrow area of foreign policy, who would not only have to be confirmed by the Senate but could also be removed only pursuant to certain carefully designed restrictions? . . . Or a special Assistant Secretary of Defense for Procurement? . . . The possibilities are endless, and the Court does not understand what the separation of powers . . . is all about, if it does not expect Congress to try them. As far as I can discern from the Court's opinion, it is now open season upon the President's removal power for all executive offices, with not even the superficially principled restriction of *Humphrey's Executor* as cover. The Court essentially says to the President: "Trust us. We will make sure that you are able to accomplish your constitutional role." I think the constitution gives the President—and the people—more protection than that.[26]

## Political Discretion

Justice Scalia has also supported the second ingredient of Alexander Hamilton's administrative theory: the conception of administrators as political appointees who exercise discretion. In the late nineteenth century, a theory of public administration developed that challenged the classical approach associated with the Federalist Party and, in particular, Alexander Hamilton. Borrowing from German political philosophy, the Progressives sought a more "enlightened" system of administration. Believing that public administration had become too corrupt and that a more technical and scientific expertise was needed to solve the problems of modern government, the Progressives sought to remove politics from the field of administration. In general, the Progressive theory of administration "regarded agencies as politically insulated, self-starting, and technically sophisticated. The expectation was that neutral experts, operating above the fray, would be able to discern the public interest."[27] Perhaps the most famous exponent of the Progressive theory of administration was Woodrow Wilson, who stated in his classic essay on public administration:

> The field of administration is a field of business. It is removed from the hurry and strife of politics; it at most points stands apart even from the debatable grounds of constitutional study. It is a part of political life only as . . . machinery is part of the manufactured product. . . . Administrative questions are not political questions. Although politics sets the tasks for administration, it should not be suffered to manipulate its offices.[28]

Justice Scalia has expressed strong disagreement with the Wilsonian apolitical conception of public administration. Like Hamilton, Scalia believes that administrative heads exercise political discretion. This was evident in his dissenting opinion in *Morrison v. Olson*,[29] where he described the Office of Special Counsel as a political office that should be held accountable to the president. It has also been evident in his long-standing criticism of "independent" regulatory agencies,[30] where he has disagreed with the description of these agencies as "impartial" and "scientific":

> Justice Sutherland's decision in *Humphrey's Executor* . . . is stamped with some of the political science preconceptions characteristic of its era and not of the present day. . . . It is not obvious today as it seemed in the 1930s that there can be such things as genuinely "independent" regulatory agencies, bodies of impartial experts whose independence from the President does not entail correspondingly greater dependence upon the committees of Congress to which they are then immediately accountable; or, indeed, that the decisions of such agencies so clearly involve scientific judgment rather than political choice that it is even theoretically desirable to insulate them from the democratic process.[31]

In the early 1980s, Scalia's political conception of administration was evident at several forums in which he participated, as well as in his scholarly publications. For example, during the annual conference of the D.C. Court of Appeals, then-judge Scalia described the "Age of Deregulation," which he equated with the "Age of the Enlightenment" and the "Age of the Industrial Revolution," as "largely the very antithesis of expertise." "In a way," he continued, "deregulation is an antiexpertise movement."[32] As Judge Scalia saw it, independent regulatory agencies operating under the Progressive view of public administration may have employed a rational and scientific technique in making rules, but they did not adequately account for the overall cost of their regulations:

> The felt fault with the existing system was that yes, you have a lot of individual experts out there, individual agencies, each of which is expert in its field, and each of them may be making perfectly sound decisions for the particular field; but the sum total of those individually expert decisions doesn't make any sense. . . . So I think you have to regard the deregulation movement as to some extent a reaction to conferring too much power upon the expertise of individual agencies at the expense of the overall picture.[33]

Moreover, as editor of *Regulation*, Scalia criticized what he called the "Saxbe Hypothesis"[34]—the idea about the two major political parties which posits that the Democrats want to govern, while the Republicans want to prevent them from doing so.[35] At a time when Republicans controlled the White

House and one house of Congress, Scalia described this minimalist, limited-government philosophy as disastrous for "genuine regulatory reform." All that can be done by followers of such a hypothesis is to slow down the rate of regulation. In order to eliminate the "encrusted" regulations of the past, Scalia advocated a new Republican attitude about the national government in general, and the executive branch in particular, which would entail a vigorous use of the machinery of government to accomplish conservative goals. For this reason, Scalia sharply criticized several congressional proposals then under consideration that would have made regulatory change more difficult, including bills limiting the amount of discretion agencies could exercise; requiring more formal adjudicatory procedures in rule making; and subjecting administrative decisions to legislative vetoes, particularly one-house vetoes. In the battle between Democrats and Republicans over the administrative state, these measures, in Scalia's view, would relegate Republicans to fighting a modern war with foot soldiers:

> What [these executive-enfeebling measures] deter is change. Imposed upon a regulation-prone executive, they will on balance slow the increase of regulation; but imposed upon an executive that is seeking to dissolve the encrusted regulation of past decades, they will impede the dissolution. Regulatory reformers who do not recognize this fact, and who continue to support the unmodified proposals of the past as though the fundamental game had not been altered, will be scoring points for the other team.[36]

Finally, as chair of the American Bar Association's Administrative Law Section, Scalia wrote a series of messages in which he emphasized the political nature of agency decision making. In his last message, titled "Rule-making as Politics,"[37] Scalia maintained that regulatory issues often pose questions of values, not simply facts, and that "[a]n agency may make some decisions in rulemaking not because they are the best or the most intelligent, but because they are what the people seem to want."[38] Not wishing to be confused as a populist, however, Scalia maintained that the determination of what the people want should not be ascertained by referring to "the latest Gallup poll, but to the manifestations of the popular will through the political process—the administration placed in office in the last election, the oversight and appropriations committees of Congress, the groups with political power (from the Common Cause to the U.S. Chamber of Commerce) that appear before the agency and are listened to more closely than John Doe precisely because of their political power."[39] Scalia urged that more needs to be done to bring "the political, accommodationist, value-judgment aspect of rulemaking out of the closet." [40] While Scalia admitted that some independent agencies are more scientific than others, he claimed that, by and large, administrative decisions involve political judgment "as to which there are no 'right' or 'wrong' answers":[41]

> Lest I be misunderstood, I am not suggesting that all rulemaking is appropriate for political judgment. There are, surely, instances in which Congress has given an agency a technocratic mandate that should be executed technocratically. . . . But when the Federal Trade Commission is told to prohibit "unfair or deceptive trade practices," or the Federal Communications Commission to manage the airwaves "in the public interest, convenience and necessity"—that is another matter. What such broad delegation precisely seeks is the conferral of nontechnocratic, political judgments upon the agencies. That may be good or bad; it may even, in the view of some, be unconstitutional. But if it is to *work*, if the modern complaint of the "unresponsive" bureaucracy is not to become a permanent feature of our system, the scheme of judicial review and the requirements of administrative process must permit political judgments to be made politically.[42]

As a judge, Scalia has attempted to allow administrative agencies to exercise political discretion by defending a deferential role for the courts in three major areas of administrative law: (1) during the *process* of agency rule making, (2) in reviewing agency constructions of law, and (3) in examining the *substance* of agency rules.

### Hybrid Rule Making

The Administrative Procedure Act (APA) of 1946 contemplates two types of procedures for rule making: informal and formal. Informal rule making, also known as "notice and comment" rule making, mandates that agencies satisfy certain basic due process requirements before they can issue substantive rules affecting the legal rights of private parties. These procedural requirements include giving notice of proposed rules, affording an opportunity for interested persons to participate in rule making through submission of *written* comments, and publishing the final rules with "a concise general statement of their basis and purpose."[43] Formal rule making, by contrast, imposes procedures closely akin to courtroom adjudication, where interested parties enjoy extensive rights to know and challenge opposing evidence. For example, the agency must conduct a trial-type hearing and provide interested persons with an opportunity to testify and cross-examine adverse witnesses before issuing a rule. Although the type of procedures that an agency is required to use can sometimes be ambiguous, a reviewing court is supposed to consult the APA or some other federal statute, such as the one conferring rule-making authority on the agency, to determine what procedures are necessary.

A major controversy surrounding the rule-making process is that even when the APA or some other statute does *not* require formal rule making, courts (particularly the D.C. Circuit Court, which hears the vast majority of government agency cases) have required agencies to use a variety of formal procedures (e.g., oral hearings and/or the right to cross-examine witnesses) in the process of *informal* rule making. These additional judge-made requirements on administrative agencies are called "hybrid rule making."

In *Vermont Yankee Nuclear Power Corp. v. Natural Resources Defense Council*,[44] the Supreme Court attempted to put an end to judicially imposed hybrid rule making. The case involved a D.C. Circuit Court ruling that mandated additional formal rule-making procedures be used before the Atomic Energy Commission could issue individual nuclear power licenses. Justice Rehnquist, who wrote the unanimous opinion, chastised the lower court for engaging in "Monday morning quarterbacking," and held that except in "extremely rare" circumstances, courts cannot force agencies to utilize rule-making procedures beyond those prescribed in the APA or some other statutory provision. Otherwise, courts violate "the very basic tenet of administrative law that agencies should be free to fashion their own rules of procedure."[45] The *Vermont Yankee* justices worried that the additional court-imposed procedural requirements would be unpredictable and would lead agencies to resort to formalized rule making in order to avoid litigation. Barring a specific requirement by the APA or some other statute, the justices ruled that the choice of what procedures the agencies should use should be left to the agencies themselves.

One year later, Antonin Scalia, then a law professor at the University of Chicago, authored a sixty-four-page article devoted entirely to the Court's decision in *Vermont Yankee*.[46] Scalia described *Vermont Yankee* as a "major watershed" in administrative law and lauded the opinion for its judicial restraint. He also rebuked the D.C. Court of Appeals for imposing the additional procedural requirements on the Atomic Energy Commission, which he believed flouted Supreme Court precedent. In Scalia's view, the hybrid rule making imposed by courts gives agencies less flexibility in determining what procedures to use, and allows too much backdoor judicial legislating under the guise of common law rule making. Even though he ironically took issue with the Court's reliance on the plain meaning of the APA,[47] a statute that Scalia said no longer deserved (and perhaps never did) the fundamental stature it has received, he viewed *Vermont Yankee* as an important step toward a more deferential judicial approach to administrative decision making.

Equally important, as a member of the Supreme Court, Justice Scalia has defended the Court's decision in *Vermont Yankee* from being, in his judgment, effectively overruled. In *Pension Benefit Guaranty Corp. v. LTV Corp.*,[48] the Court examined whether the Pension Benefit Guaranty Corporation (PBGC)—the federal agency that insures pension benefits for private-sector employees under the Employee Retirement Income Security Act of 1974—had the authority to require LTV Corporation, a large private steel company going through Chapter 11 bankruptcy, to resume responsibility for a terminated and underfunded pension plan previously taken over by the agency. The Second Circuit Court of Appeals held that the PBGC had not done a sufficiently detailed analysis to justify its restoration order and had acted arbitrarily and capriciously by failing to inform LTV of the basis for its determination. It also held that PBGC failed to give the company an opportunity to offer contrary evidence. In an eight-to-one decision, the Supreme Court overturned that decision. Prior to the decision being announced, however, Scalia was able to secure a major concession from Harry Blackmun, the author of the Court's opinion, in how the case should be analyzed. In the original draft of the opinion, Blackmun seemed to agree with the court of appeals that under some circumstances the APA imposes general procedural requirements on agencies to develop records that enable the courts to evaluate their reasoning at the time of decision. In two separate, lengthy "Ninograms" to his colleagues, Scalia contended that this analysis was fundamentally incompatible with *Vermont Yankee*. According to Scalia's reading of the APA, the PBGC did not have to provide any reasons for its decision:

> The APA specifically sets forth when it is that an agency must give reasons for its action or inaction. It must do so in formal rulemaking and adjudication . . . and in informal rulemaking. . . . According to your opinion, however, [the APA] "mandates that an agency take whatever steps it needs to provide an explanation that will enable the court to evaluate the agency's rationale at the time of the decision." I do not think that is correct. The agency need provide a rationale only where the APA or some other law apart from [the APA] so requires. Absent such a requirement, the agency's action (much like a statute) must be accepted by the court as rational if there is a plausible basis of rationality.[49]

Consistent with his law review article supporting *Vermont Yankee*, Scalia expressed concern that hybrid rule making by the Courts "confers enormous discretion upon the courts to mandate procedures not specifically set forth in the APA." Such a position, Scalia wrote, "contradicts the central proposition of *Vermont Yankee*, which was 'that Congress intended the discretion of agencies and not that of the courts to be exercised in determining when extra procedural devices should be employed.'"[50] After several of the other justices expressed agreement with Scalia's reading of *Vermont Yankee*, Blackmun altered the original draft of his opinion to accommodate Scalia's views.

## Judicial Review of Agency Constructions of Law

In *Chevron v. National Resources Defense Council*,[51] the Supreme Court established a two-prong test for determining the proper scope of review regarding agency interpretations of law. Under the first prong, a reviewing court must determine if Congress has "directly spoken" to the underlying issue being regulated. If it has done so, then the court "must give effect to the unambiguously expressed intent of Congress."[52] On the other hand, if Congress has not specifically addressed the underlying issue, *Chevron*'s second prong requires that a reviewing court respect the agency's construction of the statute so long as it is permissible.

Justice Scalia is an avid champion of *Chevron*,[53] describing it as "perhaps the most important [decision] in the field of administrative law since *Vermont Yankee*. . . ."[54] In his aforementioned Duke University Law School speech, where he unabashedly defended the decision, Scalia considered three different rationales for the principle of deference announced therein. First is the superior competence of administrative agencies to understand the purposes behind statutes and to reach "correct" results. On this view, courts should defer to administrative agencies because the persons who serve in these agencies have scientific training and expertise in their respective fields and can change the law in light of new information. Not surprisingly, Scalia rejected this rationale as a theoretical justification for *Chevron*. While as a practical matter, administrative agencies may have more competence than courts in effectuating the purposes behind statutes, Scalia did not believe this is a sufficient reason for the courts to shirk their responsibility under *Marbury v. Madison*[55] "to say what the law is." The second rationale for *Chevron* discussed by Scalia was separation of powers. According to this view, the courts should defer to reasonable agency constructions of ambiguous statutes, because the resolution of that ambiguity necessarily involves policy judgment, and under the U.S. constitutional system, administrative agencies (as part of the executive branch) are political entities that have the authority to make policy, while courts are legal institutions that are not supposed to make policy judgments. Remarkably, Scalia rejected this rationale as well. According to Scalia, in discerning the purpose behind statutes, courts also make policy judgments, and therefore administrative agencies cannot claim any superior constitutional authority over courts in considering and evaluating legislative intent. It was the third justification—the real or presumed intent of Congress—that Scalia defended as the most plausible theoretical justification for *Chevron*. On this view, if Congress has no clear intent, then the courts should defer to an agency interpretation since this comports with the probable desire of Congress. Even though he said that the search for legislative intent is often "a wild-goose chase," Scalia thought that such an approach would put Congress on notice that if it is not clear with its statutes, then administrative agencies (not courts) will ultimately resolve the issue. Scalia regarded this as a desirable solution for several reasons: (1) members of Congress likely know the political views of agencies better than they do the policy views of judges; (2) in contrast to courts, agencies can apply a more flexible political solution to their interpretations of statutes, thereby allowing laws to change with new executive administrations; and (3) administrative agencies (in contrast to courts) are participants in and are more accountable to the administrative process.[56]

Significantly, Scalia not only defended *Chevron*, but he called for an expansive interpretation of its principle of deference. For example, Scalia argued that judges should not second-guess agency decisions by themselves searching for the "correct" interpretation of a statute; in his view, a reasonable interpretation will suffice.[57] He also argued that judicial deference should be accorded not only to agency interpretations of law during the process of rule making, but to the positions that agencies take during the course of litigation, such as those interpretations found in court briefs or opinion letters. Interestingly, Scalia argued that *Chevron*'s deferential approach would have long-term consequences that might not be noticeable at the time. In his view, there no longer will be "correct" meanings of statutes, deference to "agency expertise," or "consistent and longstanding agency positions." These are the old terms of the game. In order to accommodate broad delegations of authority to the executive branch, which is the "hallmark of the modern administrative state," agency changes to laws should not be looked at with suspicion by the courts.[58] In Scalia's view, "The agency [is] simply 'changing the law,' in light of new information or even new social attitudes impressed upon it through the political process—all within the limited range of discretion to 'change the law' conferred by the governing statue."[59] Scalia expressed great hope that if *Chevron* is to have any importance, judicial deference should be the norm, and that under *Chevron*'s first prong, deference to agency interpretations will apply (and thus a statute will be deemed ambiguous) "when two or more reasonable, though not necessarily equally valid, interpretations exist."[60]

With some notable exceptions,[61] Scalia has consistently followed *Chevron*'s principle of deference in court opinions. In *Fort Stewart Schools v. Federal*

*Labor Relations Authority* (1990),[62] Scalia wrote the unanimous opinion deferring to the Federal Labor Relations Authority's requirement that schools collectively bargain with the union over a proposed salary increase and fringe benefits. In *Sullivan v. Everhart* (1990),[63] Scalia wrote the five-to-four opinion deferring to the "netting" regulations established by the secretary of health and human services for determining payments under the Social Security Act. In *General Dynamics Land Systems v. Cline* (2004)[64] and *Smith v. City of Jackson* (2005),[65] Scalia wrote separate opinions arguing that the Court should defer to the Equal Employment Opportunity Commission's determinations that the Age Discrimination in Employment Act of 1967 prohibits discrimination against younger covered employees in favor of older covered employees and authorizes disparate-impact claims. And in *Gonzales v. Oregon* (2006),[66] Scalia dissented from the Court's ruling that the U.S. attorney general overstepped his authority in prohibiting Oregon doctors from prescribing a lethal dose of drugs to terminally ill patients under the Controlled Substances Act.

With respect to judicial deference to agency constructions of law, Scalia did however suffer a major defeat in the 2001 decision *United States v. Mead Corp.*[67] In his Duke University Law School speech,[68] as well as in Court opinions,[69] Scalia argued that if congressional statutes are ambiguous, judges are bound by agency interpretations of law regardless of the format they come in—ranging from adjudicatory opinions and formalized rules in the Federal Register to agency policy statements, opinion letters, manuals, guidelines, and court briefs—as long as these interpretations of law represent the official position of the agency. In *Mead*, the Court resoundingly rejected Scalia's across-the-board presumption of deference. In an eight-to-one decision, the Court devised a new test for judicial review of agency interpretations of law, which is premised on whether the agency's construction of law comes in a format bearing the "force of law." Striking a balance between complete deference to agency constructions of law and no deference at all, the Court rekindled an earlier test announced in *Skidmore v. Swift and Co.*,[70] and applied a sliding-scale analysis to agency decision making. According to the *Mead* test, "Administrative implementation of a particular statutory provision qualifies for *Chevron* deference when it appears that Congress delegated authority to the agency generally to make rules carrying the force of law, and that the agency interpretation claiming deference was promulgated in the exercise of that authority."[71] Thus, as a condition precedent to the application of *Chevron* deference, courts must examine whether Congress delegated authority that has the force of law to the agency. Specific examples of force of law authority would be an agency's power to enact formal or informal rules and to make adjudicatory determinations. Under the second part of the *Mead* test, the agency must then act pursuant to that authority. For example, if the Food and Drug Administration issues a new rule after employing notice-and-comment procedures, then it has promulgated a rule pursuant to its force of law authority. What the *Mead* test means in practice is that informal formats of agency constructions of law, such as policy statements, opinion letters, manuals, enforcement guidelines, and court briefs, will not normally be accorded *Chevron*-type deference. While the *Mead* Court stopped short of saying that *Chevron* deference never applies to these informal formats, *Chevron*'s principle of deference is primarily reserved for formal agency rulings. An agency policy statement may be persuasive to a court in interpreting a statute, but it does not have controlling authority. Under these circumstances, the court must independently determine whether the agency's interpretation is correct. Accordingly, in what many scholars view as a counterrevolution to *Chevron*,[72] the *Mead* Court adopted a middle-ground approach to judicial review of agency constructions of law. Agency constructions of law made pursuant to delegated force of law authority will be accorded judicial deference, while agency interpretations of law that come in informal formats (to which force of law authority has not been delegated) will not be given such deference. *Mead* can be seen as an attempt by the Court (after years of experience with a toothless nondelegation doctrine) to reassert some supervisory authority over a burgeoning and increasingly powerful federal bureaucracy.

Dissenting alone, Justice Scalia argued that the Court's new test for agency constructions of law contradicted Court precedent, was wrong in principle, and would have several negative practical effects. As for Court precedent, Scalia maintained that neither *Chevron* nor any other Court case made a distinction between formal and informal formats for purposes of determining the degree of deference owed to agency interpretations of law. Rather, *Chevron* established a simple bright-line test that when Congress has not directly spoken to the precise question at issue, judicial deference must be given to reasonable agency interpretations of law. This judicial deference was rooted in the principle that Congress intended for agencies (not courts) to exercise the discretion necessary to apply ambiguous statutes to a new set of facts. According to Scalia, the *Mead* Court now reverses *Chevron*'s principle of deference by requiring an affirmative force of law mandate by Congress in order for judicial deference to apply. And with respect to informal formats of agency construction, *Chevron*'s principle of deference may not even apply. Scalia pointed out that some agency decisions are statutorily required to be made personally by cabinet secretaries where rule-making or adjudicatory authority is not even applicable. In his view, it is "quite absurd" to argue that these cabinet-level decisions are entitled to less deference than those decisions made by administrative law judges.

Justice Scalia also contended that the Court's new sliding-scale test has several practical defects. First, it will lead to protracted confusion. Under *Mead*'s sliding-scale analysis, or what Scalia pejoratively called the "totality of the circumstances" test, judges will no longer have guidance as to when they should defer to agency interpretations of law, thus leading to "uncertainty, unpredictability, and endless litigation." For a justice who sees "the rule of law as a law of rules,"[73] this is a most unwelcome development. Second, *Mead* will result in an increase in informal rule making, "since formal adjudication is not an option but must be mandated by statute or constitutional command." Consequently, Scalia sarcastically advised people to "[b]uy stock in the GPO [Government Printing Office]." Finally, the Court's new test will lead to an "ossification" of large portions of statutory law. Since courts under *Mead* will more frequently require agencies to follow court interpretations of statutes, the agencies' ability to change the law in light of new circumstances will be reduced. "For the indeterminately large number of statutes taken out of *Chevron* by today's decision," wrote Scalia, "ambiguity (and hence flexibility) will cease with the first judicial resolution." As Scalia saw it, "*Skidmore* deference gives the agency's current position some vague and uncertain amount of respect, but it does not, like *Chevron*, leave the matter within the control of the Executive Branch for the future. Once the court has spoken, it becomes *unlawful* for the agency to take a contradictory position; the statute now says what the court has prescribed."[74] Scalia's frustration and anger in *Mead* were palpable. In addition to referring to the Court's reasoning as "quite absurd" and "mak[ing] no sense," he described the new test for judicial review of agency constructions of law as "irresponsible." Not unlike the views of some scholars in the academic community, Scalia said that *Mead* will result in "an avulsive change in judicial review of federal administrative action," and predicted that "[i]ts consequences will be enormous, and almost uniformly bad."[75] In subsequent cases, Scalia has continued to sharply criticize *Mead*.[76]

## *Judicial Review of Substantive Agency Decisions*

The final area in which Justice Scalia has defended a deferential approach toward agency action is court supervision of the substance of agency decisions. In contrast to judicial review of agency interpretations of law, the concern here is with the proper judicial posture toward agencies' factual or policy determinations. For example, in reviewing agency adjudications, courts will seek to determine whether administrative-law judges' findings are supported by the whole record.[77] In rule making, courts ask one or several of the following questions: Did the agency deviate from a prior rule or practice, rely on factors that Congress intended it to consider, consider all important aspects of the problem, or fail to offer an explanation for its policy? The APA establishes two basic tests. In adjudication and formal on-the-record rule making, the agency's decision must be supported by "substantial evidence." In informal rule making, the courts apply a similar test to rational basis scrutiny in constitutional cases, that is, whether the policy is "arbitrary and capricious." Traditionally, the substantial evidence test has had more bite than the arbitrary-and-capricious test, but there are several instances in which courts have applied heightened review using the latter test.[78] Ultimately, both tests seek to determine whether the agency's policy determination is reasonable. While courts usually extend more deference to agencies' factual determinations than to their legal conclusions, several judges[79] and academics[80] have defended a hard-look approach to substantive agency action. Justice Scalia vehemently opposes hard-look review, which is evident in several of his judicial opinions, two of which will be discussed here.

In *Chaney v. Heckler* (1983),[81] the Food and Drug Administration's (FDA's) refusal to investigate and regulate the unapproved use of lethal injection as a method of capital punishment. Eight prison inmates under sentence of death brought suit in federal court claiming that the drugs used for lethal injection violated the Food, Drug, and Cosmetic Act's (FDCA's) requirements that all "new drugs" be safe and effective for the use prescribed, and that the labeling of all drugs bear adequate warnings against unapproved uses of drugs.[82] Petitioners claimed that the use of barbiturates and paralytics as capital punishment devices posed a substantial threat of torturous pain to persons being executed. The FDA, however, refused to investigate or regulate the use of the drugs as a method of capital punishment, citing (among other reasons) its inherent enforcement discretion *not* to take any action. A majority of the D.C. Court of Appeals ruled in favor of the petitioners. Judge Skelly Wright found that the FDA had acted arbitrarily and capriciously by not investigating the unapproved use of lethal injections for capital punishment. In Judge Wright's view, the FDA does not have absolute discretion over decisions concerning the enforcement of the unapproved use of drugs; the courts, too, must make "a careful and searching review" to determine if the agency has acted reasonably.

Judge Scalia wrote an excoriating dissent, which was substantially followed by the U.S. Supreme Court on appeal.[83] In contrast to the majority, Scalia argued that there was a strong presumption against reviewing the enforcement decisions of administrative agencies: "Generally speaking, enforcement priorities are not the business of this Branch, but of the Executive—to whom, and not to the courts, the Constitution confides the responsibility to 'take Care that the Laws be faithfully executed.'"[84] Scalia also argued that even if the FDA does not have complete enforcement discretion in investigating violations under the FDCA, there was no clear error (or "right" or "wrong" answer) in this case: "Without belittling the human concerns associated with the present complaint, it must be acknowledged that the public health interest at issue is not widespread death or permanent disability, but (at most) a risk of temporary pain to a relatively small number of individuals."[85] On this basis, Scalia accused the majority of substituting its own policy views for those of the agency:

> [T]here is ultimately no special factor to support the extraordinary assertion of authority to control the agency's enforcement discretion in the present case— nothing, except the majority's disagreement with the agency's determination that no serious danger to the public health exists. But we are not the only public officials endowed with intelligence and worthy of trust, and our system of laws has committed the relative evaluation of public health concerns to others.[86]

Another opinion by Antonin Scalia illustrating his deferential approach toward agency substantive decisions came in the Supreme Court case *Webster v. Doe*.[87] John Doe was dismissed by the Central Intelligence Agency (CIA) after voluntarily informing a CIA security officer that he was a homosexual. Without providing the particular reasons for his dismissal, the director of the CIA "deemed it necessary and advisable in the interests of the United States to terminate [Doe's] employment with this Agency."[88] For support of this decision, the director relied on the National Security Act (NSA) of 1947, which provides, "Notwithstanding . . . the provisions of any other law, the director of central intelligence may, in his discretion, terminate the employment of any officer or employee of the Agency whenever he shall deem such termination necessary or advisable in the interests of the United States."[89]

Doe challenged his dismissal, contending that it was an abuse of discretion under the APA, and that the director's termination of his employment deprived him of property and liberty interests under the Due Process Clause of the Fifth Amendment, privacy rights under the First, Fourth, Fifth, and Ninth Amendments, and equal protection of the laws under the Fifth Amendment. He sought a declaratory judgment and reinstatement to the position he held prior to his dismissal. The District Court for the District of Columbia granted an injunction, finding that the director's actions failed to follow procedures described in the Agency's own regulations.

In an opinion by Chief Justice William Rehnquist, the Supreme Court reversed. According to Rehnquist, judicial review under the APA is circumscribed when "agency action is committed to agency discretion by law,"[90] which he contended was the case here, since the NSA left employment dismissals to the discretion of the CIA director. The act, Rehnquist reasoned, "allows termination of an Agency employee whenever the director 'shall *deem* such termination necessary or advisable in the interests of the United States,' not simply when the dismissal *is* necessary or advisable to those interests. This standard fairly exudes deference to the director, and appears to foreclose the application of any meaningful judicial standard of review."[91] Nevertheless, while the majority did not rule in favor of Doe's APA claim, it remanded the case for a determination on the constitutional issues. According to Chief Justice Rehnquist, nothing in the statute "persuades us that Congress meant to preclude consideration of colorable constitutional claims arising out of the actions of the Director."[92] A "'serious constitutional question' . . . would arise," Rehnquist wrote, "if a federal statute were construed to deny any judicial forum for a colorable constitutional claim."[93]

Justice Scalia filed a solo dissent. He agreed with the majority on the APA claim, but he disagreed with his colleagues on the constitutional claims. According to Scalia, the "ominous warning" of the Court concerning the lack of a judicial forum for colorable constitutional claims cannot be taken seriously. Federal courts, he argued, are denied judicial review in many areas of the law, and it is incorrect to say "that there must be a judicial remedy for every constitutional violation."[94] "I think it entirely beyond doubt that if Congress intended, by the APA . . . to exclude judicial review of the President's decisions (through the Director of Central Intelligence) to dismiss an officer of the Central Intelligence Agency, that disposition would be constitutionally permissible."[95] Scalia also accused the majority of "the impossible feat of having its cake and eating it too."[96] According to Scalia, if the director really has the discretion to remove an employee for whatever reason he decides is in the best interest of the country, then that decision cannot be questioned by a court of law. "Even if the basis of the Director's assessment was the respondent's homosexuality, and even if the connection between that and the interests of the United States is an irrational and hence an unconstitutional one, if that assessment is really 'the Director's alone' there is nothing more to litigate about."[97] Finally, Justice Scalia lamented the fact that the decisions of the intelligence community could now be taken to the courts:

> The harm done by today's decision is that, contrary to what Congress knows is preferable, it brings a significant decisionmaking process of our intelligence services into a forum where it does not belong. Neither the Constitution, nor our laws, nor common sense gives an individual a right to come into court to litigate the reasons for his dismissal as an intelligence agent. It is of course not just *valid* constitutional claims that today's decision makes the basis for judicial review of the Director's action, but all *colorable* constitutional claims, whether meritorious

or not. . . . Today's result . . . will have ramifications far beyond creation of the world's only secret intelligence agency that must litigate the dismissal of its agents. If constitutional claims can be raised in this highly sensitive context, it is hard to imagine where they cannot. The assumption that there are any executive decisions that cannot be hauled into the courts may no longer be valid.[98]

## Administration as Policy Making

Consistent with a Hamiltonian conception of administration, Justice Scalia has also defended the legislative powers of the president. Anticipating strong presidents who would use the veto for political purposes, Hamilton once observed that the veto power "supposes the duty of objecting, when [the president] is of opinion, that the object of any bill is either *unconstitutional* or *pernicious*." Approval of a bill, by contrast, implies "that he does not think it either the one or the other. And it makes him responsible to the community for this opinion. The measure becomes his by adoption."[99] The importance Hamilton placed in the executive's legislative role is also reflected in the comprehensive financial program he introduced to and pushed through Congress in the early 1790s. Hamilton wanted to forge the United States into a prosperous and well-respected nation. To this end, he proposed that the debt accumulated by the Continental Congress be paid in full, that the federal government assume all state debts, and that the Bank of the United States be chartered. These policies were intended to promote commercial development and create economic interests that would tie the interests of the American people to the national government. Many members of Congress were so distressed by Hamilton's far-reaching legislative programs that he was disparagingly called the "prime minister" under the Washington administration.

Under the Constitution, the president has two major ways of acting in a legislative capacity. Pursuant to Article II, Section 3—the Recommend Clause—the president is authorized to give to "Congress Information on the State of the Union, and recommend to their Consideration such Measures as he shall judge necessary and expedient."[100] Moreover, every bill or resolution passed by the Congress must be presented to the president for his approval.[101] Both of these provisions give the president a substantial role in the legislative process and, in court opinions and extrajudicial writings, Scalia has defended them both.

### The Recommend Clause

As a member of the D.C. Court of Appeals, Judge Scalia participated in a case implicating the president's legislative role under the Recommend Clause. In its capacity as trustee, the federal government can litigate claims on behalf of

Native Americans whose land the government holds in trust. Prior to 1966, some 17,000 Indian claims, involving such matters as old-age assistance, unapproved rights of way, unauthorized transfers of Indian trust lands, mineral rights, and welfare claims, had been identified as potential actions for monetary damages. However, no action had been taken to resolve any of these disputes. In 1980, after numerous extensions of the statute of limitations, Congress required "the Secretary of the Interior, after consultation with the Attorney General, [to] submit to the Congress legislative proposals to resolve those Indian claims . . . not appropriate [for] . . . litigation."[102]

On October 21, 1982, Secretary of the Interior James Watt submitted a brief proposal covering only a few of the claims. The Native Americans sued for a declaratory judgment and injunctive relief, claiming that the Department of the Interior had failed to satisfy the request made by Congress. The government defended, claiming that (among other things) it would be a violation of the separation of powers for the Congress to require the secretary of interior to submit additional legislative proposals. In *Covelo Indian Community v. Watt*,[103] a divided three-judge panel of the D.C. Court of Appeals held that Congress could require the executive branch to submit additional legislative proposals. According to the majority, since there was "a major shortfall" in the secretary's performance in identifying or litigating Indian claims, "Congress might have reasonably believed that it was necessary to require the Department to submit legislative proposals by a set date."[104] "It is not unusual," the majority reasoned, "for Congress to instruct the executive branch to draft regulations incorporating certain principles and priorities with which the drafting agency may not agree."[105] In response to the government's separation of powers concerns, the majority concluded:

> The government maintains that it must be allowed ultimate discretion to submit only those legislative proposals that it considers worthy of enactment. We believe, however, that its separation-of-powers objection is ameliorated by the option of submitting proposals together with a report that discusses the proposals' benefits and deficiencies. Control of the substance of the legislative proposals required by Section 2 remains in the hands of the executive branch.[106]

Judge Scalia dissented. Scalia argued that the Native Americans lacked standing because there was no assurance that Congress would enact the legislation needed to redress their injuries. As he put it, "[I]t is no more than conjecture that the relief here sought (the Secretary's submission of legislative proposals he disapproves) will remedy" the monetary claims of the Indians.[107] Interestingly, Scalia also contended that the law requiring the secretary of interior to submit legislative proposals jeopardized the president's legislative role under the Recommend Clause. "It is questionable whether Congress has the power to compel the President to submit draft legislation—especially draft legislation of which he disapproves. The constitutional provision that the President 'shall . . . recommend to [the Congress's] Consideration such Measures as he shall judge necessary and expedient' . . . may well be read to insulate him from compulsion to submit measures he does not judge to be so."[108] Finally, Scalia contended that the congressional mandate was in all likelihood a violation of separation of powers:

> It does not take a naive faith in hermetically sealed separation of the three branches to believe that the Executive's power to submit or not submit legislation is an important element in the checks and balances that the Constitution establishes. Nor an acute perception of political realities to understand how congressional authority to compel such submission might be put to uses that weaken the second branch. One can envision the Executive's being required to submit proposals that are in opposition to legislative alternatives it has introduced; or a mandated legislative proposal "to place the Social Security System on an actuarilly sound basis," labelled the "Administration Bill," despite its submission under protest. . . . The very scarcity of such legislative provisions suggests that Congress has sensed the impropriety of dictating the legislative activities of the Executive Branch.[109]

### The Presentment Clause and the Legislative Veto

In the interest of making the bureaucracy more accountable, Congress began a practice in the early 1930s of subjecting executive branch decision making to a legislative veto. How this normally worked in practice is that Congress built into an agency's enabling statute the authority to disapprove of its decisions by either a one-house or two-house veto. This practice raised constitutional concerns, however, because it enabled the Congress to revoke executive action "by mere resolution—not formal legislation—thus avoiding the President's veto power and (in the case of the one-house veto) the requirement of approval by both houses."[110] By the time the Supreme Court struck down the practice in *Immigration and Naturalization Service v. Chadha*,[111] some two hundred laws were passed with a legislative veto attached,[112] prompting Justice Lewis F. Powell, in a concurring opinion in that case, to observe: "The breadth of this holding gives one pause."[113]

During the 1970s, Justice Scalia exhibited no such pause. In various forums and writings,[114] Scalia argued that the legislative veto was an unconstitutional and impractical device for monitoring the actions of the federal bureaucracy. In terms of the constitutional defects, Scalia argued that the legislative veto violated general separation of powers principles as well as the text of the Constitution. According to Scalia, the legislative veto violated the doctrine of separation of powers, because it allowed Congress to do an end run around the president's legislative function. Quoting Hamilton, Scalia said that the primary purpose of the president's veto was "to enable the President to defend himself. Otherwise, he might be gradually stripped of his authorities by successive resolutions or annihilated by a single vote."[115] Scalia also argued that the legislative veto violated the Presentment Clause of the Constitution, which requires that all bills passed by Congress be presented to the president for his approval.[116] That "bill veto" clause, Scalia pointed out, is succeeded by the following provision:

> Every order, resolution, or vote, to which the concurrence of the Senate and House of Representatives may be necessary (except on a question of adjournment) shall be presented to the President of the United States; and before the same shall take effect, shall be approved by him, or being disapproved by him, shall be repassed by two thirds of the Senate and House of Representatives, according to the rules and limitations prescribed in the case of a bill.[117]

According to Scalia, the purpose of this extra-precautionary measure was to prevent Congress from evading the president's legislative role by simple resolution. The provision was meant "to ensure presidential participation in *all* lawmaking, under whatever form it might disguise itself."[118] In terms of the one-house veto, Scalia also argued that it suffered from the additional defect of violating the bicameral provision of the Constitution.[119]

Aside from the constitutional infirmities, Scalia also pointed out that the legislative veto suffered from several practical defects. The purpose of the legislative veto was to rein in a "runaway bureaucracy" and thereby make government more accountable to the people. But Scalia argued that the problem of government excess is not directly attributable to the bureaucracy. Rather, the "main culprit" is Congress. By delegating broad authority to administrative agencies without specific guidelines, Congress has abdicated its legislative responsibilities:

> Congress has shrunk from providing standards for many years. Nor has there been "usurpation" of power; for that implies that power has been yielded unwillingly—and Congress has in fact rushed to abdicate for many years, often conferring upon the agencies authority which the incumbent administration itself did not desire. The main culprit, in other words, has not been the agencies but Congress itself.[120]

As Scalia saw it, the legislative veto would not go far in correcting this problem; in fact, he argued that it would only worsen it. Since Congress as a whole does not have time to review agency action, the responsibility of oversight will fall on its committees. The result, Scalia argued, is that "[i]nstead of government by one bureaucracy, we will have government by two—hardly a step towards more democratic government."[121] Moreover, because Congress will be lulled into thinking that the legislative veto is an effective remedy for checking administrative action, it will be "all the more ready to continue and expand the transfer of basic policy decisions to the agencies."[122] "It is significant in this regard," Scalia argued, "that some of the most prominent examples of legislative vetoes enacted in the past were proposed by the executive branch itself—to induce the congressional transfer of power which would otherwise not have been accorded."[123] Finally, Scalia argued that "most of the criticism of the legislative veto has originated in the executive branch, and thus has focused on the propensity of the device to alter the constitutional balance of power between the first and second branches of government"[124]—an argument he certainly agreed with.[125] But the greater problem, in Scalia's view, is that the legislative veto will alter the balance of power between the two political branches and the people. As he put it, "[T]he legislative veto is an excellent mechanism for enabling the president and the Congress to facilitate the passage of unpopular laws by eliminating the congressional burden of having to vote for them."[126] "[T]he only remedy," Scalia maintained, "if we really want a remedy, is to take some of those tasks away and to perform them instead by legislation, or not perform them at all."[127]

## CONCLUSION

Justice Scalia has defended a theory of administration strikingly similar to Hamilton's. He has defended a unified executive that will allow the president to exercise leadership over his administrative staff, and that will allow for a comprehensive and systematic administration of the nation's laws. In contrast to the Progressive theory of administration, Scalia believes that administrative decisions primarily involve political discretion for which there are no discernible "right" or "wrong" answers. He therefore has vigorously defended a deferential judicial posture toward agency action. Scalia's opinions in *Chaney* and *Doe* indicate that his deferential approach to substantive agency decisions is virtually limitless. Finally, Scalia has defended the president's legislative role against attempts by Congress to force the executive branch to submit particular legislative proposals, and against attempts by Congress to bypass the president's legislative role through the mechanism of a legislative veto.[128] What is clear is that Justice Scalia does not believe the president is the "errand boy" of Congress.[129] Like Hamilton, Scalia believes that the executive branch not only serves as an important check against unconstitutional usurpations of power by Congress, but that it has its own legislative agenda to pursue.

Justice Scalia's view of "rulemaking as politics" is particularly Hamiltonian. Scalia believes that agencies exercise mainly political (not scientific) judgment, which requires that they balance various interests and be responsive to the political process. When coupled with his narrow interpretation of legal standing,[130] opposition to the legislative veto,[131] and broad view of the president's removal power,[132] Scalia's deferential approach toward agency action would confer substantial independent power on the executive branch. Moreover, as seen in chapter 3, Scalia does not follow a strict interpretation of the nondelegation doctrine. While Scalia has found one unconstitutional delegation of power by Congress,[133] he has also supported broad conferrals of authority on administrative agencies where there has been hardly any legislative guidance at all.[134] In fact, in his dissenting opinion in *Clinton v. City of New York*,[135] Scalia tellingly argued that the line-item veto was a permissible delegation of power to the executive branch. Scalia's *real* position with respect to the nondelegation doctrine is that broad delegations of power are now a fact of life, and that courts (except at the extreme margins) should not involve themselves in regulating congressional delegations of power. Scalia's views regarding judicial review of agency action, as well as those involving administrative law generally, are strong evidence of his Hamiltonian political philosophy.

## NOTES

1. Leonard D. White, *The Federalists: A Study in Administrative History* (New York: MacMillan Co., 1961), 125–26.

2. FP (No. 68), 395.

3. Ibid., at 412. Hamilton's understanding of what fell under the administrative authority of the executive branch was quite extensive: "The actual conduct of foreign negotiations, the preparatory plans of finance, the application and disbursement of the public moneys in conformity to the general appropriations of the legislature, the arrangement of the army and navy, the direction of the operations of war—these, and other matters of a like nature, constitute what seems to be most properly understood by the administration of government." FP (No. 72), 412.

4. For an excellent synopsis of Hamilton's administrative theory, see James W. Ceaser et al., *American Government: Origins, Institutions, and Public Policy*, 5th ed. (Dubuque, IA: Kendall/Hunt, 1998), 510–11. For longer treatments of the same subject, see White, *The Federalist*; and Lynton K. Caldwell, *The Administrative Theories of Hamilton and Jefferson: Their Contribution to Thought on Public Administration*, 2nd ed. (New York: Holmes & Meier, 1988).

5. FP (No. 72), 413.

6. Ibid., 403.

7. Ibid., 405.

8. Ibid., 412.

9. *The Effective Republic: Administration and Constitution in the Thought of Alexander Hamilton* (Durham, NC: Duke University Press, 1992).

10. See Richard Brisbin, *Justice Antonin Scalia and the Conservative Revival* (Baltimore, MD: Johns Hopkins University Press, 1997), 76–84; and Peter B. Edelman, "Justice Scalia's Jurisprudence and the Good Society: Shades of Felix Frankfurter and the Harvard Hit Parade of the 1950s," *Cardozo Law Review* 12 (1991): 1799–1815.

11. See G. Edward White, "The Evolution of Reasoned Elaboration: Jurisprudential Criticism and Social Change," in *Patterns of American Legal Thought* (Indianapolis, IN: Bobbs-Merrill Co., 1978), 136–63; Neil Duxbury, "Faith in Reason: The Process Tradition in American Jurisprudence," *Cardozo Law Review* 15 (1993): 601–705.

12. See, e.g., Cass Sunstein, "In Defense of the Hard Look: Judicial Activism and Administrative Law," *Harvard Journal of Law and Public Policy* 7 (1984): 51–59.

13. Antonin Scalia, "Judicial Deference to Administrative Interpretations of Law," *Duke Law Journal*, 1989, 511.

14. Scalia taught administrative law as a law professor at Virginia and Chicago law schools. He also served as the chair for the Administrative Conference, was the cofounder and editor of *Regulation*, and was the chair of the ABA's Administrative Law Section. From 1982 to 1986, Scalia served on the D.C. Court of Appeals, a court noted for its specialization in government agency law.

15. *Ramirez de Arellano v. Weinberger*, 745 F.2d. 1500, 1562 (D.C. Cir. 1984).

16. 521 U.S. 898 (1997).

17. Ibid., 922–23.

18. See "Deregulation HQ: An Interview on the New Executive Order with Murray L. Wiedenbaum and James C. Miller III," *Regulation*, March–April 1981, 14–23; Scalia, "Reagulation—The First Year: Regulatory Review and Management," *Regulation* 6, no. 1 (January–February 1982): 19–21.

19. Scalia, "Reagulation—The First Year," 21.

20. 295 U.S. 602 (1935).

21. 487 U.S. 654 (1988).

22. Ibid., 689–91.

23. Ibid., 725.

24. 488 U.S. 361 (1989).

25. Ibid., 424.

26. *Morrison*, 487 at 726–27.

27. Cass R. Sunstein, "Constitutionalism after the New Deal," *Harvard University Law Review* 101 (1987): 440–41.

28. "The Study of Administration," *Political Science Quarterly* (1887): 209–10. See also Frank Goodnow, *Politics and Administration: A Study in Government* (New York: MacMillan Co., 1900).

29. 487 U.S. 654 (1988).

30. Scalia's view of independent regulatory agencies was in lockstep at the time with similar criticisms expressed by the Reagan administration and, in particular, Attorney General Edwin Meese. See, e.g., Howard Kurtz, "Agencies' Authority Chal-

lenged: Justice Department Seems to Side with Conservatives on Regulating Power," *Washington Post*, January 3, 1985, A17.

31. *Synar v. United States*, 626 F. Supp. 1374, 1398 (D. D.C. 1986).

32. "Proceedings of the Forty-Fifth Judicial Conference of the District of Columbia Circuit," Williamsburg, Virginia (May 21–22, 1984), located in *Federal Rules Decisions* 105:251, 323, 345.

33. Ibid., 345.

34. This hypothesis was attributed to William Bart Saxbe, the attorney general that Scalia initially served under during the Ford administration.

35. "Regulatory Reform—The Game Has Changed," *Regulation* 5, no. 1 (1981): 13–15.

36. Ibid., 14.

37. "Rulemaking as Politics," *Administrative Law Review* 34 (1982): vii.

38. Ibid., v.

39. Ibid., vi.

40. Ibid., vii, xi.

41. Scalia, "The Legislative Veto: A False Remedy for System Overload," *Regulation* 3 (1979): 24.

42. Scalia, "Rulemaking as Politics," x. For Scalia's understanding of the political role played by administrative agencies, see also "The Judges are Coming," reprinted in *Congressional Record* 126 (1980): 18920–22.

43. U.S.C.A. sec. 553 (b) and (c).

44. 435 U.S. 519 (1978).

45. Ibid., 544.

46. Scalia, "Vermont Yankee: The APA, the D.C. Circuit, and the Supreme Court," *The Supreme Court Review* (1978): 345–409.

47. Scalia acknowledged that several post-APA developments, particularly the trend by many agencies to use informal rulemaking procedures when previously they had used formal procedures, made some of the court-imposed hybrid rulemaking understandable and perhaps more true to the original intent of the APA.

48. 496 U.S. 633 (1990).

49. "*PBGC v. LTV Corp.*," memo from Antonin Scalia to Harry Blackmun, June 6, 1990, HABP, box 558, folder 1.

50. "*PBGC v. LTV Corp.*," memo from Antonin Scalia to Harry Blackmun, May 29, 1990, HABP, box 558, folder 1. See also Bernard Schwartz, "'Shooting the Piano Player'?, Justice Scalia and Administrative Law," *Administrative Law Review* 47 (1995): 18–21.

51. 467 U.S. 837 (1984).

52. Ibid., 843.

53. See, e.g., Scalia, "Judicial Deference to Administrative Interpretations of Law," 511–21; Scalia, "The Role of the Judiciary in Deregulation," *Antitrust Law Journal* 55 (1986): 191–98; Scalia, "Responsibilities of Federal Regulatory Agencies under Environmental Laws," *Houston Law Review* 24 (1987): 97–109.

54. Scalia, "Judicial Deference to Administrative Interpretations of Law," 512. See also *INS v. Cardoza-Fonseca*, 480 U.S. 421, 454 (1987) (Scalia, J., concurring) ("This

Court has consistently interpreted *Chevron*—which has been an extremely important and frequently cited opinion, not only in this Court but in the Court of Appeals—as holding that courts must give effect to a reasonable agency interpretation of a statute unless that interpretation is inconsistent with a clearly expressed congressional intent").

55. 5 U.S. (1 Cranch) 137, 177 (1803).

56. See also Scalia, "Responsibilities of Regulatory Agencies under Environmental Laws," 107 ("The major factor for our exclusion [from administrative decisions], I suggest, is that the decisions are supposed to be political ones—made by institutions whose managers change with each presidential election and which are under the constant political pressure of the congressional authorization and appropriations processes").

57. See also *INS v. Cardoza-Fonseca*, 480 U.S. 421, 452 (1987) (Scalia, J., concurring in judgment); *NLRB v. United Food & Commercial Workers Union, Local 23*, 484 U.S. 112 (1987).

58. Scalia, "Judicial Deference to Administrative Interpretations of Law," 512.

59. Ibid., 518–19.

60. Ibid., 520.

61. Post-*Chevron*, the federal courts have favored deference in over 80 percent of cases involving agency constructions of statutes. See Peter H. Schuck and E. Donald Elliot, "To the *Chevron* Station: An Empirical Study of Federal Administrative Law," *Duke Law Journal* (1990): 984. Among his Supreme Court colleagues, Scalia somewhat surprisingly has voted in favor of deference in only 60.5 percent of such cases, placing him last among his colleagues in terms of judicial deference toward administrative interpretations of law.* This can be attributed in all likelihood to his plain meaning approach to reading statutes—a point he acknowledged in his Duke University Law School lecture—which has made him less likely to find congressional intent ambiguous and thus less prone to defer to administrative constructions of law. See, e.g., *Immigration and Naturalization Service v. Cardoza-Fonseca*, 480 U.S. 421, 452 (1987) (Scalia, J., concurring); *Babbitt v. Sweet Home Chapter of Communities for a Great Oregon*, 515 U.S. 687, 714 (1995) (Scalia, J., dissenting); *Food and Drug Administration v. Brown & Williamson Tobacco Corp.*, 529 U.S. 120 (2000); *Alaska Department of Environmental Conservation v. EPA*, 540 U.S. 461 (2004) (Scalia, J., dissenting); and *National Cable & Telecommunications Association v. Brand X Internet Services*, 125 S. Ct. 2688 (2005) (Scalia, J., dissenting). *From 1986–2005, the ranking of the Rehnquist Court justices in terms of the percentages of cases in which each justice supported judicial deference toward agency action is as follows: Breyer (83.3 percent), Rehnquist (81.6 percent), Souter (70 percent), Ginsburg (66.7 percent), Stevens (65.8 percent), Kennedy (63.6 percent), O'Connor (63.2 percent), Thomas (63 percent), and Scalia (60.5 percent). The aforementioned statistics were computed from the United States Supreme Court Judicial Database: 1953–2005 terms (Harold J. Spaeth, principal investigator), Michigan State University, 2005.

62. 495 U.S. 641 (1990).

63. 494 U.S. 83 (1990).

64. 540 U.S. 581 (2004) (Scalia, J., dissenting).

65. 125 S. Ct. 1536 (2005) (Scalia, J., concurring).

66. 126 S. Ct. 904 (2006).

67. 533 U.S. 218 (2001).

68. Scalia, "Judicial Deference to Administrative Interpretations of Law," 519–20.

69. *Christensen v. Harris County*, 529 U.S. 576, 589 (2000) (Scalia, J., concurring in part and concurring in judgment) (*"Skidmore* deference to authoritative agency views is an anachronism, dating from an era in which we declined to give agency interpretations [including interpretative regulations, as opposed to 'legislative rules'] authoritative effect").

70. 323 U.S. 134 (1944).

71. 533 U.S. at 226–27.

72. See, e.g., Eric R. Womack, "Into the Third Era of Administrative Law: An Empirical Study of the Supreme Court's Retreat from *Chevron* Principles in *United States v. Mead," Dickinson Law Review* 107 (2002): 289.

73. Scalia, "The Rule of Law as a Law of Rules," *University of Chicago Law Review* 56 (1989): 1175.

74. 533 U.S. at 247.

75. Ibid., 239, 261.

76. See, e.g., *National Cable & Telecommunications Association v. Brand X Internet Services*, 125 S. Ct. 2688 (2005) (Scalia, J., dissenting).

77. *Universal Camera Corp. v. NLRB*, 340 U.S. 474 (1951).

78. See, e.g., *Motor Vehicle Mfrs. Assn. v. State Farm Mutual Automobile Ins. Co.*, 463 U.S. 29 (1983).

79. The late Judge Harold Leventhal of the D.C. Circuit Court was a leading champion of hard-look scrutiny. See, e.g., *Greater Boston Television Corp. v. FCC*, 444 F.2d 841, 851–52 (D.C. Cir. 1970), cert. denied, 403 U.S. 923 (1971).

80. See, e.g., Sunstein, "In Defense of the Hard Look"; Sidney A. Shapiro and Richard E. Levy, "Heightened Scrutiny of the Fourth Branch: Separation of Powers and the Requirement of Adequate Reasons for Agency Decisions," *Duke Law Journal* (1987): 387–455.

81. 718 F.2d 1174 (D.C. Cir. 1983).

82. Ibid., 1176.

83. *Heckler v. Chaney*, 470 U.S. 821 (1985).

84. 718 F.2d at 1192.

85. Ibid., 1197.

86. Ibid.

87. 486 U.S. 592 (1988).

88. Ibid., 595.

89. Ibid., 616 (quoting 50 U.S.C. sec. 403[c]).

90. Ibid., 597 (quoting 5 U.S.C. sec. 701 [a][2]).

91. Ibid., 600 (emphasis added).

92. Ibid., 603.

93. Ibid. (quoting *Bowen v. Michigan Academy of Family Physicians*, 476 U.S. 667, 681n12 [1986]).

94. Ibid., 613.

95. Ibid., 615.

96. Ibid., 616.
97. Ibid., 617.
98. Ibid., 620–21.
99. PAH, 12:616. In *The Federalist*, Hamilton defended the president's veto power in a similar fashion:

> It not only serves as a shield to the executive, but it furnishes an additional security against the enaction of improper laws. It establishes a salutary check upon the legislative body, calculated to guard the community against the effects of faction, precipitancy, or of any impulse unfriendly to the public good, which may happen to influence a majority of that body. (FP [No. 73], 418)

100. U.S. Const. art. II, sec. 3.
101. U.S. Const. art. I, sec. 7, cl. 2.
102. No. 82-2377 and No. 82-2417 (1982) (slip opinion), 4.
103. Ibid.
104. Ibid., 6.
105. Ibid., 7.
106. Ibid.
107. Ibid., 12.
108. Ibid., 14.
109. Ibid., 15.
110. Scalia, "The Legislative Veto: A False Remedy for System Overload," 19.
111. 462 U.S. 919 (1983).
112. As Justice White noted in his dissent in *Chadha*, the legislative veto had been employed "in every field of governmental concern: reorganization, budgets, foreign affairs, war powers, and regulation of trade, safety, energy, the environment and the economy." Ibid., 968.
113. Ibid., 959.
114. See, e.g., Scalia, "The Legislative Veto: A False Remedy for System Overload," 176; and "1976 Bicentennial Institute—Oversight and Review of Agency Decisionmaking," *Administrative Law Review* 28, no. 4 (1976): 685–716. Justice Scalia also coauthored the brief for the American Bar Association in *INS v. Chadha* and testified before Congress on numerous occasions in the 1970s and 1980s, arguing that the legislative veto violated separation of powers principles and the Presentment Clause of the Constitution. As a judge of the D.C. Court of Appeals, Scalia testified against a constitutional amendment to restore the legislative veto as a form of congressional oversight of the executive branch. U.S. Senate, *Constitutional Amendment to Restore Legislative Veto: Hearing before the Subcommittee on the Constitution of the Committee on the Judiciary*, 98th Cong., 2nd sess., March 2, 1984, 245–52.
115. U.S. House of Representatives, *Congressional Review of International Agreements: Hearings before the Subcommittee on International Security and Scientific Affairs of the Committee on International Relations*, 94th Cong., 2nd sess., July 22, 1976, 186 (quoting *Federalist* 73).
116. U.S. Const. art. I, sec. 7, cl. 2.

117. Scalia, "The Legislative Veto: A False Remedy for System Overload," 20 (quoting U.S. Const. art. I, sec. 7, cl. 3).

118. Ibid.

119. Ibid., at 22 (quoting U.S. Const. art. I, sec. 1).

120. Ibid., 23.

121. Ibid., 25.

122. Ibid.

123. Ibid.

124. Ibid.

125. In hearings before Congress involving the use of legislative vetoes in executive agreements, then Assistant Attorney General Scalia testified:

> I think the defect of that argument is that it analogizes the relationship between the Congress and the President to the relationship between a principal and his agent. That is simply not what the Constitution establishes. The President is not merely the errand boy of the Congress. The Congress has authority to give him powers or to take the powers away; but when it gives powers, the President is not simple [*sic*] like any other agent. The Congress cannot say "you can do it," and then change its mind the next day and withdraw the power without any Presidential consent. (U.S. Senate, *Congressional Oversight of Executive Agreements—1975: Hearings before the Subcommittee on Separation of Powers of the Committee on the Judiciary*, 94th Cong., 1st sess., May 15, 1975, 197)

126. Scalia, "The Legislative Veto: A False Remedy for System Overload," 26.

127. Ibid.

128. In stark contrast, Scalia has argued that congressional conferral of line-item veto authority on the president does not violate the Presentment Clause of the Constitution. *Clinton v. City of New York*, 524 U.S. 417 (1998) (Scalia, J., dissenting).

129. *Congressional Oversight of Executive Agreements—1975*, 197.

130. Scalia, "The Doctrine of Standing as an Essential Element of the Separation of Powers," *Suffolk University Law Review* 17 (1983): 881–99.

131. See, e.g., Scalia, "The Legislative Veto: A False Remedy for System Overload," 19–26.

132. See *Synar v. United States*, 626 F. Supp. 1374 (D. D.C. 1986); *Morrison v. Olson*, 487 U.S. 654, 697 (1988) (Scalia, J., dissenting).

133. *Mistretta v. United States*, 488 U.S. 361, 413 (Scalia, J., dissenting).

134. See, e.g., *Synar v. United States*, 626 F. Supp. 1374 (D. D.C. 1986).

135. 524 U.S. 417, 453 (1998) (Scalia, J., dissenting).

## Chapter Six

# The Conservative Role of Judges in a Democratic System of Government

Alexander Hamilton referred to the judiciary as "beyond comparison the weakest of the three departments of power." Having "neither FORCE nor WILL but merely judgment," the judiciary presented the least danger to the basic liberties of the people.[1] But Hamilton regarded the judiciary as vitally important to the U.S. governmental system. Properly constituted, the judicial branch would have a moderating (or conservative) influence on republican government in three ways. First, with its power of judicial review, the judiciary could guard against violations of rights by Congress, which in a republican system of government was regarded as the dominant branch. In *Federalist* 78, Hamilton observed,

> [T]he judicial magistracy is of vast importance in mitigating the severity and confining the operation of . . . [unjust and impartial] laws. It not only serves to moderate the immediate mischiefs of those which may have been passed but it operates as a check upon the legislative body in passing them; who, perceiving that obstacles to the success of an iniquitous intention are to be expected from the scruples of the courts, are in a manner compelled, by the very motives of the injustice they mediate, to qualify their attempts. This is a circumstance calculated to have more influence upon the character of our governments than but few may be aware of.[2]

Second, Hamilton viewed the courts as an important check on the people themselves. Since the Constitution was understood as more fundamental than ordinary law, Hamilton maintained that "the solemn and authoritative act" of the people in ratifying it ought to outweigh their "momentary inclination[s]," which could "occasion dangerous innovations in the government, and serious

169

oppressions of the minor party in the community."[3] As Hamilton explained in his draft of Washington's farewell address,

> The basis of our political systems is the right of the people to make and to alter their constitutions of Government. But the constitution for the time, and until changed by an explicit and authentic act of the whole people, is sacredly binding upon all. The very idea of the right and power of the people to establish Government presupposes the duty of every individual to obey the established Government.[4]

Finally, Hamilton regarded the judges who serve on the federal judiciary as, in Ralph Lerner's words, republican schoolmasters who fulfill "the role of an educator, molder, or guardian of those manners, morals, and beliefs that sustain republican government."[5] Since federal judges have life tenure and are appointed at some remove from the immediate influence of the people, Hamilton believed that they had the capacity to keep the people faithful to their basic document. "What is the most sacred duty and the greatest source of security in a Republic?," Hamilton asked at the time the Washington administration was confronted with the Whiskey Rebellion of 1794. "[T]he answer would be, [a]n inviolable respect for the Constitution and Laws—the first growing out of the last."[6] Moreover, as Alexis de Tocqueville and Rufus Choate would later argue, judges could have a significant conservative influence on democratic forms of government because of their aristocratic status and legal training.[7] Judges, who are endowed with "the tastes and habits of an aristocracy," are trained to respect laws, not only because they benefit from them (e.g., the protection of property rights), but also because their legal education and training emphasize fidelity to law through such concepts as *stare decisis*.[8] Thus, even though Hamilton regarded the judiciary as the "weakest" of the three departments of government, he lauded it as "the most essential [institution] to the efficiency and stability of Government; to the security of property; to the safety and liberty of the person."[9]

Justice Antonin Scalia shares Hamilton's conception of the judicial branch. Scalia is acutely aware of the judiciary's significant role in checking against usurpations of power by Congress, as evidenced by the numerous occasions in which he has voted to strike down or limit federal statutes.[10] Scalia is also cognizant of the anti-democratic role played by courts in the U.S. system of government. "My most important job as a judge," Scalia has observed, "is to say no to the people."[11] In one speech where he expanded on this theme, Scalia explained that the reason judges have life tenure is so that they "can tell the people to go take a walk." "The most important thing I do in my job is to tell the majority that it can't do what it wants to do, because the Constitution forbids it. I stand between you and the majority, with the Constitution in my hand. And essentially, I tell the people, you know, 'people be damned, you cannot do this. The Constitution forbids you.'"[12] Scalia has embraced this anti-democratic view of the federal judiciary in Court opinions where he has not hesitated to strike down laws that he believes conflict with the text or structure of the Constitution. In *Maryland v. Craig*,[13] for example, he dissented from a Court ruling allowing a judge to receive, by one-way closed-circuit television, the testimony of an alleged child abuse victim after determining that the child's courtroom testimony would result in the child's suffering serious emotional distress:

> Seldom has this Court failed so conspicuously to sustain a categorical guarantee of the Constitution against the tide of prevailing current opinion. The Sixth Amendment provides, with unmistakable clarity, that "[i]n all criminal prosecutions, the accused shall enjoy the right . . . to be confronted with the witnesses against him." The purpose of enshrining this protection in the Constitution was to assure that none of the many policy interests from time to time pursued by statutory law could overcome a defendant's right to face his or her accusers in court. . . . Because the text of the Sixth Amendment is clear, and because the Constitution is meant to protect against, rather than conform to, current "widespread belief," I respectfully dissent.[14]

Justice Scalia's anti-democratic view of courts is also revealed in his criticism of the increasing politicization of the confirmation process for federal judges. According to Scalia, today's process of selecting federal judges has turned out to be a "mini-plebiscite" on such fundamental issues as abortion, capital punishment, and the right to die. Scalia's dismay with the selection process has become so acute that after John Roberts was confirmed to be chief justice in 2005, he said in a television interview that he would not want to go through it again.[15] As Scalia sees it, the current process of selecting federal judges will have devastating consequences for the protection of rights, and will transform what the framers regarded as a countermajoritarian institution into a majoritarian one:

> The American people have been converted to belief in The Living Constitution, a "morphing" document that means, from age to age, what it ought to mean. And with that conversion has inevitably come the new phenomenon of selecting and confirming federal judges, at all levels, on the basis of their views regarding a whole series of proposals for constitutional evolution. If the courts are free to write the Constitution anew, they will, by God, write it the way the majority wants; the appointment and confirmation process will see to that. This, of course, is the end of the Bill of Rights, whose meaning will be committed to the very body it was meant to protect against: the majority.[16]

It is also apparent that Justice Scalia takes his role as republican schoolmaster quite seriously. Each year, Scalia travels around the country delivering speeches on law and democracy where he makes the case for an originalist interpretation of the Constitution. Scalia unabashedly tells audiences that he believes in a "dead" (or more recently, an "enduring") Constitution, as opposed to a living Constitution, which posits that judges can create new rights by interpreting the Constitution to reflect current social values.[17] While Scalia concedes that there is no agreed-upon theory of constitutional interpretation, he says that he cannot support a living Constitution philosophy because it conflicts with democratic principles and does not contain a limiting principle on the willful judge. If people want rights in addition to those mentioned in the Constitution, Scalia advises that they can secure them through the political process or by amending the Constitution. In Scalia's view, his understanding of the Constitution is flexible, while the living Constitution philosophy is inflexible, because once the Supreme Court creates unenumerated rights, they apply to every person in the United States, which has the effect of discouraging states from experimenting with rights. "In my Constitution," expounds Scalia, "if you want the death penalty, pass a statute. If you don't want the death penalty, pass a statute the other way. You want a right to abortion, create it the way most rights are created in a democracy: Pass a law. If you don't want it, pass a law the other way. And if you want a right to [physician-assisted] suicide, the same."[18] Scalia laments that the Constitution is no longer revered like it used to be. While it is perhaps an imperfect document, Scalia regards the Constitution as "the symbol of our nation," which was produced under "irreplicable circumstances" that many of the founders believed were "providential."[19] When students ask Scalia for additional reading material on how to understand the U.S. Constitution and political system, he always recommends *The Federalist* and *Democracy in America*.[20]

Justice Scalia also touches on moral themes in his addresses across the country. Reminiscent of pre–Marshall Court era Federalist judges, Scalia stresses the importance of civic virtue as vitally important to sustaining republican government. In 1987 remarks at Rutgers Law School, Scalia observed that "great societies . . . are built upon the effect of one good person upon another," and he gave as examples "Pericles' Athens," "Cicero's Rome," "Dante's Florence," "Elizabeth's England," and "Washington's United States." Like Chief Justice John Jay and Associate Justice Samuel Chase, who preached about the importance of civic virtue while riding circuit in the 1790s,[21] Scalia contended in his Rutgers speech that republican government requires citizens to take responsibility for their actions. Referring to law as "second best," Scalia reminded his audience that "legal constraint, the opposite of freedom, is in most of its manifestations a cure for human vice or folly." "The Bill of Rights," he added, is "a charter of freedom from the law. A law that restricts the lawmakers, not the governed—a law restricting the law." Scalia maintained that "laws are more a manifestation and a product of the goodness of our society than they are the cause of it." Consequently, the more virtuous the people are, the less there is a need for laws, and "to the extent we have fewer laws, we are happy." In Scalia's view, in order to preserve freedom, people must exercise their rights responsibly. For example, while he said that he supports the remark attributed to Voltaire—"I disagree with what you say, but I will fight to the death for your right to say it"—he noted that irresponsible use of freedom of speech can result in socially undesirable outcomes, such as libel, which if engaged in enough will lead to laws eroding free speech rights. "It is a strange and poetically just phenomenon," Scalia observed, "that even as unthinking appeal to legal freedoms erodes moral responsibility, the erosion of moral responsibility in turn destroys legal freedom. That progress, I think, is inexorable."[22]

In this chapter, Hamilton's and Scalia's views on the judiciary will be compared in two areas: (1) the importance of the standard of "good behavior" in attracting meritorious persons to federal judgeships, and (2) the importance of that same standard in preserving judicial independence.

## A NATURAL ARISTOCRACY

Hamilton defended the standard of good behavior for federal judgeships as "one of the most valuable of the modern improvements in the practice of government."[23] One of the advantages he cited is that, along with an undiminishable salary, it would furnish an enticement for "a few choice spirits" in society to "[quit] a lucrative line of practice . . . [and] accept a seat on the bench."[24] In the same way that he defended reeligibility for the president, Hamilton sought to tie the interests of the person to the duties of the office. "It is a general principle of human nature," Hamilton reasoned, "that a man will be interested in whatever he possesses, in proportion to the firmness or precariousness of the tenure by which he holds it."[25] Only with permanency in office did Hamilton believe that "fit characters"—that is, those individuals "who unite requisite integrity with the requisite knowledge"—would be willing to undertake the arduous task of being a federal judge.[26] In contrast to the two political branches of government, Hamilton emphasized previous training or knowledge as a qualification for federal judgeships. The study of laws, he explained, "must demand long and laborious study to acquire a competent knowledge of them. Hence it is that there will be but few men in society who will have sufficient skill in the laws to qualify them for the stations of judges."[27] On this basis, Hamilton rejected temporary appointments for federal judgeships, because they would "throw the administration of justice into hands less able and less well qualified to conduct it with utility and dignity."[28]

In contemporary times, Justice Scalia has also defended an elite federal judiciary. In a 1987 speech he gave before the American Bar Association, Scalia implored the nation's lawyers to consider taking steps to preserve the prestige and reputation of federal judgeships.[29] Scalia related that when he graduated from law school in 1960, the federal judiciary had a reputation for the "big case":

> The federal courts, as I knew them then, were forums for the "big case"—major commercial litigation under the diversity jurisdiction, and federal actions under such laws regulating interstate commerce as the Sherman Act, the Securities Exchange Act, and the National Labor Relations Act. They were not the place where one would find many routine tort and employment disputes. They had FELA and Jones Act cases, to be sure—but those seemed to be the exception proving the rule, a touch of the mundane in a docket that was at least substantially exotic. . . . In Cleveland, where I first went to practice it was possible, as I do not think it is any more, to speak of the "federal bar"—an elite group of practitioners quite distinct from another group of lawyers who never appeared in federal court. In short, there was, in 1960, real meaning to the phrase "Don't make a federal case out of it."[30]

In contrast to the federal judiciary of that time, Scalia compared today's judiciary to a "bureaucracy," and its judges to "case processors." With the tremendous increase in the federal courts' docket, Scalia contended that judges are spending more time on "cases of overwhelming triviality" and less time on "cases of major importance." He warned that if this problem persists, "the stature of the job, and the quality of the people it attracts, will decline":

> Unless some structural changes are made, . . . it is unrealistic not to expect substantial alteration in the nature of the federal courts. The character of their business, and the amount of time they have to do it, have already changed enormously; the nature of the personnel they attract is bound to change as well. Not at the Supreme Court level. There are still only nine of us, and we can control our own docket so that only significant cases occupy our attention. But what of the circuit and district courts? If there is as yet no scarcity of the best and brightest eager to accept federal judicial appointment, that can only be, I suggest, because the candidates—being, most of them, not much younger than I—have the 1960 image in mind. As the image catches up to the modern reality—federal judges in much more abundance, each of them processing many more cases, not necessarily easier cases, but much less significant ones—then I suggest the attractiveness of the jobs will disappear.[31]

In his remarks to the ABA, Scalia maintained that most of the reforms that have been suggested in recent years—increase the number of federal judges, eliminate the courts' diversity jurisdiction, and/or establish an intercircuit tribunal—will not remedy the problem and, even worse, will lessen the prestige of federal judgeships. For example, Scalia rejected the idea of an inter-circuit tribunal—an appellate court "below the Supreme Court that would review cases presenting issues on which the circuit courts were in conflict."[32] While this new appellate tribunal might reduce the workload at the Supreme Court, Scalia contended that it would transform the status of circuit court judges "from second-level federal judges to third-level federal judges, hardly a step designed to enhance their importance and prestige."[33] Thus, albeit reluctantly, Scalia suggested a different structural change: greater specialization among Article III tribunals. Although he was not enthralled by the idea, Scalia argued that specialized courts—such as "a national Social Security Court"—could divert a substantial amount of the mundane business from regular federal courts, thereby allowing the judges who sit on those courts to concentrate on more significant cases. Only in this way did Scalia believe that the "cream of the profession" would continue to be attracted to federal judgeships:

> Now perhaps it is not necessary, or even desirable, to have a system of elite federal courts. Elitism has never been popular in democratic society—though the Founding Fathers, if one can believe the *Federalist Papers*, thought that the life-tenured judges they were creating would constitute a "natural aristocracy" (of ability rather than wealth). But if it is desirable, then I think the time is well past due to consider the means of preserving it.[34]

## JUDICIAL INDEPENDENCE

Another advantage that Hamilton gave for the standard of good behavior was that it would provide judges with the necessary courage to withstand encroachments by the political branches of government. The "inflexible and uniform adherence to the rights of the Constitution, and of individuals," Hamilton argued, will require "an uncommon portion of fortitude in the judges."[35] Since the federal judiciary is the weakest of the three branches of government, it "is in continual jeopardy of being overpowered, awed, or influenced by its coordinate branches."[36] Hamilton thus argued that the standard of good behavior may "justly [be] regarded as an indispensable ingredient in its constitution."[37] On this basis, Hamilton supported neither a mandatory retirement age for federal judges nor congressional power to reverse particular judicial decisions. Instead, he maintained that impeachments were "alone a complete security" against judicial usurpation of the functions of the legislature.[38]

As mentioned in chapter 2, Hamilton had the occasion to defend the standard of good behavior for federal judges after Congress passed the Judiciary

Act of 1802. This act, which was passed at the suggestion of President Thomas Jefferson during his First Annual Message to Congress, eliminated six new federal circuit courts and seven additional district courts established under the Judiciary Act of 1801. Before and after the act was adopted, Hamilton wrote a series of essays contending that the measure violated the "Good Behaviour" Clause of Article III and severely jeopardized the independence of the federal judiciary. Elaborating on arguments he had made in *The Federalist*, Hamilton described the federal judiciary as "naturally the weakest of the three" branches of government:

> The Judiciary . . . can ordain nothing. It commands neither the purse nor the sword. It has scarcely any patronage. Its functions are not active but deliberative. Its main province is to declare the meaning of the laws; and in extraordinary cases it must even look up to the Executive aid for the execution of its decisions. Its strength is in the veneration which it is able to inspire by the wisdom and rectitude of its judgments.[39]

In eighteen essays as "Lucius Crassus," Hamilton uncharacteristically hemmed and hawed about whether Congress could abolish lower federal courts without violating the "good Behaviour" provision.[40] One thing he was certain about, however, was that the Judiciary Act of 1802 constituted a substantial threat to an independent judiciary and a republican system of government. Prior to the bill's passage, Hamilton argued that the abolition of federal courts would make the judiciary subservient to the will of the legislature, and predicted that even before his remarks were read, the "Constitution will be no more!":[41]

> The real danger is on the side of that foul and fatal doctrine, which emboldens its votaries, with daring front and unhallowed step, to enter the holy temple of Justice and pluck from their seats the venerable personages, who, under the solemn sanction of the Constitution, are commissioned to officiate there; to guard that sacred compact with jealous vigilance; to dispense the laws with a steady and impartial hand; unmoved by the storms of faction, unawed by its powers, unseduced by its favors; shielding right and innocence from every attack; resisting and repressing violence from every quarter. 'Tis from the triumph of that execrable doctrine that we may have to date the downfall of our Government and with it, of the whole fabric of Republican Liberty.[42]

Justice Scalia has also defended the independence of the federal judiciary—although not as dramatically as Hamilton. During his confirmation hearings, Judge Scalia was asked about his views concerning the impeachment process for federal judges. Senator Howell Heflin (D-AL) asked the nominee if any changes should be made to the current "cumbersome process" of indictment by the House and trial by the Senate. Judge Scalia cautioned against making any changes. Even though the impeachment process is cumbersome, Scalia said, "[I]t's the major protection for the independence of the judiciary."[43] According to Scalia, any reforms along the lines of making the impeachment process easier would affect the ability of judges to decide cases as they see them:

> [The framers] were out of step with many of the Colonies at the time in what they provided for the judiciary. One of the major debates at the Convention was the provision on the judiciary, giving them life tenure, for example.
>
> Our federal judiciary is out of step with the States in many other respects. Many States have mandatory retirement ages, as you know; many States still, I believe, have election of judges. And all of those things were considered and rejected in favor of an extraordinarily strong—extraordinarily, more so than most of the states now—an extraordinarily strong and independent Federal judiciary. I think it was a conscious decision by the framers, and I happen to think that it was a good one.[44]

Similarly, Justice Scalia has rejected other proposed structural changes to the Constitution that would jeopardize the independence of the federal judiciary. For example, in 1997 remarks before the Anti-Defamation League, Scalia disagreed with a proposal by his friend and former colleague Robert Bork to have a constitutional amendment allowing any federal court decision to be overturned by a simple majority vote in both houses of Congress. Bork defended such an amendment as a way to curb what he perceived as a liberally activist Supreme Court bent on stamping out the moral values of the American people.[45] In his appearance before the Anti-Defamation League, Scalia questioned whether "Bork has essentially given up," adding that he himself was not yet "ready to throw in the towel." During his remarks, Scalia also derided proposed efforts by conservative members of Congress to impeach liberal judges.[46]

## Court Decisions Protecting Judicial Independence

As a member of the Supreme Court, Justice Scalia has written several important decisions concerning the independence of the federal judiciary. In *Freytag v. Commissioner of Internal Revenue*,[47] for example, Scalia wrote a concurring opinion in which he referred to the standard of good behavior as one of the chief means to protect the judiciary from legislative encroachment. With this security (as well as an irreducible salary), Scalia argued that Article

III courts could be safe repositories for the appointment of inferior officers under the Excepting Clause of Article II:

> Like the President, the Judicial Branch was separated from Congress not merely by a paper assignment of functions, but by endowment with the means to resist encroachment—foremost among which, of course, are life tenure (during "good behavior") and permanent salary. These structural accoutrements not only assure the fearless adjudication of cases and controversies . . . they also render the Judiciary a potential repository of appointment power free of congressional (as well as Presidential) influence.[48]

In *Mistretta v. United States*,[49] Justice Scalia dissented from the Court's decision upholding the U.S. Sentencing Commission, which was created under the Sentencing Reform Act of 1984 as an independent body located within the judicial branch. Scalia not only viewed the creation of the U.S. Sentencing Commission as a violation of the nondelegation doctrine (see chapter 2), but he raised a number of concerns about how judicial power was diminished and compromised by the establishment of the commission. First, Scalia noted that the determinate sentencing guidelines imposed by the sentencing commission replaced the wide discretion federal district court judges used to exercise in making sentencing determinations. As Scalia saw it, sentencing judges now have little discretion under the new sentencing guidelines and "will be reversed" if they disregard them. Moreover, Scalia regarded the placement of the sentencing commission in the judicial branch as extremely odd and troublesome to the concept of judicial independence. Scalia maintained that an independent agency within the judicial branch does not make any sense, since judicial power has never been thought to be delegable. Unlike the president, who can delegate authority to subordinate officials within the executive branch, judges do not have the ability to delegate judicial power to law clerks or special masters. Thus, even though there are many precedents for establishing "independent agencies" within the executive branch, Scalia argued that "here we have an anomaly beyond equal: an independent agency exercising governmental power on behalf of a Branch where all governmental power is supposed to be exercised personally by the judges of courts."[50] If an independent body such as this can survive separation of powers analysis, Scalia warned of further erosion of judicial power by the creation of additional independent agencies that are not controllable by courts or judges, and who perform functions previously exercised by the judiciary:

> Today's decision may aptly be described as the *Humphrey's Executor* of the Judicial Branch, and I think we will live to regret it. Henceforth there may be agencies "within the Judicial Branch" (whatever that means), exercising gov-

ernmental powers, that are neither courts nor controlled by the courts, nor even controlled by judges. If an "independent agency" such as this can be given the power to fix sentences previously exercised by district courts, I must assume that a similar agency can be given powers to adopt rules of procedure and rules of evidence previously exercised by this Court. The bases for distinction would be thin indeed.[51]

Justice Scalia has also defended the authority of the federal judiciary against erosion of its jurisdiction under the so-called "public rights" doctrine. Historically, there have been three main exceptions to the exercise of judicial power by Article III courts: territorial courts, courts-martial, and administrative and legislative courts. With respect to the last-mentioned courts, Congress traditionally has been able to create such courts to adjudicate cases involving "public rights." Justice Scalia has been a strenuous critic of an expanded interpretation of the public rights doctrine, which would allow private rights, "so closely integrated into a public regulatory scheme," to be adjudicated by non–Article III courts.[52] In the 1989 case *Granfinanciera, S.A. v. Nordberg*,[53] the Court had before it a challenge to a provision of the 1984 amendments to the Bankruptcy Act, which designated fraudulent conveyances in bankruptcy as "core" proceedings triable by non–Article III bankruptcy judges sitting without a jury. Petitioners, who were accused of being the recipients of a fraudulent monetary transfer within one year of the date of a bankruptcy petition, claimed that they had a constitutional right to a jury trial under the Seventh Amendment of the Constitution.[54] The Eleventh Circuit Court of Appeals ruled against the petitioners, holding that under the Bankruptcy Act, a fraudulent transfer was a "core" proceeding of the bankruptcy court, which under the common law was a nonjury issue. It also held that fraudulent conveyances are equitable in nature and thus do not fall within the safeguards of the Seventh Amendment. In an opinion by Justice William Brennan, the Supreme Court reversed. Brennan pointed out that while fraudulent conveyances for money could be brought in a court of equity, the respondent here was seeking monetary (not equitable) relief, and thus petitioners have a right to jury trial under the Seventh Amendment if they request it. Brennan also held that Congress is circumscribed under the public rights doctrine in assigning private legal actions to non–Article III judges. "If a statutory right is not closely intertwined with a federal regulatory program Congress has power to enact, and if that right neither belongs to nor exists against the Federal Government, then it must be adjudicated by an Article III court."[55] Nonetheless, Brennan acknowledged that some private rights, closely intertwined with a federal regulatory program, could be decided by non–Article III courts.

Justice Scalia filed an opinion, concurring in part and concurring in judgment. After reviewing the public rights doctrine from its inception, Scalia concluded that Congress could not constitutionally assign adjudicatory functions to a non–Article III court unless the government is a party to the case. Relying upon the text of Article III and the Court's precedent in *Murray's Lessee v. Hoboken Land & Improvement Co.*,[56] where the public rights doctrine was first formulated, Scalia maintained that the public rights doctrine has not meant "rights important to the public, or rights created by the public, but rights *of the public*—that is, rights pertaining to claims brought by or against the United States."[57] He based this interpretation on the principal rationale of the public rights doctrine, which provides that under the concept of sovereign immunity, the government may attach conditions to its consent to be sued. Scalia rejected pragmatic arguments about the desirability of having non–Article III tribunals adjudicate certain causes of action, and instead made the case for a formalistic distinction in powers between the three branches of government. "I do not think one can preserve a system of separation of powers on the basis of such intuitive judgments regarding 'practical effects,'" wrote Scalia. The separation of powers "must be anchored in rules, not set adrift in some multifactored 'balancing test'—and especially not in a test that contains as its last and most revealing factor 'the concerns that drove Congress to depart from the requirements of Article III.'"[58]

Finally, Justice Scalia has defended judicial independence from legislative interference with particular Court decisions. In *Plaut v. Spendthrift Farm, Inc.*,[59] the Court had before it a congressional amendment to the Securities Exchange Act of 1934 that allowed for the reinstatement of civil actions alleging fraud in the sale of stock, which had been previously dismissed as time barred as the result of two Court decisions. When petitioners filed a motion to reinstate their suit, the district court found that petitioners satisfied the conditions required under the amended act, but denied their motion on the ground that the act violated the doctrine of separation of powers by reopening a final judgment of the Supreme Court. In an opinion by Justice Scalia, the Supreme Court affirmed. According to Scalia, the act violated a postulate deeply rooted in our law: "Article III establishes a 'judicial department' with the 'province and duty . . . to say what the law is' in particular cases and controversies."[60] While Congress has the authority to amend or repeal a law, Scalia contended that it could not retroactively require federal courts to reopen final judgments:

> [A] distinction between judgments from which all appeals have been foregone or completed, and judgments that remain on appeal (or subject to being appealed), is implicit in what Article III creates: not a batch of unconnected courts, but a judicial department composed of "inferior Courts" and "one supreme Court." Within that hierarchy, the decision of an inferior court is not (unless the time for appeal has expired) the final word of the department as a whole. It is

the obligation of the last court in the hierarchy that rules on the case to give effect to Congress's latest enactment, even when that has the effect of overturning the judgment of an inferior court, since each court, at every level, must "decide according to existing laws." . . . Having achieved finality, however, a judicial decision becomes the last word of the judicial department with regard to a particular case or controversy, and Congress may not declare by retroactive legislation that the law applicable to that very case was something other than what the courts said it was.[61]

Justice Scalia also rejected the argument made by Justice Stephen Breyer in a concurring opinion that retroactive legislation that reopens a final decision of the court may *sometimes* be permissible if the law is generally applicable. According to Scalia, it does not matter if the law affects one or many cases; it is still an intrusion on judicial authority:

The nub of that infringement consists not of the Legislature's acting in a particularized and hence (according to the concurrence) nonlegislative fashion; but rather of the Legislature's nullifying prior, authoritative judicial action. It makes no difference whatever to that separation-of-powers violation that it is in gross rather than particularized (e.g., "we hereby set aside all hitherto entered judicial orders"). . . . [T]he doctrine of separation of powers is a structural safeguard rather than a remedy to be applied only when specific harm, or risk of specific harm, can be identified. In its major feature (of which the conclusiveness of judicial judgments is assuredly one) it is a prophylactic device, establishing high walls and clear distinctions because low walls and vague distinctions will not be judicially defensible in the heat of interbranch conflict. . . . We think legislated invalidation of judicial judgments deserves the same categorical treatment accorded by *Chadha* to congressional invalidation of executive action. . . . Separation of powers, a distinctly American political doctrine, profits from the advice authored by a distinctly American poet: Good fences make good neighbors.[62]

## Judicial Branch Encroachments on the Powers of the Political Branches

While Justice Scalia has formalistically defended the federal judiciary from diminution of its authority and from encroachment by a coordinate branch of government, he has also drawn limits on judicial power when he believes that Article III does not prescribe such authority. We shall see in chapter 7 that Scalia has been a forceful critic of judicially created rights outside of the four corners of the Constitution, arguing that the creation of such rights intrudes upon the policy-making functions of the coordinate branches of government as well as the state governments. Moreover, unlike under Article II, where

Scalia has recognized inherent presidential power, he has sharply restricted the scope of judicial "inherent" authority under Article III. This can be seen in the 1987 case *Young v. United States ex rel. Vuitton et Fils S.A.*,[63] where the Court examined whether judges can appoint private attorneys to represent the government in investigating and prosecuting violations of court orders. In that case, a judge appointed two special prosecutors after making a probable cause determination that petitioners were in contempt for violating a previously imposed permanent injunction. The two special prosecutors were not disinterested in the contempt proceedings, however. One of the special prosecutors represented one of the petitioners in the earlier civil litigation, and the other special prosecutor was his colleague. Over the course of a month, the two special prosecutors made more than one hundred audio- and video-tapes of meetings and telephone conversations between petitioners and investigators. Based on this evidence, the petitioners either pled guilty or were found guilty of criminal contempt or of aiding and abetting criminal contempt, and received sentences ranging from six months to five years. On appeal, the Second Circuit Court of Appeals rejected petitioners' argument that the appointment of two interested attorneys as special prosecutors violated their right to be prosecuted by an impartial prosecutor.

In an opinion by Justice William Brennan, the Court reversed the convictions and held that the appointment of interested parties as special prosecutors was improper. At the same time, however, the Court expansively defined the judiciary's inherent power to appoint prosecutors to vindicate their judgments. According to Brennan, judges have the authority to punish in-court contempts that interfere with the judicial process, and they can appoint special prosecutors to investigate and prosecute out-of-court contempts of their judicial orders. In the latter situation, Brennan suggested that it would be proper to request the local prosecutor to undertake the investigation, but he said that was not necessary, since the power to appoint special prosecutors is inherent in the judicial function and is a matter of necessity. As Justice Brennan explained, "If the Judiciary were completely dependent on the Executive Branch to redress direct affronts to its authority, it would be powerless to protect itself if that Branch declined prosecution."[64]

Justice Scalia filed a solo concurring opinion in which he agreed with the Court that the appointment of interested parties as special prosecutors in this case was improper, but he disagreed with its expansive interpretation of judicial authority to appoint private attorneys to vindicate judicial orders. As Scalia saw it, judges only have inherent authority to prosecute individuals for contempt when it is necessary to protect the court's ability to conduct its proceedings. The primary authority conferred on judges under Article III, Scalia explained, is the power to decide cases and controversies. Courts generally do not have the authority to prosecute crime, a power which belongs to the executive branch.

Scalia rejected the majority's argument that unless courts had the inherent authority to prosecute violations of their orders, they would be at the mercy of the executive branch. Consistent with his support of broad prosecutorial discretion in administrative law cases, Scalia observed, "There are numerous instances in which the Constitution leaves open the theoretical possibility that the actions of one Branch may be brought to nought by the actions or inactions of another." Scalia noted the stark contrast between the Court's understanding of inherent judicial power and Hamilton's observation in *Federalist* 78:

> [T]he judiciary, from the nature of its functions, will always be the least dangerous to the political rights of the constitution; because it will be least in a capacity to annoy or injure them. . . . The judiciary . . . has no influence over either the sword or the purse, no direction either of the strength or of the wealth of the society, and can take no active resolution whatever. It may truly be said to have neither Force nor Will but merely judgment; *and must ultimately depend upon the aid of the executive arm for the efficacy of its judgments.*"[65]

Scalia claimed that the Court's expansive interpretation of inherent judicial power conflicted with separation of powers principles. According to Scalia's understanding of inherent judicial authority, judges can "prosecute for contempt those who interfere with the orderly conduct of their business," but this authority does not extend to prosecuting and punishing those who "disregard . . . the *product* of their functioning, their judgments." Inherent judicial power, in Scalia's view, is limited by separation of powers principles, which forbid "a judge to promulgate a rule of behavior, prosecute its violation, and adjudicate whether the violation took place."[66]

## CONCLUSION

Alexander Hamilton and Antonin Scalia share a very similar conception of the federal judiciary. It would be natural to assume that because of Scalia's strenuous criticism of what he calls the "imperial judiciary," he does not support the exercise of judicial power. Properly understood, however, this is not the case. Like Hamilton, Scalia regards the judicial role as vitally important to the stability of republican government. Through the exercise of judicial review, judges provide an important check against congressional usurpation of presidential and judicial powers. Moreover, the standard of good behavior gives judges the fortitude to curb majoritarian measures that violate clearly prescribed rights. For both Hamilton and Scalia, however, the authority of judicial review is carefully cabined. If the text or structure of the Constitution does not require intervention by the courts, then the decision should be left to the political process.

# NOTES

1. FP, (No. 78), 437.
2. Ibid., 441.
3. Ibid., 440.
4. PAH, 20:275.
5. Lerner, "The Supreme Court as Republican Schoolmaster," *The Supreme Court Review* (1967): 127–80, 128.
6. PAH, 17:159.
7. Alexis de Tocqueville, *Democracy in America*, ed. J. P. Mayer (Garden City, NY: Doubleday & Co., Inc. 1969), 263–70; Rufus Choate, "The Position and Functions of the American Bar, as an Element of Conservatism in the State," *The Works of Rufus Choate* (Boston: Little, Brown and Co., 1862), 1:414–38.
8. The concept of *stare decisis* means that judges should abide by decided cases and not disturb things that are already established.
9. PAH, 25:529.
10. See, e.g., *Morrison v. Olson*, 487 U.S. 654 (1988) (Scalia, J., dissenting); *Mistretta v. United States*, 488 U.S. 361 (1989) (Scalia, J., dissenting); *Lujan v. Defenders of Wildlife*, 504 U.S. 555 (1992); *Friends of the Earth v. Laidlaw Environmental Services*, 528 U.S. 167 (2000) (Scalia, J., dissenting); *United States v. Lopez*, 514 U.S. 549 (1990); *Printz v. United States*, 521 U.S. 898 (1997); *United States v. Morrison*, 529 U.S. 598 (2000); *City of Boerne v. Flores*, 521 U.S. 507 (1997) (Scalia, J., concurring).
11. Remarks by Justice Antonin Scalia to Dr. Henry J. Abraham's "Seminar in American Constitutional Law and Theory" class from the University of Virginia, Supreme Court Building, Washington, DC, December 2, 1996.
12. Antonin Scalia, address given at Thomas Aquinas College, January 24, 1997, student-www.uchicago.edu/~jfmitche/scalia/tac.html.
13. 497 U.S. 836 (1990) (Scalia, J., dissenting).
14. Ibid., 860–61.
15. "Justice Scalia says 'Not a chance' to cameras." MSNBC Interview by Maria Bartiromo. http://msnbc.msn.com/id/9649724/print/1/displaymode/1098.
16. Antonin Scalia, *A Matter of Interpretation: Federal Courts and the Law* (Princeton, NJ: Princeton University Press, 1997), 47.
17. See, e.g., Antonin Scalia, "Interpreting the Constitution," address given at the Woodrow Wilson International Center for Scholars, Washington, DC, March 14, 2005. C-SPAN broadcast.
18. Glen Johnson, "Deciding Abortion, Suicide Issues is Duty of Congress, Scalia Says," *Washington Post*, March 3, 1998, A7.
19. Antonin Scalia, "Sibley Lecture," address given at the University of Georgia School of Law, 1989, student-www.uchicago.edu/~jfmitche/scalia/uga.html.
20. See, e.g., Diane Carroll, "Justice Scalia Speaks at KU; Students Question High Court's Role," *Kansas City Star*, November 16, 2001, B3.
21. Lerner, "The Supreme Court as Republican Schoolmaster," 127–80.
22. Antonin Scalia, "The Limits of the Law," *New Jersey Law Journal* 119 (1987), 4–5, 22–23.
23. FP (No. 78), 437.

24. Ibid., 442.
25. Ibid., 409.
26. Ibid., 442.
27. Ibid.
28. Ibid.
29. Antonin Scalia, "To Preserve Elite Federal Courts," *L.A. Times Daily Journal*, February 20, 1987, p. 4, col. 3.
30. Ibid.
31. Ibid.
32. Ibid.
33. Ibid.
34. Ibid. It is interesting that in another speech, Justice Scalia raised serious doubts about whether a "natural aristocracy," akin to the one the framers supported, was possible in the modern era:

When Madison described them [federal judges] as a "natural aristocracy," I am sure he had in mind an aristocracy of property as well as manners. But with the proliferation and consequent bureaucratization of the courts, the relative modesty of judicial salaries, and above all the development of lawyers (and hence of judges) through a system of generally available university education which, in this country as in others, more often nurtures collectivist than capitalist philosophy, one would be foolish to look for Daddy Warbucks on the bench. (Antonin Scalia, "Economic Affairs as Human Affairs," in *Economic Liberties and the Judiciary*, ed. James A. Dorn and Henry G. Manne [Fairfax, VA: George Mason University Press, 1987], 35–36)

35. FP (No. 78), 441.
36. Ibid., 438.
37. Ibid.
38. Ibid., 444, 452–53.
39. "Examination No. XIV," PAH, 25:550–51.
40. Initially, Hamilton suggested that Congress could abolish lower federal courts pursuant to its express authority to create inferior tribunals below the Supreme Court under Article III, so long as judges who were already appointed could continue in office. PAH, vol. 25 (Examination No. VI), 488. Then after the Senate passed the repeal act of 1802, Hamilton took the more inflexible position that Congress could not abolish lower federal courts once they had been established, since any *implied* authority that Congress might have to abolish federal courts must give way to the "express and positive right" of judges to hold their offices during good behavior. Ibid., (Examination No. XII), 529–35. Finally, after the House passed the repeal act and President Jefferson signed it into law, Hamilton returned to his more moderate initial position that Congress has *"a right to change or abolish Inferior Courts, but not to abolish the actual Judges."* Ibid., (Examination No. XVI), 567. For support of this interpretation, Hamilton relied upon a rule of interpretation, which holds that two different constitutional provisions addressing the same subject, "ought to be construed, as, if possible, to comport with each other, and give a reasonable effect to all." Ibid., (Examination No. XII), 533. Hamilton believed this middle ground position "substantially" preserved the independence of the federal judiciary, because once "it was understood not to be in the

power of the Legislature to deprive the Judges of their offices and emoluments, it would be a great restraint upon the factious motives, which might induce the abolition of a court." Ibid., (Examination No. XVI), 569. Interestingly, the question of whether Congress can abolish federal courts without interfering with the "good Behavior" Clause of Article III has never been definitively answered by the Supreme Court. In *Stuart v. Laird*, 5 U.S. (1 Cranch) 299 (1803), a decision handed down one year after the Judiciary Act of 1802 was passed, the Court upheld the act on the ground that Congress, pursuant to its authority to ordain and establish inferior courts, could transfer a case from one court to another. But the Court avoided the larger constitutional issue.

41. "Examination No. XII," PAH, 25:529–30.

42. "Examination No. XIV," PAH, 25:549.

43. U.S. Senate, *The Nomination of Judge Antonin Scalia: Hearings before the Committee on the Judiciary of the United States Senate*, 99th Cong., 2nd. sess., August 5–6, 1986, 99.

44. Ibid., 99–100.

45. Robert Bork, *Slouching Towards Gomorrah: Modern Liberalism and American Decline* (New York: Regan Books, 1996), 117; and "The Conservative Case for Amending the Constitution," *Weekly Standard*, March 3, 1997, 21.

46. Glenn Elsasser, "No Contest: Top Court's Top Fighter is Scalia," *Chicago Tribune*, May 27, 1997, 1.

47. 501 U.S. 868 (1991).

48. Ibid., 907.

49. 488 U.S. 361 (1989).

50. Ibid., 425.

51. Ibid., 425–26.

52. See, e.g., *Thomas v. Union Carbide Agricultural Products*, 473 U.S. 568 (1985); *Commodity Futures Trading Commission v. Schor*, 478 U.S. 833 (1986).

53. 492 U.S. 33 (1989).

54. The Seventh Amendment provides: "In Suits at common law, where the value in controversy shall exceed twenty dollars, the right of a trial by jury shall be preserved."

55. 492 U.S. at 54–55.

56. 59 U.S. 272 (1856).

57. 492 U.S. at 68.

58. Ibid., 70.

59. 514 U.S. 211 (1995).

60. Ibid., 218 (quoting *Marbury v. Madison*, 5 U.S. [1 Cranch] 137, 177 [1803]).

61. Ibid., 227.

62. Ibid., 239–40.

63. 481 U.S. 787 (1987).

64. Ibid., 801.

65. Ibid., 818 (quoting *Federalist* 78, 522–23 [J. Cooke ed. 1961]) (emphasis added).

66. Ibid., 821, 824.

*Chapter Seven*

# The "Science" of Interpreting Texts

Even though Alexander Hamilton and Antonin Scalia view judges as performing an important conservative function in republican government, they still regard the judiciary as the least dangerous branch of government. For Hamilton, judges were interpreters of law, not policy makers. As he explained, "the general liberty of the people can never be endangered" by judges, "so long as the judiciary remains truly distinct from both the legislature and the executive."[1] If judges assume functions more properly belonging to the other branches of government, Hamilton warned that they would be violating Montesquieu's maxim: "There is no liberty if the power of judging be not separated from the legislative and executive powers."[2] Thus, while Hamilton did not deny the existence of natural rights, and at times spoke favorably about the "spirit" of the law as a tool for interpreting legal texts, he viewed judges primarily as textualists who were supposed to enforce the plain meaning of laws. To this end, Hamilton proposed certain rules of construction to limit an "arbitrary discretion in the courts."[3] For Hamilton, the true test of a just interpretation of law was the "natural and obvious" sense of a provision.[4]

Like Hamilton, Justice Scalia also believes that judges are interpreters of law, not policy makers. In construing statutory and constitutional texts, he has employed the same commonsense rule of construction that Hamilton proposed in *The Federalist*: the "natural and obvious" meaning of words. One of the claimed strengths of a textualist approach to interpreting laws is that it limits judicial discretion, which can be seen in some of Scalia's decisions. For example, even though on a personal level Scalia finds flag burning to be a disagreeable form of political protest, he has sided with his liberal colleagues in finding this practice to be protected political speech under the First Amendment.[5] Moreover, while Scalia supports tort reform limiting the amount of money juries can award as punitive damages, he has disagreed with his conservative colleagues that corporations are protected against excessive punitive damages awards under the Due Process Clauses of the Fifth and Fourteenth Amendments.[6] While Scalia's textualist approach to interpreting laws has not always been consistently applied in cases,[7] it has served to limit his discretion in particular areas of his jurisprudence. This chapter examines Hamilton's and Scalia's textualist approach to construing laws. Not only do the similarities between the two men in this area provide substantial additional evidence of their shared vision of the judicial role in the U.S. political system, but their similar textualist approaches to interpreting laws also illuminate several important areas of disagreement between Scalia and his colleagues (both liberal and conservative) on the Supreme Court.

## HAMILTON'S TEXTUALISM

In *Federalist* 78, Hamilton made the case for federal courts exercising the authority of judicial review—that is, the power to review congressional legislation and executive orders and declare them null and void when they conflict with the Constitution. Although this was not the first occasion Hamilton defended such a power belonging to the courts,[8] it was the first time he defended it at the federal level, and it was his most systematic treatment of the doctrine. In contrast to Chief Justice John Marshall's opinion in *Marbury v. Madison*,[9] which defended the power of judicial review on both textual and republican grounds, Hamilton rested his argument for judicial review exclusively on the latter. According to Hamilton, the ultimate source of authority in America "rest[s] on the solid basis of THE CONSENT OF THE GOVERNED,"[10] as expressed in the fundamental law of the land, the Constitution. The members of Congress are only the agents of the people. Thus, if a law passed by the legislative branch violates a constitutional provision, it must be declared void. "To deny this," Hamilton wrote, "would be to affirm that the deputy is greater than his principal; that the servant is above his master; that the representatives of the people are superior to the people themselves."[11] As the guardians of the Constitution, Hamilton contended that the courts must have the authority of judicial review, since the alternative would lead to legislative supremacy. In contrast to Thomas Jefferson, who defended the concept of departmental review,[12] Hamilton argued that if the legislative branch had the power to enact and interpret laws, its authority would be superior to the will of the people. To those who objected that judicial review would create an omnipotent federal judiciary, Hamilton denied such an implication. The power of judicial review "only supposes that the power of the people is superior to both, and that where the will of the legislature, declared in its statutes, stands in opposition to that of the people, declared in the Constitution, the judges ought to be governed by the latter rather than the former."[13]

Hamilton conceded, however, that the claim of judicial supremacy would have more force if courts acted like legislatures. As he put it, if the judicial branch exercised "WILL instead of JUDGMENT, the consequence would equally be the substitution of their pleasure for that of the legislative body." In order to avoid this possibility, Hamilton claimed that judges must be "bound down by strict rules and precedents."[14] Following the English jurist William Blackstone,[15] Hamilton's standard for interpreting texts (both statutory and constitutional) was the "natural and obvious" sense of a provision:

> The rules of legal interpretation are rules of *common sense*, adopted by the courts in the construction of the laws. The true test therefore, of a just application of them, is its conformity to the source from which they are derived. . . . Even if these maxims had a precise technical sense, corresponding with the ideas of those who employ them upon the present occasion, which, however, is not the case, they would still be inapplicable to a constitution of government. In relation to such a subject, the natural and obvious sense of its provisions, apart from any technical rules, is the true criterion of construction.[16]

Some commentators have claimed that Hamilton's favorable view of natural rights and judicial reliance upon the "spirit of laws" makes him a less than committed textualist, or even an early defender of judicial activism.[17] It is true that Hamilton was a steadfast believer in natural rights. One year before the Declaration of Independence was authored, Hamilton gave a powerful defense of natural rights in *The Farmer Refuted* (1775), where he wrote, "The sacred rights of mankind are not to be rummaged for, among old parchments, or musty records. They are written, as with a sun beam, in the whole *volume* of human nature, by the hand of the divinity itself; and can never be erased or obscured by mortal power."[18] In that same pamphlet, Hamilton repudiated the legal positivism of Thomas Hobbes for drawing into question "the existence of an intelligent superintending principle, who is the governor, and will be the final judge of the universe," and recommended for a true understanding of the rights of man the works of "Grotius, Puffendorf, Locke, Montesquieu, and Burlemaqui."[19] Moreover, in his legal opinion in the early stages of the famous Yazoo land fraud case, Hamilton (as would Chief Justice John Marshall[20]) relied on natural principles of justice, as well as a broad construction of the Contracts Clause, in arguing that a state law rescinding a land grant was unconstitutional.

Prior to the adoption of the Constitution, Hamilton also occasionally spoke effusively about "the spirit of laws" as a justifiable methodology in making judicial decisions. In his "Phocion" letters, authored in 1784, Hamilton contended that when a Constitution is "silent on particular points," judges should "consult and pursue its spirit" in order to "conform to the dictates of reason and equity."[21] And in his sixth legal brief filed in the 1784 New York case *Rutgers v. Waddington*,[22] Hamilton proclaimed, "In law as in Religion THE LETTER KILLS," but "The SPIRIT MAKES ALIVE."[23] Finally, in response to the Anti-Federalist concern that federal judges would subvert republican government by resting their decisions on the spirit of the Constitution, Hamilton gave the feeble response in *Federalist* 81 that the Constitution does not *directly* authorize such power.[24]

There are a variety of reasons, however, for not expansively interpreting Hamilton's natural rights philosophy or favorable statements about judicial reliance upon the spirit of the laws. First and foremost, Hamilton learned from Blackstone that if the language of the law is clear (according to its natural and obvious sense), then judicial reliance upon a law's spirit is unwarranted. Hamilton made this point in many of the constitutional and policy debates in which he participated, where he utilized a textual or positivistic approach to interpreting the Constitution. In his "Camillus" essays, for example, Hamilton defended the Jay Treaty from oversight and review by the House by relying upon "the natural import of the terms of the Constitution."[25] In his articles as "Lucius Crassus," in which Hamilton argued that the Judiciary Act of 1802 conflicted with the Good Behavior Clause of the Constitution, he placed reliance on "a positive written Constitution" and recommended "[t]aking the literal import of the terms" of the Good Behavior provision "as the criterion of their true meaning." In those same articles, Hamilton described the tenure conferred on judges by the Good Behavior clause as an "express and positive right."[26] And in his "Phocion" letters, in which Hamilton mentioned that judges should consult the spirit of the Constitution when it does not address a particular subject, Hamilton also mentioned "the natural and obvious scope of the words" as a rule of construction, and asked, "What is the plain language of the proposal?" In those same letters, Hamilton placed reliance upon "the plain and authentic language of [a] solemn treaty" and employed a "simple and candid construction."[27]

Moreover, Hamilton's own rejection of the use of extratextual sources when the provisions of the Constitution were neither silent nor unclear provides additional grounds for not exaggerating his statements about natural rights and judicial reliance on a law's spirit. In his "Camillus" essays, Hamilton buttressed his textual argument with congressional practice. Under both the Articles of Confederation and the newly adopted Constitution, Hamilton noted that many treaties had been entered into without being challenged as unlawful. Congressional practice, he argued, "fixed" the sense of the constitutional provision in question. But Hamilton also recognized that this congressional practice was unnecessary to his textual argument, because Article II's treaty provision was itself "clear and decisive."[28] Moreover, Hamilton was not an intentionalist when it came to interpreting laws, as has been suggested by some constitutional scholars.[29] According to this view, the most important consideration in properly construing laws is the intention of the drafters who authored the provision, which in some instances might conflict with the actual words of the provision. For Hamilton, extratextual sources, such as the framers' intent, could not be relied upon to displace the actual words of a constitutional provision; they could only be used to buttress the natural and obvious meaning of the words. On at least three different occasions, Hamilton discussed the views of the delegates to the Constitutional Convention during the course of subsequent constitutional debates. The first occasion was in the famous debate with Thomas Jefferson over the constitutionality of the national bank, in which Jefferson relied upon the framers' intent to conclude that Congress could not establish such a national institution. The second was in Hamilton's defense of the Jay Treaty where he cited framers' intent to support his constitutional analysis of the treaty-making provision. And finally, in Hamilton's "Examination" articles defending the independence of the federal judiciary, he cited passages from *The Federalist* in attempting to understand what the delegates to the Constitutional Convention thought about judicial independence. In the latter two instances, Hamilton used framers' intent to buttress the natural and obvious meaning of a constitutional provision. As he explained in the controversy over the Republican attempt to restructure the federal judiciary, contemporary explanations of a provision "by men who had had a perfect opportunity of knowing the views of its framers must operate as a weighty collateral reason for believing the construction agreeing with this explanation to be right, rather than the opposite one." But, Hamilton continued, such intent could not displace the clear language of the provision: "In recurring to the comments which have been cited, it is not meant to consider them as evidence of any thing but of the views with which the Constitution was framed. After all, the Instrument must speak for itself."[30] It is for this reason that, eleven years earlier, Hamilton had accused Thomas Jefferson, then secretary of state, of improperly using framers' intent in the debate over the bank bill:

> The Secretary of State will not deny, that whatever may have been the intention of the framers of a constitution, or of a law, that intention is to be sought for in the instrument itself, according to the usual & established rules of construction. Nothing is more common than for laws to *express* and *effect*, more or less than was intended. If then a power to erect a corporation, in any case, be deducible by fair inference from the whole or any part of the numerous provisions of the

constitution of the United States, arguments drawn from extrinsic circumstances, regarding the intention of the convention, must be rejected.[31]

It was only when the language of the Constitution was silent or ambiguous
on a particular point that Hamilton (following Blackstone) believed judicial
reliance on the Constitution's spirit was permissible, which raises the question
of what Hamilton meant by the Constitution's spirit. Three possible explanations deserve consideration. One explanation of what Hamilton had in mind
by judicial reliance on the Constitution's spirit was the political discretion federal judges might need to shore up the powers of the national government.
Hamilton, the founding father who so strongly believed in the concept of authority in maintaining an effective republican government, did not exclude the
possibility that federal judges might need to rely upon the Constitution's spirit
to buttress national authority when a particular power was not explicitly mentioned in the Constitution or contemplated by the framers. Implicit in Hamilton's reply to the Anti-Federalist charge that judges would destroy republican
government by relying upon the Constitution's spirit was the understanding
that judges *indirectly* had such authority. Hamilton's defenses of judicial review, according to general principles of republican government, and the right
of prerogative under Article II, can both be said to derive from the Constitution's spirit as understood by him. In fact, there is historical evidence to support this. In the case in which Hamilton for the first time defended the power
of judicial review, *Rutgers v. Waddington* (1784), he argued that the defendant
in that case was not liable under New York's Trespass Act, because the state
law violated common law principles of New York's Constitution and the plain
language of the Treaty of Paris. Interestingly, under New York's Constitution
at that time, the Council of Revision (a body whose members included the
governor and judges) had the authority to revise all bills passed by the legislature that were inconsistent with the "spirit of this constitution" *or with the
public good*.[32] Moreover, in *Federalist* 81, where Hamilton claims that the
Constitution did not directly empower federal courts to construe laws according to their spirit, he admits "that the Constitution ought to be the standard of
construction for the laws, and that wherever there is an evident opposition, the
laws ought to give place to the Constitution," which is a power "not deducible
from any circumstance peculiar to the plan of convention, but from the general theory of a limited Constitution."[33]

Second, for Hamilton (as was true for Blackstone), the Constitution's spirit
meant the exercise of equity in particular cases. The equity power was what
Hamilton was referring to when he wrote in his brief in *Rutgers*, "In law as in
Religion THE LETTER KILLS," but "The SPIRIT MAKES ALIVE." In that case,
Joshua Waddington was the agent for two British merchants who during the

Revolutionary War occupied the brewery of Elizabeth Rutgers, an eighty-year-old widow and New York resident, without paying her compensation. After the British captured New York City in 1776, Rutgers fled her brewery, and the defendants operated it rent free from September 1778 until May 1780, when they were forced to pay rent to the British government. On November 23, 1783, two days before the British evacuated New York City, a fire broke out in the brewery and reduced it to ashes. After Rutgers reclaimed her property, she sued Waddington under New York's Trespass Act, which permitted residents of the state to sue for damages "any Person or Persons who may have occupied, injured, or destroyed his, her or their Estate, either real or personal, with the Power of the Enemy." The act also did not permit defendants to plead as a defense any military order of the enemy.[34] In a case in which Hamilton was criticized for displaying pro-Tory sentiment, he argued in defense of Waddington that the Trespass Act was unconstitutional because it conflicted with the law of war, as incorporated into the common law of New York, which absolved foreign nationals from paying rent to two different sovereignties when they occupy land at the direction of an enemy nation. Hamilton also argued that the Trespass Act was unconstitutional because it violated the plain language of the Treaty of Paris, which gave a "general amnesty" to crimes committed during the war. Alternatively, Hamilton argued that if the judges of New York's Mayor's Court did not find the Trespass Act to be unconstitutional, they should construe the word "Person" under the Trespass Act not to include British citizens, which would follow the "spirit" rather than the "letter" of the law and make it conform to the law of nations. As Hamilton viewed it, for British subjects to be forced to pay rent to two different countries during an armed conflict violates natural principles of justice. Although he would have preferred that the court strike down the law as unconstitutional, he favored a construction of the Trespass Act that would avoid "inconvenient consequences." As Hamilton put it, "Many things within the letter of a statute are not within its Equity & Vice versa," and "[G]eneral words are to receive a construction according to the subject matter and so as to exclude inconvenient consequences."[35] Hamilton's statutory construction argument was the one adopted by the Mayor's Court. Chief Judge Mayor Duane, who wrote the court's opinion, concluded as follows:

> The supremacy of the Legislature need not be called into question; if they think fit *positively* to enact a law, there is no power which can controul them. When the main object of such a law is clearly expressed, and the intention manifest, the Judges are not at liberty, altho' it appears to them to be *unreasonable*, to reject it: for this were to set the *judicial* above the legislative, which would be subversive of all government.

But when a law is expressed in *general words*, and some *collateral matter*, which happens to arise from those words is *unreasonable*, there the Judges are in decency to conclude, that consequences were not foreseen by the Legislature; and therefore they are at liberty to expound the statute by *equity*, and only *quoad hoc* to disregard it.[36]

It is important to note, however, that Hamilton understood equity in the traditional Blackstonian sense: it was an "extraordinary" remedy where judges could exercise mercy in particular cases when the law itself was deficient or did not comport with reason. Hamilton agreed with Blackstone that the equitable power should not be "indulged too far; lest thereby we destroy all law, and leave the decision of every question entirely in the breast of the judge."[37] As political scientist Gary McDowell points out, traditional equitable relief applied to specific individuals and concrete rights, such as the right of property, while modern equitable relief applies to broad social groups and abstract rights, such as equality.[38] That Hamilton understood equity in the traditional way is confirmed by his discussion of the equitable power in *The Federalist*, where he observed that "[t]he great and primary use of a court of equity is to give relief in *extraordinary cases*, which are *exceptions* to general rules." Hamilton cited as examples of equitable remedies, relief from "hard bargains" and enforcement of "agreements to convey lands."[39] Thus, while Hamilton urged the Mayor's Court to rely upon the spirit of the Trespass Act in *Rutgers*, he did not believe that under the banner of "equity," judges could effectuate broad policy goals, which he regarded as a responsibility consigned to the legislature.

A third explanation of what Hamilton understood by "the spirit of the law" were certain basic natural rights so essential to a republican system of government that their denial would make a mockery of a system of justice. Not unlike Justice Samuel Chase's defense of the ex post facto provision in *Calder v. Bull*,[40] and a similar defense of that right and the rights prohibiting bills of attainder and laws impairing the obligation of contract by James Madison in *The Federalist*,[41] Hamilton maintained that there are certain natural rights that could not be denied to the individual in a republican system of government. In his "Phocion" letters, for example, Hamilton argued that if a defendant's right to a jury trial was not guaranteed under New York's constitution, a judge following the spirit of the Constitution should find such a right. All of the natural rights Hamilton supported, however, ultimately found positive expression in the federal Constitution, including Article I, Section 10's Contracts Clause, which prohibits any state from impairing the obligation of contract. The framers, mostly propertied men who were concerned about the increase in state-enacted debtor relief laws, skillfully managed to get this provision into the original articles of the Constitution. The ability to buy, sell, lease, or use property, as guaranteed by a legally binding contract, which the states could not interfere with, was regarded as a natural right closely tied to the right of property. In *Federalist* 44, James Madison captured the prevailing sentiment of his fellow delegates when he reasoned that laws impairing the obligation of contracts "are contrary to the first principles of the social compact and to every principle of sound legislation."[42] And in Hamilton's legal opinion regarding the famous Yazoo land fraud case, dated March 1796, he argued that the liberty interest protected by the Contracts Clause was rooted in natural law principles:

> Without pretending to judge of the original merits or demerits of the purchasers, it may be safely said to be a contravention of the first principles of natural justice and social policy, without any judicial decision of facts, by a positive act of the legislature, to revoke a grant of property regularly made for valuable consideration, under legislative authority, to the prejudice even of third persons on every supposition innocent of the alleged fraud or corruption; and it may be added, that the precedent is new of revoking a grant on the suggestion of corruption of a legislative body.[43]

## HAMILTON AND THE LIVING CONSTITUTION

While Hamilton was a defender of traditional natural rights and said favorable things about judicial reliance upon the spirit of laws, there are three reasons why he would not likely support the modern idea of a living Constitution, or the concept that judges can fashion new rights under the Bill of Rights to keep the Constitution current with the times. First, his textualist approach to interpreting laws strongly suggests that he thought the words of the Constitution were of paramount importance. Throughout his writings on constitutional interpretation, Hamilton talks about the "plain language," "literal meaning," and "natural and obvious sense" of constitutional provisions. In his "Examination" essays, which contain his last protracted discussion of constitutional interpretation, Hamilton refers to "a positive written Constitution." It is true that Hamilton supported a broad interpretation of the national government's powers, but that does not make him a defender of a living Constitution philosophy. Chief Justice John Marshall's opinion in *McCulloch v. Maryland* is often cited for support of such an interpretation of the Constitution,[44] where in making the case for a broad construction of national power, Marshall distinguished the minute details of ordinary statutes from the great outlines of the Constitution, and said with respect to the latter, "[W]e must never forget, that it is *a constitution* we are expounding," one which is "intended to endure for ages to come, and, consequently, to be adapted to the various *crises* of human affairs."[45] But these statements do not support the modern living Constitution philosophy as defined above. What Marshall was arguing in *McCulloch* was the same thing that Hamilton argued in his defense of the Bank Bill: the *legislature's* powers must be interpreted broadly in order for it to have the capacity to adjust to new situations. Hamilton and Marshall did not believe that constitutional language was indeterminate or boundlessly malleable, or why make the case for a broad construction of national power in the first place? Even Hamilton, the ardent nationalist, believed there were things that Congress could not do in exercising its power under the Commerce Clause.[46] In short, Hamilton would have disagreed with Chief Justice Charles Evans Hughes's famous aphorism: "We are under a Constitution, but the Constitution is what the Supreme Court says it is."[47]

Second, even assuming that the Constitution is ambiguous in places, which it is, Hamilton's understanding of separation of powers suggests that he would not place the authority for updating the Constitution with federal judges. As conceived by Hamilton, judges were interpreters of law, not lawmakers. If the people want to change the Constitution, Hamilton contended that they had to go through the formal process of amending the Constitution. As he put it in *Federalist* 78, "Until the people have, by some solemn and authoritative act, annulled or changed the established form, it is binding upon themselves collectively, as well as individually."[48] It is important to acknowledge that Hamilton's textualist approach to constitutional interpretation did not regard constitutional provisions as self-evident or subject to only one interpretation; as understood by him, judges do have discretion. But Hamilton's belief that the judiciary was the least dangerous branch of government provides an important limiting principle on that judicial discretion. Hamilton would likely view judicial creation of rights beyond the four corners of the Constitution as an abuse of that discretion and a violation of the social contract. For judges to create unenumerated rights under the vague and open-ended provisions of the Constitution, such as the Due Process Clause, would intrude upon the democratic process and create separation of powers difficulties with the legislature. This interpretation of Hamilton is consistent with his rule of law philosophy. In order to preserve a government of laws, not men, judges must faithfully attempt to construe the words of the Constitution. If they do not do this, then the people will become less respectful of law, which Hamilton desperately did not want to happen. While federal judges have discretion, it is discretion cabined by a distinction between judicial interpretation and lawmaking.

Third, it is important to take account of Hamilton's overall philosophy of rights. Hamilton's statements about natural rights can be greatly exaggerated if not understood within the context in which he defends them. As the person who argued *against* even having a bill of rights, Hamilton is not a likely candidate to support the expansion of the people's rights by judges. In *Federalist* 84, he disparaged declarations of rights as more appropriate "in a treatise of ethics than in a constitution of government."[49] It should also be recalled that while Hamilton objected to a bill of rights as both unnecessary and dangerous, another unstated reason for why he likely opposed a bill of rights was that excessive claims of rights by the people would impede the authority of the federal government and, in particular, the executive branch. For Hamilton, judges were to preserve private rights enumerated in the Constitution, and natural rights absolutely essential to republican government, all of which (as understood by him) were ultimately placed *within* the four corners of the document. While Hamilton's conservative political philosophy led him to defend traditional natural rights, such as the right of property, those same conservative instincts would likely have seen him reject judicially created substantive due process rights, including those recognized during both the *Lochner* and *Roe* eras. The natural rights Hamilton favored were those already listed in the Constitution, which could be defended on both natural law and textualist grounds. Hamilton would thus have agreed with Chief Justice Marshall's observation that "although the spirit of an instrument, especially of a constitution, is to be respected not less than its letter, yet the spirit is to be collected chiefly from its words."[50]

## JUSTICE SCALIA'S TEXTUALISM

In Court opinions and extrajudicial writings, Justice Scalia has described his method of interpreting legal texts as the traditional approach of textualism and has utilized the same commonsense rule of construction that Hamilton used: the "plain meaning" or the "natural and obvious" sense of a provision. In statutory cases, Scalia has rejected intentionalist and purposive approaches to understanding the meaning of statutes, and in constitutional cases, he has eschewed reliance upon extratextual sources (e.g., natural law and international law) as a substitute for the original meaning of a provision. In all cases of legal interpretation, Scalia claims that the words and phrases of laws are what should matter most for the judge. What concerns Scalia is the possibility that judges will use extratextual sources to support whatever results they want. As he put it, "The main danger in judicial interpretation of the Constitution—or, for that matter, in judicial interpretation of any law—is that judges will mistake their own predilections for the law."[51] Justice Scalia's most systematic treatment of his approaches to interpreting statutes and the U.S. Constitution came in his 1995 Tanner Lectures at Princeton University, which were later published in the book called *A Matter of Interpretation: Federal Courts and the Law* (1997). In this work, as well as in Court opinions, Scalia makes the case for a textualist approach to interpreting law.

## Statutory Interpretation

In *A Matter of Interpretation*, Scalia laments that there is no agreed-upon method of interpreting *statutory* texts and is frankly surprised by the lack of scholarly attention given to the subject, since approximately 80 percent of the Court's business deals with "the meaning of federal statutes and federal agency regulations."[52] Scalia observes that the state of statutory interpretation is in such disarray that there is not even agreement over what the *objective* is in construing statutes. For many, the purpose of interpreting statutes is to give effect to the *intent* of the legislature. Scalia rejects this view for several reasons. First and most fundamentally, Scalia argues that reliance on legislative intent is inconsistent with democratic theory. According to Scalia, the guiding principle of the U.S. republic is that we have "[a] government of laws, not of men."[53] Lawmakers may intend what they will, but the only laws that bind people are those adopted by a majority of both houses of Congress and approved by the president. Scalia contends that for judges to give effect to what legislators *meant*, instead of what they actually enacted, violates democratic theory. "It is our task . . . not to enter the minds of members of Congress—who need have nothing in mind in order for their votes to be both lawful and effective—but rather to give fair and reasonable meaning to the text of the United States Code, adopted by various Congresses at various times."[54] If this understanding of democracy sounds formalistic, writes Scalia, so be it: "Long live formalism."[55]

In *A Matter of Interpretation*, Justice Scalia also argues that there are several practical problems with using legislative intent as a substitute for the language of the law. First, it is next to impossible to find *the* sole intent of a law. Revealing an unflattering view of the legislative process, Scalia has contended in court opinions that legislators vote on laws for many different reasons, most of which have nothing to do with the intent or purpose of the law:

> In the present case, for example, a particular legislator need not have voted for the Act either because he wanted to foster religion or because he wanted to improve education. He may have thought the bill would provide jobs for his district, or may have wanted to make amends with a faction of his party he had alienated on another vote, or he may have been a close friend of the bill's sponsor, or he may have been repaying a favor he owed the majority leader, or he may have hoped the Governor would appreciate his vote and make a fundraising appearance for him, or he may have been pressured to vote for a bill he disliked by a wealthy contributor or by a flood of constituent mail, or he may have

been seeking favorable publicity, or he may have been reluctant to hurt the feelings of a loyal staff member who worked on the bill, or he may have been settling an old score with a legislator who opposed the bill, or he may have been intoxicated and utterly *un*motivated when the vote was called, or he may have accidentally voted "yes" instead of "no," or, of course, he may have had (and very likely did have) a combination of some of the above and many other motivations. To look for *the sole purpose* of even a single legislator is probably to look for something that does not exist.[56]

A second practical concern cited by Justice Scalia is that the sources relied on to assess legislative intent—such as floor debates, committee testimony, and committee reports—are not reliable indicators of the will of Congress. According to Scalia, most members of Congress are not present during floor debates and are "blissfully unaware" of the substance of committee reports. Moreover, committee reports are often used for strategic purposes; staff members place them in the congressional record in order to influence the judges who read them. As a D.C. Court of Appeals judge, Scalia warned about "routine deference to the detail of committee reports," which he argued was "converting a system of judicial construction into a system of committee-staff prescription."[57] In Scalia's view, the lawmaking power, unlike executive authority, is nondelegable; members of Congress cannot authorize individual committees to make laws, nor can a committee's report be taken as the authoritative view of Congress. In a concurring opinion in the 1989 case *Blanchard v. Bergeron*, Scalia stressed precisely this point:

> That the Court should refer to . . . a document issued by a single committee of a single house as the action *of Congress* displays the level of unreality that our unrestrained use of legislative history has attained. . . . As anyone familiar with modern-day drafting of congressional committee reports is well aware, the references to the cases were inserted, at best by a committee staff member on his or her own initiative, and at worst by a committee staff member at the suggestion of a lawyer-lobbyist; and the purpose of those references was not primarily to inform the members of Congress what a bill meant . . . but rather to influence judicial construction. What a heady feeling it must be for a young staffer, to know that his or her citation of obscure district court cases can transform them into the law of the land, thereafter dutifully to be observed by the Supreme Court itself.[58]

A final practical concern cited by Justice Scalia is that reliance on legislative history allows judges to reach whatever results they want. If the plain language of a statute does not produce a desirable outcome, the results-oriented judge can pore through the legislative history and find something that will. In one case, Scalia cited former D.C. Court of Appeals Judge Harold Leventhal's description of the use of legislative history as "the equivalent of entering a crowded cocktail party and looking over the heads of the guests for one's friends."[59] For Scalia, judges are interpreters of laws, not reconstructors of legislative intent. As a consequence, Scalia has sworn off the use of legislative history, or what he calls the "St. Jude of the hagiology of statutory construction,"[60] as both illegitimate and indeterminate. In the absence of a patent absurdity (i.e., a scrivener's error), Scalia has argued that judges must give effect to the clear language of a statute.[61] "My view on legislative history," Scalia has written, "is, quite simply, that it ought not to be used as an authoritative indication of the meaning of a statute. Ordinarily, this means that it should be consulted *not at all*."[62]

Justice Scalia's textual approach to statutory interpretation can be seen in many of his opinions. In *Chisom v. Roemer* (1991),[63] for example, he dissented from a ruling that the Voting Rights Act's "results" test applies to state judicial elections, on the grounds that judges are not "representatives" under the plain language of the statute. In *United States v. Thompson/Center Arms Co.* (1992),[64] Scalia concurred in a holding that a tax payment for "making" a firearm under the National Firearms Act was not required where the pistol and kit, which allows for conversion of the pistol into a firearm, are packaged as a unit. In *Immigration and Naturalization Service v. Elias-Zacarias* (1992),[65] Scalia held for the Court that a guerilla organization's attempt to coerce a person into performing military service does not necessarily constitute "persecution on account of . . . political opinion" under the Immigration and Nationality Act. In *Babbitt v. Sweet Home Chapter of Communities for a Great Oregon* (1995),[66] Scalia dissented from the majority's deference to the secretary of interior's construction of the Endangered Species Act to define "harm" to include "significant habitat modification or degradation where it actually kills or injures wildlife." And in *Koons Buick Pontiac GMC, Inc. v. Nigh* (2004),[67] Scalia filed a solo dissent to the Court's ruling that the 1995 amendment to the Truth in Lending Act left unaltered the limits prescribed for violations of the act involving loans secured by personal property. In the last-mentioned case, Scalia criticized the majority for placing reliance upon legislative history, which he said "lends itself to ventriloquism," because "[t]he Congressional Record or committee reports are used to make words appear to come from Congress's mouth which were spoken or written by others (individual members of Congress, congressional aides, or even enterprising lobbyists)."[68] While he acknowledged that the Court's conclusion in the case might be desirable, Scalia said that "[i]t is beyond our province to rescue Congress from its drafting errors, and to provide what we might think is the preferred result."[69]

## Purposeful Statutory Interpretation and Gender-Based Affirmative Action

Consistent with his criticism of judicial reliance on legislative intent as an aid to interpreting statutes, Justice Scalia has strenuously objected to judicial attempts to effectuate the purpose or spirit of a statute. On this view, rather than attempting to discern the intention of the legislators who passed the law, the interpreter should choose the interpretation that best carries out the statute's purpose. The purposeful method of statutory interpretation gained popularity in the 1950s when Legal Process theorists defended an intelligible or reasonable reading of statutes.[70] One case illustration of a purposeful interpretation of the law came in the Supreme Court decision *Church of Holy Trinity v. United States*.[71] In that case, a church contracted with a British citizen to move to the United States and become its rector and pastor. However, an 1885 federal law made it unlawful for "any corporation . . . to . . . in any way assist or encourage the importation or migration of any alien . . . into the United States." A plain reading of this statute would make this employment contract unlawful, but the Court limited its prohibitive effect to manual laborers. In an opinion by Justice David Brewer, the Court reasoned, "It is a familiar rule, that a thing may be within the letter of the statute and yet not within the statute, because not within its spirit, nor within the intention of its makers."[72]

Justice Scalia, who is sometimes mistakenly associated with the Legal Process School,[73] has been a sharp critic of *Church of Holy Trinity* and the purposeful method of statutory interpretation.[74] Rather than trying to discern the purpose or spirit of statutes, Scalia seeks the "plain meaning" of the words. The majority and dissenting opinions in *Johnson v. Transportation Agency, Santa Clara County*,[75] provide a good illustration of the differences between the plain meaning and purposeful approaches to statutory interpretation. In 1978, the Santa Clara County Transportation Agency (Agency) voluntarily adopted an affirmative action plan for hiring and promoting women. Under the plan, the Agency was authorized to consider sex as a "plus" in making promotions to positions within a traditionally segregated job classification in which women had been significantly underrepresented. The plan did not set aside a specific number of positions for women but rather established annual goals as guidelines in making employment decisions. In 1979, a vacancy for the job of road dispatcher was announced. Of the 238 positions in the skilled-craft category, which included the dispatcher position, none had ever been held by a woman. Nine qualified applicants for the position were interviewed, including Paul E. Johnson, a male employee, and Diane Joyce, a female employee. Both of these candidates were deemed "well qualified" for the road dispatcher position, but Joyce ultimately received it. The director of the agency, James Graebner, explained his decision as follows: "I tried to look at the whole picture, the combination of her qualifications and Mr. Johnson's qualifications, their test scores, their expertise, their background, affirmative action matters, things like that. . . . I believe it was a combination of all those."[76] Johnson filed a reverse discrimination suit claiming that the Agency's plan violated Title VII of the Civil Rights Act of 1964, which makes it unlawful for any employer "to refuse to hire . . . any individual . . . because of such individual's . . . sex."

The Supreme Court held that the affirmative action plan did not violate Title VII of the Civil Rights Act. For the majority, Justice William Brennan relied upon the 1979 decision *United Steelworkers of America v. Weber*,[77] an opinion he also wrote, where the Court held that Title VII did not prohibit private, voluntary race-conscious affirmative action programs where they are necessary to "eliminate manifest racial imbalances in traditionally segregated job categories." In *Weber*, the Court rejected a literal reading of Title VII and cited the aforementioned language from *Holy Trinity*: "It is a familiar rule, that a thing may be within the letter of the statute and yet not within the statute, because not within its spirit, nor within the intention of its makers."[78] Brennan buttressed his purposive reading of Title VII by noting that Congress had not amended the civil rights statute to reject the *Weber* Court's construction of it, nor had any such amendment ever been proposed to do so.[79] Following the reasoning of *Weber*, Brennan held that the Santa Clara Transportation Agency plan was attempting to remedy an imbalance between the percentage of women working in the area's labor market (36.4 percent) and the percentage of women working at the agency itself (22.4 percent), and that "women were most egregiously underrepresented in the Skilled Craft job category, since *none* of the 238 skilled craft positions was occupied by a woman."[80]

Justice Scalia filed a heated dissent, contending that the Agency's affirmative action plan violated the plain language of Title VII. Scalia also claimed that *Weber* rewrote Title VII by relying upon its spirit rather than its plain words, and he regarded it as a "canard" to say that Congress has acquiesced in *Weber*'s interpretation of Title VII by not enacting legislation disapproving of that decision. Rather than demonstrating congressional approval of the Court's interpretation of Title VII, Scalia contended that there are plenty of other reasons for congressional inaction, including (1) "inability to agree upon how to alter the status quo," (2) "unawareness of the status quo," (3) "indifference to the status quo," or (4) "political cowardice." On this basis, he concluded that "*Weber* should be overruled."

In sum, Justice Scalia's textualist approach in statutory cases has sparked what one commentator has referred to as "a jurisprudence of lexicography."[81] If the words of the statute are "plain" or "clear," Scalia will follow their obvious meaning. If words are unclear or lead to absurd results, he consults the entire statute, other statutes using the same words,[82] or a dictionary.[83] Scalia is the Court's most forceful critic of the two major alternative approaches to statutory interpretation: judicial reliance on legislative history and judicial attempts to effectuate the purpose or spirit of statutes. Scalia's textualist approach in statutory cases has had some influence on his colleagues. Justice Clarence Thomas and, to a lesser degree, Justice Anthony Kennedy have relied upon plain meaning approaches in statutory cases, and there is some evidence that Scalia's harsh and uncompromising criticism of legislative history has led all of his colleagues to cite these sources less often in their opinions.[84] But Scalia has been fighting an uphill battle. While his major point—that is, words do matter in construing statutes—is uniformly accepted by his colleagues, almost all modern-day federal judges do not agree with his extreme position that legislative history should not be consulted at all, and many have been willing to use legislative history to carry out the intent or purpose of a law, even when such an interpretation arguably conflicts with the plain meaning of the statute's words.[85] While Scalia does not have wide support by contemporary judges for his textualist method of construing statutes, his emphasis on the plain meaning of statutes does have support in the writings of Alexander Hamilton[86] and in early Supreme Court opinions.[87]

## Constitutional Interpretation

Justice Scalia defends a similar textualist approach to interpreting the Constitution: original meaning. This mode of interpretation places great weight on the words and historical meaning of constitutional provisions. Unlike in statutory cases, where Scalia rejects placing any reliance on legislative history in gleaning the meaning of statutes, he is willing to consult the debating history of the Constitution in construing ambiguous constitutional provisions. Scalia defends this seeming inconsistency by claiming that while he consults the framers' intent in constitutional cases, he does so not to glean the subjective intentions of individual framers, but rather to understand how the text of the Constitution was originally understood.[88] While this might not be a satisfactory explanation for Scalia's starkly different approaches to drafters' intent in statutory and constitutional cases,[89] the important thing for our purposes is that in interpreting the Constitution, as in interpreting statutes, Scalia puts a premium on the plain meaning of the words used. For example, while Scalia regards tradition as critically important in interpreting the Constitution, he has explained that the role of tradition supplies "content only to *ambiguous* constitutional text," because "no tradition can supersede the Constitution."[90] Even though Scalia has not always been consistent in the application of his textualist approach in constitutional cases, his textualist methodology has seen him reach results that run against his personal preferences.

## Case Illustrations

Justice Scalia's focus on constitutional language gives his jurisprudence a literalist quality reminiscent of Justice Hugo Black's. In *Coy v. Iowa*,[91] Scalia wrote the majority opinion striking down a state law allowing for screens to be placed in the courtroom between the accused and child victims of sexual abuse, on the grounds that the Sixth Amendment's Confrontation Clause requires face-to-face confrontation between the accuser and the defendant. Tracing the lineage of the Confrontation Clause back to Roman law, Scalia argued that the purpose of face-to-face encounters is that they limit the ability of accusers to lie. As he put it, "It is always more difficult to tell a lie about a person 'to his face' than 'behind his back.'" To support this "irreducible literal meaning" of the Confrontation Clause, Scalia dissected the Latin meaning of "confront," which "ultimately derives from the prefix 'con-' (from 'contra' meaning 'against' or 'opposed') and the noun 'frons' (forehead)." Similarly, under the Fourth Amendment, Scalia has defended a literal definition of what constitutes a "search." The Fourth Amendment requires police officers to have "probable cause" before they can conduct warrantless searches. In *Arizona v. Hicks*,[92] police officers, who were investigating a shooting incident in which a person was injured, arrived at Hicks's apartment and found incriminating evidence in plain view, including a sawed-off shotgun and a ski mask. They also noticed expensive stereo equipment in the otherwise "squalid" apartment, which they regarded as "suspicious." By lifting several components of the stereo system, the officers were able to read off the serial numbers and determine that the equipment was stolen. Hicks claimed that the stereo equipment must be excluded from trial because there was no probable cause to inspect it to see if it was stolen. Justice Scalia, for the majority, agreed with Hicks and held that even a "cursory inspection" of stereo equipment constitutes a search for which probable cause is required. "It matters not that the search uncovered nothing of any great personal value to respondent—serial numbers rather than (what might conceivably have been hidden or under the equipment) letters or photographs. A search is a search, even if it happens to disclose nothing but the bottom of a turntable."

Justice Scalia usually does not take such a technical or definitional approach to constitutional language, however, and has criticized strict constructionist interpretations of the Constitution. For example, Scalia believes that the Free Speech and Free Press Clauses of the First Amendment protect forms of communication other than simply the spoken or written word. On this basis, Scalia has ruled that flag burning is a protected form of expression under the First Amendment,[93] and that cross burnings are protected political speech, if done without the intention to intimidate.[94] He has also ruled that floating buffer zones outside of health facilities violate the free speech rights of abortion protesters.[95] In order to have some First Amendment protection, however, the "speech" in question must have communicative value. Scalia, for example, has refused to extend First Amendment protection to nude dancing or sleeping demonstrations by the homeless.[96]

The importance Justice Scalia places on constitutional language has seen him defend other rights as well—albeit not consistently. Consonant with his decision in *Arizona v. Hicks*, Scalia has held that suspicionless searches of customs agents violate the probable cause requirement of the Fourth Amendment.[97] On the other hand, Scalia has declined to reexamine the Court's stop-and-frisk exception to the Fourth Amendment,[98] which more than any other Fourth Amendment exception has gutted the literal requirement that police have "probable cause" before they can conduct warrantless searches and seizures. He has also voted (arguably against the plain meaning of the Fourth Amendment) to extend the Court's lenient "reasonableness" test in the area of administrative searches.[99] Scalia has been an occasional ally of the rights of the accused under the Fifth Amendment's Double Jeopardy Clause, believing that the provision embodies "technical, prophylactic rules that require the government to turn square corners,"[100] and has been the Court's most strenuous defender of property rights under the Takings Clause.[101] Scalia has been particularly sensitive to encroachments upon the right to a jury trial in criminal cases under the Sixth Amendment,[102] as well as in civil cases under the Seventh Amendment.[103] In opposition to the plain language and original meaning of the Tenth Amendment, Scalia has authored an opinion extending the Court's novel "anticommandeer" principle as a limit on Congress's authority to regulate commerce.[104] After some initial hemming and hawing, Scalia has also rejected a plain reading of the Eleventh Amendment and has written or joined decisions that place substantial limits on Congress's ability to abrogate state sovereign immunity under the Commerce Clause and the Fourteenth Amendment.[105] Surprisingly, under the Fourteenth Amendment's Privileges or Immunities Clause, Scalia voted to strike down California's durational residency law for welfare benefits, which limited new residents' welfare benefits for the first year to the amount receivable in the person's state of former residence.[106] Finally, Scalia has strictly enforced the Suspension Clause of the habeas corpus provision of Article I, Section 9 of the Constitution.[107]

Justice Scalia supplies meaning to constitutional language by examining what the framers understood by a given provision. This is not an easy task, he admits, and is "sometimes better suited to the historian than the lawyer." Scalia describes the task of the originalist judge as something akin to learning a foreign language. It requires "immersing oneself in the political and intellectual atmosphere of the time—somehow placing out of mind knowledge that we have which an earlier age did not, and putting on beliefs, attitudes, philosophies, prejudices and loyalties that are not those of our day."[108] Scalia insists, however, that originalism is not the "narrow and hidebound" science it is sometimes caricatured as.[109] Originalism, in his view, is not mechanical (or slot-machine) jurisprudence, and it often requires judges to exercise judgment. Scalia also acknowledges that two originalists looking at the same historical evidence can come to different conclusions. A good illustration of this came in the 1995 case *McIntyre v. Ohio Elections Commission*,[110] where the issue before the Court was whether a state could prohibit the distribution of anonymous campaign literature without violating the Free Speech Clause of the First Amendment. The Court's two originalists—Scalia and Justice Thomas—wrote long and extensively researched opinions examining the historical record but ultimately arrived at different results. Based on his original understanding of the First Amendment, Justice Thomas concurred with the majority's ruling that laws prohibiting anonymous campaign literature violate free speech rights. Meanwhile, Justice Scalia argued in dissent that anonymous leafleting is not a core value of the Free Speech Clause and has traditionally been prohibited by the states.

What does the originalist judge do when both constitutional language and original meaning are uncertain on a particular legal issue? There are some technological advances, for example, that the framers could not have anticipated, such as those used by police to combat crime. In *Kyllo v. United States* (2001),[111] the Supreme Court was faced with the question of whether the use of thermal-imaging devices to detect relative amounts of heat from inside the home constitutes a search under the Fourth Amendment. The Court, with Justice Scalia authoring the opinion, ruled that they do. Taking "the long view, from the original meaning of the Fourth Amendment forward," Scalia held that a bright line must be established to protect homeowners' privacy—which he claimed was the core purpose of the Fourth Amendment—from technological advances that with increasing sophistication can penetrate into the privacy of the home. "Where, as here, the Government uses a device that is not in general public use, to explore details of the home that would previously have been unknowable without physical intrusion, the surveillance is a 'search' and is presumptively unreasonable without a warrant."[112]

More typically, when constitutional language and original meaning are not determinative on a particular constitutional question, Scalia looks to American tradition for guidance, which he gleans primarily from common law decisions and state legislative practices. In a dissenting opinion filed in the 1990 decision *Rutan v. Republican Party of Illinois*, a case in which the Court extended First Amendment protection to prohibit hiring decisions based on political patronage, Scalia explained the importance of tradition in interpreting the Constitution:

> The provisions of the Bill of Rights were designed to restrain transient majorities from impairing long-recognized personal liberties. They did not create by implication novel individual rights overturning accepted political norms. Thus, when a practice not expressly prohibited by the text of the Bill of Rights bears the endorsement of a long tradition of open, widespread, and unchallenged use that dates back to the beginning of the Republic, we have no proper basis for striking it down. Such a venerable and accepted tradition is not to be laid on the examining table and scrutinized for its conformity to some abstract principle of First Amendment adjudication devised by this Court. To the contrary, such traditions are themselves the stuff out of which the Court's principles are to be formed.[113]

Sometimes an American tradition will favor the right in question, but that is the rare exception. For example, Scalia dissented from a decision in which the Court held that suspects could be detained without a warrant for up to forty-eight hours without a probable cause determination of whether their arrest was lawful. Scalia argued in dissent that under the common law, suspects could not be held for more than twenty-four hours without a probable cause hearing.[114] More frequently, Scalia finds that American tradition does not support the right at hand, and has been sharply critical of his colleagues for "inventing" rights through abstract legal tests that erode traditional values and practices. In Court opinions, Scalia despairs about "elite" judges drawn from a "law-profession culture" who support the liberal agenda of secular humanism, abortion rights, affirmative action, opposition to the death penalty, and homosexual rights, and are willing to impose those values on the majority. "[W]hen judges test their individual notions of 'fairness' against an American tradition that is deep and broad and continuing," Scalia has written, "it is not the tradition that is on trial, but the judges."[115] On the issue of capital punishment, for example, Scalia has suggested that judges who cannot bring themselves to impose death sentences, which he claims are clearly contemplated by the words of the Constitution, ought to resign from the bench.[116] Based on Scalia's reading of constitutional text and tradition, he has held that libel and obscenity are not protected under the First Amendment; that the Free Speech Clause does not trump the historical practice of political patronage;[117] that various forms of religious accommodation are permissible under the Establishment Clause; that the ceremonial use of peyote by Native Americans is not permitted under the Free Exercise Clause;[118] that the Fifth Amendment does not require *Miranda* warnings;[119] that the Eighth Amendment does not prohibit death sentences for the mentally retarded[120] or minors;[121] that laws prohibiting abortion,[122] the withdrawal of life support,[123] physician-assisted suicide,[124] or the right of sexual preference[125] do not offend the Due Process Clause; and that same-sex military academies[126] and discrimination against homosexuals[127] do not violate the Equal Protection Clause.

## Religion

A closer examination of the Court's Establishment Clause jurisprudence illustrates Scalia's concerns about judicially "invented" legal principles eroding American moral traditions, and also serves to demonstrate another important area of agreement between Hamilton and Scalia. The First Amendment prohibits any law "respecting an establishment of religion." In deciding whether government conduct violates this constitutional command, the Court uses (albeit not consistently) a three-part test derived from the 1971 case *Lemon v. Kurtzman*.[128] In order to survive constitutional scrutiny under the *Lemon* test, the government conduct in question (1) must have a secular purpose, (2) must have a principal or primary effect that neither advances nor inhibits religion, and (3) must not foster an excessive government entanglement with religion. If a law violates any one of these three prongs, it must be struck down. Justice Scalia has been a sharp critic of the *Lemon* test. In one case in which he filed a dissent from a denial of certiorari, Scalia contended that the Court should have granted review "if only to take the opportunity to inter the *Lemon* test once for all."[129] In another case, Scalia memorably described the *Lemon* test as "some ghoul in a late-night horror movie that repeatedly sits up in its grave and shuffles abroad, after being repeatedly killed and buried."[130] In cases in which he has grudgingly applied the *Lemon* test, Scalia has done his best to limit it.[131] As Scalia sees it, the *Lemon* test, as well as other tests the Court sometimes uses to decide church-state issues, are judicial glosses on the Establishment Clause, which he believes are hostile to traditional religious practices in the United States. The "foremost principle" that Scalia applies to the Establishment Clause is "fidelity to the longstanding traditions of our people."[132]

The *Lemon* test is symptomatic of what Justice Scalia perceives to be government hostility toward religion. In *Board of Education of Kiryas Joel Village v. Grumet*, Scalia described a concurring opinion by his colleague John Paul Stevens as "less a legal analysis than a manifesto of secularism. It surpasses mere rejection of accommodation, and announces a positive hostility to religion—which, unlike all other noncriminal values, the state must not assist parents in transmitting to their offspring."[133] In 1996 remarks at the First Baptist Church in Jackson, Mississippi, Scalia criticized the modern secular ideology that regards Christians as "simple-minded" and casts doubt on the possibility of miracles. "We are fools for Christ's sake," Scalia told the audience, and "[w]e must pray for the courage to endure the scorn of the sophisticated world." Scalia sharply criticized secularists—"the worldly wise," he called them—for disparaging those who believe in miracles or the resurrection of the dead. "It is really quite absurd," Scalia observed, that "everything from the Easter morning to the Ascension had to be made up by the groveling enthusiasts as part of their plan to get themselves martyred."[134]

In contrast to Establishment Clause tests like *Lemon*, Scalia has defended an accommodationist approach to the Establishment Clause. On this view, government can support religion as long as it does not prefer one religion to another. "Religion," in Scalia's view, is not "some purely personal avocation that can be indulged entirely in secret, like pornography, in the privacy of one's room."[135] Like other conservatives, including Hamilton, Scalia believes that religion plays a crucial role in supporting republican government. On this basis, in Court opinions and extrajudicial comments, Scalia has supported school vouchers;[136] equal access to school facilities and student-activity fees by religious groups;[137] clergy-read prayers at public graduation ceremonies;[138] student-led prayers at football games;[139] the Pledge of Allegiance in public schools;[140] the teaching of creation science on an equal footing with evolution theory;[141] and religious displays on government property,[142] including the Ten Commandments.[143]

Justice Scalia's dissenting opinion in *Lee v. Weisman*[144] showcases his accommodationist approach toward religion, as well as his belief that elite secularism is the main culprit to religious toleration in the United States. In that case, the Court had before it the constitutionality of clergy-led prayers at graduation ceremonies. In Providence, Rhode Island, principals had the authority to invite members of the clergy to give invocations and benedictions at middle and high school graduations. Four days before the June 1989 graduation exercise, Daniel Weisman, whose daughter attended the middle school, requested that a prayer not be given at his daughter's graduation. Principal Robert E. Lee declined Weisman's request. Weisman then filed suit against Lee and the school district, claiming that state-sponsored religious ceremonies conflicted with the Establishment Clause. Applying the Court's *Lemon* test, the First Circuit Court of Appeals ruled against the school district.

On appeal, the Supreme Court was closely divided. After the justices met in conference to discuss the case, they tentatively voted to reverse the lower court. After writing a first draft of the Court's opinion, however, Justice

Anthony Kennedy circulated a memo to his colleagues stating that his "draft looked quite wrong," so he rewrote it to rule "in favor of the objecting student."[145] Accordingly, the Court affirmed the lower court, albeit on different grounds. Quoting famous language from the Court's 1962 school prayer case, Kennedy declared that "it is no part of the business of government to compose official prayers for any group of the American people to recite as a part of a religious program carried on by government."[146] Declining to use or reexamine the Court's *Lemon* test, Kennedy instead relied on what is now called the "coercion" test, which prohibits states from placing students in the untenable position of choosing between participating in an exercise with religious content or protesting. While acknowledging that graduation ceremonies are in a formal sense "voluntary," and that students are not required to participate in invocations or benedictions, Kennedy held that the school's sponsorship of the exercises exacted pressure on the students to participate. Emphasizing that the Establishment Clause was ratified to protect individual rights, not majoritarian rights, Kennedy cautioned that "if citizens are subjected to state-sponsored religious exercises, the State disavows its own duty to guard and respect that sphere of inviolable conscience and belief which is the mark of a free people."[147]

In dissent, Scalia blasted the majority's analysis as "psychology practiced by amateurs," and referred to the coercion test as "the bulldozer of [the Court's] social engineering" that will have a devastating impact on religious practices in the United States. Examining the Establishment Clause from the perspective of an originalist, Scalia noted that since July 1868, when the nation's first public high school graduation is believed to have taken place, prayers have been part of graduation ceremonies. And since the time of the republic's founding, nonsectarian prayers have been given at public celebrations and included in official proclamations. Scalia accused the majority of overlooking this long and continuous history of religious accommodation and of inventing a novel test for the Establishment Clause that is not rooted in its original meaning.[148] But even if he were forced to apply the Court's coercion test (no pun intended), Scalia said he would still side with the school district. Scalia ridiculed the majority's psychological evidence showing that state officials "coerced" students into taking part in graduation prayers. According to Scalia, the middle school students were not coerced into participating in the invocation and benediction, but rather had several options: they could stand and participate in the religious exercises, they could stand in respectful silence of others who wanted to participate in the exercises, or they could express their dissent by remaining seated during the exercises. The assertion that students were being forced into participating in the invocation and benediction, Scalia maintained, "is nothing short of ludicrous." But, he continued, even if it could be assumed that someone would feel coerced into participating in these exercises, maintaining respect for another's religion is part of the civic responsibility of every individual:

> I may add, moreover, that maintaining respect for the religious observances of others is a fundamental civic virtue that government (including the public schools) can and should cultivate—so that even if it were the case that the displaying of such respect might be mistaken for taking part in prayer, I would deny that the dissenter's interest in avoiding *even the false appearance of participation* constitutionally trumps the government's interest in fostering respect for religion generally.[149]

Framing the culture war over religion as a conflict between "elite" secular judges and the religious values and practices of a majority of the people, Scalia stated, "Today's opinion shows more forcefully than volumes of argumentation why our Nation's protection, that fortress which is our Constitution, cannot possibly rest upon the changeable philosophical predilections of the Justices of this Court, but must have deep foundations in the historic practices of our people."[150]

One founder who supported Justice Scalia's accommodationist approach to the Establishment Clause was Alexander Hamilton. In his draft of Washington's Farewell Address, Hamilton observed,

> To all those dispositions which promote political prosperity, Religion and Morality are essential props. In vain does that man claim the praise of patriotism who labours to subvert or undermine these great pillars of human happiness—these firmest foundations of the duties of men and citizens. . . . Nor ought we to flatter ourselves that morality can be separated from religion. Concede as much as may be asked to the effect of refined education in minds of a peculiar structure—can we believe—can we in prudence suppose that national morality can be maintained in exclusion of religious principles? Does it not require the aid of a generally received and divinely authoritative Religion?[151]

In 1802, after the Jeffersonian Republicans gained full control of the government, and after the tragic death of his eldest son, Philip, in a duel, Hamilton turned to religion. Perplexed by how the American people were enamored with Thomas Jefferson, whom Hamilton regarded as "an *Atheist* in Religion and a *Fanatic in politics*,"[152] Hamilton proposed the creation of a political party called the Christian Constitutional Society, which would attempt to counteract the popularity of the Republican Party by "promot[ing] the election of *fit men*" to public offices. The governing structure for this society would consist of a national council and subnational councils within each of the states, and the two main objects of the society were (1) the support of Christian religion and (2) the support of the Constitution of the United States.[153] Both Scalia and Hamilton believe that religion is an absolutely necessary pillar to republican government. At the conclusion of his *Lee v. Weisman* dissent, Scalia made the following *policy* observation:

> The Founders of our Republic knew the fearsome potential of sectarian religious belief to generate civil dissension and civil strife. And they also knew that nothing, absolutely nothing, is so inclined to foster among religious believers of various faiths a toleration—no, an affection—for one another than voluntarily joining in prayer together, to the God whom they all worship and seek. . . . To deprive our society of that important unifying mechanism, in order to spare the nonbeliever what seems to me the minimal inconvenience of standing or even sitting in respectful nonparticipation, is as senseless in policy as it is unsupported by law.[154]

Scalia's view that state "encouragement" of religion can be an "important unifying mechanism" in a diverse religious society has support in Hamilton's writings. Hamilton, who drafted Washington's Thanksgiving Proclamation sometime before it was issued on January 1, 1795, was questioned by Secretary of State Edmund Randolph about the political ramifications of the president's message, particularly since it came so shortly after the suppression of the Whiskey Rebellion. Hamilton responded to Randolph's inquiry as follows: "A proclamation of a Government which is a national act, naturally embraces objects which are political—This [proclamation] is a mere benevolent sentiment or unifier with public feeling."[155] Because both men believe that religion is an essential ingredient of republican government, Hamilton and Scalia have been willing to take on the "nonbelievers" of their day. Hamilton wrote passionately about the moral decay and threat to republican government posed by the "atheist" ideology of the French philosophes,[156] and in modern times, Scalia is "the gladiator," as Justice Souter so appropriately described him,[157] slaying the philosophy of secular humanism both on and off the Court.

## Natural Rights

Justice Scalia has also been critical of judicial reliance upon natural rights in interpreting the Constitution. In an important speech he gave at the Gregorian University in Rome, Italy, in 1996,[158] Scalia argued that natural rights theories were incompatible with democratic theory, because they allow the government (i.e., judges) to impose them on the majority of the people who might not agree with them. Like Hamilton, Scalia does not deny the existence of natural rights,[159] but he objects to judges imposing their interpretations of those rights on the people. Scalia, for example, has criticized his colleagues for finding fundamental "liberty" rights under the Due Process Clause of the Fourteenth Amendment, such as a woman's right to obtain an abortion, a qualified right to die, and a right of sexual preference. Scalia claims that these unenumerated rights are inconsistent with the traditional understanding of due process, which only requires that certain procedural protections be provided when someone has been incarcerated, such as notice of the charges and a right to be heard. The bottom line for Scalia is that judicially created rights under the Fourteenth Amendment's Due Process Clause violate democratic theory and the will of the majority.

In his Gregorian University speech, as well as in his Court opinions, Scalia has also expressed an unwillingness to rely upon the Declaration of Independence as a guide to interpreting the Constitution. In Scalia's view, the Constitution is a practical legal document, which specifies the rights that judges can and should protect and, by implication, those they should not. By contrast, the Declaration of Independence is an aspirational document that judges should not rely upon in interpreting the Constitution. Scalia's aversion to judges relying upon the Declaration of Independence as a source for interpreting the Constitution was first suggested in his and Justice Thomas's separate concurring opinions in *Adarand Constructors, Inc. v. Pena* (1995).[160] In that case, the Court imposed for the first time its strict scrutiny analysis to a federal affirmative action program. While Justices Thomas and Scalia agreed with that decision, they wrote separate concurrences expressing their views about the particular affirmative action program under review. Thomas, substantiating speculation about his natural law leanings during his Senate confirmation hearings, argued that the federal government's affirmative action program violated the principle of equality embedded in the Declaration of Independence.[161] Meanwhile, Scalia based his opinion solely on the Equal Protection Clause and argued that "the concept of racial entitlement" underlying the federal affirmative action program was incompatible with the Constitution's focus on individual rights.[162]

A more explicit example of Scalia's unwillingness to use the Declaration of Independence as a source of constitutional construction is seen in his dissenting opinion in the 2000 case *Troxel v. Granville*.[163] In that case, the Court had before it a permissive visitation rights law, which allowed "any person" to petition a superior court in the state of Washington for visitation rights "at any time" whenever it is in "the best interest of the child." The mother of two daughters challenged the petition of her deceased husband's parents who wanted visitation with their granddaughters for two weekends of overnight visitation per month and two weeks of visitation each summer. The mother claimed that the state law violated the fundamental right of parents to rear their children as they see fit under the liberty provision of the Fourteenth Amendment's Due Process Clause.

In an opinion by Justice Sandra Day O'Connor (which was joined by Justice Thomas), the Court sided with the mother and struck down the law. According to Justice O'Connor, the application of the state law to the mother and her family "violated the due process right to make decisions concerning the care, custody, and control of her daughters."[164] In dissent, Scalia expressed strong support for the right in question, but argued that the Court had no business finding such a right under the Due Process Clause. As Scalia explained, "[A] right of parents to direct the upbringing of their children is among the 'unalienable Rights' with which the Declaration of Independence proclaims 'all Men . . . are endowed by their Creator,'" and is "among the 'other [rights] retained by the people' which the Ninth Amendment says the Constitution's enumeration of rights 'shall not be construed to deny or disparage.'" But he concluded that judges could not rely upon the Declaration of Independence as a source of constitutional interpretation, because it "is not a legal prescription conferring powers upon the courts." He also reasoned that "the Constitution's refusal to 'deny or disparage' other rights" under the Ninth Amendment "is far removed from affirming any one of them, and even farther removed from authorizing judges to identify what they might be, and to enforce the judges' list against laws duly enacted by the people."[165]

## International Law

Similarly, Justice Scalia has been a sharp critic of judicial reliance on international law in interpreting constitutional provisions. In a 2005 debate with Justice Stephen Breyer, Scalia questioned the relevance of international law as a basis for understanding the U.S. Constitution.[166] Sympathetic to the notion of American exceptionalism, Scalia argued that "[the United States does not] have the same moral and legal framework as the rest of the world, and never had." The framers, Scalia maintained, looked unfavorably upon foreign law and practices as they wrote the Constitution. For Scalia, America is a special and unique society, which is reflected in the fact that there is no similar concept in the world to what is called "un-American." In his debate with Justice Breyer, Scalia also questioned the selective use of international law in judicial opinions, believing that the use of these sources lends itself to manipulation. He contended, for example, that the United States is the only country in the world with the exclusionary rule, and one of only six countries that allows for abortion upon demand prior to viability. Why don't federal judges rely upon international law in those constitutional areas, Scalia wondered? In the Court's 2005 decision prohibiting capital punishment for minors, Scalia filed a blistering dissent in which he accused the majority of selectively using international law in constitutional cases:

> The Court should either profess its willingness to reconsider all these matters [e.g., the exclusionary rule and abortion] in light of the views of foreigners, or else it should cease putting forth foreigners' views as part of the *reasoned basis* of its decision. To invoke alien law when it agrees with one's thinking, and ignore it otherwise, is not reasoned decisionmaking, but sophistry.[167]

In sum, with the exception of constitutional provisions explicitly protecting individual rights, Scalia believes it is the fundamental premise of a democracy that the majority rules and can adopt whatever laws it wants. On this basis, and drawing the ire of natural law conservatives,[168] Scalia says that if the majority wants to legalize abortion, physician-assisted suicide, or homosexual rights, it has the right to do so. Reminiscent of a famous remark by William F. Buckley Jr.,[169] the conservative founder of the *National Review*, Scalia wrote in a case involving constitutional standards for the withdrawal of life support, "[T]he point at which life becomes 'worthless,' and the point at which the means necessary to preserve it become 'extraordinary' or 'inappropriate,' are neither set forth in the Constitution nor known to the nine Justices of this Court any better than they are known to nine people picked at random from the Kansas City telephone directory."[170]

## Living versus Dead (or Enduring) Constitution

Like Hamilton, Justice Scalia believes that in order for the federal government to have the capacity to adjust to new circumstances, its powers must be interpreted expansively rather than narrowly. In *A Matter of Interpretation*, Scalia distinguished his version of textualism from "so-called strict constructionism," which he said is "a degraded form of textualism that brings the whole philosophy into disrepute":

> I am not a strict constructionist, and no one ought to be—though better that, I suppose, than a nontextualist. A text should not be construed strictly, and it should not be construed leniently; it should be construed reasonably, to contain all that it fairly means. . . . In textual interpretation, context is everything, and the context of the Constitution tells us not to expect nit-picking detail, and to give words and phrases an expansive rather than narrow interpretation—though not an interpretation that the language will not bear.[171]

At the same time, Scalia is not a proponent of the living Constitution philosophy. While constitutional language should be given an expansive interpretation, Scalia believes that words have a "fixed" or a "limited range of meaning" that does not change over time. "[T]he good textualist," Scalia has written, "is not a literalist," but "neither is he a nihilist."[172] In extrajudicial writings and at various forums, Scalia has argued that the living Constitution philosophy suffers from two fatal defects.[173] First, it is inconsistent with democratic theory. As Scalia sees it, it is not the responsibility of judges to keep the Constitution up with the times. In fact, he believes that judges are especially ill equipped to do this since they are not supposed to base their decisions on public opinion. According to Scalia, "[A] constitution whose meaning changes as our notions of what it *ought* to mean changes is not worth a whole lot. To keep government up-to-date with modern notions of what good government ought to be, we do not need a constitution but only a ballot-box and a legislature."[174] Scalia believes that the Constitution is at bottom a majoritarian compact. It protects some rights, but not all rights. If the people want to secure additional rights, they can pass laws to that effect. As he explained during his confirmation hearings,

> [A] constitution has to have ultimately majoritarian underpinnings. To be sure a constitution is a document that protects against future democratic excesses. But when it is adopted, it is adopted by democratic process. That is what legitimates it.
>
> [I]f the majority that adopted it did not believe this unspecified right, which is not reflected clearly in the language, if their laws at the time do not reflect that that right existed, nor do the laws at the present date reflect that the society believes that right exists, I worry about my deciding that it exists. I worry that I am not reflecting the most fundamental, deeply felt beliefs of our society, which is what a constitution means, but rather, I am reflecting the most deeply felt beliefs of Scalia, which is not what I want to impose on society.[175]

The second major defect of a living Constitution philosophy, according to Scalia, is that it can result in the loss of rights. Many of the proponents of a living Constitution defend it on the ground that it will lead to an expansion of individual rights, but Scalia disputes this. As a historical matter, Scalia contends that nonoriginalist arguments have led to a diminution of some rights. For example, Scalia cites the Contracts Clause where the Court in *Home Building & Loan Association v. Blaisdell*[176] rejected an originalist interpretation of Article I, Section 10 in upholding Minnesota's law allowing for a temporary moratorium on the payment of mortgages during the Great Depression.[177] Similarly, in his dissenting opinion in *Maryland v. Craig*,[178] Scalia claimed that the majority neglected the original meaning of the Confrontation

Clause and instead paid attention to modern psychological evidence about the emotional trauma experienced by children who confront their alleged assailants in court.

While recognizing that originalism is not without its own warts—including the difficulty of accurately plumbing the historical record, and in some instances being "medicine too strong to swallow"[179]—Scalia contends that it is the lesser of two evils. In his view, theories of constitutional interpretation that attempt to keep the Constitution current with the times do not contain a limiting principle on the willful judge. "Are the 'fundamental values' that replace original meaning," Scalia asks, "to be derived from the philosophy of Plato, or of Locke, or Mills, or Rawls, or perhaps the latest Gallup poll?" At least with originalism, Scalia believes there is an agreed-upon point of departure. Like members of Congress and the president, Scalia contends that judges must be held accountable to the law, or as Hamilton put it, "bound down by rules." While he admires a jurist like Justice Felix Frankfurter for his sense of self-restraint and humility, Scalia does not think it is sufficient to place the responsibility of judicial restraint on the individual judge. Like Justice Hugo Black, Scalia believes that judges cannot always be counted on to exercise self-restraint. Even though Scalia admits that originalism does not completely curb judicial discretion, he does believe it limits it. As he put it, "Originalism does not aggravate the principal weakness of the system, for it establishes a historical criterion that is conceptually quite separate from the preferences of the judge himself."[180] Revealing his own conservative orientation toward the law, Scalia has argued that the philosophy of a living Constitution is antithetical to the whole idea of a written constitution, which he believes is antiprogressive in purpose. As he explains, "It certainly cannot be said that a constitution naturally suggests changeability; to the contrary, its whole purpose is to prevent change—to embed certain rights in such manner that future generations cannot readily take them away. A society that adopts a bill of rights is skeptical that 'evolving standards of decency' always 'mark progress,' and that societies always 'mature,' as opposed to rot."[181] For Scalia, a constitution is an anchor; it contains certain fixed principles that should not be changed without careful consideration by the people. The role of the judge, in his view, is to preserve (not update) the *original* values of the founding generation:

> The purpose of constitutional guarantees—and in particular those constitutional guarantees of individual rights that are at the center of this controversy—is precisely to prevent the law from reflecting certain *changes* in original values that the society adopting the Constitution thinks fundamentally undesirable. Or, more precisely, to require the society to devote to the subject the long and hard consideration required for a constitutional amendment before those particular values can be cast aside.[182]

# CONCLUSION

Hamilton and Scalia support a similar textualist approach to interpreting laws. For both men, the cardinal principle in legal interpretation is the "natural and obvious" sense of a provision. One of the professed merits of such an interpretative philosophy is that it allows judges to enforce the letter of the law, while at the same time limiting their ability to reach desirable results in particular cases. Both Hamilton and Scalia support positivistic conceptions of the law, pursuant to which judges perform an important *moral* function. By giving primacy to the plain meaning of a law's words, judges teach people to respect the law. In a democratic system of government, Hamilton and Scalia emphasize that the makers of the law are the people. If the people want to change the law, they have the capacity to do so; judges, in their view, are not supposed to exercise this authority. For the positivist, laws that change through creative forms of judicial interpretation subvert the democratic process and result in a loss of respect for the laws. Scalia's strict textualism in statutory cases can be seen as a deliberate and self-conscious way to eliminate the element of discretion from the judicial role. And his backward-looking methodology of interpreting the Constitution—originalism—which is not supportive of modern claims of constitutional rights, is designed to return the federal courts to their traditional role of protecting constitutionally prescribed minority rights.

# NOTES

1. FP, 437.
2. FP (No. 78), 437 (quoting *The Spirit of the Laws*).
3. Ibid., 442.
4. Ibid., 463.
5. *Texas v. Johnson*, 491 U.S. 397 (1989); *United States v. Eichman*, 496 U.S. 310 (1990).
6. *BMW of North America, Inc. v. Gore*, 517 U.S. 559 (1996) (Scalia, J., dissenting).
7. See, e.g., *Minnesota v. Dickerson*, 508 U.S. 366 (1993) (Scalia, J., concurring) (accepting "reasonable suspicion" as the constitutional standard for conducting stop and frisks under the Fourth Amendment); *Printz v. United States*, 521 U.S. 898 (1997) (striking down the temporary provisions of the Brady Handgun Violence Prevention Act of 1993 as violative of constitutional principles of federalism); and *Pennsylvania v. Union Gas Co.*, 491 U.S. 1, 29 (1989) (Scalia, J., concurring) (rejecting a plain reading of the Eleventh Amendment).
8. See Hamilton's legal briefs filed in *Rutgers v. Waddington* (1784), where he argued that New York's Trespass Act of 1783 violated common law principles and the Treaty of Paris. LPAH, 1:338–92.
9. 5 U.S. (1 Cranch) 137 (1803).

10. FP (No. 22), 184.

11. FP (No. 78), 438.

12. According to this theory, each department of government should decide for itself whether its laws or actions violate the Constitution.

13. FP, 439.

14. Ibid., 440 and 442.

15. In his *Commentaries on the Laws of England*, Blackstone noted that the first rule of interpreting the will of the legislator is the words themselves, as "understood in their usual and best known signification; not so much regarding the propriety of grammar, as their general and popular use." *Blackstone's Commentaries*, 1:59. Similarly, Joseph Story, in his *Commentaries on the Constitution of the United States*, provided this rule of construction:

> The Constitution is to be expounded in its plain, obvious, and common sense, unless the context furnishes some ground to control, qualify, or enlarge it. Constitutions are not designed for metaphysical or logical subtleties, for niceties of expression, for critical propriety, for elaborate shades of meaning, or for the exercise of philosophical acuteness, or judicial research. They are instruments of a practical nature, founded on the common business of human life, adopted to common wants, designed for common use, and fitted for common understandings. The people make them, the people adopt them; the people must be supposed to read them, with the help of common sense; and cannot be presumed to admit in them any recondite meaning or any extraordinary gloss. (*Commentaries*, 2:436–37)

16. FP, 462–63.

17. See, e.g., Sotirios A. Barber, *The Constitution of Judicial Power* (Baltimore, MD: Johns Hopkins University Press, 1993), 26–65.

18. PAH, 1:122.

19. Ibid., 86–87.

20. *Fletcher v. Peck*, 10 U.S. (6 Cranch) 87 (1810).

21. PAH, 3:548.

22. The *Rutgers* opinion is not found in any contemporary reporter, but the opinion and briefs filed in the case can be found in LPAH, 1: 317–419.

23. LPAH, 1:391.

24. FP, 450–51.

25. "The Defence No. XXXVIII," PAH, 20:30–31.

26. "Examination No. XII," PAH, 25:530, 533, 534.

27. PAH, 3:487–88, 547, 555.

28. PAH, 20:31–33.

29. See, e.g., Raoul Berger, "'Original Intention' in Historical Perspective," *George Washington Law Review* 54 (1986): 296–337; Lino A. Graglia, "How the Constitution Disappeared," *Commentary* 81 (February 1986): 19–27.

30. "Examination No. 15," PAH, 25:558.

31. PAH, 8:111.

32. LPAH, 1:286 (emphasis added).

33. FP (No. 81), 451.

34. LPAH, 1:200–201, 289–93

35. Ibid., 383, 390.

36. Ibid., 415.

37. *Blackstone's Commentaries*, ed. St. George Tucker (New York: Augustus M. Kelley, 1969), 1:61.

38. Gary L. McDowell, *Equity and the Constitution: The Supreme Court, Equitable Relief, and Public Policy* (Chicago: University of Chicago Press, 1982), 3–47.

39. FP (Nos. 80, 83), 448–49, 469.

40. 3 U.S. (3 Dall.) 386 (1798).

41. FP (No. 44), 287.

42. Ibid.

43. "CASE and ANSWER," by Alexander Hamilton (March 25, 1796), LPAH, 4:431.

44. 17 U.S. (4 Wheat.) 316 (1819).

45. Ibid., 407, 415.

46. In his opinion on the national bank, Hamilton makes this clear: "There will be cases clearly within the power of the National Government; others clearly without its power; and a third class, which will leave room for controversy & difference of opinion, & concerning which a reasonable latitude of judgment must be allowed." PAH, 8:107. Hamilton maintained, for example, that Congress could not establish a corporation "for superintending the police of the city of Philadelphia because they are not authorised to *regulate* the *police* of that city." Ibid., 100 (emphasis in the original).

47. Charles Evans Hughes, *Addresses and Papers of Charles Evans Hughes* (New York: Putnam's Sons, 1908), 139.

48. FP (No. 78), 440.

49. Ibid., 476.

50. *Sturges v. Crowninshield*, 17 U.S. (4 Wheat.) 122, 202 (1819).

51. Antonin Scalia, "Originalism: The Lesser Evil," *University of Cincinnati Law Review* 57 (1989): 863.

52. Antonin Scalia, *A Matter of Interpretation: Federal Courts and the Law*, ed. Amy Gutmann (Princeton, NJ: Princeton University Press, 1997), 13–14.

53. Ibid., 17 (quoting the Massachusetts constitution).

54. *Pennsylvania v. Union Gas Co.*, 491 U.S. 1, 29, 30 (1989) (Scalia, J., concurring in part and dissenting in part).

55. Scalia, *A Matter of Interpretation*, 25.

56. *Edwards v. Aguillard*, 482 U.S. 578, 637 (1987) (Scalia, J., dissenting).

57. *Hirschey v. F.E.R.C.*, 777 F.2d 1, 8 (D.C. Cir. 1985) (Scalia, J., concurring).

58. 489 U.S. 96, 98–99 (1989) (Scalia, J., concurring).

59. *Conroy v. Aniskoff*, 507 U.S. 511, 519 (1993) (Scalia, J., concurring in judgment).

60. *United States v. Thompson/Center Arms Co.*, 504 U.S. 505, 521 (1992) (Scalia, J., concurring in judgment).

61. See, e.g., *Green v. Bock Laundry Machine Co.*, 490 U.S. 504 (1989) (Scalia, J., concurring in judgment); *INS v. Cardoza-Fonseca*, 480 U.S. 421, 452 (1987) (Scalia, J., concurring in judgment).

62. Antonin Scalia, "Use of Legislative History: Judicial Abdication to Fictitious Legislative Intent," unpublished speech delivered to various law schools in 1985–1986 (on file with the author).

63. 501 U.S. 380 (1991) (Scalia, J., dissenting).

64. 504 U.S. 505 (1992) (Scalia, J., concurring).

65. 502 U.S. 478 (1992).

66. 515 U.S. 687, 714 (1995) (Scalia, J., dissenting).

67. 125 S. Ct. 460 (2004) (Scalia, J., dissenting).

68. Ibid., 474.

69. Ibid., 476 (quoting *Lamie v. United States Trustee*, 540 U.S. 526, 542 [2004]).

70. See, e.g., Henry M. Hart Jr. and Albert M. Sacks, *The Legal Process: Basic Problems in the Making and Application of Law*, ed. William N. Eskridge Jr. and Philip P. Frickey (Westbury, NY: Foundation Press, 1994).

71. 143 U.S. 457 (1892).

72. Ibid., 459.

73. See Richard Brisbin, *Justice Antonin Scalia and the Conservative Revival* (Baltimore, MD: Johns Hopkins University Press, 1997), 76–84; and Peter B. Edelman, "Justice Scalia's Jurisprudence and the Good Society: Shades of Felix Frankfurter and the Harvard Hit Parade of the 1950s," *Cardozo Law Review* 12 (1991): 1799–1815.

74. See Scalia, *A Matter of Interpretation*, 14–23.

75. 480 U.S. 616 (1987).

76. Ibid., 625.

77. 443 U.S. 193 (1979).

78. Ibid., 201 (quoting *Church of Holy Trinity*, 143 U.S. at 459).

79. 480 U.S. at 629n7.

80. Ibid., 621, 636.

81. David O. Stewart, "By the Book: Looking up the Law in the Dictionary," *ABA Journal* (July 1993): 47–48.

82. See, e.g., *West Virginia University Hospitals v. Casey*, 499 U.S. 83 (1991).

83. Interestingly, the edition of the dictionary has not always corresponded with the year in which the statute was enacted, leading some scholars to speculate whether the justices are "dictionary shopping" and searching through various editions of dictionaries to find the definition that supports their point of view. Scalia defends this "jurisprudence of lexicography" as more objective than looking at legislative history, while others say it is less reliable and conservative in orientation. See, e.g., William N. Eskridge, Jr., Philip P. Frickey, and Elizabeth Garrett, *Cases and Materials on Legislation: Statutes and the Creation of Public Policy*, 3rd ed. (St. Paul, MN: West Group, 2001), 770–72.

84. Thomas Merrill, "Textualism and the Future of the *Chevron* Doctrine," *Washington University Law Quarterly* 72 (1994): 351, 365.

85. See, e.g., Felix Frankfurter, "Some Reflections on the Reading of Statutes," *Columbia Law Review* 47 (1947): 527–46; Stephen Breyer, "On the Uses of Legislative History in Interpreting Statutes," *Southern California Law Review* 65 (1992): 845–74.

86. Hamilton, as well as many of his contemporaries, rejected the idea that the meaning of laws was to be gleaned from the subjective intentions of their drafters; rather, the "intention" of laws was to be gathered from the actual language of the laws themselves. While Hamilton might not have objected to all modern judicial uses of legislative history—for example, he might have supported attempts by judges to

corroborate the plain meaning of a statute—he would likely agree with Scalia that these sorts of materials should not be used to contradict the actual words of statutes. Scalia's complete rejection of judicial reliance upon a law's spirit does present a conflict with Hamilton's brief in *Rutgers v. Waddington* (1784), where he defended judicial reliance upon the spirit rather than the letter of the law when a particular construction would lead to an unjust result. But Hamilton (following Blackstone) maintained a narrow conception of the equitable power and would not likely support judicial attempts to bring about broad social policy changes, such as affirmative action, through a purposive construction of a statute. This method of statutory interpretation is inconsistent with Hamilton's view of judges as interpreters of law, not policy makers. Scalia's more rigid, literalistic approach to interpreting statutes is likely attributable to his concern about judicial policy making in the modern era.

87. *United States v. Fisher*, 6 U.S. (2 Cranch) 358 (1805) (Marshall, C.J.) ("That these words, taken in their natural and usual sense, would embrace the case before the court, seems not to be controverted. . . . But other parts of the act involve this question in much embarrassment. It is undoubtedly a well established principle in the exposition of statutes, that every part is to be considered, and the intention of the legislature to be extracted from the whole. It is also true, that where great inconvenience will result from a particular construction, that construction is to be avoided, unless the meaning of the legislature be plain; in which case it must be obeyed"); *Aldridge v. Williams*, 44 U.S. (3 How.) 9, 24, (1845) (Taney, C.J.) ("In expounding this law, the judgment of the court cannot, in any degree, be influenced by the construction placed upon it by individual members of Congress in the debate which took place on its passage, nor by the motives or reasons assigned by them for supporting or opposing amendments that were offered. The law as it passed is the will of the majority of both houses, and the only mode in which that will is spoken is in the act itself; and we must gather their intention from the language there used, comparing it, when any ambiguity exists, with the laws upon the same subject, and looking, if necessary, to the public history of the times in which it was passed").

88. See Scalia, *A Matter of Interpretation*, 38.

89. See William N. Eskridge Jr., "Textualism and Original Understanding: Should the Supreme Court Read *The Federalist* But Not Statutory Legislative History?" *George Washington Law Review* 66 (1998): 1301–23.

90. *Rutan v. Republican Party of Illinois*, 497 U.S. 62, 95n1 (1990).

91. 487 U.S. 1012 (1988); see also *Maryland v. Craig*, 497 U.S. 836 (1990) (Scalia, J., dissenting).

92. 480 U.S. 321 (1987).

93. *Texas v. Johnson*, 491 U.S. 397 (1989); *United States v. Eichman*, 496 U.S. 310 (1990).

94. *R.A.V. v. City of St. Paul*, 505 U.S. 377 (1992); *Virginia v. Black*, 538 U.S. 343 (2003) (Scalia, J., concurring in part and dissenting in part).

95. *Hill v. Colorado*, 530 U.S. 703 (2000) (Scalia, J., dissenting).

96. *Barnes v. Glen Theatre*, 501 U.S. 560 (1991); *City of Erie v. Pap's A.M. TDBA "Kandyland,"* 529 U.S. 277 (2000); *Community for Non-Violence v. Watt*, 703 F.2d 586 (D.C. Cir. 1983) (Scalia, J., dissenting).

97. *National Treasury Employees Union v. Von Raab*, 489 U.S. 656 (1989) (Scalia, J., dissenting).

98. *Minnesota v. Dickerson*, 508 U.S. 366 (1993) (Scalia, J., concurring).

99. *Vernonia School Dist. 47J. v. Acton*, 515 U.S. 646 (1995); *Board of Education of Pottawatomie Co. v. Earls*, 536 U.S. 822 (2002); *Ferguson v. City of Charleston*, 532 U.S. 67 (2001) (Scalia, J., dissenting).

100. *Jones v. Thomas*, 491 U.S. 376 (1989) (Scalia, J., dissenting). See also *United States v. Richardson*, 702 F.2d 1079 (1983) (Scalia, J., dissenting). But see *Sattazahn v. Pennsylvania*, 537 U.S. 101 (2003).

101. *Nollan v. California Coastal Commission*, 483 U.S. 825 (1987); *Lucas v. South Carolina Coastal Council*, 505 U.S. 1003 (1992). See also *Dolan v. City of Tigard*, 512 U.S. 374 (1994); *Kelo v. City of New London*, 125 S. Ct. 2655 (2005) (Scalia, J., dissenting).

102. See, e.g., *Apprendi v. New Jersey*, 530 U.S. 466 (2000); *Ring v. Arizona*, 536 U.S. 584 (2002); *Blakely v. Washington*, 542 U.S. 296 (2004); *United States v. Booker*, 125 S. Ct. 738 (2005). In each of these cases, the justices in the majority worried that judges (acting pursuant to state or federal law) were usurping the important role played by juries in the U.S. judicial system.

103. *Gasperini v. Center for Humanities*, 518 U.S. 415 (1996) (Scalia, J., dissenting).

104. *Printz v. United States*, 521 U.S. 898 (1997) (striking down the temporary provisions of the Brady Handgun Violence Prevention Act of 1993 as violative of constitutional principles of federalism).

105. Initially, Justice Scalia had reservations about extending the Eleventh Amendment bar to a state's own citizens. See *Welch v. Texas Department of Highways & Public Transp.*, 483 U.S. 468, 495 (1987) (Scalia, J., concurring). The "plain language" of the Eleventh Amendment prohibits only suits against a state by citizens of another state. But the Court in *Hans v. Louisiana*, 134 U.S. 1 (1890), interpreted the amendment to prohibit suits brought against a state by its own citizens. Scalia has now adopted that interpretation, and in fact wrote the concurring opinion in *Pennsylvania v. Union Gas Co.*, 491 U.S. 1, 29 (1989) (Scalia, J., concurring), relied on by the Court in *Seminole Tribe of Florida v. Florida*, 517 U.S. 44 (1996), which places severe restrictions on Congress's ability to abrogate state sovereign immunity. See also *Alden v. Maine*, 527 U.S. 706 (1999); *Kimel v. Florida Board of Regents*, 528 U.S. 62 (2000); *Board of Trustees of the University of Alabama v. Garrett*, 531 U.S. 356 (2001); *Nevada Dept. of Human Resources v. Hibbs*, 538 U.S. 721 (2003) (Scalia, J., dissenting); and *Tennessee v. Lane*, 124 S. Ct. 1978 (2004) (Scalia, J., dissenting).

106. *Saenz v. Roe*, 526 U.S. 489 (1999).

107. *Hamdi v. Rumsfeld*, 124 S. Ct. 2633 (2004) (Scalia, J., dissenting).

108. Scalia, "Originalism: The Lesser Evil," 856–57.

109. Scalia, *A Matter of Interpretation*, 140.

110. 514 U.S. 334 (1995).

111. 533 U.S. 27 (2001).

112. Ibid., 40.

113. 497 U.S. 62, 95–96 (1990) (Scalia, J., dissenting).

114. *County of Riverside v. McLaughlin*, 500 U.S. 44 (1991) (Scalia, J., dissenting).

115. *Schad v. Arizona*, 501 U.S. 624, 650 (1991) (Scalia, J., concurring).

116. Antonin Scalia, "God's Justice and Ours," *First Things: A Monthly Journal of Religion & Public Life* 123 (May 2002), 18.

117. *Rutan v. Republican Party of Illinois*, 497 U.S. 62 (1990) (Scalia, J., dissenting); *Bd. of County Comm'rs v. Umberhr*, 518 U.S. 668 (1996) (Scalia, J., dissenting); and *O'Hare Truck Service Inc. v. City of Northlake*, 518 U.S. 712 (1996) (Scalia, J., dissenting).

118. *Employment Division, Dept. of Human Resources of Oregon v. Smith*, 494 U.S. 872 (1990).

119. *Dickerson v. United States*, 530 U.S. 428 (2000) (Scalia, J., dissenting).

120. *Atkins v. Virginia*, 536 U.S. 304 (2002) (Scalia, J., dissenting).

121. *Thompson v. Oklahoma*, 487 U.S. 815 (1988) (Scalia, J., dissenting); *Roper v. Simmons*, 125 S. Ct. 1183 (2005) (Scalia, J., dissenting).

122. *Webster v. Reproductive Health Services*, 492 U.S. 490, 532 (1989) (Scalia, J., concurring in part); and *Planned Parenthood of Southeast Pennsylvania v. Casey*, 505 U.S. 833 (1992) (Scalia, J., concurring in judgment and dissenting in part).

123. *Cruzan v. Director, Missouri Department of Health*, 497 U.S. 261, 292 (1990) (Scalia, J., concurring).

124. *Washington v. Glucksberg*, 521 U.S. 702 (1997).

125. *Lawrence v. Texas*, 539 U.S. 558 (2003) (Scalia, J., dissenting).

126. *United States v. Virginia*, 518 U.S. 515 (1996) (Scalia, J., dissenting).

127. *Romer v. Evans*, 517 U.S. 620 (1996) (Scalia, J., dissenting).

128. 403 U.S. 602 (1971).

129. *Tangipahoa Parish Bd. of Educ. v. Freiler*, 530 U.S. 1251, 1253 (2000) (Scalia, J., dissenting from denial of certiorari).

130. *Lamb's Chapel v. Center Moriches Union Free Sch. Dist.*, 508 U.S. 384, 398 (1993) (Scalia, J., concurring in judgment).

131. *Edwards v. Aguillard*, 482 U.S. 578 (1987) (Scalia, J., dissenting) (arguing that under *Lemon's* first prong, a state law must be motivated wholly by religious considerations in order to be struck down, and if it is supported by *a* secular purpose it satisfies that part of the test).

132. *Bd. of Educ. of Kiryas Joel Village v. Grumet*, 512 U.S. 687, 751 (1994) (Scalia, J., dissenting).

133. Ibid., 749.

134. Joan Biskupic, "Justice Makes the Case for Christianity: Scalia Affirms Beliefs at Prayer Breakfast," *Washington Post*, April 10, 1996, A7.

135. *Lee v. Weisman*, 505 U.S. 577, 645 (1992) (Scalia, J., dissenting).

136. *Zelman v. Simmons-Harris*, 536 U.S. 639 (2002).

137. *Bd. of Educ. of the Westside Cmty. Sch. v. Mergens*, 496 U.S. 226 (1990); *Lamb's Chapel v. Center Moriches Union Free Sch. Dist.*, 508 U.S. 384 (1993) (Scalia, J., concurring in judgment); *Rosenberger v. Rector & Visitors of the Univ. of Va.*, 515 U.S. 819 (1995); *Good News Club v. Milford Central School*, 533 U.S. 98 (2001).

138. *Lee v. Weisman*, 505 U.S. 577 (1992) (Scalia, J., dissenting).

139. *Santa Fe Indep. Sch. Dist. v. Doe*, 530 U.S. 290 (2000) (Scalia, J., dissenting).

140. Gina Holland, "Scalia Withdraws from Pledge of Allegiance Decision," *Kansas City Star*, October 20, 2003, A4.

141. *Edwards v. Aguillard*, 482 U.S. 578 (1987) (Scalia, J., dissenting).

142. *County of Allegheny v. American Civil Liberties Union, Greater Pittsburg Chapter*, 492 U.S. 573 (1989).

143. *McCreary County v. A.C.L.U.*, 125 S. Ct. 2722 (2005) (Scalia, J., dissenting); *Van Orden v. Perry*, 125 S. Ct. 2854 (2005) (Scalia, J., concurring).

144. 505 U.S. 577 (1992).

145. *"Lee v. Weisman,"* memo from Anthony Kennedy to Harry Blackmun, March 30, 1992, HABP, box 586, folder 6.

146. 505 U.S. at 588 (quoting *Engel v. Vitale*, 370 U.S. 421, 425 [1962]).

147. Ibid., 592.

148. See Mark Tushnet, *A Court Divided: The Rehnquist Court and the Future of Constitutional Law* (New York: W. W. Norton, 2005), 180–203.

149. 505 U.S. at 628 (Scalia, J., dissenting) (emphasis in the original).

150. Ibid., 632.

151. PAH, 20: 280.

152. "Letter to John Jay" (May 7, 1800), PAH, 24:465.

153. "Letter to James A. Bayard" (April 16–21, 1802), PAH, 25:605–10.

154. 505 U.S. at 646.

155. "Hamilton's Draft [undated] of Washington's Thanksgiving Proclamation," issued on January 1, 1795, Record Group 11 (General Records of the United States Government), Presidential Proclamations Series, Proclamation No. 6, containing handwritten comments/annotations in the margins. National Archives Microfilm Publication T1223, Roll 1. See also "Madison's 'Detached Memoranda,'" ed. Elizabeth Fleet, *William and Mary Quarterly* 3 (1945): 534, 560–62.

156. See, e.g., "The Stand No. III," PAH, 21:402–8.

157. *Bd. of Educ. of Kiryas Joel Village v. Grumet*, 512 U.S. at 708.

158. Scalia, "Of Democracy, Morality and the Majority," *Origins: CNS Documentary Service* 26, no. 6 (June 26, 1996): 81–90.

159. In his Gregorian University address, Scalia said that he loved natural law and approvingly referred to the natural right of the people to establish a new system of government. Scalia, "Of Democracy, Morality and the Majority," 87–88. See also Scalia, "The Two Faces of Federalism," *Harvard Journal of Law and Public Policy* 6 (1982): 20 ("The individual possesses, as the Declaration of Independence points out, a God-given freedom, which rightly counsel an attitude of suspicion if not hostility towards novel impositions of governmental constraint").

160. 515 U.S. 200 (1995).

161. 515 U.S. at 240. See also Scott D. Gerber, *First Principles: The Jurisprudence of Clarence Thomas* (New York: New York University Press, 1999).

162. 515 U.S. at 239.

163. 530 U.S. 57 (2000).

164. Ibid., 75.

165. Ibid., 91 (Scalia, J., dissenting).

166. "Foreign Courts and U.S. Constitutional Law," debate between Antonin Scalia and Stephen Breyer, American University, January 13, 2005. C-SPAN broadcast.

167. *Roper v. Simmons*, 125 S. Ct. 1183, 1228 (2005) (Scalia, J., dissenting).

168. See, e.g., Harry V. Jaffa, *Storm over the Constitution* (Lanham, MD: Lexington Books, 1999), 115–26. For a more moderate criticism of Justice Scalia's views on natural rights, see Douglas W. Kmiec, "Natural-Law Originalism—Or Why Justice Scalia (Almost) Gets It Right," *Harvard Journal of Law & Public Policy* 20, no. 3 (1997): 627.

169. Buckley once said "that he would rather be governed by the first two thousand people in the phone book than by the members of the Harvard faculty." Michael M. Uhlmann, "Justice Scalia and His Critics," *Perspectives on Political Science* 28, no. 1 (Winter 1999), 31.

170. *Cruzan v. Director, Missouri Dep't of Health*, 497 U.S. 261, 293 (1990) (Scalia, J., concurring).

171. Scalia, *A Matter of Interpretation*, 23, 37.

172. Ibid., 24.

173. See, e.g., Scalia, "Originalism: The Lesser Evil," 849–65.

174. Antonin Scalia, "Assorted Canards of Contemporary Legal Analysis," *Case Western Reserve Law Review* 40 (1989–1990): 581, 594–95.

175. U.S. Senate, *The Nomination of Judge Antonin Scalia: Hearings Before the Committee on the Judiciary of the United States Senate*, 99th Cong., 2nd sess., August 5–6, 1986, 89.

176. 290 U.S. 398 (1934).

177. Scalia, "Originalism: The Lesser Evil," 855–56.

178. 497 U.S. 836 (1990).

179. Scalia admits that he would not sustain a state law allowing for "public lashing, or branding of the right hand, as punishment for certain criminal offenses," even if it could be demonstrated that the framers did not regard them as cruel and unusual under the Eighth Amendment. See Scalia, "Originalism: The Lesser Evil," 861.

180. Scalia, "Originalism: The Lesser Evil," 864.

181. Scalia, *A Matter of Interpretation*, 40–41, 44.

182. Scalia, "Originalism: The Lesser Evil," 862.

*Chapter Eight*

# Early Hamiltonian Leanings in the Area of Federalism

In his first inaugural address, President Ronald Reagan promised to take steps "aimed at restoring the balance between the various levels of government," and declared at one point that "the Federal Government did not create the States; the States created the Federal Government."[1] In Justice Sandra Day O'Connor, Reagan had a tested champion of states' rights. But Justice Antonin Scalia was not as predictable. In fact, if his pre-appointment speeches were any indication, Scalia would not assist much in "restoring the balance between the various levels of government." Scalia represented a unique breed of conservative: a Hamiltonian conservative. This chapter considers the various sources of Scalia's early Hamiltonian leanings: (1) statements made in speeches in the 1980s, as well as at both of his confirmation hearings, in which he either referred to the Tenth Amendment as a "constitutional redundancy" or expressed support for the political process approach toward federalism; (2) his early federalism decisions, in which he supported a broad construction of the national government's powers; (3) 1982 remarks before the Federalist Society wherein he urged fellow conservatives to place more confidence in the federal government to accomplish conservative policy goals; and (4) his preemption decisions.

## POLITICAL PROCESS APPROACH

In 1976, the Supreme Court sent a shock wave through the legal community with its five-four ruling in *National League of Cities v. Usery*.[2] There the Court struck down the 1974 amendments to the Fair Labor Standards Act, which extended minimum wage and maximum hour coverage to state and local employees, on the ground that they interfered with "traditional" state functions.

What came as a surprise to many was the Court's interpretation of the Tenth Amendment. According to then Justice William Rehnquist, the author of the Court's opinion, the Tenth Amendment, like the other original amendments to the Constitution, places "an affirmative limitation" on the exercise of national power. "We have repeatedly recognized," Rehnquist wrote, "that there are attributes of sovereignty attaching to every state government which may not be impaired by Congress, not because Congress may lack an affirmative grant of legislative authority to reach the matter, but because the Constitution prohibits it from exercising the authority in that manner."[3]

The Court's decision in *Usery* was short lived, however. No subsequent case followed its reasoning, and only nine years later, the decision was explicitly overturned. In *Garcia v. San Antonio Metropolitan Transit Authority*,[4] the Court rejected the idea that the Tenth Amendment places a substantive limit on Congress's authority to regulate commerce. Justice Harry Blackmun, who switched the position he had taken in *Usery*, found that attempts to draw boundaries of state regulatory immunity in terms of "traditional" governmental functions had proven "unworkable in practice," and that judicially created limitations on national authority invited "an unelected federal judiciary to make decisions about which state policies it favors and which ones it dislikes."[5] The Court instead endorsed a political process approach to federalism, according to which "the principal means chosen by the Framers to ensure the role of the States in the federal system lies in the structure of the Federal Government itself."[6]

## Origins of the Political Process Approach

James Madison is often given credit for being the originator of the political process approach to federalism disputes,[7] but that accolade should actually go to Alexander Hamilton. Hamilton can more properly be described as the inventor of the political process approach to federalism for two distinct reasons.[8] First, Hamilton placed little weight on the Tenth Amendment as a check on national power. Like Madison, Hamilton viewed the Tenth Amendment as declaratory of what was implied by the structure of the federal system.[9] Second, Hamilton did not make formalistic distinctions between national and state powers, as Madison and Thomas Jefferson did. Hamilton, for example, never maintained, as Madison did in *Federalist* 45, that "the powers delegated by the proposed Constitution to the federal government are few and defined. Those which are to remain in the State governments are numerous and indefinite."[10] As Hamilton said in his opinion on the national bank, "The means by which national exigencies are to be provided for, national inconveniences obviated, national prosperity promoted, are of such infinite variety, extent and complexity, that there must, of necessity, be great latitude of discretion in the selection & application of those means."[11] For Hamilton, the question of the distribution of powers between the general and state governments was not primarily a legal question but a prudential consideration: "The question then, of the division of powers between the general and state governments, is a question of convenience: It becomes a prudential enquiry, what powers are proper to be reversed [*sic*] to the latter; and this immediately involves another enquiry into the proper objects of the two governments."[12] On this basis, Hamilton did not see much of a role for the federal courts in enforcing the line between the national and state governments:

> To ascertain this division of objects is the proper business of legislation: It would be absurd to fix it in the constitution, both because it would be too extensive and intricate, and because alteration of circumstances must render a change of the division indispensable. Constitutions should consist only of general provisions: The reason is, that they must necessarily be permanent, and that they cannot calculate for the possible changes of things. I know that the states must have their resources; but I contend that it would be improper to point them out particularly in the constitution.[13]

Hamilton thought that the limits on national power would come from the structure of the federal system, as well as from the enumeration of powers under Article I. In terms of the former, he wrote in *Federalist* 31, "I repeat here what I have observed in substance in another place, that all observations founded upon the danger of usurpation ought to be referred to the composition and structure of the government, not to the nature or extent of its powers."[14] And in terms of the latter, he observed that "congress can in no case exercise any power not included in those enumerated in the constitution."[15]

## Scalia's Political Process Views

In Justice Scalia's early statements on federalism, one sees little indication that he believed the Tenth Amendment places a substantive limit on national power. In fact, contrary to *Usery*, he regarded the Tenth Amendment as a mere parchment barrier. In remarks before the Cato Institute in 1984, then Judge Scalia observed that the Tenth Amendment states the principle "that the federal government is a government of limited powers."[16] What Scalia did not say, however, was that the Tenth Amendment places an affirmative limit on national power. That Scalia does not believe the amendment has such a restrictive value was confirmed by a response he gave to a later question regarding the meaning of the Tenth Amendment. In remarks to a class visiting the Supreme Court for oral arguments, Scalia was asked about his general

views regarding the Tenth Amendment. In response he said: "The Tenth
Amendment does not mean anything. What limits the national government's
powers are the enumerated powers."[17]

A nutshell account of Scalia's structural and political process views regarding federalism can be found in his confirmation hearings and in several
speeches he gave in the late 1980s. During his 1986 confirmation hearings for
the Supreme Court, Scalia was asked by Senator Howell Heflin (D-AL) to
give his "general philosophy of the role of judiciary relative to federalism."[18]
His response is illuminating:

> The fact is, it seems to me, that the primary defender of the constitutional bal-
> ance, the Federal Government versus the States — maybe "versus" is not the way
> to put it — but the primary institution to strike the right balance is the Congress.
> It is a principle of the Constitution that there are certain responsibilities that be-
> long to the State and some that belong to the Federal Government, but it is es-
> sentially the function of Congress — the Congress, which takes the same oath to
> uphold and defend the Constitution that I do as a judge, to have that constitu-
> tional prescription in mind when it enacts the laws.[19]

Not fully satisfied, Senator Heflin pushed a little further. Explaining that
"certain people of diverse ideologies" seemed to want a national solution to a
wide variety of social and economic issues, including abortion, gun control,
tort reform, and labor violence, the senator asked if there was anything the
courts could do. Scalia conceded that if he were a legislator, he would be
sympathetic to devolving more of these issues to the state and local governments, but he regarded the question as irrelevant "in the vast majority if not
all of the cases" he had to decide.[20] "The Supreme Court decisions on the subject," Scalia added, "show that it is very hard to find a distinct justiciable line
between those matters that are appropriate for the states and those that are appropriate for the Federal Government, that finding that line is much easier for
a legislator than for a court, and by and large the courts have not interfered."
Scalia concluded, however, by saying that he expected there would be more
arguments urging the courts to play a more active role, and that he "will of
course keep an open mind."[21]

In a subsequent speech, Scalia's structural and political process views were
even more apparent. In comments at a panel discussion on separation of powers, Scalia explicitly referred to *Garcia*:

> To what extent can the federal government affect the powers of the states? The
> *Garcia* case and all of that. Can the federal government require states to pay a
> certain minimum wage? What are the limits? I am persuaded that it is a losing
> battle and has been a losing battle since the adoption of the Seventeenth

Amendment, because it was the original election of the Senate that was the structure which preserved the relative balance between the states and the Federal Government. The states as states controlled the Senate. The senators were elected by the state legislatures. So, really, as formal institutions, as state governments, they had an arm inside the federal structure. Once the Seventeenth Amendment eliminated that, the ultimate result was clear—the decline of federalism, which we've seen and which the Court will be unable to remedy to any significant degree.[22]

Scalia's remarks demonstrate the importance he places on constitutional structure in maintaining the balance between the federal and state governments. Note that he says absolutely nothing about the Tenth Amendment. The Tenth Amendment does not provide any protection to the states. What limits national power is the structure of the federal system. During his confirmation hearings for the D.C. Court of Appeals, Scalia was asked by Senator Strom Thurmond (R-SC), chairman of the Senate Judiciary Committee, if he thought the Tenth Amendment provided "an affirmative grant of authority to the States." In response, Scalia said,

As to whether the 10th amendment is a grant of authority to the States, the States did not need a grant of authority. The Supreme Court has said in some cases that the 10th amendment is redundant, and I think that is accurate. It is redundant because it is clear that under the original Constitution that the Federal Government is a government of specified powers, and that unless those powers have been affirmatively granted to the Federal Government, they automatically remain with the States.[23]

In *Garcia*, the Court mentioned several structural provisions that protect the sovereign interests of the states, including (1) the states' role in the selection of congressional representatives and the president,[24] (2) the equal representation of each state in the Senate,[25] and (3) the prohibition of any constitutional amendment divesting a state of this equal representation.[26] Of particular importance to the Court was the states' role in choosing representatives for the national political branches of government. Since the states have a significant role in selecting members of Congress and the president, the Court reasoned that the political process adequately "ensures that laws that unduly burden the States will not be promulgated."[27] Thus, it concluded that "[a]ny substantive restraint on the exercise of Commerce Clause powers must . . . be tailored to compensate for possible failings of the national political process."[28]

Justice Scalia's comments regarding the Seventeenth Amendment make his reliance on the structure of the Constitution apparent. In a 1988 speech at American University, Scalia observed that the Seventeenth Amendment

marked "the beginning of the end for the states."[29] Under the original Constitution, the senators were chosen by state legislatures and thus could be held
accountable by those legislatures for their decisions. But that all changed in
1913 with the passage of the Seventeenth Amendment. Senators are now
elected by popular vote and are less beholden to the interests of the states.
Scalia lamented this fact but said there is little the Court can do. Federalism
"is a losing battle and has been a losing battle since the adoption of the Seventeenth Amendment."[30]

Implicit in everything Scalia has said up to this time is that the courts do
not have much of a role in policing the boundary between the national and
state governments. During his confirmation hearings, Scalia said that the
"main protection" of the states "is in the policymaking area, is in the Congress."[31] Scalia took the position then that federalism controversies involve
basic questions of policy, the resolution of which was more appropriate for a
legislature than for a court. Moreover, he maintained that it was primarily
Congress's responsibility, "in the vast majority if not all of the cases," to
judge whether its laws comply with the Constitution. Thus, in the delicate
balance between the federal and state governments, Scalia would have left
much of the line drawing to Congress. Scalia's early support of the political
process approach toward federalism makes his views similar to those of
Alexander Hamilton and the Federalist Party.

## Early Supreme Court Decisions

Justice Scalia's early decisions as a member of the Supreme Court also gave
little indication that he believed the Tenth Amendment constituted an affirmative limitation on national power. During his first couple of terms on the
Court, Scalia participated in two important Tenth Amendment decisions,
which provide further evidence that he regarded the courts as having only a
minimal role to play in federalism disputes. In the first case, he supported a
broad construction of the federal government's spending power; in the second, he supported the political process approach toward federalism.

In *South Dakota v. Dole* (1987),[32] Scalia joined a decision by Chief Justice
William Rehnquist upholding the Minimum Drinking Age Amendment Act of
1984. Under this law, Congress directed the secretary of transportation to
withhold a percentage of federal highway funds from states whose drinking
age was lower than twenty-one. South Dakota, which permitted persons nine-
teen years of age or older to purchase beer containing up to 3.2 percent alco-
hol, brought suit. It claimed that the condition on the receipt of federal funds
violated the constitutional limitations on Congress's spending power, as well
as the reserved powers of the states under the Twenty-first Amendment.

The Constitution empowers Congress to "lay and collect Taxes, Duties, Imposts, and Excises, to pay the Debts and provide for the common Defence and general Welfare of the United States."[33] The latter phrase—the General Welfare Clause—has been the subject of a longstanding debate over whether Congress can authorize the expenditure of public moneys for purposes beyond the direct grants of legislative authority listed under Article I. The Jeffersonian Republicans answered this question in the negative; the Federalists answered it in the affirmative. In various writings and public addresses, James Madison provided the theoretical argument for the Republican position. In his opinion on the national bank, for example, Madison argued that Congress's spending authority under the General Welfare Clause was limited to expenditures made pursuant to one of its enumerated powers under Article I. In support of this view, he relied upon a general principle of government as well as a rule of constitutional construction said to follow therefrom. Madison noted "the peculiar manner in which the federal government is limited," and argued, "It is not a general grant, out of which particular powers are excepted—it is a grant of particular powers only, leaving the general mass in other hands."[34] What follows from this general principle of government, according to Madison, is an equally fundamental rule of constitutional interpretation: "An interpretation that destroys the very characteristic of the government cannot be just."[35] Thus, Madison's first rule of "right interpretation" took into account the consequences of a proposed method of interpreting the Constitution. If the proposed method had the tendency to subvert "[t]he essential characteristic of the government, as composed of limited and enumerated powers," then it had to be wrong and the action unconstitutional.[36]

Alexander Hamilton took up the Federalist side of the debate. In his opinion on the national bank, Hamilton also began with a first principle of government:

> [T]hat every power vested in a Government is in its nature *sovereign*, and includes by *force* of the *term*, a right to employ all the *means* requisite, and fairly *applicable* to the attainment of the *ends* of such power; and which are not precluded by restrictions & exceptions specified in the constitution; or not immoral, or not contrary to the essential ends of political society.[37]

What followed from this was a Hamiltonian rule of "right interpretation." It is a "sound maxim of construction," Hamilton wrote, that "the powers contained in the Constitution of government, especially those which concern the general administration of the affairs of a country, its finances, trade, defence &c ought to be construed liberally, in advancement of the public good."[38] To rule otherwise, he believed, would be to endanger the safety and liberty of the people, since "[n]othing . . . can be more fallacious than to infer the extent of any power proper to be lodged in the national government from an estimate of its immediate necessities."[39] With respect to the spending power, Hamilton rejected any substantive limitation on the objects for which public moneys could be spent, except that they "be *General* and not *local*."[40] In his "Report on the Subject of Manufactures" in 1791, Hamilton explained his position as follows:

> The terms "*general Welfare*" were doubtless intended to signify more than was expressed or imported in those which Preceded; otherwise numerous exigencies incident to the affairs of a Nation would have been left without a provision. The phrase is as comprehensive as any that could have been used; because it was not fit that the constitutional authority of the Union, to appropriate its revenues shou'd have been restricted within narrower limits than the "General Welfare" and because this necessarily embraces a vast variety of particulars, which are not susceptible neither of specification nor of definition.
>
> It is therefore of necessity left to the discretion of the National Legislature, to pronounce, upon the objects, which concern the general Welfare, and for which under that description, an appropriation of money is requisite and proper.[41]

It was not until 1936 that the Supreme Court took sides in this important interpretative debate. In *United States v. Butler*,[42] the Court, while striking down the Agricultural Adjustment Act of 1933, endorsed the Hamiltonian view. In an opinion by Justice Owen Roberts, the Court held that while "the power to tax is not unlimited, its confines are set in the clause which confers it, not in those of section 8 which bestow and define the legislative powers of Congress."[43] Since *Butler*, the Hamiltonian construction of the General Welfare Clause had basically gone unchallenged. But *Dole* presented an opportunity for the conservative Rehnquist Court to rein in Congress's spending power. Yet that did not happen.

In the beginning of his opinion for the Court in *Dole*, Chief Justice Rehnquist mentioned "a longstanding debate over the scope of the Spending Clause."[44] While he did not go into the details of this debate, he approvingly quoted *Butler*'s language that "the power of Congress to authorize expenditure of public moneys for public purposes is not limited by the direct grants of legislative power found in the Constitution."[45] Rehnquist thus concluded that even if an object of Congress does not fall squarely within one of Article I's legislative fields, it "may nevertheless be attained through the use of the spending power and the conditional grant of federal funds."[46] In assessing whether an expenditure is for the "general welfare," Rehnquist also maintained that lower courts should defer substantially to the judgment of Congress.[47]

In examining the condition placed on the receipt of federal funds in the case at hand, Rehnquist had little difficulty finding that it served the general welfare. Both Congress and a presidential commission appointed to study alcohol-related accidents reported that "the differing drinking ages in the States created particular incentives for young persons to combine their desire to drink with their ability to drive, and that this interstate problem required a national solution."[48] And the means chosen by Congress to address teenage drunk driving, the Chief Justice concluded, were reasonably calculated to advance the general welfare: "The condition imposed by Congress is directly related to one of the main purposes for which highway funds are expended—safe interstate travel."[49] Although Rehnquist did not say so, his opinion in *Dole* was a ringing endorsement of the Hamiltonian construction of the spending power, which differed dramatically from the dissent filed by Justice Sandra Day O'Connor, which embraced a Madisonian interpretation of the General Welfare Clause.

Justice Scalia joined Chief Justice Rehnquist's opinion in *Dole*, indicating his agreement with the Hamiltonian construction of the General Welfare Clause. This should not be surprising in light of Scalia's testimony at his confirmation hearings, where he said that it was primarily the responsibility of Congress to determine whether or not its laws comply with the Constitution. Ten years after *Dole*, Scalia still maintained an expansive view of the general welfare provision. In a 1997 speech at the Manhattan Institute in New York, Scalia claimed that the Constitution does not protect the right of parents to raise their children as they choose. Edward Crane, the founder and president of Cato, asked "if the Tenth Amendment didn't cover that since nowhere in the enumerated powers of Congress was control over how we raise our kids given to the federal government." In response, Scalia said "there is such a thing as the General Welfare Clause," to which Crane replied "that none other than James Madison had said an expansive view of the General Welfare Clause would make the Constitution incoherent." Scalia then answered, "That was then, this is now."[50] Moreover, Scalia's vote in *Dole* is consistent with his support of a Hamiltonian construction of other national powers. In *Synar v. United States*,[51] for example, Scalia supported a Hamiltonian construction of the Necessary and Proper Clause.[52]

The second important early federalism ruling in which Justice Scalia participated is *South Carolina v. Baker* (1988).[53] Based on reports about the growth in cases of tax evasion, Congress enacted the Tax Equity and Fiscal Responsibility Act (TEFRA) of 1982, which contained a variety of provisions designed to promote compliance with the nation's tax laws. In particular, section 310(b)(1) of TEFRA removed the federal income tax exemption for interest earned on bonds issued by state and local governments, unless those bonds were issued in registered (as opposed to bearer) form. South Carolina challenged the constitutionality of this provision under the Tenth Amendment and the doctrine of intergovernmental tax immunity. Although the case is perhaps best remembered for the Court's overturning its one-hundred-year-old precedent in *Pollock v. Farmers' Loan & Trust Co.*,[54] it also contains interesting Tenth Amendment analysis.

Justice William Brennan, who authored the Court's opinion, held that section 310(b)(1) did not violate "the Tenth Amendment" or "constitutional principles of federalism." Since it was discovered that most of the states felt obligated under the new law to comply with the condition, Brennan assumed for purposes of the Tenth Amendment analysis that Congress had directly regulated the states by prohibiting outright the issuance of bearer bonds. The importance of this is that the Court had before it a *Garcia* type of case: Congress was applying a generally applicable law to the states. The question for the justices was whether the Tenth Amendment (or some other "constitutional principles of federalism") prevented Congress from doing so. Justice Brennan first examined the Court's decision in *Garcia*. According to Brennan, *Garcia* stands for the proposition that the limits on Congress's authority to regulate state activities are structural (not substantive), and that the states must find their protection from congressional regulation through the national political process rather than through judicially defined spheres of unregulatable state activity. Although *Garcia* left open the possibility that some extraordinary defects in the national political process might render congressional regulation of state activities invalid under the Tenth Amendment, Brennan determined that no such extraordinary defects were present in this case. "It suffices to observe," he wrote, "that South Carolina has not even alleged that it was deprived of any right to participate in the national political process or that it was singled out in a way that left it politically isolated and powerless."[55]

Second, Brennan considered the claim made by the National Governors Association (NGA) that the law was invalid because it "commandeered" the state legislative and administrative processes by coercing states into having to enact legislation authorizing bond registration and then having to administer the registration scheme. The NGA relied, in particular, on the Court's decision in *FERC v. Mississippi*,[56] which left open the possibility that the Tenth Amendment might set some limits on Congress's power to compel states to regulate on behalf of federal interests. With respect to this claim, Brennan first questioned the extent to which a *FERC* type of claim survived the Court's decision in *Garcia*, which left the protection of state sovereignty primarily to the national political process. But, assuming *arguendo* the validity of such a claim, Brennan found it inapplicable to the facts of this case. Section 310 regulates state activities; it does not, as did the statute in *FERC*, seek to control or influence the manner in which states regulate private parties. Thus, the majority held that the Tenth Amendment did not bar the national government from removing the income tax exemption for unregistered state bonds.

Justice Scalia wrote a short concurring opinion—the only opinion he would write on the Tenth Amendment prior to his decision for the Court in *Printz v. United States* (1997). Scalia objected to the reasoning of the majority opinion on two separate grounds. First, he argued that the majority "unnecessarily cast doubt upon *FERC v. Mississippi*," and second, it "misdescribe[d] the holding in *Garcia*." On the latter point, he added,

> I do not read *Garcia* as adopting—in fact I read it as explicitly disclaiming— the proposition attributed to it in today's opinion, . . . that the "national political process" is the States' only constitutional protection, and that nothing except the demonstration of "some extraordinary defects" in the operation of that process can justify judicial relief. We said in *Garcia*: "These cases do not require us to identify or define what affirmative limits *the constitutional structure* might impose on federal action affecting the States under the Commerce Clause." I agree only that that structure does not prohibit what the Federal Government has done here.[57]

That was Scalia's entire opinion. What he meant, though, remains ambiguous. The reason for his mentioning *FERC* is certainly clear. Scalia wanted to leave open the possibility for the Court to reexamine whether Congress can "command" the states into legislating or administering a federal program— which it will in time do. But what Scalia meant by his criticism of the majority's reading of *Garcia* is puzzling. Brennan's reading of *Garcia* certainly seems justifiable. Justice Blackmun made it clear in *Garcia* that "[a]ny substantive restraint on the exercise of Commerce Clause powers . . . must be tailored to compensate for possible failings in the national political process."[58] And while he said that "[t]hese cases do not require us to identify or define what affirmative limits the constitutional structure might impose on federal action affecting the States under the Commerce Clause," he then cited Justice Felix Frankfurter's observation in *New York v. United States*: "The process of Constitutional adjudication does not thrive on conjuring up horrible possibilities that never happen in the real world and devising doctrines sufficiently comprehensive in detail to cover the remotest contingency."[59] Moreover, Justice Scalia did not identify how the constitutional structure places "affirmative limits" on "federal action affecting the States under the Commerce Clause," or why the constitutional structure did not prohibit the federal government from taxing the interest on bearer bonds issued by the states. We know what Justice Scalia thinks about the Tenth Amendment. If it is not the Tenth Amendment that places restrictions on Congress's authority to regulate commerce, then what structural provision of the Constitution does? When the framers referred to "constitutional structure," they had in mind the actual provisions of the Constitution that protected state interests, such as the selection process for U.S. senators. We shall see in chapter 9 a similar ambiguity in Scalia's analysis of "constitutional structure" in his opinion for the court in *Printz*.

Justice Scalia's opinion in *Baker* remains cryptic and vague, but the bottom line is that he joined the opinion of the Court, giving added support (albeit with some qualifications) to his political process approach toward federalism.[60] His opinions in *Dole* and *Baker* give little indication (other than the *FERC* type of possibility) that he believed the Court has a significant role to play in federalism disputes. He wrote very little, and what he did write was not a ringing endorsement of the values of federalism. Unlike Justice O'Connor, who often stressed these values in her federalism opinions,[61] Scalia seemed to regard federalism as a matter primarily consigned to the national political process. Scalia's ambivalence about federalism was so marked that scholars began to question his commitment to its principles. In one 1988 article, for example, the authors had this to say about Scalia's views on the subject:

> When Antonin Scalia joined the Supreme Court in 1986, we all knew what we were getting—a smart, often eloquent, and highly conservative Justice. Those who favor strong state and local governments were hopeful that this meant Justice Scalia would be a friend of federalism issues. But by the end of his first Term, Justice Scalia has given state and local governments more reason to worry than to hope. Although the jury is still out, Justice Scalia is emerging as at best, an occasional—perhaps only an accidental—advocate of federalism.[62]

## NATIONAL POLICY MAKING

Justice Scalia's strongest identification with the nationalist ideas of Alexander Hamilton came in 1982 remarks at a conference on federalism sponsored by the Federalist Society.[63] His comments were short but important in underscoring his reliance on Hamilton, not Madison (the sometime champion of states' rights), for his views on the subject. Scalia began by saying that when he started to prepare some thoughts for the conference, he came to the conclusion that "if a resurrected and updated Alexander Hamilton had been invited to this conference the subjects he would have expected to hear addressed are quite different from—and the tenor of his own remarks would have been quite the opposite of—what we have heard over the past few days."[64] It is clear that Scalia was not himself impressed with the substance or tenor of the papers he had heard. The conference was in need of a nationalist perspective, which Scalia was only too happy to provide.

Scalia defined federalism as "a form of government midway between two extremes." "At one extreme," he explained, is "the autonomy, the disunity, the conflict of independent states; at the other, the uniformity, the inflexibility, the monotony of one centralized government."[65] As a consequence, federalism "is a stick that can be used to beat either dog."[66] Scalia chided his fellow conservatives for forgetting this important truth. The general hostility among conservatives toward the national government, Scalia maintained, has limited them to fighting only a one-sided battle:

> To be sure, decision at a lower level of government tends to maximize overall satisfaction, by permitting diversity instead of submerging large regional majorities beneath a narrow national vote. But that is a practical rather than a transcendental concern, to be laid beside other practical concerns such as the need for national rather than local enforcement of certain prescriptions. It justifies a predisposition towards state and local control—but not, I think, the degree of generalized hostility towards national law which has become a common feature of conservative thought.[67]

Scalia could understand why some conservatives have an antagonistic view toward the national government. A natural rights philosophy, which has been passed down to us from the Declaration of Independence, counsels against an overzealous confidence in centralized power. Moreover, conservatives have simply been "out-gunned" at the federal level for half a century. "Unfortunately, a tactic employed for half a century," Scalia warned, "tends to develop into a philosophy. And an anti-federalist philosophy on the part of conservatives seems to me simply wrong."[68] Scalia maintained that once in power, this approach "is ultimately self-defeating," and added: "When liberals are in power they do not shrink from using the federal structure for what they consider to be sound governmental goals. But when conservatives take charge, the most they hope to do is to keep anything from happening."[69]

Scalia mentioned that he had heard that in some of the offices of the Reagan administration there were signs on the wall which read, "Don't just stand there; undo something."[70] This was an inadequate approach, in Scalia's view, because it will take *positive* legislation by the federal government to achieve the policy objectives conservatives want. Instead of fighting only a one-sided war, which in the end conservatives will ultimately lose, Scalia proposed a more activist approach. Since most conservatives are defenders of the free market, Scalia suggested floating federal legislation that prohibits (or at least limits) state regulation in such areas as the cable, construction, or housing industries. Why not limit the ability of state courts to create novel tort theories of "enterprise liability" or "design defect," which subject interstate businesses to greatly increased damages? Or what about "antitrust" and "anti-escape" laws that excessively penalize businesses? Scalia lamented the fact that there was not a single federal statute that simply said, "The states shall not regulate."[71] He urged the members of the conference—"as Hamilton would have urged [them]—to keep in mind that the federal government is not bad but good. The trick is to use it wisely."[72]

At the end of the conference, Scalia also took part in an interesting exchange over the federal regulation of abortion rights. Professor (now Judge) John T. Noonan Jr. defended the pro-life movement's support of the Hatch Amendment, which contained three important provisions: (1) "A right of abortion is not secured by this Constitution," (2) "[t]he Congress and the several states shall have concurrent power to restrict and prohibit abortion," and (3) "a provision of a law of a state which is more restrictive than a conflicting provision of a law of Congress shall govern."[73] Noonan conceded that the Hatch Amendment would effectively "federalize" abortion law, but he regarded this as the only realistic choice after the Court nationalized the issue in *Roe v. Wade*.[74] According to Noonan, abortion law will be "federalized one way or the other."[75] At least with the Hatch Amendment, it will be federalized in "a way that it protects life."[76] During the question and answer period, Noonan was sharply criticized for his support of the Hatch Amendment. One questioner described the abortion issue as "a test case for conservativism [*sic*]—whether people really mean what they say when they say they want liberty and decentralization or whether it is just hypocrisy."[77] Scalia, listening to this exchange, chimed in as follows:

> [T]he world in general and the political process in particular do not work on logic. I did not understand Professor Noonan's response to be "Well, it is your own fault." I took his response to be "It is an improvement over the existing situation, at least. It still violates the principle of federalism but certainly no more, and indeed, somewhat less, than the *status quo*." The realistic choice presented is compared to what? You do not like it. Do you like it any better than the existing situation? That is the realistic choice before the house, not whether it is best of all possible worlds. I think his defense on that point is absolutely correct, unless those who believe in federalism strongly enough come up with something that is not only an improvement over the *status quo*, but also is perfection, and get that on the floor of the Congress. Then we can argue that the Hatch Amendment is no good. I do not like the Hatch Amendment compared to perfection, but I certainly prefer it to the *status quo*. It is both substantively more congenial, and it is more congenial from the sole standpoint of federalism.[78]

Here one sees clear evidence of Justice Scalia's Hamiltonian side: an affectionate view of national power and of how it can be used to achieve conservative policy goals. As the nation's first treasury secretary, Hamilton was an expert at using the instruments of federal power to effectuate the policy goals of the Washington administration. One also sees in Justice Scalia's comments the Hamiltonian temperament, which is unique among conservatives. Traditional conservatives typically take a cautious approach to change. In his *Reflections on the Revolution in France*, the eighteenth-century English philosopher and statesman Edmund Burke captured this traditional conservative attitude: "[I]t is with infinite caution that any man ought to venture upon pulling down an edifice which has answered in any tolerable degree for ages the common purposes of society, or on building it up again, without having models and patterns of approved utility before his eyes."[79] While Burke was not opposed to all forms of change, he advocated a gradual, almost imperceptible, type of change:

> By a slow but well-sustained progress, the effect of each step is watched; the good or ill success of the first, gives light to us in the second; and so, from light to light, we are conducted with safety through the whole series. We see, that the parts of the system do not clash. The evils latent in the most promising contrivance are provided for as they arise. One advantage is as little as possible sacrificed to another. We compensate, we reconcile, we balance. We are enabled to unite into a consistent whole the various anomalies and contending principles that are found in the minds and affairs of men.[80]

Hamilton and Scalia do not share the Burkean temperament. Their temperaments are more inclined toward bold, innovative, and decisive action. In fact, one of the reasons often cited for exempting Hamilton from the conservative tradition was his temperament.[81] Scalia's remarks at the conference on federalism were a clarion call for conservatives to be more aggressive at the national level. His objection to what he regarded as "inaction" by conservatives had less to do with disagreement on basic policies than with "the unfortunate tendency of conservatives to regard the federal government, at least in its purely domestic activities, as something to be resisted, or better yet (when conservatives are in power) undone, rather than as a legitimate and useful instrument of policy."[82]

## FEDERAL PREEMPTION

Under the U.S. federal system, what happens when there is a conflict between national and state law? If there were no way to peacefully resolve these sorts of disputes, the United States would be in a constant state of civil war. The doctrine of preemption, which is derived from the Supremacy Clause,[83] provides the answer. According to this doctrine, "[A]ny state law, however clearly within a State's acknowledged power, which interferes with or is contrary to federal law, must yield."[84] As Justice O'Connor has recognized, the doctrine of preemption gives the federal government "a decided advantage in

[the] delicate balance" between the states and the federal government, because "[a]s long as [Congress] is acting within the powers granted it under the Constitution," it may reach areas traditionally regulated by the states.[85]

Alexander Hamilton assumed that some notion of preemption is inherent in a federal system of government. In *Federalist* 33, he set forth how political power was to be divided in a republic. According to Hamilton, the laws of the larger political entity—into which smaller political societies agree to join— are the supreme law of the land. If otherwise, the relationship would constitute "a mere treaty, dependent on the good faith of the parties, and not a government, which is only another word for POLITICAL POWER AND SUPREMACY."[86] As he explained,

> A LAW, by the very meaning of the term, includes supremacy. It is a rule which those to whom it is prescribed are bound to observe. This results from every political association. If individuals enter into a state of society, the laws of that society must be the supreme regulator of their conduct. If a number of political societies enter into a larger political society, the laws which the latter may enact, pursuant to the powers intrusted to it by its constitution, must necessarily be supreme over those societies and the individuals of whom they are composed.[87]

There are three major ways in which the federal government can preempt state law. The first is by expressly stating so. A federal law might simply say that it is preempting state law, either partially or entirely. The second and third ways are implied methods. One implied method is "field" preemption, "where Congress's legislation is so complete and the area is one requiring national uniformity of regulation, that Congress can be said to have intended to occupy the field."[88] For example, comprehensive and uniform federal regulations fully occupy the field of foreign affairs. The other implied method is "conflict" preemption, "where the federal and state regulations are in such conflict that state law must yield to the federal because either (a) there is an actual conflict in that it is impossible for a party to comply with both federal and state regulation, or (b) state law 'stands as an obstacle' to the accomplishment of federal objectives and, therefore, must yield."[89] This last-mentioned implied preemption doctrine, known as "obstacle" preemption, presents the most difficulty for the reviewing Court, because it must discern Congress's objectives or purposes when it passed the statute. The basic issue in all preemption cases is one of congressional intent. In contrast to Tenth Amendment cases, where the central question is whether Congress has the constitutional *authority* to regulate a particular activity, preemption cases ask whether Congress statutorily *intended* to regulate a particular area.

Since taking his seat on the Supreme Court, Justice Scalia has participated in a number of decisions involving federal preemption. What should become obvious from the cases discussed below is that he is not opposed to ruling in favor of the federal government. In fact, from 1986 to 2005, Scalia ranked first among members of the Rehnquist Court in voting in favor of the federal government in preemption cases (see Table 8.1). Scalia is not alone, however. Table 8.1 also shows that Scalia's conservative colleagues have been favorably disposed toward national power in preemption cases. Remarkably, and a clear sign that the Rehnquist Court's federalism jurisprudence was not principled, the ranking of the justices in terms of the percentage of cases in which they supported the federal government in preemption cases is dramatically different from the individual voting behavior of the justices in all types of federalism cases, including the Tenth and Eleventh Amendments. While the conservative bloc of the Rehnquist Court made modest strides in protecting the sovereign interests of the states under the Tenth and Eleventh Amendments (particularly under the latter), it was the chief defender of the national government in preemption cases. In an age in which the federal courts are deciding more statutory cases,[90] this is an important development in judicial policy

**Table 8.1.   U.S. Supreme Court Justices' Support for the Federal Government in Federalism and Preemption Cases, 1986–2005**

| Federalism (Including Tenth and Eleventh Amendment Cases) | |
| --- | --- |
| Stephen Breyer | 65.6% |
| David Souter | 61.7 |
| Ruth Bader Ginsburg | 60.6 |
| John Paul Stevens | 56.1 |
| Anthony Kennedy | 50.9 |
| Antonin Scalia | 50.0 |
| Sandra Day O'Connor | 50.0 |
| William H. Rehnquist | 46.8 |
| Clarence Thomas | 41.6 |
| Preemption | |
| Antonin Scalia | 62.7% |
| Sandra Day O'Connor | 59.2 |
| Anthony Kennedy | 59.2 |
| William H. Rehnquist | 56.6 |
| Clarence Thomas | 50.0 |
| David Souter | 50.0 |
| Stephen Breyer | 44.4 |
| Ruth Bader Ginsburg | 43.3 |
| John Paul Stevens | 42.3 |

*Source:* Harold J. Spaeth, principal investigator, "United States Supreme Court Judicial Database: 1953–2005 Terms" (Michigan State University, 2005).

making. As one constitutional scholar of federal preemption has observed, the Supreme Court conservatives are no longer operating under the traditional presumption against preemption, but rather have substituted in its place a presumption in its favor.[91]

## The Regulation of Cigarette Advertisements

In one form or another, the regulation of tobacco products has been before the Court on several occasions.[92] In the 1992 case *Cipollone v. Liggett Group*[93] the Court had to decide whether two federal laws regulating the labeling and advertisement of cigarette products preempted state common law damages claims against three tobacco companies. In 1965, Congress enacted the Federal Cigarette Labeling and Advertising Act (FCLAA), which mandated health warnings on cigarette packages but did not require similar warnings in cigarette advertising. The stated purposes of the act were to (1) "adequately [inform] the public that cigarette smoking may be hazardous to health, and to (2) [protect] the national economy from the burden imposed by diverse, nonuniform and confusing cigarette labeling and advertising regulations."[94] In furtherance of the second purpose, section 5 of the act (under the caption "Preemption") provided that

(a) No statement relating to smoking and health, other than the statement required by Section 4 of this Act [i.e., smoking may be hazardous to your health], shall be required on any cigarette package, and

(b) No statement relating to smoking and health shall be required in the advertising of any cigarettes the packages of which are labeled in conformity with the provisions of this Act.[95]

In 1969, Congress passed the Public Health Cigarette Smoking Act,[96] which amended the 1965 act in several ways. Under the 1969 act, the warning label was strengthened by requiring that the word "dangerous" be substituted for the word "hazardous," and following a recommendation by the Federal Communications Commission,[97] the act prohibited cigarette commercials on the radio and television. Finally, and most important for our purposes, the 1969 act modified the preemption provision as follows: "No requirement or prohibition based on smoking and health shall be imposed under State law with respect to the advertising or promotion of any cigarettes the packages of which are labeled in conformity with the provisions of this Act."[98]

In 1983, Rose Cipollone and her husband brought suit against three tobacco companies, claiming that she developed lung cancer as a result of smoking cigarettes manufactured and sold by the companies. Their complaint alleged several theories of recovery, including failure to warn, breach of express warranty, fraudulent misrepresentation, and conspiracy to defraud, all of which were based on New Jersey common law. The tobacco companies defended by arguing that these common law damages claims were preempted by the federal laws.

The plurality opinion by Justice John Paul Stevens found *some*, but not all, of the common law claims preempted. According to Stevens, the 1965 preemption provisions only "prohibited state and federal rule-making bodies from mandating particular cautionary statements on cigarette labels," and therefore did not foreclose additional obligations imposed under state common law.[99] As for the 1969 preemption provision, however, Stevens found a broader purpose in mind: The later act barred "not 'simply statements' but rather 'requirement[s] or prohibition[s] . . . imposed under State law,'" and it reached "beyond statements 'in the advertising' to obligations 'with respect to the advertising or promotion' of cigarettes.'"[100] Thus, the later act could be read to prohibit not only positive enactments concerning the health risks associated with smoking, but common law damages actions which impose a "requirement or prohibition" under state law. Applying such an analysis to the claims in this case, the plurality found the failure-to-warn and fraudulent-misrepresentation claims preempted "to the extent that those claims rel[ied] on omissions or inclusions in respondents' advertising or promotion."[101] However, other aspects of those claims, as well as the express-warranty and conspiracy-to-defraud claims, were allowed to go forward.

Significantly, in reaching its conclusion, the plurality relied on two rules of statutory construction. First, it applied a plain statement rule.[102] According to Stevens, under the Supremacy Clause, "the historic police powers of the States [are] not to be superseded" by federal law unless there is a "clear and manifest purpose" to do so.[103] Second, the Court reasoned that "[w]hen Congress has considered the issue of pre-emption and has included in the enacted legislation a provision explicitly addressing that issue," the Court need not infer congressional intent to preempt state authority beyond the explicit language.[104] In other words, Congress's enactment of a provision defining the preemptive reach of a statute means that all doctrines of implied preemption are foreclosed.

Justice Scalia (who was joined by Justice Clarence Thomas) concurred in part and dissented in part. Scalia would have found federal preemption of the failure-to-warn claims under the 1965 act, and preemption of *all* the common law actions under the 1969 act. Scalia strongly objected to the plurality's "novel" and "unprecedented" principles of statutory construction. First, he questioned the Court's application of a plain statement rule in preemption cases. According to Scalia, since the Court can find federal preemption in cases where there is no explicit statement of preemptive intent by Congress (i.e., implied "field" or "conflict" preemption), a requirement of a plain statement rule in cases where explicit statements do exist "is more than somewhat odd":

> To be sure, our jurisprudence abounds with rules of "plain statement," "clear statement," and "narrow construction" designed variously to ensure that, absent unambiguous evidence of Congress's intent, extraordinary constitutional powers are not invoked, or important constitutional protections eliminated, or seemingly inequitable doctrines applied. . . . But *none* of those rules exists alongside a doctrine whereby the same result so prophylactically protected from careless explicit provision can be achieved by *sheer implication*, with no express statement of intent at all. That is the novel regime the Court constructs today.[105]

Second, Scalia took aim at the Court's other rule of statutory construction— if there is an express preemption provision in a federal statute, then the Court will not infer congressional intent to preempt state authority beyond the scope of the explicit language. As Scalia saw it, this rule conflicts with the prior decisions of the Court and "works mischief" in the area of implied "conflict" preemption:

> If taken seriously, it would mean, for example, that if a federal consumer protection law provided that no state agency or court shall assert jurisdiction under state law over any workplace safety issue with respect to which a federal standard is in effect, then a state agency operating under a law dealing with a subject other than workplace safety (e.g., consumer protection) could impose requirements entirely contrary to federal law—forbidding, for example, the use of certain safety equipment that federal law requires.[106]

Taken together, Scalia found the plurality's canons of "narrow construction" to be "extraordinary," and argued that they would place a presumption against federal preemption in the Court's jurisprudence:

> The statute that says *anything* about pre-emption must say *everything*; and it must do so with great exactitude, as any ambiguity concerning its scope will be read in favor of preserving state power. If this be the law, surely only the most sporting of congresses will dare to say anything about pre-emption.[107]

Justice Scalia's opinion in *Cipollone* strongly supports federal preemption of state law. Unlike the plurality, he was much more willing to assume federal preemption of the common law damages claims, which has been shown in subsequent cases as well.[108] Although the determinative question in all preemption cases is one of congressional intent, there is wide latitude in these types of cases for judges to reach the results they want. Moreover, *Cipollone* was not crystal clear. In an opinion concurring in part and dissenting in part, Justice Harry Blackmun (who was joined by Justices David Souter and Anthony Kennedy) found *no* intent by Congress under either statute to preempt any of the common law actions. The types of lawsuits that Scalia would have preempted are also worth mentioning: those involving state court theories of liability. These are the same types of suits that he suggested should be preempted by the federal government in his pre-Court remarks before the Federalist Society.[109] Scalia's concern about reading preemptive statutes too narrowly has been heeded by his conservative colleagues in subsequent products liability cases. For example, in the 1996 case *Medtronic v. Lohr*,[110] four of the Court's conservatives,[111] concurring in part and dissenting in part, argued that the Medical Device Amendment's premarket clearance procedures preempted several common law tort theories alleging injuries as a result of a defective pacemaker. And in *Geier v. American Honda Motor Company* (2000),[112] four conservative justices[113] plus Justice Stephen Breyer ruled that the 1984 version of the Federal Motor Vehicle Safety Standard 208, as promulgated by the Department of Transportation, *impliedly* preempted state common law suits against car manufacturers for failing to install airbags as passive-restraint devices. What was particularly remarkable about the latter ruling was that the Motor Vehicle Safety Act of 1966, which authorizes the Department of Transportation to promulgate national safety standards for motor vehicles, contained a saving clause explicitly exempting common law actions from the preemption provision.

## The Government Contractor Defense

Justice Scalia has also written an important implied preemption decision involving the government contractor defense, which extends the federal government's sovereign immunity to independent contractors that have executed design specifications developed or approved by the government. Traditionally, government contractors who have strictly complied with government design specifications have been able to plead two types of defense for any damages resulting from such specifications: (1) the government agency defense, and (2) the contract specification defense. Under the former, courts have applied principles of agency to shield government contractors from liability when the contractor acts pursuant to the authority and direction of the federal government.[114] This defense is rarely invoked and has been applied only in public works cases. It also suffers from a severe limitation: it does not cover government contractors that are not employees of the federal government.

The contract specification defense shields government contractors from ordinary negligence claims. If a contractor (private or public) manufactures products to the order of another party, it will not be liable for any damages caused by the product's design unless the specifications provided were so clearly defective and dangerous that a reasonably prudent contractor should have realized that the product was unsafe.[115] This defense has been invoked mostly in public works cases,[116] but also (with limited success) in products liability suits.[117] The problem in the latter type of case has been the advent of strict liability, which allows plaintiffs to recover from government contractors even if the contractors are not responsible for the defectively designed equipment that caused the injuries.

In response to the limitations of these two defenses, the federal courts fashioned a new defense: the government contractor defense.[118] Under this defense, courts have recognized that if a contractor manufactures a product according to the government's specifications, that contractor should be entitled to share in the government's sovereign immunity defense and thus be protected to the same extent that the government would have been protected had it manufactured the product itself. Significantly, government contractors can plead this defense even if they are not employees of the government, and since the defense is based on a shared sovereign immunity concept, they will be immune from all theories of tort liability. In recent years, this defense has been applied almost exclusively to the area of military procurement contracts and thus is sometimes referred to as the "military contractor defense." Despite a flurry of lower federal court decisions on the subject, the Supreme Court had not weighed in on the government contractor defense. Since there was a split in the circuits over which test to apply in such cases, the Court took the opportunity to do so by granting certiorari in *Boyle v. United Technologies Corp.*[119]

On April 27, 1983, a United States Marine helicopter crashed off the coast of Virginia Beach, Virginia, carrying four crew members. Three of the crew members were able to escape from the helicopter without serious injury, but the co-pilot, Lieutenant David Boyle, could not open his escape hatch and drowned. Boyle's father brought suit against the manufacturer of the helicopter, the Sikorsky Division of United Technologies Corporation (Sikorsky), alleging two theories of liability under Virginia tort law. First, he claimed that Sikorsky negligently repaired the helicopter's automatic flight control system, which resulted in the pilot's losing control of the helicopter and its eventual crash into the ocean. Second, he claimed that Sikorsky defectively designed the co-pilot's emergency escape system: "the escape hatch opened out instead of in (and was therefore ineffective in a submerged craft because of water pressure), and access to the escape hatch handle was obstructed by other equipment."[120] A federal district court jury returned a general verdict in favor of Boyle and awarded him $725,000. The Fourth Circuit Court of Appeals, however, reversed. It found, in part, that Sikorsky was immune from the state tort claims because it satisfied the "military contractor defense," which that court recognized the same day in *Tozer v. LTV Corp.*[121] Boyle appealed.

Due to the retirement of Justice Lewis Powell—the Court's swing vote—*Boyle* was originally argued before only eight of the Supreme Court's justices on October 13, 1987. At conference, the justices were deadlocked, and the case was set for reargument in April 1988, when Powell's successor was expected to be named. After reargument, Justice Anthony Kennedy, Powell's replacement, cast the decisive vote to affirm the lower court.[122] As the author of the Court's opinion, Justice Scalia examined whether there was a basis in law for the federal courts to create a government contractor defense. As pointed out by Justice William J. Brennan in dissent, despite repeated requests for it to do so, Congress had refused to legislate such a defense.[123] Scalia, however, held that the federal courts had the authority to fashion such a defense under federal common law. Even "in the absence of legislation specifically immunizing Government contractors from liability for design defects," Scalia ruled that there are a few areas of "uniquely federal interest" where the federal courts have preempted state law under federal common law.[124] Scalia mentioned two such areas of uniquely federal interest: (1) obligations to and rights of the United States under its contracts, and (2) civil liability of federal officials for actions taken in the course of their duty.[125] Scalia had to concede, however, that neither of these two examples of uniquely federal interest were at issue here, since neither the federal government, nor one of its officials, was a party to this lawsuit. Nevertheless, Scalia extended these two earlier examples of "peculiarly federal concern" to cover government contractors. According to Scalia, "It makes little sense to insulate the Government against financial liability for the judgment that a particular feature of military equipment is necessary when the Government produces the equipment itself, but not when it contracts for the production."[126] It is also apparent that the Court was concerned about the ability of the federal government to procure military contracts in the future if suits like this one were permitted to go forward. "The imposition of liability on Government contractors," Scalia reasoned, "will directly affect the terms of Government contracts: either the contractor will decline to manufacture the design specified by the Government, or it will raise its price. Either way, the interests of the United States will be directly affected."[127]

Significantly, Justice Scalia tied the justification for the government contractor defense to the discretionary function exception of the Federal Tort

Claims Act (FTCA) of 1946—a point not even argued by counsel in the case.[128] This exception immunizes federal officials from liability arising from the exercise of, or the failure to exercise, a discretionary function or duty. The purpose of the defense is to prevent litigants from bringing suits against the government in order to challenge the correctness of policy decisions by members of the executive branch. Interestingly, all of the federal courts that had previously recognized the government contractor defense had based it not on the discretionary function exception of the FTCA but on the *Feres* doctrine.[129] This doctrine, which originated in *Feres v. United States*,[130] immunizes the federal government from suits brought by servicemen who are injured in the line of duty. Unlike the discretionary function exception of the FTCA, where the courts must determine whether the activity in question involved a policy choice by a government official for the sovereign immunity defense to apply, the *Feres* doctrine provides blanket immunity only in the narrow area of service-related suits. Although several sketchy rationales have been given for this doctrine, the most common construction of the decision is that such immunity will preserve military discipline.

Justice Scalia explicitly rejected grounding the government contractor defense on the *Feres* doctrine, finding that such a rationale would make the defense both too broad and too narrow.[131] It would be too broad because it would absolve government contractors from suits by military personnel even when no policy judgment has been made by the federal government. It would be too narrow because it arbitrarily limits immunity to suits brought by servicemen and not by civilians that might be the incidental victims of poorly designed equipment. In Scalia's view, the discretionary function exception of the FTCA conforms better with the central purpose of the government contractor defense: it prevents injured parties from indirectly questioning the wisdom of governmental decisions by bringing tort suits against the contractors that implement those decisions.

Scalia's decision in *Boyle* illustrates the extent to which he will go to find federal preemption of state law. Since there was no governing statute in the case, the Court was, by any objective analysis, on shaky ground in fashioning a government contractor defense. Not only this, but Scalia expanded the scope of the defense beyond what the federal courts had previously recognized by shielding government contractors from civilian claimants who are injured by defectively designed products. Scalia's willingness to invoke federal common law in a preemption case is hard to reconcile with his sharp criticism of substantive due process rights under the "liberty" provision of the Fifth and Fourteenth Amendments,[132] and with his positivist, Benthamite disapproval of federal common law in international law cases.[133] *Cipollone* and

*Boyle* suggest that Scalia is favorably disposed toward federal preemption. In addition to these two cases, he has voted in favor of federal preemption in cases involving foreign affairs,[134] occupational safety,[135] consumer protection,[136] environmental regulation,[137] and bankruptcy.[138] This is not meant to suggest that Scalia has supported preemption in every case. He has not.[139] But his preemption opinions strongly demonstrate a predisposition in favor of preemption rather than the traditional presumption against it, and the Hamiltonian understanding that the federal government can be "a legitimate and useful instrument of policy." The latter perspective has been particularly apparent in products liability cases, where Scalia and his conservative colleagues have read federal statutes in such a way as to forbid state courts from imposing higher standards of conduct on manufacturers through traditional common law damages actions.[140] By so doing, they have fulfilled the conservative political agenda of protecting "big business" from various forms of tort liability.

## CONCLUSION

This chapter has demonstrated several areas of agreement between Alexander Hamilton and Justice Scalia in the area of federalism. Like Hamilton, Scalia does not believe the Tenth Amendment places an affirmative limit on national power, but rather agrees with the Court's conclusion in *United States v. Darby*[141] that the amendment states a constitutional redundancy. Scalia's vote in *Dole* and concurring opinion in *Baker* also support a broad construction of national power, as does his 1997 speech at the Manhattan Institute, where he embraced a Hamiltonian conception of the general welfare provision. In remarks to the Federalist Society's inaugural national convention in 1982, Scalia likely surprised some of its members by invoking Hamilton, not Madison or Jefferson, on the subject of federalism, and urged the conference participants—"as Hamilton would have urged [them]—to keep in mind that the federal government is not bad but good. The trick is to use it wisely." And finally, Scalia's preemption decisions indicate that his movement toward Madison in the area of federalism in the 1990s is not wholly complete. His voting behavior in preemption cases, which placed him *first* among members of the Rehnquist Court in terms of supporting federal power, still indicates an acute awareness that the instruments of national power can be used for conservative purposes. Even though there is substantial evidence of a Hamiltonian influence in Scalia's early federalism jurisprudence, we shall see in the next chapter a steady movement in the direction of Madison's views on the subject.

# NOTES

1. "Inaugural Address of President Ronald Reagan," *Weekly Compilation of Presidential Documents* 17 (January 20, 1981): 1, 2–4.
2. 426 U.S. 833 (1976).
3. Ibid., 845.
4. 469 U.S. 527 (1985).
5. Ibid., 546.
6. Ibid., 550.
7. See, e.g., Herbert Wechsler, "The Political Safeguards of Federalism: The Role of the States in the Composition and Selection of the National Government," *Columbia Law Review* 54 (1954): 543, 558.
8. For a more extended discussion of the differences between Hamilton and Madison over the issue of federalism, see James B. Staab, "The Tenth Amendment and Justice Scalia's 'Split Personality,'" *Journal of Law & Politics* 16, no. 2 (2000): 231–379.
9. In fact, at the New York Ratifying Convention, Hamilton objected to the inclusion of the word "expressly" in a proposed constitutional amendment reserving the powers of the states, noting that there are "a thousand things" the national government must be able to do that are not expressly mentioned in the Constitution. Interestingly, Hamilton cited the debates at the Virginia Ratifying Convention for support of this view. PAH, 5:182.
10. FP (No. 45), 296. In fact, Hamilton said the complete opposite:

> [T]o the care of the Federal Government are confided . . . those great, general interests on which all particular interests materially depend: our safety in respect to foreign nations; our tranquility in respect to each other; the foreign and mutual commerce of the states; the establishment and regulation of the money of the country; the management of our national finances. . . . In a word, it is the province of the general Government to manage the greatest number of those concerns in which its provident *activity* and *exertion* are of most importance to the people; and we have only to compare the state of our country antecedent to its establishment, with what it has been since, to be convinced that the most operative causes of public prosperity depend upon that general Government. (PAH, 25:503 [emphasis in original])

11. PAH, 8:105.
12. PAH, 5:97. See also PAH, 8:104.
13. PAH, 5:118–19.
14. FP (No. 31), 219. At the New York State Ratifying Convention, Hamilton elaborated on his structural view:

> [T]he most powerful obstacle to the members of the Congress betraying the interests of their constituents, is the state legislatures themselves; who will be standing bodies of observation, possessing the confidence of the people, jealous of federal encroachments, and armed with every power to check the first essays of treachery. . . . Thus, it appears that the very structure of the confederacy affords the surest preventives from error, and the most powerful checks to misconduct. (PAH, 5:57)

15. PAH, 8:99.

16. Antonin Scalia, "Economic Affairs as Human Affairs," in *Economic Liberties and the Judiciary*, ed. James A. Dorn and Henry G. Manne (Fairfax, VA: George Mason University Press, 1987), 36–37.

17. Remarks by Justice Antonin Scalia to Dr. Henry J. Abraham's "Seminar in American Constitutional Law and Theory" class from the University of Virginia, Supreme Court Building, Washington, DC, December 2, 1996.

18. U.S. Senate, *The Nomination of Judge Antonin Scalia, To Be Associate Justice of the Supreme Court of the United States: Hearings before the Committee on the Judiciary of the United States Senate*, 99th Cong., 2nd sess., August 5–6, 1986, 81.

19. Ibid., 82.

20. Ibid.

21. Ibid.

22. Remarks by Justice Antonin Scalia at a roundtable discussion on "Separation of Powers in the Constitution," sponsored by the U.S. Court of Appeals, Washington, DC, November 15, 1988. C-SPAN video.

23. U.S. Senate, *Confirmation of Federal Judges: Hearings before the Committee on the Judiciary of the United States Senate*, 97th Cong., 2nd sess., 1982, 92.

24. Art. 1, sec. 2 and art. 2, sec. 1.

25. Art. 1, sec. 3.

26. Art. 5.

27. 469 U.S. at 556. See also *Nat'l. League of Cities v. Usery*, 426 U.S. 833, 876 (Brennan, J., dissenting).

28. 469 U.S. at 554.

29. Antonin Scalia, "Reflections on the Constitution," address to the Kennedy Political Union at American University, Washington, DC, November 17, 1988. C-SPAN video.

30. Ibid.

31. U.S. Senate, *Nomination of Judge Antonin Scalia*, 82.

32. 483 U.S. 203 (1987).

33. U.S. Const. art. I, sec. 8, cl. 1.

34. "The Bank Bill" (February 2, 1791), PJM, 13:374. For an excellent analysis of Madison's and Hamilton's interpretation of the General Welfare Clause, see H. Jefferson Powell, "Enumerated Means and Unlimited Ends, *Michigan Law Review* 94 (1995): 651–73.

35. Ibid.

36. Ibid., 376.

37. "Final Version of an Opinion on the Constitutionality of an Act to Establish a Bank" (February 23, 1791), PAH, 8:98.

38. Ibid., 105.

39. FP (No. 34), 227.

40. "Final Version of the Report on the Subject of Manufactures" (December 5, 1791), PAH, 10:303.

41. Ibid.

42. 297 U.S. 1 (1936).

43. Ibid., 66.

44. 483 U.S. at 207.
45. Ibid. (quoting *United States v. Butler*, 297 U.S. at 66).
46. 483 U.S. at 207.
47. Ibid.
48. Ibid., 208–9.
49. Ibid., 208.
50. Edward H. Crane, "The Era of Big Government Ain't Over," *Cato Online Policy Report* 19, no. 6 (November–December 1997). See also *United States v. American Library Association*, 539 U.S. 194 (2003) (upholding the Children's Internet Protection Act of 2000 under Congress' spending authority).
51. 626 F. Supp. 1374 (D. D.C. 1986).
52. In his opinion in *Synar*, authored for a special three-judge panel of the D.C. District Court, Scalia made the following observation about the Necessary and Proper Clause:

> Nor is it the law, as plaintiffs assert, that a broad delegation such as this must be supported by some rigorous "principle of necessity" which is allegedly not met here because Congress has exercised sole power over appropriations in the past and presumably could continue to do so. To be sure, in delegation cases the Supreme Court has occasionally recognized the "necessity" for delegation. . . . It is doubtful, however, that the word "necessity" in that context, any more than the word "necessary" in the "necessary and proper" clause of the Constitution, refers to an "absolute physical necessity." . . . Rather, necessity refers to a strong utility and convenience, which can certainly be considered to exist here. (626 F. Supp. at 1386 [internal citation omitted])

53. 485 U.S. 505 (1988).
54. 157 U.S. 429 (1895).
55. 485 U.S. at 512–13.
56. 456 U.S. 742 (1982).
57. 485 U.S. at 528 (Scalia, J., concurring).
58. 469 U.S. at 554.
59. Ibid., at 556 (quoting 326 U.S. 572, 583 [1946]).
60. After all, even if one takes Scalia's reading of *Garcia* at face value, he did not argue that the Tenth Amendment places a bar on Congress's authority to regulate commerce; rather, he argued that some structural provision imposes such a limit.
61. See, e.g., *FERC v. Mississippi*, 456 U.S. 742, 775 (1982) (O'Connor, J., dissenting); *Gregory v. Ashcroft*, 501 U.S. 452 (1991).
62. Stewart Abercrombie Baker and Katherine H. Wheatley, "Justice Scalia and Federalism: A Sketch," *The Urban Lawyer* 20, no. 2 (1988): 353.
63. The conference was held at Yale Law School April 23–25, 1982—only four months prior to Scalia's appointment to the D.C. Court of Appeals. See, generally, "A Symposia on Federalism," *Harvard Journal of Law and Public Policy* 6 (1982): 1–147.
64. Antonin Scalia, "The Two Faces of Federalism," *Harvard Journal of Law and Public Policy* 6 (1982): 19–22, 19.
65. Ibid.
66. Ibid.
67. Ibid., 20.

68. Ibid.

69. Ibid.

70. President Reagan himself gave vent to the conservative hostility toward the national government. In his first inaugural address, Reagan said that "government is not the solution to our problem; government is the problem." "Inaugural Address of President Ronald Reagan," p. 2.

71. Scalia, "The Two Faces of Federalism," 21–22.

72. Ibid., 22.

73. John T. Noonan, Jr., "The Hatch Amendment and the New Federalism," *Harvard Journal of Law and Public Policy* 6 (1982): 93, 98.

74. 410 U.S. 113 (1973).

75. Noonan, "The Hatch Amendment and the New Federalism," 101.

76. Ibid.

77. Ibid., 100.

78. Ibid., 101–2.

79. "Reflections on the Revolution in France," SWEB, 2:153.

80. Ibid., 275–76.

81. See, e.g., Russell Kirk, *The Conservative Mind: From Burke to Santayana* (Chicago: Henry Regnery Company, 1953), 65–70; see also Clinton Rossiter, *Conservatism in America: The Thankless Persuasion*, 2nd ed. (New York: Alfred A. Knopf, Inc., 1962), 105–10.

82. Scalia, "The Two Faces of Federalism," 22.

83. The Supremacy Clause provides: "This Constitution, and the Laws of the United States which shall be made in Pursuance thereof; . . . shall be the supreme Law of the Land; . . . any Thing in the Constitution or Laws of any State to the Contrary notwithstanding." U.S. Const. art. VI, cl. 2.

84. *Free v. Bland*, 369 U.S. 663, 666 (1962).

85. *Gregory v. Ashcroft*, 501 U.S. 452, 460 (1991).

86. FP, 225.

87. Ibid.

88. Mary J. Davis, "Unmasking the Presumption in Favor of Preemption," *South Carolina Law Review* 53 (2002): 967, 970.

89. Ibid.

90. See Guido Calabresi, *A Common Law for the Age of Statutes* (Cambridge, MA: Harvard University Press, 1982), 1–7.

91. Davis, "Unmasking the Presumption in Favor of Preemption," 968.

92. See also *Food and Drug Admin. v. Brown & Williamson Tobacco Corp.*, 529 U.S. 120 (2000); *Lorillard Tobacco Co. v. Reilly*, 533 U.S. 525 (2001).

93. 505 U.S. 504 (1992).

94. Ibid., 514 (quoting 15 U.S.C. sec. 1331).

95. Ibid. (quoting 15 U.S.C. sec. 1334).

96. Public Health Cigarette Smoking Act of 1969, Pub. L. No. 91-222, 84 Stat. 87 (1970) (codified as amended at 15 U.S.C. secs. 1331–38).

97. Advertisement of Cigarettes, 34 Fed. Reg. 1959 (Feb. 11, 1969) (to be codified at 47 C.F.R. pt. 73).

98. Pub. L. No. 91-222 (codified as amended at 15 U.S.C. sec. 1334[b]).

99. 505 U.S. at 518.

100. Ibid., 520 (quoting 15 U.S.C. sec. 1334[b]).

101. Ibid., 531.

102. Ibid., 516 (citing *Rice v. Santa Fe Elevator Corp.*, 531 U.S. 218, 230 [1947]).

103. Ibid.

104. Ibid., 517.

105. Ibid., 546, 547.

106. Ibid., 547.

107. Ibid., 548.

108. See, e.g., *Bates v. Dow Agrosciences LLC*, 125 S. Ct. 1788 (Thomas, J., concurring in the judgment in part and dissenting in part, in which Scalia, J., joined).

109. Scalia, "The Two Faces of Federalism," 19–22.

110. 518 U.S. 470, 509 (1996).

111. Justice Sandra Day O'Connor wrote the opinion, which was joined by Chief Justice Rehnquist and Justices Scalia and Thomas.

112. 529 U.S. 861 (2000).

113. Chief Justice Rehnquist and Justices O'Connor, Scalia, and Kennedy.

114. See, e.g., *Yearsley v. W. A. Ross Construction Co.*, 309 U.S. 18 (1940).

115. See, e.g., *Bynum v. FMC Corp.*, 770 F.2d 556, 560 (5th Cir. 1985).

116. See, e.g., *Merritt, Chapman & Scott Corp. v. Guy F. Atkinson Co.*, 295 F.2d 14 (9th Cir. 1961); *Ryan v. Feeney & Sheehan Building Co.*, 239 N.Y. 43 (1924).

117. See, e.g., *Challoner v. Day & Zimmermann, Inc.*, 512 F.2d 77 (5th Cir. 1975); *Garrison v. Rohm & Haas Co.*, 492 F.2d 346 (6th Cir. 1974); *Spangler v. Kranco, Inc.*, 481 F.2d 373 (4th Cir. 1973); *Johnston v. United States*, 568 F. Supp. 351 (D. Kan. 1983).

118. See, e.g., *Tozer v. LTV Corp.*, 792 F.2d 403 (4th Cir. 1986); *Shaw v. Grumman Aerospace Corp.*, 778 F.2d 736 (11th Cir. 1985); *Koutsoubos v. Boeing Vertol*, 755 F.2d 352 (3d Cir. 1985); *Tillett v. J. I. Case Co.*, 756 F.2d 591 (7th Cir. 1985); *Bynum v. FMC Corp.*, 770 F.2d 556 (5th Cir. 1985); *McKay v. Rockwell Int'l Corp.*, 704 F.2d 444 (9th Cir. 1983); *In re "Agent Orange" Product Liab. Litig.*, 534 F. Supp. 1046 (E.D.N.Y. 1982).

119. 487 U.S. 500 (1988).

120. Ibid., 503.

121. 792 F.2d 403 (4th Cir. 1986).

122. For the conference votes in *Boyle*, see HABP, box 490, folder 8.

123. 487 U.S. at 515n1 (Brennan, J., dissenting).

124. Ibid., 504.

125. Ibid., 504–6.

126. Ibid., 512.

127. Ibid., 507.

128. Scalia raised this issue several times during oral argument, but counsel for Sikorsky (as well as for the government) explicitly disclaimed reliance on the discretionary function exception of the FTCA. See reargument in *Boyle v. United Technologies Corp.*, (April 27, 1988), original transcripts, U.S. Supreme Court Library, Washington, DC. In making this point, Scalia likely relied upon a recent law review article, which the author appears to have sent to each of the justices, contending that

the government contractor defense was more soundly based on the FTCA discretionary function exception than on the *Feres* doctrine. See Richard Ausness, "Surrogate Immunity: The Government Contract Defense and Products Liability," *Ohio State Law Journal* 47 (1986): 985; Letter from Richard Ausness to Harry Blackmun, July 7, 1987, HABP, box 490, folder 8. In any event, resting the defense on the discretionary function exception of the FTCA does substantially expand the scope of the government contractor defense.

129. See, e.g., *McKay v. Rockwell Int'l Corp.*, 704 F.2d 444 (9th Cir. 1983); *Tillett v. J. I. Case Co.*, 756 F.2d 591 (7th Cir. 1985); *Bynum v. FMC Corp.*, 770 F.2d 556 (5th Cir. 1985); *Tozer v. LTV Corp.*, 792 F.2d 403 (4th Cir. 1986).

130. 340 U.S. 135 (1950).

131. Justice Scalia might have also avoided basing the government contractor defense on the *Feres* doctrine, because only one year earlier he sharply criticized the Court's decision recognizing such an immunity. See *United States v. Johnson*, 481 U.S. 681, 692 (1987) (Scalia, J., dissenting).

132. See, e.g., *Webster v. Reproductive Health Services*, 492 U.S. 490, 532 (1989) (Scalia, J., concurring) ("The outcome of today's case will undoubtedly be heralded as a triumph of judicial statesmanship. It is not that, unless it is statesmanlike needlessly to prolong this Court's self-awarded sovereignty over a field [abortion] where it has little proper business since the answers to most of the cruel questions posed are political and not juridical."); *Cruzan v. Director, Missouri Dep't of Health*, 497 U.S. 261, 293 (1990) (Scalia, J., concurring) ("While I agree with the Court's analysis today, and therefore join its opinion, I would have preferred that we announce, clearly and promptly, that the federal courts have no business in this field; that American law has always accorded the State the power to prevent, by force if necessary, suicide— including suicide by refusing to take appropriate measures necessary to preserve one's life").

133. *Sosa v. Alvarez-Machain*, 542 U.S. 692 (2004) (Scalia, J., concurring in part and concurring in judgment) ("In Benthamite terms, creating a federal command [federal common law] out of 'international norms,' and then constructing a cause of action to enforce that command through the purely jurisdictional grant of the [Alien Tort Statute], is nonsense on stilts").

134. See, e.g., *Crosby v. Nat'l Foreign Trade Council*, 530 U.S. 363, 388 (2000).

135. See, e.g., *Gade v. Nat'l Solid Wastes Mgmt. Ass'n.*, 505 U.S. 88 (1992).

136. See, e.g., *Morales v. Trans World Airlines, Inc.*, 504 U.S. 374 (1992).

137. See, e.g., *Engine Manufacturers Ass'n v. South Coast Air Quality Management District*, 541 U.S. 246 (2004); *United States v. Locke*, 529 U.S. 89 (2000); *Int'l Paper Co. v. Ouellette*, 479 U.S. 481 (1987); *California Coastal Comm'n v. Granite Rock Co.*, 480 U.S. 572, 607 (1987) (Scalia, J., dissenting).

138. See, e.g., *Owen v. Owen*, 500 U.S. 305 (1991).

139. See, e.g., *Lukhard v. Reed*, 481 U.S. 368 (1987); *Wisconsin Public Intervenor v. Mortier*, 501 U.S. 597, 616 (1991) (Scalia, J., concurring).

140. See James B. Staab, "Conservative Activism on the Rehnquist Court: Federal Preemption is No Longer a Liberal Issue," *Roger Williams University Law Review* 9 (2003): 129–85.

141. 312 U.S. 100, 124 (1941).

## Chapter Nine

# The Transformation from a Hamiltonian to a Madisonian in Federalism Disputes

This chapter examines Antonin Scalia's movement during the 1990s in the direction of a more balanced approach to federalism, which was represented most prominently at the time of the founding by James Madison. Four cases will be unpacked in some detail in order to show this transformation: *Gregory v. Ashcroft* (1991), *United States v. Lopez* (1995), *U.S. Term Limits, Inc. v. Thornton* (1995), and *Printz v. United States* (1997). In each of these decisions, Scalia either wrote or joined an opinion that indicates a more moderate Madisonian approach to federalism disputes. In fact, Scalia claimed in his majority opinion in *Printz* that "it was Madison's—not Hamilton's—[view] that prevailed" on the subject of federalism.[1] However, these four decisions, and Scalia's statement in *Printz*, must be reconciled with two other important developments in Scalia's federalism jurisprudence. First, Scalia wrote a separate concurring opinion in *Gonzales v. Raich* (2005), where the Court ruled that Congress had the authority to prohibit the local cultivation and use of marijuana for medicinal purposes, in which he defended an expansive interpretation of Congress's commerce and necessary and proper powers. Moreover, as discussed in chapter 8, Scalia is the Court's leading defender of national power in preemption cases. Thus, rather than a major transformation in political principles, Scalia's self-conscious movement in the 1990s toward a more nuanced Madisonian approach in federalism cases can be seen as strategic. By proclaiming that it was Madison's, not Hamilton's, view that prevailed in federal-state relations, Scalia can now stake out a middle-ground position in the federalism disputes that come before the Court.

## *GREGORY V. ASHCROFT*: THE "PLAIN STATEMENT" RULE

In *Gregory v. Ashcroft*,[2] the issue before the Court was whether the federal Age Discrimination in Employment Act (ADEA) of 1967, as amended, prevented the states from imposing mandatory retirements on their judges. The ADEA makes it unlawful for an employer to discharge any individual who is at least forty years old because of such individual's age. In 1974, Congress extended the substantive provisions of the act to include states as employers. At the same time, Congress amended the definition of "employee" to exclude all state elected officials as well as "appointee[s] on the policymaking level."[3]

In 1976, voters in Missouri passed a constitutional amendment requiring that all judges, except for municipal courts, retire at the age of seventy years.[4] Petitioners, three state judges who were initially appointed by the governor of Missouri, brought suit, claiming that the state law violated the ADEA. John Ashcroft, then governor of Missouri, defended the constitutional provision by arguing that state judges were not included within the coverage of the ADEA, because they were "appointee[s] on the policymaking level." The U.S. District Court granted the governor's motion to dismiss, and the U.S. Court of Appeals for the Eighth Circuit affirmed the dismissal.

In an opinion by Justice Sandra Day O'Connor, the Supreme Court affirmed. While O'Connor acknowledged that the central issue in the case involved federal preemption, she began the Court's opinion with an extended discussion of the values of federalism. "As every schoolchild learns," wrote O'Connor, "our Constitution establishes a system of dual sovereignty between the States and the Federal Government."[5] This "dual sovereignty" was recognized by the Court over 120 years ago when it held that "[t]he Constitution, in all its provisions, looks to an indestructible Union, composed of indestructible States."[6] Under the U.S. federal system, O'Connor continued, the States "retain substantial sovereign authority," which as a textual matter is made clear by the reservation of state powers under the Tenth Amendment. O'Connor then quoted James Madison from *Federalist* 45: "The powers delegated by the proposed Constitution to the federal government are few and defined. Those which are to remain in the State governments are numerous and indefinite."[7]

Justice O'Connor also cited "numerous advantages" of the federal system: (1) sensitivity to the diverse interests and preferences of a heterogeneous population, (2) increased opportunity for citizen involvement in the democratic process, (3) innovation and experimentation in the policies adopted by government, and (4) a government that is more responsive to the needs of the people by putting the states in competition with each other for a mobile citizenry. But the "principal benefit" of the federal system, in O'Connor's view, is the added security it provides to liberty. A properly designed separation of powers system will "prevent the accumulation of excessive power in any one branch, [while] a healthy balance of power between the States and the Federal Government will reduce the risk of tyranny and abuse from either front." "In the tension between federal and state power," O'Connor observed, "lies the promise of liberty."[8]

After this extended discussion of federalism, O'Connor turned to the legal question presented in the case: whether the 1974 amendments to the ADEA preempt a state law requiring judges to retire by the age of seventy. O'Connor acknowledged that the Supremacy Clause gives the federal government "a decided advantage" in federalism disputes, because "[a]s long as it is acting within the powers granted it under the Constitution, Congress may impose its will on the States," and it may do so "in areas traditionally regulated by the States." Having made this concession, however, O'Connor proceeded to describe the importance of the governmental function involved. The right to establish qualifications for judges, she maintained, is a function that "lies at the 'heart of representative government." "Through the structure of its government, and the character of those who exercise governmental authority," she added, "a State defines itself as a sovereign." Determining the qualifications of those who sit as judges "goes beyond an area traditionally regulated by the States; it is a decision of the most fundamental sort for a sovereign entity."[9]

Due to the important nature of the state function involved, O'Connor reasoned that application of the ADEA to cover state court judges "would upset the usual constitutional balance of federal and state powers." As a result, she determined that "it is incumbent upon the federal courts to be certain of Congress' intent before finding that federal law overrides this balance." Rather than rely upon conventional methods of interpreting statutes, the Court thus applied a plain statement rule. "If Congress intends to alter the usual constitutional balance between the States and the Federal Government," wrote O'Connor, "it must make its intention to do so unmistakably clear." "This plain statement rule," she continued, "is nothing more than an acknowledgement that the States retain substantial sovereign powers under our constitutional scheme, powers with which Congress does not readily interfere." The concern about federal overreaching of state power was made clear when O'Connor warned that Congress's authority under the Supremacy Clause to preempt state law "in areas traditionally regulated by the States" is "an extraordinary power in a federalist system" that "we must assume Congress does not exercise lightly."[10]

Applying this new plain statement rule to the facts of this case, O'Connor found that the amendments to the ADEA did not cover state judges. Even though she conceded that "'appointee at the policymaking level,' particularly in the context of the other exceptions that surround it, is an odd way for Congress to exclude judges," she contended that "[w]e will not read the ADEA to cover state judges unless Congress has made it clear that judges are included."[11] Moreover, the burden of satisfying this new plain statement rule was particularly heavy in this case. While O'Connor claimed that the ADEA did not have to mention judges, it had to be plain to anyone reading the act that judges were covered. Thus, the Court refused to consider the legislative history of the act. "In the context of a statute that plainly excludes most important state public officials," O'Connor reasoned, "'appointee on the policymaking level' is sufficiently broad that we cannot conclude that the statute plainly covers appointed state judges. Therefore, it does not."[12]

Justice Scalia joined the majority decision. Aside from the fact that a plain statement rule conflicts with his well-known textualist approach to interpreting statutes, Scalia's vote in *Gregory* raises two separate concerns about his previous Hamiltonian orientation to federalism disputes. First, where is the textual support for the Court's plain statement rule?[13] The Court borrows its plain statement rule from its Eleventh Amendment jurisprudence,[14] but in that area at least (though still problematic), a stronger textual argument can be made.[15] For support of a plain statement rule in cases affecting the "traditional functions" of the states, the majority relied, in part, on the Tenth Amendment. But the original meaning of that amendment gives no support to the Court's novel plain statement rule.

Second, the Court's plain statement rule conflicts with the political process approach to federalism disputes, which was adopted by the Court in *Garcia v. San Antonio Metropolitan Transit Authority.*[16] In *Garcia*, the Court ruled that "the principal means chosen by the Framers to ensure the role of States in the federal system lies in the structure of the Federal Government itself."[17] The Court thus reasoned that "[a]ny substantive restraint on the exercise of Commerce Clause powers must . . . be tailored to compensate for possible failings of the national political process."[18] The Court also rejected as "unsound in principle and unworkable in practice" any test for state immunity that requires a judicial determination of which state activities are "traditional."[19] Why, then, all the discussion in *Gregory* about the importance of the people of each state determining the qualifications of their judges? The central inquiry post-*Garcia* would seem to be whether the states have in some way been prevented from participating in the national political process, and there was no evidence in *Gregory* to suggest that Missouri, or any other state, was excluded from participating in the enactment of the 1974 amendments to the ADEA. The Court's discussion of the "traditional functions" of the states therefore seems beside the point and only clouds the central inquiry in the case: whether a conflict exists between the federal and state law. If so, then that is the end of the matter.

Justice Scalia's vote in *Gregory* marks the first clear sign of a Madisonian approach creeping into his federalism jurisprudence. His vote demonstrates that he is not willing to leave all federalism issues to the political process which is inconsistent with previous statements he has made that support such an approach. Recall that during his confirmation hearings Scalia said that the "main protection" of the states "is in the policymaking area, is in the Congress," and that it was primarily Congress's responsibility, "in the vast majority if not all of the cases," to judge whether its laws comply with the Constitution.[20] Moreover, Scalia had previously supported the *Darby* Court's interpretation of the Tenth Amendment as a mere constitutional redundancy.

Scalia's vote in *Gregory* also conflicts with his textualist approach to interpreting statutes. Unless the plain meaning of a statute is absurd on its face, Scalia has rejected resorting to external sources (e.g., committee reports and floor speeches) in ascertaining the legislative purpose behind a law. According to Scalia, the language of a statute should be the controlling factor in determining the meaning of a law. But plain statement rules necessarily involve substantive considerations external to the legislative text.[21] As one Court observer has noted, "Such rules operate to foreclose a particular interpretation of a statute even though consideration of the legislative text alone—its language and structure—might point to a different meaning than the one dictated by the rule."[22] In fact, Scalia has himself criticized the Court's use of plain statement rules for this very reason.[23] Interestingly, Scalia initially wrote a brief concurring opinion in *Gregory* in which he criticized the Court's use of a plain statement rule, but then decided to withhold it. In that opinion, Scalia objected that the application of a plain statement rule to the ADEA "would compel Congress to prepare laundry lists of covered state functionaries, with no assurance that any given degree of specificity is enough." He also believed that "judges have no power to prescribe for Congress particular formulas of statutory enactment, such as the 'name-the-judges' rule the Court favors."[24]

In sum, the Court's decision in *Gregory* represents a Madisonian compromise in the area of federalism. It is neither as drastic as overturning a congressional law using the traditional functions analysis of *National League of Cities v. Usery*,[25] nor as lenient as the political process approach of *Garcia*. A plain statement rule is a practical (and rather ingenious) way for the Court to restrict Congress's commerce authority without drawing much attention to itself.[26] The upside of a plain statement rule is that it will make legislators be more accountable for the laws they enact. In order for Congress to apply its laws to the traditional functions of the states, it will have to be explicit. The downside of the plain statement rule is that the justices are imposing their own value judgments (absent clear constitutional support) on the legislative process. The importance of the Court's plain statement rule will depend on how often it is used and under what circumstances. To date, and perhaps not surprisingly, the Court has not used it consistently.[27] Scalia's support of a plain statement rule in cases affecting the traditional functions of the states is difficult to explain. He must believe that the political process does not adequately protect the sovereign interests of the states, but because plain statement rules necessarily involve considerations external to text, they remain controversial. They would seem to involve the Court in the same type of judicial policy making of which Scalia has been famously critical.


## *UNITED STATES V. LOPEZ*: A "TRUE AND FAIR" CONSTRUCTION OF NATIONAL POWER

In 1990, Congress enacted the Gun-Free School Zone Act, making it a federal crime to possess a gun within one thousand feet of a private or public school. On March 10, 1992, Alfonso Lopez was arrested and charged with carrying a concealed .38-caliber handgun and five bullets into Edison High School in San Antonio, Texas. Lopez was initially charged under Texas law for possessing a firearm on school premises, but the next day, the state charges were dismissed, and federal agents charged him with violating the Gun-Free School Zone Act. A federal district judge found Lopez guilty and sentenced him to six months' imprisonment and two years' probation. On appeal, Lopez's attorneys challenged his conviction on the ground that the Gun-Free School Zone Act went beyond Congress's authority to regulate commerce. The Court of Appeals for the Fifth Circuit agreed and overturned his conviction.

In a five-to-four decision,[28] the Supreme Court affirmed—marking the first time in almost sixty years that the Court struck down a federal law for exceeding Congress's authority to regulate commerce. Writing for the majority, Chief Justice Rehnquist began the Court's opinion with "first principles" of federalism. "The Constitution creates a federal government of enumerated powers," wrote Rehnquist.[29] As the Court had done in *Gregory*, Rehnquist also quoted James Madison: "The powers delegated by the proposed Constitution to the federal government are few and defined. Those which are to remain in the State governments are numerous and indefinite."[30] According to Rehnquist, the federal system of divided powers "was adopted by the Framers to ensure protection of our fundamental liberties."[31] Again citing *Gregory*, Rehnquist maintained, "Just as the separation of powers serves to prevent the accumulation of excessive power in any one branch of government, a healthy balance of power between the States and the Federal Government will reduce the risk of tyranny and abuse from either front."[32]

The Court next reviewed its long history of Commerce Clause decisions. It did so for two reasons. First, it sought to show that while Congress's authority to regulate commerce has greatly expanded in the modern era, there are still "outer limits" to this authority. These limits, Rehnquist claimed, "are inherent in the very language of the Commerce Clause," and were first recognized by Chief Justice John Marshall in *Gibbons v. Ogden*, when he wrote, "The enumeration [of powers] presupposes something not enumerated."[33] Second, the Court reviewed its Commerce Clause jurisprudence in order to determine the appropriate standard of review to apply in the case. While the Court acknowledged some ambiguity on this question, it determined that the proper standard was the "substantial effects" test. Under this test, the Court asks whether there is a rational basis that a given intrastate activity has a substantial effect on interstate commerce. Applying this test to the case before it, the Court found no rational basis for concluding that firearm possession in and around schools has a substantial effect on interstate commerce. According to Rehnquist, the possession of guns "has nothing to do with 'commerce' or any sort of economic enterprise, however broadly one might define those terms."[34]

Justice Scalia joined Chief Justice Rehnquist's majority opinion. What are the implications of his vote for purposes of assessing his previously expressed Hamiltonian leanings in the area of federalism? At first blush, Scalia's vote in *Lopez* seems perfectly consistent with a Hamiltonian approach. Hamilton, after all, never said that the federal government's powers were unlimited.[35] The limits, identified by Hamilton, were contained in the structure of the federal system as well as in the checklist of enumerated powers under Article I. Indeed, there is much to commend in the majority opinion from a Hamiltonian perspective. Noticeably absent from Chief Justice Rehnquist's opinion is any mention of the Tenth Amendment. Unlike his opinion in *Usery*, Rehnquist does not rely on the Tenth Amendment (at least in an explicit way) as an affirmative limit on national power. Rather, the Court determined that gun possession in and around schools is not commercial activity subject to the regulatory authority of Congress. By focusing the majority's analysis on "commerce," Rehnquist was at least implicitly following a Hamiltonian approach to federalism.

Having said this, however, several observations can be made that indicate that the *Lopez* majority was influenced more by a Madisonian construction of national power than by a Hamiltonian interpretation. First, it is important to remember that Madison did not place much weight on the Tenth Amendment either. Unlike the leading Anti-Federalists of his day, Madison did not think a reserved power amendment was even necessary, because the principle of limited government was already implied by the structure of the Constitution.[36] Moreover, Madison rejected the idea that the Tenth Amendment, as ratified, constituted an affirmative limit on national power.[37] Rather, like Hamilton, he regarded the limits on national power as implied by the enumeration of powers under Article I.[38]

Second, a Madisonian influence on the *Lopez* majority is reflected in its emphasis on the *limits* of national power. In the great constitutional debates with Hamilton in the 1790s, Madison tended to stress the limits of national power. As he observed in his opinion on the national bank, a rule of construction cannot be just that would convert a limited government into an unlimited one.[39] Hamilton, by contrast, emphasized that the powers delegated to the national government were more properly regarded as grants, not limits. He did not contemplate a strict division of powers between the national and state levels of government. Indeed, he assumed (and thought it desirable) that the national government would extend its authority into the internal concerns of the states.[40]

When seen in this light, the *Lopez* majority speaks more to a Madisonian construction of national power than to a Hamiltonian one. While Chief Justice Rehnquist rejects a strict construction of the national government's powers,[41] he appears to be more concerned with the limits of federal authority than with whether the national government had a rational basis for concluding that gun possession at schools had a substantial effect on commerce. In fact, the Chief Justice does not even consider the federal government's arguments on their own merits. Rather, the *Lopez* majority disagreed substantively with Congress's conclusion that gun-free school zones substantially affect interstate commerce. As several observers of the Court have pointed out, the *Lopez* majority appears to have applied a rational basis test with a bite.[42]

Third, the *Lopez* majority speaks to a Madisonian construction of national power in that it regards the supervision of federalism issues as ultimately a judicial function. Even though Madison sometimes emphasized a political process approach toward federalism, he ultimately came to regard the federal judiciary as the final arbiter of federal-state relations.[43] By contrast, while Hamilton did not completely deny a judicial role in federalism controversies, he regarded the political branches as better able to resolve these disputes.[44] For the *Lopez* majority, the issue of whether Congress overstepped its boundaries by enacting the Gun-Free School Zone Act was quintessentially a judicial question. As Rehnquist put it, "Simply because Congress may conclude that a particular activity substantially affects interstate commerce does not necessarily make it so."[45] The determination of whether a particular activity comes within Congress's commerce power, Rehnquist concluded, "is ultimately a judicial rather that a legislative question, and can be settled finally only by this Court."[46]

Finally, the rhetoric of a Madisonian construction of national power runs throughout the majority opinion. First, Rehnquist quoted Madison for the proposition that the federal government's powers are "few and defined," while the states' powers are "numerous and indefinite."[47] This quote is emblematic of the central paradox of the *Lopez* decision: while the Court sounds pragmatic in its approach toward federalism, its analysis marks a return to a moderate form of formalism in this area. Moreover, as law professor H. Jefferson Powell points out,[48] Rehnquist concluded the Court's opinion with a method of reasoning strikingly similar to the one used by Madison in his opinion on the national bank: "To uphold the Government's contentions here, we would have to pile inference upon inference in a manner that would bid fair to convert congressional authority under the Commerce Clause to a general police power of the sort retained by the States. . . . This we are unwilling to do."[49]

Justice Scalia's vote in *Lopez* represents another pragmatic compromise to his political process approach toward federalism. During his confirmation hearings, Scalia said that the "main protection" of the states "is in the policy-making area, is in the Congress," and that it was primarily Congress's responsibility, "in the vast majority if not all cases," to judge whether its laws comply with the Constitution.[50] But the Court in *Lopez* did not defer to the legislative judgment of Congress; rather, it made its own determination of whether gun possession in and around schools substantially affects interstate commerce. Following *Lopez*, the same five-justice majority applied a similar sort of analysis to Congress's commerce authority in striking down a provision of the Violence Against Women Act of 1994.[51] That provision granted a federal civil remedy, enforceable in state or federal court, to victims of gender-based hate crimes. Chief Justice Rehnquist, again speaking for the Court, reiterated that in order for intrastate activity to have a substantial affect on interstate activity, the activity in question must be economic in nature. "Gender-motivated crimes of violence are not, in any sense of that phrase, economic activity," concluded Rehnquist.[52] Even though Scalia joined his conservative colleagues in *Lopez* and *Morrison*, he dramatically broke ranks with them in a high profile case involving the federal regulation of drugs.

## THE MEDICINAL USE OF MARIJUANA

During the first campaign of the "war on drugs," Congress passed the Comprehensive Drug Abuse Prevention and Control Act of 1970, Title II of which is called the Controlled Substances Act (CSA). The main purpose of the CSA is to control drug abuse and regulate the legitimate and illegitimate traffic in controlled substances. The act places controlled substances into five schedules "based on their accepted medical uses, the potential for abuse, and their psychological and physical effects on the body."[53] Since 1970, marijuana has been listed as a Schedule I drug, meaning it has a high potential for abuse and lacks any accepted medical use. Except when used during government-approved research studies, the act makes it a federal crime to manufacture, distribute, or possess marijuana. Despite many attempts to reschedule marijuana over the years, it remains a Schedule I drug.

In 1996, California voters approved a measure titled the "Compassionate Use Act," which decriminalized the use of marijuana for "seriously ill" residents of the state when recommended by a licensed physician. Since then, ten other states have passed similar laws. Angel Raich and Diane Monson, two California residents, suffer from a variety of serious medical conditions for which they use marijuana as a medical treatment. Raich, for example, suffers from "an inoperable brain tumor, life-threatening weight loss, a seizure disorder, nausea, and several chronic pain disorders."[54] She has found that marijuana is the only effective form of pain relief for her medical conditions that does not come with intolerable side effects. Her doctor claims that if Raich were to forego cannabis treatments, she would suffer excruciating pain that could be fatal. Both women use marijuana that is cultivated locally. Monson cultivates her own cannabis, while two caregivers supply Raich with hers free of charge. Controversy developed in 2002 when state and federal agents arrived at Monson's home and, after a three-hour standoff, seized and destroyed her six marijuana plants. While the state agents acknowledged that the possession of marijuana was not unlawful under California law, the federal agents seized the plants pursuant to their authority under the CSA. In their federal suit, Raich and Monson sought, among other things, a declaration that the application of the act to locally cultivated and used marijuana exceeded Congress's commerce authority. While Raich and Monson did not dispute that Congress had the authority to pass the CSA, they contended that its application to the intrastate, noncommercial use of marijuana for medicinal purposes went beyond federal power.

In an opinion by Justice John Paul Stevens, the Court sided with the federal government. Relying on its 1942 precedent in *Wickard v. Filburn*[55] — widely regarded as one of the Court's most far-reaching Commerce Clause decisions — the Court held that Congress has the authority to regulate purely intrastate, noncommercial activity if it substantially affects interstate commerce. In *Wickard*, the Court upheld a fine imposed on a family-owned farm for violating the Agricultural Adjustment Act of 1938, which, in order to control the price of wheat, restricted the amount of wheat individual farmers could produce. Instead of growing his allotted 11.1 acres of wheat, Roscoe

Filburn sowed 23 acres and was fined for the overage. Filburn contested his fine on the ground that the nearly 12 acres of extra wheat he produced did not affect interstate commerce since it was intended entirely for use on his farm. The Court unanimously, with Justice Robert Jackson writing the majority decision, ruled that even locally used wheat could substantially affect interstate commerce. According to Jackson, even if economic incentives do not compel someone to introduce the wheat into the market, the homegrown use of wheat reduces the demand for the product in the market. And while the loss of Filburn's demand for wheat on the market might not be significant, the aggregate loss of demand from other similarly situated farmers doing the same thing could substantially affect the market price for wheat. Following this line of reasoning, Stevens argued that an exemption for marijuana grown and used locally for medicinal purposes could substantially affect the supply and demand for marijuana in the unlawful drug market. "The likelihood that all [marijuana] production will promptly terminate when patients recover or will precisely match the patients' medical needs during their convalescence seems remote," observed Stevens.[56] And the high demand for marijuana in the interstate market, despite vigorous criminal enforcement efforts to ban transactions of the drug, will lead "no small number of unscrupulous people [to] make use of the California exemption to serve their own ends whenever it is feasible to do so."[57] In light of the fact that California is one of eleven states that authorize the medical use of marijuana, Stevens concluded that Congress could have rationally believed that any sort of national exemption for locally used and cultivated marijuana could impact interstate commerce substantially. While Stevens expressed concern that Raich and Monson will suffer irreparable harm if they are prevented from using marijuana as a medical treatment, and admitted that their arguments regarding the medical benefits of marijuana were "strong," he recommended that any change to the classification of marijuana as a Schedule I drug take place in the political process, "in which the voices of voters allied with these respondents may one day be heard in the halls of Congress."[58]

Demonstrating his Hamiltonian instincts, Justice Scalia broke from his conservative states' rights colleagues and filed a concurring opinion.[59] While Scalia agreed with the majority's holding in the case, he wrote separately to explain what he regarded as his more "nuanced" approach to interstate commerce cases. Scalia emphasized that Congress's authority to regulate intrastate activities that substantially affect interstate commerce derives from two distinct provisions of the Constitution: the Commerce Clause and the Necessary and Proper Clause. These different sources of authority are important, according to Scalia, because when Congress is relying upon its necessary and proper authority, it can reach intrastate noncommercial activities that do not themselves substantially affect interstate commerce. Scalia pointed out that Court precedent shows that Congress may regulate intrastate activities necessary and proper for the regulation of interstate commerce in two circumstances. First, as part of its authority to regulate commerce among the states, Congress can pass regulations "to facilitate interstate commerce by eliminating potential obstructions, or to restrict it by eliminating potential stimulants."[60] These sorts of regulation have been analyzed under the Court's substantial effects test, and will be upheld if it can be shown that the underlying intrastate activity has a substantial effect on interstate commerce. But Congress can also regulate intrastate noneconomic activity "as an essential part of a larger regulation of economic activity, in which the regulatory scheme could be undercut unless the intrastate activity were regulated."[61] For Scalia, this type of regulation ensures that Congress's regulation of interstate commerce is effective and extends to intrastate noneconomic activity that does not itself substantially affect commerce. Based on these doctrinal clarifications, Scalia distinguished both *Lopez* and *Morrison* in two ways. First, there was no evidence in those cases that the underlying activities—gun possession around schools and violence against women—had a substantial effect on commerce. Moreover, those activities were not part of a more comprehensive interdependent legislative scheme in which the failure to regulate them could undercut the federal objective. By contrast, Scalia said that the possession of marijuana—the intrastate noneconomic activity involved in this case—was part of a larger comprehensive regulatory scheme that, if unregulated, could undermine the purpose of the law. "That simple possession [of marijuana] is a noneconomic activity" was irrelevant to Scalia.[62] The sole question was whether the prohibition of the possession of marijuana was a necessary and proper measure to effectuate the goals of the CSA, and Scalia thought that it was. For Scalia, "it hardly makes sense" to try to distinguish "'controlled substances manufactured and distributed intrastate' from 'controlled substances manufactured and distributed interstate,'" and he agreed with the majority that the former can just as easily find their way into the streams of interstate commerce.[63] As Scalia saw it, the federal government does not have to "accept on faith that state law will be effective in maintaining a strict division between a lawful market for 'medical' marijuana and the more general marijuana market." Citing Chief Justice John Marshall's language from *McCulloch v. Maryland* (1819), Scalia wrote, "To impose on [Congress] the necessity of resorting to means which it cannot control, which another government may furnish or withhold, would render its course precarious, the result of its measures uncertain, and create a dependence on other governments, which might disappoint its most important designs, and is incompatible with the language of the constitution."[64]

Justice Scalia's separate opinion in *Raich* is strong evidence of his Hamiltonian leanings. As long as the intrastate noneconomic activity is part of a larger regulatory scheme, Congress can regulate it even if the intrastate activity does not itself have a substantial impact on commerce. As Justice O'Connor pointed out in her dissent, the comprehensive nature of the federal legislation did not appear to be crucial to the Court's holdings in *Lopez* and *Morrison*, but rather the determinative question was whether the underlying activity involved was "economic" in nature. If Congress has the authority to regulate intrastate noneconomic activities that are part of a larger regulatory scheme, then the constitutionality of federal regulation will now depend on how it is drafted, reasoned O'Connor. Scalia's emphasis on Congress's ability to make federal legislation effective under the Necessary and Proper Clause furnishes little *legal* restriction on Congress's ability to regulate intrastate noneconomic activities. Although he still maintains that *Lopez* and *Morrison* are good law, and that there is a meaningful distinction between what is truly national and what is truly local, Congress (under Scalia's analysis) has been given ample discretion to regulate intrastate noneconomic activity. It might be true that for political reasons Congress will be less willing to regulate broadly, but that is a prudential question, not a legal impediment to Congress's commerce and necessary and proper powers. Scalia's opinion in *Raich* confirms his Hamiltonian political process approach toward federalism disputes, as well as his broad constructions of the Commerce Clause and the Necessary and Proper Clause. It also illustrates how Hamiltonian means can be used to accomplish conservative goals. Unlike in *Lopez* and *Morrison*, which involved gun possession and violence against women—two issues that Scalia arguably did not want to see nationalized—Scalia saw a need for federal involvement in regulating the availability of marijuana. Scalia did not likely approve of marijuana being described as medical treatment, and was concerned about the Compassionate Use Act being misused and marijuana becoming more prevalent in interstate commerce.

## *U.S. TERM LIMITS, INC. V. THORNTON*: TERM LIMITS

In the 1990s, popular frustration with the "career" politician, and with what voters perceived as an unresponsive and unaccountable Congress, sparked the national term limits movement. By the time the Supreme Court made a decision on the subject, twenty-three states had passed term limits laws. Although the laws varied from state to state, they all had one thing in common: to prevent a candidate who had already served a maximum number of terms in Congress from running for reelection. Typically, the laws were passed by large majorities, and voters overwhelmingly favored them.[65] But the term limits movement faced an uphill battle. No court (federal or state) ever upheld a term restriction for members of Congress, making the close vote (five to four) at the nation's high court a surprise to many.

The case before the Supreme Court, *U.S. Term Limits, Inc. v. Thornton*,[66] involved a constitutional amendment passed by popular initiative in the state of Arkansas. Like most term limits laws, the Arkansas amendment restricted U.S. representatives to three terms, and U.S. senators to two.[67] The central legal question for the justices was whether the Qualifications Clauses—which provide age, citizenship, and residency requirements for members of both houses of Congress[68]—forbid the states from supplementing those qualifications with what amounts to an ineligibility ("nonincumbency") restriction.

Justice John Paul Stevens wrote the majority opinion, which was joined by Justices David Souter, Anthony Kennedy, Ruth Bader Ginsburg, and Stephen Breyer. The majority held that the Qualifications Clauses did not permit the states to impose additional qualifications for members of Congress. For support of this position, Stevens made two central arguments. First, he argued that the power to add qualifications for representatives to Congress was not part of the "original powers" of state sovereignty and thus could not be *reserved* to the states by the Tenth Amendment. Second, Stevens reasoned that even if it could be assumed that the states possess as part of their original powers some control over congressional qualifications, there is abundant evidence to demonstrate that the Qualifications Clauses were intended to preclude them from exercising any such authority. For support of this view, Stevens relied upon the text and structure of the Constitution, the Court's decision in *Powell v. McCormack*,[69] the views of Hamilton and Madison in *The Federalist*, scholarly and judicial opinion, congressional and state ratification debates, fundamental principles of democratic government, and early state practices. All of this evidence, Stevens argued, pointed to the irrefutable position that the Qualifications Clauses were intended to be fixed and exclusive.

The dissent was written by Justice Clarence Thomas and joined by Chief Justice William H. Rehnquist and Justices Sandra Day O'Connor and Antonin Scalia. Thomas strongly objected to the majority's "original powers" thesis, which in his view "fundamentally misunderstands the notion of 'reserved powers'" under the Tenth Amendment.[70] According to Thomas, the people of the individual states are "[t]he ultimate source of the Constitution's authority," not any "undifferentiated people of the Nation as a whole."[71] In fact, Thomas maintained, there is no such thing as the popular sovereignty of a collective people in the United States, since the Constitution does not contemplate that the collective "people will either exercise power or delegate it," nor does it "recognize any mechanism for action by the undifferentiated people of the Nation."[72] According to Justice Thomas, the fact that ultimate sovereignty resides with the people of the several states is "enshrined" by the Tenth Amendment, which declares that "[t]he powers not delegated to the United States by the Constitution, nor prohibited by it to the states, are reserved to the States respectively, or to the people."[73] Even though the Tenth Amendment does not specify, when it uses the phrase "or to the people," whether it is referring to the people of each state or the people of the nation as a whole, Thomas argued that only the former makes any sense. "There would have been no reason," Thomas contended, "to provide that where the Constitution is silent about whether a particular power resides at the state level, it might or might not do so."[74] Since the people of the several states are the only "true source of power" recognized by the Constitution, they do not need to point to any affirmative constitutional grant of power to supplement the qualifications for their representatives to Congress. If a power is not granted, it must remain with the people of the several states. On the question of state-imposed term limits, Thomas argued that "[t]he Constitution is simply silent. . . . And where the Constitution is silent, it raises no bar to action by the States or the people."[75]

Justice Thomas also rejected the majority's more specific arguments concerning the fixed and exclusive nature of the Qualifications Clauses. While he agreed with the majority that Congress was prohibited from adding to the qualifications listed in the Constitution,[76] he did not think the states were. For support of this view, Thomas provided a different interpretation of the text and structure of the Constitution, *Powell v. McCormack*, congressional and state ratification debates, and early state practices. He also cited Thomas Jefferson as a founding father who thought that the states had the power to supplement the qualifications for their congressional representatives.[77] According to Justice Thomas, "Nothing in the Constitution deprives the people of each State of the power to prescribe the eligibility requirements for the candidates who seek to represent them in Congress."[78] The Constitution sets a qualifications floor; it does not deprive the states of the power to impose additional qualifications.[79]

While each side in the *Term Limits* decision presents strong arguments for its respective position, the important question for our purposes is what Hamilton thought about term limits. On this point, there can be no question: he strongly disapproved of them. This can be gleaned from *The Federalist*, where both Hamilton and Madison speak of the fixed and exclusive nature of the Qualifications Clauses, and it can also be gleaned from the New York ratification debates (1788), where Hamilton and other leading Federalists opposed a proposed constitutional amendment requiring the rotation of U.S.

senators. While Thomas's opinion is persuasive and commendable in many respects, his total neglect of Madison's and Hamilton's views in *The Federalist*, as well as of the substantive arguments at the New York ratification debates, weakens his originalist interpretation of the Qualification Clauses substantially.


## The Qualifications Clauses

The language of the Qualifications Clauses is not dispositive on whether the states can supplement or alter the qualifications for their representatives to Congress. These clauses provide that "[n]o Person shall be a Representative who shall not have attained to the Age of twenty five Years, and been seven Years a Citizen of the United States, and who shall not, when elected, be an Inhabitant of that State in which he shall be chosen,"[80] and "[n]o Person shall be a Senator who shall not have attained to the Age of thirty Years, and been nine Years a Citizen of the United States, and who shall not, when elected, be an Inhabitant of that State for which he shall be chosen."[81] On their face, the Qualifications Clauses prohibit certain classes of individuals from serving in Congress: those under a certain age, those who have not been citizens of the United States for a specified period of time, and nonresidents of the state in which the election is being held. Nothing in the language of these clauses, however, suggests that they were intended to be an exclusive list of disqualifications. The clauses do not, for example, declare that all persons who possess the required qualifications shall be eligible. As Justice Thomas points out, an exclusive formulation of the qualifications would have read something like this: "Every Person who shall have attained to the age of twenty five Years, and been seven Years a Citizen of the United States, and who shall, when elected, be an Inhabitant of that State in which he shall be chosen, shall be eligible to be a Representative."[82]

Moreover, the canons for interpreting legal texts do not conclusively determine whether the states can supplement the qualifications for congressional representatives. On the one hand, there is the maxim *expressio unius est exclusio alterius*—the expression of one thing is the exclusion of the other. If this maxim were applied to the Qualifications Clauses, it would forbid the states from adding qualifications for representatives to Congress: the explicit enumeration of age, citizenship, and residency qualifications implies the exclusion of all other requirements. On the other hand, the *expressio unius* maxim is only a rule of construction whose application must be weighed against other considerations, such as whether applying it to other constitutional provisions affecting federal elections would lead to inconsistent results. The Religious Test Clause, for example, prohibits religious oaths for any public office in the United States.[83] If the *expressio unius* maxim were applied to this clause, it would mean that other qualifications for those seeking to run for Congress are permissible. Thus, Justice Thomas's textual argument is persuasive.[84] On their face, the Qualifications Clauses do not prohibit the people of each state from establishing additional eligibility requirements for their representatives to Congress.

However, while the language of the Qualifications Clauses is not stated in exclusive terms, the original understanding of these clauses indicates that they were intended to contain an exclusive list of the qualifications for membership in Congress. In *Federalist* 52, Madison discussed the political compromise reached over the selection of congressional representatives. On the one hand, the *electors* for members of Congress were to have the same qualifications as the electors for the state legislatures.[85] This arrangement was designed to appease the states' rights delegates at the Constitutional Convention by giving the states some control over who could represent them in the Congress. On the other hand, the qualifications of the *elected*, Madison argued, are more "susceptible of uniformity."[86] The Federalists were put on the defensive by Anti-Federalist charges that the new Congress would be composed of only the rich and powerful. In fact, Charles Pinckney of South Carolina urged his fellow delegates at the Constitutional Convention to adopt a property qualification for all three branches of the new government.[87] In order to reassure a nervous public that service in the national legislature would not be limited to a privileged few, Madison explained in *Federalist* 52,

> The qualifications of the elected, being less carefully and properly defined by the State constitutions, and being at the same time *more susceptible of uniformity*, have been very properly considered and regulated by the convention. A representative of the United States must be of the age of twenty-five years; must have been seven years a citizen of the United States; must, at the time of his election, be an inhabitant of the State he is to represent.[88]

Were he to stop here, it might be argued that Madison only contemplated a qualifications floor. As Justice Thomas contended, prior to the adoption of the Constitution, the states did not have strict qualifications for their delegates to Congress.[89] On this view, Madison may have simply wanted to ensure that members of Congress met *minimal* requirements of age, citizenship, and residency. If the states wanted to set higher qualifications, nothing in the Constitution prevented them from doing so. But Madison did not stop there. He went on to say that "[u]nder these reasonable limitations, the door of this part of the federal government is open to merit of every description, whether native or adoptive, whether young or old, and without regard to poverty or wealth, or to any particular profession of religious faith."[90]

This language makes it clear that Madison did not regard the states as having authority to alter the qualifications for their representatives to Congress. As Justice Stevens points out, "a patchwork of qualifications" by the states would defy the desire for "uniformity."[91] Moreover, if a state could impose a property qualification for members of Congress, it would *close* "the door of this part of the federal government . . . to merit of every description."[92] Rather, Madison believed that the Qualifications Clauses were exclusive and unalterable; neither the Congress nor the states could supplement the qualifications mentioned in the Constitution.

Alexander Hamilton's views were substantially the same as Madison's. In responding to the Anti-Federalist charge that the new Constitution favored the wealthy and wellborn, Hamilton observed in *Federalist* 60,

> The truth is that there is no method of securing to the rich the preference apprehended but by prescribing qualifications of property either for those who may elect or be elected. But this forms no part of the power to be conferred upon the national government. . . . The qualifications of the persons who may choose or be chosen, as has been remarked upon other occasions, *are defined and fixed in the Constitution*, and are unalterable by the legislature.[93]

While it is true that the "legislature" Hamilton was referring to was the Congress, the "defined and fixed" nature of federal qualifications would not make any sense if the states could supplement those qualifications with eligibility requirements of their own. For this reason, the Court in *Powell* correctly interpreted Hamilton to mean that the Qualifications Clauses were immutable.[94]

## Rotation Debates

Rotation in office (a type of term limit) was both practiced[95] and debated[96] at the time of the founding. At issue in these debates was the type of representative system desired in the United States. The Anti-Federalists, who advocated a "delegate" theory of representation,[97] supported rotation as the surest bulwark of republican government. By contrast, the Federalists, who supported a Burkean "trustee" theory of representation,[98] opposed rotation as, in Hamilton's words, a "feeble principle" that may in time prove "fatal to the prosperity of our country."[99] The differences between the two sides belie one important area of common ground: both sides did not believe the Constitution permitted the states to impose a system of rotation on their representatives to Congress. If this were not the case, why have the debates in the first place?[100] In fact, several leading Anti-Federalists cited the absence of a rotation provision as a primary reason for voting against the Constitution.[101]

## The Anti-Federalists

The most theoretical and extensive debate on rotation took place at the New York Ratification Convention, which met in Poughkeepsie, New York, from June to July 1788. Fearing that the Senate would be composed of a permanent and corrupt body of men, leading Anti-Federalists at that state convention proposed that the Constitution be amended to allow for the rotation of United States senators.[102] The New York Anti-Federalists made several arguments in defense of the proposal, many of which sounded like the arguments commonly heard in the early 1990s.[103] First, they argued that through a system of rotation, more people would have the opportunity to serve in public office, thereby promoting two political goals they regarded as desirable. First, service in government was important to the cultivation of civic virtue. By participating in government, the Anti-Federalists believed that individuals learn to sacrifice their own interests for the common good. Second, government service was regarded as an essential bulwark of individual freedom. By serving in government, it was believed that people educate themselves about government and thus can better hold their elected officials accountable. For the Anti-Federalists, the affairs of government were not simply the vocation of an elite few, but rather were the concern of the entire citizenry. As Melancton Smith put it, "The true policy of constitutions will be to increase the information of the country, and disseminate the knowledge of government as universally as possible. If this be done, we shall have, in any dangerous emergency, a numerous body of enlightened citizens, ready for the call of their country."[104]

The second argument made in behalf of rotation was that it would make those who serve in public office more responsible. Without rotation, the Anti-Federalist Gilbert Livingston contended, "men are apt to forget their dependence, lose their sympathy, and contract selfish habits. Factions are apt to be formed, if the body becomes permanent. The senators will associate only with men of their own class, and thus become strangers to the condition of the common people."[105] The concern that public officials would forsake their constituents' interests for their own interests was widely shared by the Anti-Federalists. By requiring representatives periodically to return home to their districts, it was hoped that a sense of attachment and dependency could be maintained. As John Lansing, Jr. put it, rotation was necessary in order to "oblige them [U.S. senators] to return, at certain periods, to their fellow-citizens, that, by mingling with the people, they may recover that knowledge of their interests, and revive that sympathy with their feelings, which power and an exalted station are too apt to efface from the minds of rulers."[106]

Finally, and somewhat paradoxically, the Anti-Federalists argued that citizens could not always be counted on to bring about the degree of turnover necessary to ensure that each individual has an opportunity to serve in public office. Without rotation, it was believed that incumbents would acquire advantages and privileges that would make it nearly impossible to get them out of office. As John Lansing explained, "The rights of the people will be best supported by checking, at a certain point, the current of popular favor, and preventing the establishment of an influence which may leave to elections little more than the form of freedom."[107] Rather than rely upon the normal electoral process, the Anti-Federalists thus sought to build into the structure of government a system of rotation. As Richard Henry Lee, a prominent Anti-Federalist from Virginia, explained,

> Were the people always properly attentive, they would, at proper periods, call their law makers home, by sending others in their room: but it is not often the case, and therefore, in making constitutions, when the people are attentive, they ought cautiously to provide for those benefits, those advantageous changes in the administration of their affairs, which they are often apt to be inattentive to in practice.[108]

## The Federalist Response

Led by Alexander Hamilton, the New York Federalists made several arguments in response to the Anti-Federalist proposal for rotation of U.S. senators. First, the Federalists argued that rotation would abridge the natural right of the people to vote for the candidates of their own choice. Robert R. Livingston, for example, objected to rotation because "[t]he people are the best judges [of] who ought to represent them. To dictate and control them, to tell them whom they shall not elect, is to abridge their natural rights."[109] Similarly, Hamilton contended that "the true principle of a republic is, that the people should choose whom they please to govern them. Representation is imperfect in proportion as the current of popular favor is checked."[110] In contrast to the Anti-Federalists, the Federalists thus placed more confidence in the electoral choices of the people. As Madison observed in *The Federalist*, "Frequent elections are unquestionably the only policy by which th[e] dependence [on] and sympathy [with the people] can be effectually secured."[111]

The second line of arguments made by the New York Federalists was institutional. First, they claimed that rotation would deprive the republic of experienced public leaders. Hamilton, for example, expressed concern that

> if you consider but a moment the purposes for which the *Senate* was instituted, and the nature of the business which they are to transact, you will see the necessity of giving them duration. They, together with the President, are to manage all our concerns with foreign nations; they must understand all their interests, and their political systems. . . . Is it desirable, then, that new and unqualified members should be continually thrown into that body?"[112]

For the Federalists, a strong and effective national government required experienced political leaders, part of the training for which could only come with actual service in government. The Federalists thus viewed rotation as dangerous to the health and stability of the political system, because it would banish from federal offices not only those perhaps undeserving of further service, but also those who have carried out their duties with the greatest competence and trust.[113] As Richard Harrison put it,

> We may suppose two of the most enlightened and eminent men in the state, in whom the confidence of the legislature and the love of the people are united, engaged, at the expiration of their office, in the most important negotiations, in which their presence and agency may be indispensable. In this emergency, shall we incapacitate them? Shall we prohibit the legislature from reappointing them? It might endanger our country, and involve us in inextricable difficulties.[114]

The second institutional argument made by the New York Federalists was that rotation would reduce the incentives for political accountability. In contrast to the Anti-Federalists, the Federalists believed that reeligibility would make elected officials more (not less) responsible to the people. The Federalists maintained that the promise of honors and rewards (what Hamilton called "the love of fame"[115]) provides the greatest stimulus for public virtue. "It is a general principle of human nature," Hamilton wrote in *The Federalist*, "that a man will be interested in whatever he possesses, in proportion to the firmness or precariousness of the tenure by which he holds it."[116] On this view, if legislators are allowed indefinite reeligibility, they will be ready to undertake "extensive and arduous enterprises for the public benefit."[117] But if they are not given this privilege, Hamilton warned that there "would be the temptation to sordid views, to peculation, and, in some instances, to usurpation."[118] On this basis, Hamilton strongly denounced the proposal for rotation of U.S. senators at the New York Ratifying Convention:

> Sir, in contending for a rotation, the gentlemen carry their zeal beyond all reasonable bounds. I am convinced that no government, founded on this feeble principle, can operate well. . . . When a man knows he must quit his station, let his merit be what it may, he will turn his attention chiefly to his own emolument: nay, he will feel temptations, which few other situations furnish, to perpetuate his power by unconstitutional usurpations. . . .
> . . . Men who have been in the Senate once, and who have a reasonable hope of a reelection, will not be easily bought by offices. This reasoning shows that a *rotation* would be productive of many *disadvantages*: under particular circumstances, it might be extremely inconvenient, if not fatal to the prosperity of our country.[119]

It is clear that both Madison and Hamilton opposed term limits for members of Congress. Not only did their interpretation of the Qualifications Clauses preclude state-imposed term limitations, but they also regarded restrictions on reeligibility to be unwise as a matter of policy. Term limits put in doubt a central premise of Madison's prescription for the large republic: "To refine and enlarge the public views by passing them through the medium of a chosen body of citizens, whose wisdom may best discern the true interest of their country and whose patriotism and love of justice will be least likely to sacrifice it to temporary or partial considerations."[120] While Madison and Hamilton were concerned that "[e]nlightened statesmen will not always be at the helm,"[121] the only way to transcend the partial interests of the states was to give legislators the necessary freedom and independence to make difficult (i.e., unpopular) political decisions. Term limits, which attempt to make national officials more dependent on the people of each state, jeopardize this view. Jefferson was the only founding father who thought that the states could place term limits on members of Congress, and even his views were lukewarm on the subject.[122] In order to impose term restrictions on representatives to Congress, a constitutional amendment would be required.

## Scalia's Vote

More than any other decision in which he has participated, Justice Scalia's vote in *Term Limits* appears to be at odds with his previously expressed positions on federalism. In fact, from a Hamiltonian perspective, his vote is not supportable. One of Hamilton's core political principles, which he fought for all of his life, was the preservation of the union over some narrow parochial interest. When members of his party talked about secession after Thomas Jefferson's election to the presidency in 1800, Hamilton viewed the idea with horror and vehemently opposed it.[123] If the dissenting view in *Term Limits* won in 1995, it could have done serious harm to a major U.S. national institution. Scalia's vote in *Term Limits* is hard to reconcile with his opinion in *City of Richmond v. J. A. Croson*,[124] where he supported a large republic theory of government. In that case, Scalia expressed concern about "the heightened danger of oppression from political factions in small, rather than large, political units,"[125] and the need for a "dispassionate objectivity" and "flexibility" at the national level to "mold a race-conscious remedy" for the effects of past or present discrimination.[126] By joining the *Term Limits* dissent, Scalia seems far afield from his 1982 remarks before the Federalist Society where he said that "the federal government is not bad but good. The trick is to use it wisely."[127] So, what accounts for Scalia's vote in *Term Limits*? One explanation for why Scalia joined the *Term Limits* dissent is that he saw it as a way of restoring some sense of responsibility and deliberative democracy in the halls of Congress. At the time of the decision, a number of high-profile congressional scandals had recently taken place, and the American people were generally frustrated by career politicians in Washington. The idea of restoring responsibility to Congress through term limits and other devices, such as a balanced budget amendment, had strong support among leading conservative politicians and commentators, including Speaker of the House Newt Gingrich (R-GA), George Will, and William Kristol.[128] But term limits also had plenty of detractors, including scholars on the right,[129] who worried that populist extraconstitutional tampering with the U.S. form of government would erode the public's support for the Constitution and diminish the quality of leadership in Congress. Scalia's rather negative opinion of Congress may have led him to support the term limits movement, but he is also a person who does not support populist extraconstitutional changes to the Constitution. Thomas's *Term Limits* dissent places more confidence (than either Hamilton or Madison would) in the people of each state to set appropriate term limits (or other types of qualifications) on congresspersons. Thus, while many people might not object to a ban on ex-felons serving in Congress, they might not be as comfortable with other types of qualifications imposed on members of Congress, such as district residency, property, mandatory retirement, or more restrictive term limits. Nothing in Thomas's opinion would prevent any of these other types of qualifications from being adopted at the state level.

A second, related explanation for Justice Scalia's *Term Limits* vote is that congressional term limits could be seen as an attempt to bring back some of the protections guaranteed to the states prior to the passage of the Seventeenth Amendment in 1913. Recall that in his speeches in the 1980s, Scalia lamented the ratification of the Seventeenth Amendment, believing that the repeal of state legislative appointment of U.S. senators marked "the beginning of the end for the states," and that without such a structural protection for the states, federalism disputes would be "a losing battle."[130] Thomas's opinion in *Term Limits* goes a long way to restoring state authority over representatives in both houses of Congress. If the people of a state, for example, do not like a particular vote cast by one of their congressional representatives, they can simply pass a term limit (or some other qualification) that would effectively bar that person from running in the next election. Moreover, Thomas argued that this discretionary authority belonging to the people of each state could be delegated to their state legislators. In fact, the *Term Limits* dissent goes one step further than the status quo that existed prior to the passage of the Seventeenth Amendment, since it would allow term limits to be imposed on both houses of Congress.

A third explanation for Scalia's vote in *Term Limits* is that he supported congressional term limits as a way of evening the score between Congress and the presidency. The Twenty-second Amendment (1951), which was proposed by a Republican-dominated Congress in 1947 out of frustration with the unprecedented four presidential victories by Franklin Delano Roosevelt, limits the number of terms a president can serve to two. While presidential term limits are supported by many sound arguments, it is unquestionable that the Twenty-second Amendment weakened the executive branch vis-à-vis the Congress. Scalia, who holds very strong pro-executivist views, might have voted the way he did in *Term Limits* in order to restore some balance in the length of service for elected officials who serve in the political branches of government.

A final explanation for why Scalia voted the way he did in *Term Limits* is Court politics. Scalia's views on congressional term limits were at best ambivalent. He did not write an opinion in the case, and during oral arguments he made the following comment to counsel arguing the case: "Mr. Cohen, maybe you think this is a clear case. Some aspects of it at least I find very close, where you have Thomas Jefferson and Joseph Story on the opposite sides of the issue, for example, whether the States have any power to add qualifications. That's a close case in my mind."[131] Since Scalia held such tepid views on the subject of congressional term limits, he may have strategically voted the way he did in order to please Justice Thomas and the other conservatives in dissent. The fact that Justice Kennedy, a moderate conservative, voted with the majority in *Term Limits* also made it easier for Scalia to side with the dissenters. While all of these explanations for Scalia's vote in *Term Limits* are plausible, they do not obviate the central fact that state-imposed term limits were not supported by the framers of the U.S. Constitution. From a Hamiltonian perspective, *Term Limits* was an easy case. Scalia's vote in *Term Limits* gives some credence to those who view him as a states' rights advocate.[132]

## *PRINTZ V. UNITED STATES*:
## THE ANTICOMMANDEER PRINCIPLE

Justice Scalia had been relatively reticent (at least in judicial opinions) regarding his views of the Tenth Amendment. That silence was broken, however, in 1997, when he authored the Court's opinion in *Printz v. United States*.[133] In a five-to-four decision, Scalia held that the temporary provisions of the Brady Handgun Violence Prevention Act of 1993 (the "Brady Bill") violated the Constitution. Unlike in *Lopez*, the majority did not object to the Brady Bill as an unwarranted exercise of Congress's commerce authority—presumably because Congress was attempting to regulate commercial activity.[134] Rather, it objected to the *means* chosen by Congress to carry out its national program.

In 1993, Congress enacted the Brady Bill as an amendment to the Gun Control Act of 1968. The primary purposes of the law were (1) to establish a waiting period before a person could purchase a handgun and (2) to create a national criminal background check database for use by firearms dealers before the transfer of any firearm. Because the U.S. attorney general would not be able to establish a national instant background check system until November 30, 1998, the act put into place certain interim provisions. Under the interim provisions, it was unlawful for a licensed firearms dealer to sell a gun to any individual who did not have a license. To receive a license, a prospective gun purchaser had to present a statement (the Brady Form) to a dealer, containing the purchaser's name, address, and date of birth, as well as a sworn statement that the buyer was not among a class of prohibited purchasers under the act. Within one day, the firearms dealer had to give this Brady Form to the chief law enforcement officer (CLEO) in the purchaser's area of residence. Upon notice, the CLEO was required to "make a reasonable effort" to ascertain within five business days whether receipt or possession of the handgun would be in violation of local, state, or federal law.

Petitioners Jay Printz and Richard Mack, the CLEOs for Ravilli County, Montana, and Graham County, Arizona, respectively, filed separate actions challenging the interim provisions of the Brady Bill. They claimed that the Brady Bill forced state law enforcement officers to carry out a federally enacted program in violation of the Tenth Amendment and basic principles of federalism. The Court of Appeals for the Ninth Circuit ruled against them, finding that none of the Brady Bill's interim provisions violated the Tenth Amendment.[135]

The Supreme Court reversed. Following the reasoning of its decision in *New York v. United States*,[136] the five-justice majority struck down the interim provisions of the Brady Bill for attempting to "conscript" state officials into administering or enforcing a federal regulatory program—the so-called anticommandeer principle.[137] While Justice Scalia admitted that "there is no constitutional text speaking to this precise question,"[138] he found support for the Court's anticommandeer principle in constitutional history and practice, the structure of the Constitution, and the jurisprudence of the Court. Each of these sources will be examined in turn.

## Constitutional History and Practice

In terms of constitutional history and practice, Scalia considered two separate sources: congressional practice and *The Federalist*. As for the former, Scalia could find no evidence that earlier Congresses had thought they had the power to impress state officials into carrying out federal law.[139] It is only with more recent statutes—which Scalia claimed had less probative value—that Congress has assumed this authority. Scalia thus reasoned that if "earlier Congresses avoided use of this highly attractive power," it must have been assumed that the power did not exist.[140] As for *The Federalist*, Scalia claimed that neither Hamilton nor Madison supported the proposition that the national government could conscript state officers into carrying out a federal program. The government cited several passages of *The Federalist* where Madison and Hamilton respond to Anti-Federalist concerns that the federal government's ability to tax individuals would produce two sets of revenue officers who would deplete the financial resources of the people. Brutus, for example, said "that the Constitution 'opens a door to the appointment of a swarm of revenue and excise officers to prey upon the honest and industrious part of the community, eat up their substance, and riot on the spoils of the country.'"[141] Publius responded by saying "that Congress will probably 'make use of the State officers and State regulations, for collecting' federal taxes,"[142] and "predicted that 'the eventual collection [of internal revenue] under the immediate authority of the Union, will generally be made by the officers, and according to the rules, appointed by the several States.'"[143]

The government also relied on more general observations in *The Federalist*, such as Hamilton's statement "that the Constitution would 'enable the [national] government to employ the ordinary magistracy of each [State] in the execution of its laws,'"[144] and Madison's statement "that it was 'extremely probable that in other instances, particularly in the organization of the judicial power, the officers of the States will be clothed with the correspondent authority of the Union.'"[145] Justice Scalia explained all of these statements by noting that none of them "necessarily implies—what is the critical point here—that Congress could impose these responsibilities *without the consent of the States*. They appear to rest on the natural assumption that the States would consent to allowing their officials to assist the Federal Government."[146]

Justice Scalia also discussed *Federalist* 27, which was not relied upon by the government, but which was cited by Justice David Souter in his dissent. Since the language of this passage is so important, it will be quoted in its entirety:

> The plan reported by the convention, by extending the authority of the federal head to the individual citizens of the several States, will enable the government to employ the ordinary magistracy of each in the execution of its laws. It is easy to perceive that this will tend to destroy, in the common apprehension, all distinction between the sources from which they might proceed; and will give the federal government the same advantage for securing a due obedience to its authority which is enjoyed by the government of each State, in addition to the influence on public opinion which will result from the important consideration of

its having power to call to its assistance and support the resources of the whole Union. It merits particular attention in this place, that the laws of the Confederacy as to the *enumerated* and *legitimate* objects of its jurisdiction will become the SUPREME LAW of the land; to the observance of which all officers, legislative, executive, and judicial in each State will be bound by the sanctity of an oath. Thus the legislatures, courts, and magistrates, of the respective members will be incorporated into the operations of the national government *as far as its just and constitutional authority extends*; and will be rendered auxiliary to the enforcement of its laws.[147]

Justice Scalia explained this passage with a nonobstructionist principle. Nothing in the passage, Scalia argued, could be regarded as requiring state officials to carry out federal law:

> [T]he calculatedly vague consequences the passage recites — "incorporated into the operations of the national government" and "rendered auxiliary to the enforcement of its laws" — are . . . nothing more (or less) than the duty owed to the National Government, on the part of *all* state officials, to enact, enforce, and interpret state law in such fashion as not to obstruct the operation of federal law.[148]

Justice Scalia does, however, offer a fallback position: a split-personality thesis. According to Scalia, while Hamilton's and Madison's views in *The Federalist* are similar on many subjects, that is not the case with respect to their views on federalism. It would be "most peculiar," he wrote, "to give the view expressed in that one piece [*Federalist* 27], not clearly confirmed by any other writer, the determinative weight he [Justice Souter] does. That would be crediting the most expansive view of federal authority ever expressed, and from the pen of the most expansive expositor of federal power."[149] The idea that Congress could command state officials into carrying out a federal program, Scalia argued, "has no clear support in Madison's writings."[150]

### Constitutional Structure

Justice Scalia also contended that the structure of the Constitution supported the Court's anticommandeer principle. As in *Gregory* and *Lopez*, Scalia began this section of his opinion by discussing several basic principles of federalism. "It is incontestible," he wrote, "that the Constitution established a system of 'dual sovereignty.'"[151] For support of this view, Scalia cited several provisions of the Constitution:

> the prohibition on any involuntary reduction or combination of a State's territory, Art. IV, § 3; the Judicial Power Clause, Art. III, § 2, and the Privileges and

Immunities Clause, Art. IV, § 2, which speak of the "Citizens" of the States; the amendment provision, Article V, which requires the votes of three-fourths of the States to amend the Constitution; and the Guarantee Clause, Art. IV, § 4, which "presupposes the continued existence of the states and . . . those means and instrumentalities which are the creation of their sovereign and reserved rights."[152]

Scalia also noted that the very fact of enumerated powers suggests (at least implicitly) that the states have "a residuary and inviolable sovereignty."[153] And last (and undoubtedly by design) comes the Tenth Amendment: "Residual state sovereignty was also implicit, of course, in the Constitution's conferral upon Congress of not all governmental powers, but only discrete, enumerated ones, Art. I, § 8, which implication was rendered express by the Tenth [Amendment]."[154]

Although it is not clear which of these provisions Scalia ultimately relies upon, he concludes that the Brady Bill violates this basic structure. For Scalia, the novelty of the U.S. federal system is the national government's ability to extend its authority to each individual residing within its territory. Under the Articles of Confederation, where the federal government could act only through the states, the system "was both ineffectual and provocative of federal-state conflict."[155] Thus, at the Constitutional Convention, Madison argued that "'[t]he practicality of making laws, with coercive sanctions, for the States as political bodies,' [had] been . . . 'exploded on all hands.'"[156]

## Prior Jurisprudence

Finally, Justice Scalia maintained that the prior jurisprudence of the Court supported the anticommandeer principle. Scalia mentioned several of the Court's precedents but relied primarily on its decision in *New York v. United States*.[157] At issue in *New York* were various provisions of the Low-Level Radioactive Waste Policy Amendments Act of 1985. Under the "take title" provision of this act, a state that failed to regulate the radioactive waste generated within its borders was given the option of either taking title to the waste or enacting a legislative plan for its disposal. Justice Sandra Day O'Connor, speaking for the Court, concluded that Congress could constitutionally require the states to do neither. "A choice between two unconstitutionally coercive regulatory techniques," she wrote, "is no choice at all."[158] While the Court conceded that Congress had the authority to regulate the disposal of nuclear waste under the Commerce Clause, the means it chose (forcing the states either to take title to the waste or to legislate a regulatory program) were unconstitutional. Accordingly, the Court struck down the "take title" provision as an unconstitutional intrusion on the independent and sovereign existence of the states.

Justice Scalia argued in *Printz* that the same anticommandeer principle should apply to state executive officials. According to Scalia, the conscription of CLEOs under the Brady Bill was no less an intrusion on the independent autonomy of the states: "We held in *New York* that Congress cannot compel the States to enact or enforce a federal regulatory program. Today we hold that Congress cannot circumvent that prohibition by conscripting the State's officers directly."[159]

## Critique

Justice Scalia's opinion in *Printz* can be criticized on several grounds, but we are primarily interested in what it reveals about his Hamiltonian political philosophy. His opinion in *Printz* marks the last stage of his transformation from a Hamiltonian to a Madisonian in the area of federalism. To say, as he did, that "it was Madison's—not Hamilton's—[view] that prevailed" on the subject of federalism leaves little room for ambiguity.[160] While one might try to dispute the accuracy of Scalia's claim,[161] there is no denying that he abandoned Hamilton in *Printz*. The remainder of this chapter will show how the Court's decision in *Printz* conflicts with a Hamiltonian understanding of federalism, and how there was no actual "split personality" between Hamilton and Madison on the subject of federal commandeering of state officials.

First, where is the textual support for the Court's novel anticommandeer principle? Put another way, what in the text of the Constitution prevents Congress from conscripting state officials into carrying out federal law? Unless there is some affirmative limit on Congress's commerce authority, the Brady Bill should have been upheld. The power to regulate the sale of handguns under the Commerce Clause, coupled with the Necessary and Proper Clause, would seem to establish the constitutional validity of the Brady Bill. In fact, in a television program taped just six months before the *Printz* decision was handed down, Scalia seemed to acknowledge that the federal government had the power to commandeer local sheriffs into supervising federal gun restrictions:

> There is no way you can read the Constitution, no matter how narrow an interpretation you give it, that would not allow the federal government to do many things that it ought not to do in a soundly operating system of federalism. And therefore the ultimate protection against that happening—and I think we are all in agreement that that should not happen—and the ultimate protection is the perception that the people have of the proper role of state and federal government. . . . What is out of kilter is that the people tend to look to Washington immediately instead of looking to their state capitols first.[162]

In discussing how the basic structure prohibits the national government from commandeering state officials, Scalia mentioned various provisions of the Constitution: the prohibition on any involuntary reduction or combination of a State's territory, the Judicial Power Clause, the Privileges and Immunities Clause, the amendment provision, and the Guarantee Clause.[163] What is not mentioned is how any of these provisions affects Congress's authority to regulate commerce. What makes Scalia's discussion of the federal structure even more troubling is that he admits (albeit in an ambiguous way) that the Tenth Amendment does not pose an affirmative limit on Congress's commerce authority. For example, he states in a footnote that the dissent's Necessary and Proper argument "falsely presumes that the Tenth Amendment is the exclusive textual source of protection for principles of federalism. Our system of dual sovereignty is reflected in numerous constitutional provisions . . . and not only those, like the Tenth Amendment, that speak to the point explicitly."[164] Thus, if the Tenth Amendment does not impose such a limit, what provision of the Constitution does?[165] In short, Scalia uses a scattershot approach. One of the provisions mentioned by him poses a limit, but it is not certain which one. For a textualist, this is not very convincing analysis. And the short shrift Scalia gave to the Tenth Amendment did not go unnoticed by his more ardent states' rights colleagues. Justices Sandra Day O'Connor and Clarence Thomas wrote separate concurring opinions, emphasizing how in their view the Brady Bill violated the Tenth Amendment.[166]

Justice Scalia's structural analysis in *Printz* is reminiscent of Justice William O. Douglas's "penumbra theory" in the area of privacy rights. In *Griswold v. Connecticut*,[167] the Warren Court held that married couples have a right of privacy to use contraceptives. Justice Douglas, for the majority, held that a right of privacy emanates from the penumbras of various provisions of the Constitution. Over the years, the opinion has been sharply criticized by conservatives for playing fast and loose with the language of the Constitution. In no one place is the right of privacy specifically mentioned in the Constitution. But Scalia's opinion in *Printz*, finding a novel anticommandeer principle in the recesses of the Constitution, is not readily distinguishable. Is he not essentially saying that the anticommandeer principle emanates from the shadows of various structural provisions of the Constitution?[168] For an opinion heralded as a "landmark," and as a major piece of the "constitutional revolution" of the Court's 1996–1997 term,[169] the *Printz* decision is rather short on textual support.

The second major problem with the *Printz* decision from a Hamiltonian perspective is that it conflicts with the political process approach of *Garcia*.[170] In *Garcia*, the Court ruled that "the principal means chosen by the Framers to ensure the role of the States in the federal system lies in the structure of the Federal Government itself."[171] The *Garcia* Court assumed that because the states participate in the selection of national legislative and executive officials, their interests would be adequately protected in the laws passed by the federal government. As Justice Harry A. Blackmun put it, the national "political process ensures that laws that unduly burden the States will not be promulgated."[172] For this reason, the Court held that "[a]ny substantive restraint on the exercise of Commerce Clause powers must . . . be tailored to compensate for possible failings of the national political process."[173]

Scalia's opinion in *Printz*, however, conflicts with this fundamental premise of *Garcia*. It was the national political process, in which the states do participate, that passed the Brady Bill in the first place, and there was no evidence cited in *Printz* to suggest that the states were prevented from participating in the enactment of the Brady Bill. In fact, the policy concerns often raised in federal commandeering cases (i.e., that the national government will avoid responsibility for its programs by passing the duties and costs of administering them onto the states) were not present in *Printz*. As Justice Stevens points out in his dissent, Sheriffs Printz and Mack "made public statements, including their decisions to serve as plaintiffs in these actions, denouncing the Brady Act."[174] Moreover, Congress subsequently passed the Unfunded Mandates Reform Act of 1995, which requires approval by a majority of both houses of Congress before a bill can impose costs in excess of $50 million on state and local governments.[175] Each of these developments indicates that the states are not as powerless in protecting their own interests as the *Printz* majority supposes. In any event, it is questionable that the federal judiciary has the *constitutional* authority to come to the states' assistance in these types of cases.

Moreover, and perhaps most decisively in terms of Justice Scalia's thesis, there was no "split personality" between Madison and Hamilton over whether the national government could commandeer state officials. Both Hamilton and Madison contemplated federal commandeering of state officials. Scalia's attempt to divide these two men over this issue is a red herring. In light of Scalia's split-personality thesis, Hamilton's and Madison's views will be examined separately.

## Hamilton

Of the two men, Hamilton's views regarding federal commandeering of state officials are easier to discern. It is true that Hamilton regarded the "radical vice" of the Articles of Confederation as "LEGISLATION for STATES" as "contradistinguished from the INDIVIDUALS of whom they consist," and that the latter were "the only proper objects of government."[176] He also said at the New York Ratifying Convention that a coercive authority over the states would be "one of the maddest projects that was ever devised."[177] But Hamilton was an ardent nationalist who would not readily relinquish any authority committed to the national government.[178]

In *Federalist* 27, for example, Hamilton states that because the national government could extend its laws to "the individual citizens of the several States" under the new Constitution, it could "employ the ordinary magistracy of each [state] in the execution of its laws."[179] Were he to stop here, as Scalia points out, he would not necessarily be speaking of anything beyond the possibility of cooperative federalism: voluntary agreements between the national and state governments. But he then addresses the combined effect of the proposed Supremacy Clause and the state officers' oath requirement, and states that "the legislatures, courts, and magistrates, of the respective members will be incorporated into the operations of the national government *as far as its just and constitutional authority extends*; and will be rendered auxiliary to the enforcement of its laws."[180] Scalia's attempt to explain the obvious implications of this passage as an attempt to prevent state officials from enacting, enforcing, and interpreting state law in such a way as to obstruct the operation of federal law rings hollow. The natural reading of Hamilton's language strongly suggests that the national government has the authority to commandeer state officials into carrying out federal laws.[181]

Moreover, during the Whiskey Rebellion of 1794, Hamilton had the occasion to defend the right of the federal government to commandeer state officials. During that uprising, the Washington administration assumed that the president could commandeer state governors pursuant to his constitutional authority "to faithfully execute the laws."[182] When hostilities finally did break out in Pennsylvania over a federal tax on "spirituous liquors," Hamilton sent a letter to Governor Thomas Mifflin informing him how he and the other state officials were *constitutionally* obligated to carry out the president's orders during the crisis:

> If in addition to these dispositions in the community at large—the officers of the Governments of the respective States, feeling it to be not only a patriotic, but a *constitutional duty (inculcated by the oath enjoined upon all the officers of a State, legislative Executive & Judicial) to support in their several stations, the Constitution of the UStates*—shall be disposed, as occasion may require (a thing as little to be doubted as the former) with sincerity and good faith to cooperate with the Government of the UStates, to second with all their influence and weight, its legal & necessary measures, by a real and substantial concert; then the enterprise to be accomplished can hardly even be deemed difficult.[183]

Later in the same letter, Hamilton complimented the governor by saying that "[t]he President receives with much pleasure the assu[r]ance you have repeated to him, that whatever requisition he may make, whatever *duty he may impose, in pursuance of his constitutional and legal powers*, will on your part be promptly undertaken and faithfully discharged."[184]

In contrast to what Justice Scalia claims in *Printz*, Hamilton fully contemplated that the national government could commandeer state officials. Scalia does raise an interesting separation of powers question (see chapter 5), but the authority of the national government (Congress, the president, and the federal courts) to commandeer state officers was fully anticipated by Hamilton.

## Madison

Madison's views concerning a coercive power on the part of the national government were (as one might expect) more cautious and circumspect, but there is still reason to believe that he thought the national government had the authority to commandeer state officials into carrying out federal laws. As a matter of prudence, Madison did express grave concerns about the practicality of conscripting state officials into serving the federal government. As Scalia points out, Madison stated at the Constitutional Convention that "'[t]he practicality of making laws, with coercive sanctions, for the States as political bodies' . . . [had] been 'exploded on all hands.'"[185] Moreover, Madison, more so than Hamilton, emphasized the cooperative nature of federal-state relations. In *Federalist* 45, for example, he argued that the national government would give the states the "option" of "supply[ing] their quotas by previous collections of their own; and that the eventual collection, under the immediate authority of the Union, will generally be made by the officers, and according to the rules, appointed by the several States."[186]

Having said this, however, there is also reason to believe that Madison understood that the national government had the authority to commandeer state officials when acting pursuant to a constitutionally prescribed power. In order to understand why this is the case, a brief recount of Madison's views concerning federal-state relations prior to and during the Constitutional Convention is necessary. Recall that at the convention Madison was no less a nationalist than Hamilton was. His "middle-ground" position on the subject of federalism sought to "leave in force the local authorities so far as they can be subordinately useful."[187] On a number of occasions during the proceedings, Madison also described the relationship of the states to the federal government as the same as that of the counties to the states, and he argued that "no fatal consequence could result" from "a tendency in the Genl. Government to absorb the State Govts."[188] For Madison, the greatest threat to the survival of the republic was the "multiplicity," "mutability," and "injustice" of state laws.[189]

In response to these concerns, Madison suggested two constitutional measures to offset what he called the "Vices of the Political System of the United States": (1) a right of coercion by the federal government over the states, and (2) a national veto over all laws passed by the state legislatures. Madison believed that the latter might make a federal coercive authority unnecessary, but he would eventually lose his campaign for a national veto. This defeat dismayed Madison greatly, and in private correspondence with Thomas Jefferson, he questioned whether the national government could "effectually *answer* its *national object* . . . [and] prevent the local *mischiefs* which every where *excite disgusts* agst the *state governments*."[190] The defeat of Madison's national veto provides at least circumstantial evidence that he would not lightly dismiss the need for a coercive authority at the national level. Although such an authority might be impractical, and could potentially lead to conflict, he would not forsake it altogether. In fact, there is some evidence to support this view.

In *The Federalist*, Madison emphasized that the national government's powers could extend to the states in their collective capacities.[191] While he regarded the instances as limited, he did not draw as sharp a line of distinction between the new and old systems of government as Scalia's opinion in *Printz* seems to suggest. Second, as Justice Souter points out in his dissent in *Printz*,[192] Madison made a similar remark regarding the agency of state officers in carrying out national laws as Hamilton did. In explaining why state officers have to swear to uphold the U.S. Constitution, while federal officials have no similar obligation regarding the state constitutions, Madison said that "[t]he members of the federal government will have no agency in carrying the State constitutions into effect. The members and officers of the State governments, on the contrary, will have an essential agency in giving effect to the federal Constitution."[193] Finally, and most conclusively, Madison conceded at the Virginia Ratifying Convention that the national government had the power to conscript state officers into carrying out federal laws. In response to those who protested the idea of having tax collectors at both the federal and state levels of government, Madison remarked, "Is it not in the power of the general government to employ state officers? Is nothing to be left to future legislation, or must everything be immutably fixed in the Constitution?"[194] In this remark, gone are the words of caution in *The Federalist*. During the Virginia ratification debates, Madison clearly recognized that the national government had the *authority* to commandeer state officials into carrying out federal laws.

It is almost certainly the case that the framers would have found the Court's novel anticommandeer principle rather fanciful. Both Federalists and Anti-Federalists alike thought the federal government had the authority to conscript state officers.[195] Even Thomas Jefferson (the so-called father of states' rights) believed that at least the president had the authority to command state governors when the occasion warranted it[196]—a power that Justice Scalia seems to deny.[197] One can debate the wisdom of federal mandates as a matter of public policy, but the evidence is fairly strong that the framers assumed the national government had the *constitutional authority* to commandeer state officials.[198] Justice Scalia's opinion in *Printz* marks yet another departure from his political process approach toward federalism. Despite his claims to the contrary, there does not appear to be any textual or historical support for the Court's novel anticommandeer principle, making judicial involvement in this area hard to reconcile with *Garcia*. What is remarkable about Scalia's decision is that it puts the Court in the middle of one of the most hotly debated policy issues of our time: federal mandates. As with *Gregory* and *Lopez*, the Court is holding itself out as *the* umpire in these disputes. And despite Scalia's attempt to draw a bright-line rule in this area, there does not appear to be any principled basis for the Court to decide these cases. In fact, in her concurring opinion, Justice O'Connor emphasized how certain federal programs (those involving purely "ministerial" assistance by state officials) will not be affected by the Court's decision.[199] In the end, one cannot help but conclude that Scalia's decision in *Printz* is a crafty attempt by him to turn back the federal programs and mandates with which he disagrees.[200]

## CONCLUSION

In comparison to other judges, Antonin Scalia is a fairly principled jurist. For him, the process of making decisions is as important as the actual results.[201] In the area of federalism, however, Scalia has been anything but consistent. In the 1980s, Scalia clearly aligned himself with Alexander Hamilton and the Federalist Party by supporting the political process approach toward federalism, a broad construction of national powers, and a generous domestic policy-making role for the federal government. In the 1990s, however, Scalia's federalism decisions moved in a steady and consistent direction toward James Madison—to the extent that he now says "it was Madison's—not Hamilton's—[view] that prevailed" on the subject of federalism.[202] What explains this rather obvious and seemingly self-conscious transformation by Scalia? Two explanations are offered here. First, Scalia honestly believes that national power has increased too much at the expense of the states. As he observed during a 1996 Fred Friendly Seminar, the American people have become habituated to look to the national government for solutions to socioeconomic problems that previously had been handled at the state and local level.[203] What needs to happen, Scalia counseled, is that the people need to be reeducated about the values of federalism, which raises an important point. Even though Scalia is a Hamiltonian, he is not a supporter of "Big Government" programs. For Scalia, the national government has its place and role in the U.S. political system, particularly in foreign affairs and the war on drugs, but large scale entitlement programs, such as the New Deal and Great Society, run against Scalia's (and Hamilton's) conservative political philosophy of individual responsibility. And Scalia's opinion in *Printz*, where he supported a novel anticommandeer principle—which will likely involve the Court in the type of ad hoc balancing he has so strongly protested against in the past—shows just how disillusioned Scalia has become with federal power. In short, even such an ardent Federalist as Scalia believes that the federal government has become too large and its mandates too severe.

The second explanation for Scalia's movement toward Madison on the subject of federalism is that it allows him to be a player in the leading federalism decisions handed down by the Supreme Court. In the early 1990s, Scalia was faced with a stark choice. Sitting on a Court that was evenly divided between four nationalist-leaning liberal colleagues and four conservative colleagues who were more sympathetic to states' rights than he was, Scalia had to choose whether he would side with his liberal colleagues or his conservative colleagues. For the most part, Scalia chose the latter. The importance of moving toward Madison in the area of federalism is that it gives Scalia a great deal of flexibility in deciding the federal-state disputes that come before the Court, where he (like Madison during the early years of the Republic) can stake out a middle-ground position in federalism controversies. The opinions Scalia either joined or wrote in *Gregory*, *Lopez*, *Morrison*, and *Printz* represent attempts by him to reach such a middle-ground position.

Having offered these explanations for why Scalia adopted a more Madisonian approach to federalism in the 1990s, it is important to reemphasize two important limitations about Scalia's transformation. First, Scalia's separate opinion in *Raich* still shows that he has an expansive view of national power and is willing to support congressional regulations that are harmonious with his conservative policy goals. Second, Scalia is the Court's biggest defender of national power in preemption cases, particularly when he can interpret federal statutes to limit state court judgments that negatively impact corporations. Thus, Scalia's conversion to a Madisonian philosophy in the area of federalism is far from complete.

# NOTES

1. 521 U.S. 898, 915n9 (1997).
2. 501 U.S. 452 (1991).

3. 29 U.S.C. sec. 630(f).
4. Mo. Const. art. V, sec. 26.
5. Ibid., 457.
6. Ibid. (quoting *Texas v. White*, 7 [Wall.] 700, 725 [1869]).
7. Ibid., 458 (quoting FP [No. 45]).
8. Ibid., 458, 459.
9. Ibid., 460, 463.
10. Ibid., 460–61.
11. Ibid.
12. Ibid., 467.
13. In a dissenting opinion in *Hilton v. South Carolina Public Railways Comm'n*, 502 U.S. 197 (1991), which was joined by Justice Scalia, Justice O'Connor argued that the plain statement rule was derived from the Constitution:

> The clear statement rule is not a mere canon of statutory interpretation. Instead, it derives from the Constitution itself. The rule protects the balance of power between the States and the Federal Government struck by the Constitution. Although the Eleventh Amendment spells out one aspect of that balance of power, the principle of federalism underlying the Amendment pervades the constitutional structure: The Constitution gives Congress only limited power to govern the Nation; the states retain power to govern locally. (Ibid., 209 [O'Connor, J., dissenting])

This analysis, however, is highly questionable. Other than the Eleventh Amendment, what constitutional provision is Justice O'Connor referring to when she says that a plain statement rule is derived from the Constitution itself? The Tenth Amendment (which has been interpreted as a constitutional redundancy) certainly does not support such a view.

14. In *Atascadero State Hospital v. Scanlon*, 473 U.S. 234 (1985), the Court required a plain statement rule before it would find congressional intent to abrogate the sovereign immunity of the states.

15. A distinction could perhaps be made between applying a plain statement rule in Eleventh Amendment cases versus applying one in cases involving the "traditional functions" of the states. By its own terms, the Eleventh Amendment extends a substantive guarantee to the states: It denies federal courts the power to decide suits against states brought by "Citizens of another State" and "Citizens or Subjects of any Foreign State." U.S. Const. amend. XI. Thus, before finding an abrogation of the states' sovereign immunity, the Court *might* be justified in requiring a plain statement by Congress. But in cases implicating the Tenth Amendment, no such similar logic can apply, since the Tenth Amendment does not guarantee to the states anything. As the Court held in *United States v. Darby*, 312 U.S. 100, 124 (1941), the Tenth Amendment "states but a truism that all is retained which has not been surrendered."

16. 469 U.S. 528 (1985).
17. Ibid., 550.
18. Ibid., 554.
19. Ibid., 546.

20. U.S. Senate, *The Nomination of Judge Antonin Scalia: Hearings before the Committee on the Judiciary of the United States Senate*, 99th Cong., 2nd sess., August 5–6, 1986, 82.

21. In the area of federalism, these policy considerations would concern the proper division of powers between the national and state levels of government.

22. "Note, Clear Statement Rules, Federalism, and Congressional Regulation of States," *Harvard Law Review* 107 (1994): 1959. In fact, plain statement rules may be a worse gauge of legislative meaning. At least with legislative histories, the Court is still trying to discern the *legislative* intent. With a plain statement rule, the justices are imposing their own value judgments onto the language of the statute.

23. During his Tanner Lectures at Princeton University, Scalia maintained: "To an honest textualist, all of these preferential rules and presumptions are a lot of trouble. It is hard enough to provide a uniform, objective answer to the question whether a statute, on balance, more reasonably means one thing than another. But it is virtually impossible to expect uniformity and objectivity when there is added, on one or the other side of the balance, a thumb of indeterminate weight. How "narrow" *is* the narrow construction that certain types of statute [*sic*] are to be accorded? . . . And how clear is an "unmistakably clear" statement? There are no answers to these questions, which is why these artificial rules increase the unpredictability, if not the arbitrariness, of judicial decisions." Scalia, *A Matter of Interpretation: Federal Courts and the Law* (Princeton, NJ: Princeton University Press, 1997), 28. Scalia then proceeded to question whether judges have the authority to impose such presumptions: "But whether these dice-loading rules are bad or good, there is also the question of where the courts get the authority to impose them. Can we really just decree that we will interpret the laws that Congress passes to mean less or more than what they fairly say? I doubt it." Ibid., 28–29.

24. First draft in *Gregory v. Ashcroft*, (Scalia, J., concurring in part and concurring in judgment), HABP, box 576, folder 2. (This opinion was later withdrawn.)

25. 426 U.S. 833 (1976).

26. See William N. Eskridge and Philip P. Frickey, "Quasi-Constitutional Law: Clear Statement Rules as Constitutional Law Making," *Vanderbilt Law Review* 45 (1992): 593.

27. See, e.g., *Hilton v. South Carolina Public Railways Comm'n*, 502 U.S. 197 (1991) (rejecting application of a plain statement rule in construing the Federal Employers' Liability Act to allow damage actions in state courts); *Chisom v. Roemer*, 501 U.S. 380 (1991) (rejecting application of a plain statement rule in a decision holding that section 2 of the Voting Rights Act applies to the election of state judges).

28. *United States v. Lopez*, 514 U.S. 549 (1995).

29. Ibid., 552.

30. Ibid. (quoting FP [No. 45], 292–93).

31. Ibid. (quoting *Gregory v. Ashcroft*, 501 U.S. 452, 458 [1991]).

32. Ibid.

33. Ibid., 553 (quoting *Gibbons v. Ogden*, 22 U.S. [9 Wheat.] 1, 194–95 [1824]).

34. Ibid., 561. The chief justice also found fault with the law because it did not contain a jurisdictional requirement "which would ensure, through case-by-case inquiry, that the firearm possession in question affects interstate commerce." Ibid.

35. In his opinion on the national bank, Hamilton makes this clear: "There will be cases clearly within the power of the National Government; others clearly without its power; and a third class, which will leave room for controversy & difference of opinion, & concerning which a reasonable latitude of judgment must be allowed." PAH, 8:107. Hamilton cited as an example that Congress could not establish a corporation "for superintending the police of the city of Philadelphia because they are not authorised to *regulate* the *police* of that city." Ibid., 100 (emphasis in the original).

36. Madison led the opposition to a reserved power amendment at the Virginia Ratifying Convention, and was primarily responsible for the absence of the word "expressly" in the final draft of the Tenth Amendment. See *Debates*, 3: 630. See also Charles A. Lofgren, "The Origins of the Tenth Amendment: History, Sovereignty, and the Problem of Constitutional Intention," in *Constitutional Government in America*, ed. Ronald K. L. Collins (Durham, NC: Carolina Academic Press, 1980).

37. In his opinion on the national bank, Madison stated, "Interference with the power of the States was no constitutional criterion of the power of the Congress. If the power was not given, Congress could not exercise it; if given, they might exercise it, although it should interfere with the laws, or even the constitution of the States." PJM, 13: 375.

38. Accordingly, the *real* difference between Hamilton and Madison over the issue of federalism was not whether the Tenth Amendment posed an affirmative limit on national power, but rather dealt with the scope of the federal government's powers.

39. PJM, 13:372–82.

40. See, e.g., FP (No. 27), 203 ("The inference is that the authority of the Union and the affections of the citizens towards it will be strengthened, rather than weakened, by its extension to what are called matters of internal concern; and that it will have less occasion to recur to force, in proportion to the familiarity and comprehensiveness of its agency").

41. Unlike Justice Thomas in his concurring opinion, Chief Justice Rehnquist does not call for a strict interpretation of the national government's powers. See 514 U.S. at 584–602 (Thomas, J., concurring).

42. See, e.g., Deborah J. Merritt, "Reflections on *United States v. Lopez*: Commerce!" *Michigan Law Review* 94 (1995): 674; Stephen M. McJohn, "The Impact of *United States v. Lopez*: The New Hybrid Commerce Clause," *Duquesne Law Review* 3 (1995): 1.

43. L&OWJM, 4:350 (the federal judiciary is "the surest expositor of . . . the boundaries . . . between the Union and its members").

44. PAH, 5:97, 118–19. See also PAH, 8:104 ("The *degree* in which a measure is necessary, can never be a test of the *legal* right to adopt it. That must ever be a matter of opinion; and can only be a test of expediency" [emphasis in original]).

45. 514 U.S. at 557n2 (quoting *Hodel v. Virginia Surface Mining & Reclamation Assn., Inc.*, 452 U.S. 264, 311 [1981] [Rehnquist, J., concurring]).

46. Ibid. (quoting *Heart of Atlanta Motel v. United States*, 379 U.S. 241, 273 [1964] [Black, J., concurring]).

47. Ibid., 552 (quoting FP [No. 45], 292–93).

48. H. Jefferson Powell, "Enumerated Means and Unlimited Ends," *Michigan Law Review* 94 (1995): 651–73.

49. 514 U.S. at 567–68. Compare Madison's analysis in his opinion on the Bank Bill: "Mark the reasoning on which the validity of the bill depends. To borrow money is made the *end* and the accumulation of capitals, *implied* as the *means*. The accumulation of capitals is then the *end*, and a bank *implied* as the *means*. The bank is then the *end*, and a charter of incorporation, a monopoly, capital punishments, &c. *implied* as the *means*. If implications, thus remote and thus multiplied, can be linked together, a chain may be formed that will reach every object of legislation, every object within the whole compass of political economy." PJM, 13: 377–78.

50. U.S. Senate, *The Nomination of Judge Antonin Scalia*, 82.

51. *United States v. Morrison*, 529 U.S. 598 (2000).

52. Ibid., 613.

53. *Gonzales v. Raich*, 125 S. Ct. 2195, 2203–4 (2005).

54. *Raich v. Ashcroft*, 352 F.3d 1222, 1225 (9th Cir. 2003).

55. 317 U.S. 111 (1942).

56. 125 S. Ct. at 2214.

57. Ibid.

58. Ibid., 2215.

59. The three dissenters in the case were Chief Justice Rehnquist and Justices O'Connor and Thomas.

60. 125 S. Ct. at 2216.

61. Ibid., 2217 (citing *United States v. Lopez*, 514 U.S. at 561).

62. Ibid., 2219.

63. Ibid.

64. Ibid., 2220 (citing *McCulloch v. Maryland*, 4 Wheat. 316, 424 [1819]).

65. In a Gallup Poll conducted in December 1989 and January 1990, 70 percent of respondents favored term limits on congressional representatives. See Troy Andrew Eid and Jim Kolbe, "The New Anti-Federalism: The Constitutionality of State-Imposed Limits on Congressional Terms of Office," *Denver Law Review* 69 (1992): 1, 2n8.

66. 514 U.S. 779 (1995).

67. Amendment 73 of the Arkansas Constitution provided:

(a) Any person having been elected to three or more terms as a member of the United States House of Representatives from Arkansas shall not be certified as a candidate and shall not be eligible to have his/her name placed on the ballot for election to the United States House of Representatives from Arkansas.

(b) Any person having been elected to two or more terms as a member of the United States Senate from Arkansas shall not be certified as a candidate and shall not be eligible to have his/her name placed on the ballot for election to the United States Senate from Arkansas. (Ark. Const. amend. 73, sec. 3 [repealed by *U.S. Term Limits, Inc. v. Thornton*, 514 U.S. 779 (1995)])

68. U.S. Const. art. I, sec. 2, cl. 2; and U.S. Const. art. I, sec. 3, cl. 3.

69. 395 U.S. 486 (1969).

70. 514 U.S. at 846 (Thomas, J., dissenting).

71. Ibid.

72. Ibid., 848.

73. U.S. Const. amend. X.

74. 514 U.S. at 848 (Thomas, J., dissenting). Justice Thomas's interpretation of the phrase "or to the people" is consistent with the early Republican view. See, e.g., *Annals of Congress* 17 (1807): 943 (John Randolph's argument supporting the states' right to impose district residency requirements on members of the House); John Taylor, *Construction Construed and Constitutions Vindicated* (Richmond, VA: Shepherd & Pollard, 1820), 39–50 (arguing that the "or to the people" language was intended to mean the people residing in the individual states). The importance of reading the last phrase of the Tenth Amendment in this manner is that it allows Justice Thomas to argue for a hard-and-fast default rule: if a power is not expressly (or impliedly) delegated to the national government, then it must reside with the people of the individual states. The Federalists took a different view of the "or to the people" phrase. During the debates over the election of William McCreery to the House of Representatives, Philip Key of Maryland argued that the terms "States" and "the people" as expressed in the Tenth Amendment were not intended to be synonymous, but rather were "used to contradistinguish one from the other." According to Key, "The meaning of this article then is, that all sovereign powers, not delegated to the United States, nor prohibited to the States respectively, remain to the States in their sovereign capacity; so in like manner all powers vested in the people of the United States, which are not delegated to Congress, nor prohibited to the people, belong to the people as the fountain of power in a republican Government. . . . To form a correct idea of this subject, and of the true meaning of the article of reserved powers, it is only necessary to trace with precision in what body the power was originally lodged; to that body it is reserved." *Annals of Congress* 17 (1807): 916–17. Key's interpretation of the last phrase of the Tenth Amendment is, I believe, the more accurate one. The Tenth Amendment takes no position on whether a particular power resides with the collective people of the nation or the people of the individual states. Justice Thomas's concern that the Tenth Amendment will be rendered "pointless" by such an interpretation is not persuasive. Some provisions of the Constitution, including the Qualifications Clauses, are simply neutral on the question of where residual authority lies. Thus, when questions addressing these provisions come before the courts, judges must determine where residual power is placed in light of the structure and political principles of the Constitution. A helpful way of looking at the "or to the people" phrase was suggested by political scientist William Anderson. According to Anderson, the Tenth Amendment should be read with the preamble to the Constitution as follows: "We the people of the United States . . . do ordain [that] The powers not delegated to the United States . . . are reserved to the States respectively, or to the people." William Anderson, *The Nation and the States, Rivals or Partners?* (Minneapolis: University of Minnesota Press, 1955), 89. As explained by Anderson, "[I]t is the people of the United States who, in ordaining the Constitution, delegate some powers to the United States government, reserve other powers to the states or to the people, and place restrictions on both the national government and the states in the interests of the people." Ibid.

75. 514 U.S. at 845 (Thomas, J., dissenting).

76. Unlike the majority, however, Justice Thomas did not maintain that Congress was prohibited from adding qualifications because the Qualifications Clauses were regarded as fixed and exclusive, but rather because "nothing in the Constitution grants Congress this power." Without such a grant of power, Thomas argued, "Congress may not act." Ibid., 875.

77. In a letter responding to a request from Joseph C. Cabell for his opinion on whether the states could add to the qualifications for members of Congress, Jefferson wrote:

> Had the Constitution been silent, nobody can doubt but that the right to prescribe all the qualifications and disqualifications of those they would send to represent them, would have belonged to the State. So also the Constitution might have prescribed the whole, and excluded all others. It seems to have preferred the middle way. It has exercised the power in part, by declaring some disqualifications. . . . But it does not declare, itself, that the member shall not be a lunatic, a pauper, a convict of treason, of murder, of felony, or other infamous crime, or a non-resident of his district; nor does it prohibit to the State the power of declaring these, or any other disqualifications which its particular circumstances may call for; and these may be different in different States. Of course, then, by the tenth amendment, the power is reserved to the State. (Letter to Joseph Cabell [January 31, 1814], WTJ 14:82–83)

This part of Jefferson's opinion must, however, be read with his later equivocation in the same letter about the constitutionality of state-imposed term limits.

78. 514 U.S. at 845.

79. See Cynthia L. Cates, "Splitting the Atom of Sovereignty: *Term Limits, Inc.*'s Conflicting Views of Popular Autonomy in a Federal Republic," *Publius: The Journal of Federalism* 26 (1996): 127 (providing excellent analysis of the contrasting views of popular sovereignty found in the majority and dissenting opinions in *Term Limits*).

80. U.S. Const. art. I, sec. 2, cl. 2.

81. U.S. Const. art. I, sec. 3, cl. 2.

82. 514 U.S. at 868 (Thomas, J., dissenting).

83. The Religious Test Clause provides that "no religious Test shall ever be required as a Qualification to any Office or public Trust under the United States." U.S. Const. art. VI, cl. 3.

84. 514 U.S. at 867–74 (Thomas, J., dissenting).

85. U.S. Const. art. I, sec. 2 ("[T]he Electors in each State shall have the Qualifications requisite for Electors of the most numerous Branch of the State Legislature").

86. FP (No. 52), 323.

87. Records, 2:248.

88. FP (No. 52), 323.

89. 514 U.S. at 898–904.

90. FP (No. 52), 323.

91. *U.S. Term Limits, Inc.*, 514 U.S. at 808n18.

92. Ibid., 807.

93. FP (No. 60), 359–60 (emphasis added).

94. 395 U.S. at 540.

95. Article V, cl. 2, of the Articles of Confederation, for example, imposed a term limit on delegates to Congress: "No state shall be represented in Congress by less than two, nor by more than seven members; and no person shall be capable of being a delegate for more than three years in any term of six years." Debates, 1:80.

96. Section 4 of the Virginia Plan declared that "members of the first branch of the National Legislature ought to be elected by the people of the several States every _____ for a term of _____." Records, 1:20. Rather than fill in the last blank space, the convention delegates at a later date voted unanimously to delete the provision. Ibid., 217. Moreover, three states (New York, Virginia, and North Carolina) debated and proposed a constitutional amendment requiring the rotation of various federal officials at their state ratification conventions. Significantly, none of these proposals made it into Madison's proposed bill of rights.

97. According to a delegate theory of representation, members of Congress are supposed to vote the preferences of their constituents. This theory is premised on a fundamental distrust of political power. In addition to rotation, the Anti-Federalists favored short terms, large delegations in Congress, and the ability to recall national representatives. Debates, 2:289.

98. According to a trustee theory of representation, members of Congress should not simply vote the preferences of their constituents, but should take into account what is in the best interest of the country—that is, they should exercise judgment. In the American tradition, no one pushed for this view of representation more than Alexander Hamilton. During the debates at the New York Ratifying Convention, Hamilton asked, "Is [a senator] simply the agent of the state? No. He is an agent for the Union, and he is bound to perform services necessary to the good of the whole, though his state should condemn them." Ibid., 320.

99. Ibid., 320–21.

100. As Richard Morris observed at the New York Ratifying Convention, "Sir, if the proposed amendment [rotation of U.S. senators] had been originally incorporated in the Constitution, I should consider it as a capital objection: I believe it would have ultimately defeated the very design of our Union." Ibid., 297.

101. Elbridge Gerry, for example, told the convention delegates that he would withhold his name from the Constitution partly because of "the duration and re-eligibility of the Senate." Records, 2:632; see also "Letter of an Officer to the Late Continental Army," CA, 3:94 (the Anti-Federalist William Findley urging the citizens of Philadelphia to reject the proposed Constitution, because "[R]OTATION, that noble prerogative of liberty, is *entirely excluded from the new system of government* and the great men may and probably will be continued in office during their lives") (emphasis added); "Observations on the New Constitution, and on the Federal and State Conventions by a Columbian Patriot," CA, 4:278 (Mercy Otis Warren of Massachusetts objected to the Constitution by stating that "[t]here is no provision for a rotation, nor any thing to prevent the perpetuity of office in the same hands for life; which by a little well timed bribery, will probably be done, to the exclusion of men of the best abilities from their share in the offices of government").

102. The proposal required "[t]hat no person be eligible as a senator for more than six years in any term of twelve years." Debates, 2:289.

103. See, generally, Mark P. Petracca, "Rotation in Office: The History of an Idea," in *Limiting Legislative Terms*, ed. Gerald Benjamin and Michael J. Malbin (Washington, DC: Congressional Quarterly, 1992), 53–62; Jean Yarbrough, "Federalism in the Foundation and Preservation of the American Republic," *Publius: The Journal of Federalism* 6 (1976): 43–60.

104. Debates, 2:310.

105. Ibid., 288.

106. Ibid., 293.

107. Ibid., 295.

108. *Letters from the Federal Farmer to the Republican*, ed. Walter Hartwell Bennett (University of Alabama Press, 1978), 74–75.

109. Debates, 2:292–93.

110. Ibid., 257.

111. FP (No. 52), 324.

112. Debates, 2:306.

113. Ibid., 293.

114. Ibid., 298. Hamilton made a similar argument at the New York Ratifying Convention: "It has been observed, that it is not possible there should be in a state only two men qualified for senators. But, sir, the question is not, whether there may be no more than two men; but whether, in certain emergencies, you could find two equal to those whom the amendment would discard." Ibid., 320.

115. FP (No. 72), 414.

116. Ibid. (No. 71), 409.

117. Ibid. (No. 72), 414.

118. Ibid.

119. Ibid., 320–21.

120. FP (No. 10), 126.

121. Ibid., 125.

122. In the same letter in which Jefferson argued that the states could require additional qualifications for representatives to Congress, he warned his friend, Joseph C. Cabell, that "on so recent a change of view, caution requires us not to be too confident, and that we admit this to be one of the doubtful questions on which honest men may differ with the purest motives; and the more readily, as we find we have differed from ourselves on it." WTJ, 14:83.

123. Ron Chernow, *Alexander Hamilton* (New York: Penguin Press, 2004), 678–79.

124. 488 U.S. 469, 520 (1989) (Scalia, J., concurring).

125. Ibid., 523.

126. Ibid., 522 (quoting *Fullilove v. Klutznick*, 448 U.S. 448, 527 [1980]).

127. Antonin Scalia, "The Two Faces of Federalism," *Harvard Journal of Law & Public Policy* 6 (1982): 22.

128. Ed Gillespie and Bob Schellhas, eds., *Contract with America* (New York: Times Books, 1994); George F. Will, *Restoration: Congress, Term Limits and the Recovery of Deliberative Democracy* (New York: Free Press, 1993); and William Kristol, "Term Limitations: Breaking up the Iron Triangle," *Harvard Journal of Law & Public Policy* 16 (1993): 95–100.

129. See Harvey C. Mansfield, "Newt, Take Note: Populism Poses Its Own Dangers," *Wall Street Journal*, November 1, 1994, A24.

130. Antonin Scalia, "Reflections on the Constitution," Address to the Kennedy Political Union at American University, Washington, DC, November 17, 1988. C-SPAN video.

131. *U.S. Term Limits, Inc. v. Thornton*, 1994 U.S. TRANS. LEXIS 169. Scalia repeated this "close case" comment later when he was asked about his vote in *Term Limits*. During a question-and-answer period following a speech by Justice Scalia, I asked him about his vote in *Term Limits*, and he responded that "it was a close case" and then proceeded to praise Justice Thomas's lengthy dissenting opinion. Antonin Scalia, "On Interpreting the Constitution," address at Bridgewater College, April 2, 1996.

132. See, e.g., Michael Lind, *Up from Conservatism: Why the Right is Wrong for America* (New York: Free Press, 1996), 208–34.

133. 521 U.S. 898 (1997).

134. It is interesting that Justice Scalia is not even clear on this basic point. While it can be assumed that the sale of handguns is commercial activity, and therefore lies within Congress's commerce authority, at no point does Scalia clearly state this. Only Justice Thomas, in a concurring opinion, discusses whether the Brady Bill goes beyond Congress's power to regulate commerce. 521 U.S. at 937–38 (Thomas, J., concurring).

135. *Mack v. United States*, 66 F.3d 1025 (1995).

136. 505 U.S. 144 (1992).

137. Justice White coined this term in *New York v. United States*, 505 U.S. at 202 (White, J., dissenting).

138. *Printz*, 521 U.S. at 905.

139. Scalia did mention two exceptions to this early congressional practice. First, earlier Congresses imposed additional duties on state court judges, such as requirements that state court judges record applications of citizenship, register aliens, and conduct naturalization proceedings. Second, under the Extradition Act of 1793, state executives were required to deliver fugitives from justice to the executive authority of the state from which they fled. Scalia distinguished each of these forms of federal commandeering, however. As for the former, he argued that even if it could be assumed that state judges were commandeered by earlier Congresses to perform certain additional duties, there is a fundamental difference between commanding state judges, on the one hand, and commanding state executives and legislatures, on the other. Under the Supremacy Clause of the Constitution, U.S. Const. art. VI, cl. 2, state court judges are required to apply "the law of other sovereigns all the time," 521 U.S. at 907. As for the latter—cases in which governors were required to deliver fugitives from justice—Scalia also saw a distinction. Unlike the Brady Bill, the Extradition Act of 1793 was enacted pursuant to a particular constitutional provision: the Extradition Clause, U.S. Const. art. IV, sec. 2, cl. 2, which explicitly contemplates federal commandeering of state executive officers. 521 U.S. at 908–9.

140. 521 U.S. at 905.

141. Ibid., 910 (quoting *Debate on the Constitution* 1:502 [B. Bailyn ed., 1993]).

142. Ibid. (quoting FP [No. 36], 221).
143. Ibid. (quoting FP [No. 45], 292).
144. Ibid. (quoting FP [No. 27], 176).
145. Ibid. (quoting FP [No. 45], 292).
146. Ibid., 910–11 (emphasis added).
147. FP (No. 27), 203–4.
148. 521 U.S. at 913.
149. Ibid. at 915n9. Scalia also wrote, "To choose Hamilton's view, as JUSTICE SOUTER would, is to turn a blind eye to the fact that it was Madison's—not Hamilton's—that prevailed, not only at the Constitutional Convention and in popular sentiment . . . but in the subsequent struggle to fix the meaning of the Constitution by early congressional practice." Ibid.
150. Ibid., 915.
151. 521 U.S. at 918.
152. Ibid., 919. What is interesting about Justice Scalia's discussion of the U.S. federal system is that (except for the idea of better safeguarding individual freedom) he does not emphasize the underlying values of federalism. In contrast to Justice O'Connor, who often emphasizes these values in her opinions, Scalia relies on textual and structural arguments. This, I believe, is a further indication of his ambivalent attitude about "our federalism."
153. Ibid. (quoting FP [No. 39], at 245).
154. Ibid., 919.
155. Ibid.
156. Ibid. (quoting *Records of the Federal Convention of 1787*, at 2:9 [M. Farrand ed., 1911]).
157. Ibid., 920; *New York v. United States*, 505 U.S. 144 (1992).
158. 505 U.S. at 176.
159. 521 U.S. at 935.
160. Ibid., 915n9.
161. A strong argument can be made that it was Hamilton's, not Madison's, view that prevailed on the subject of federalism. In previous decisions, for example, the Supreme Court has followed Hamilton's broad interpretations of the Commerce Clause, the General Welfare provision, and the Necessary and Proper Clause. For this and other reasons, Clinton Rossiter has argued that "we live today under a Hamiltonian Constitution, a fundamental law of immense merit in the shaping of which his influence was supreme above that of any man of his time, and for the success of which in years to come his interpretation of its critical clauses will be more relevant than that of any American of any time." Clinton Rossiter, *Alexander Hamilton and the Constitution* (New York: Harcourt, Brace & World, Inc., 1964), 11.
162. "Whose Law, Whose Order?" Fred Friendly Seminar, December 14, 1996. Films for the Humanities & Sciences.
163. 521 U.S. at 919.
164. Ibid., 924n13. Justice Scalia also explained that "[w]hat destroys the dissent's Necessary and Proper Clause argument, however, is not the Tenth Amendment but the Necessary and Proper Clause itself." Ibid., 923.

165. Perhaps the most novel argument made by Justice Scalia was his claim that the Necessary and Proper Clause limits the scope of national power. 521 U.S. at 923–24; see also U.S. Const. art. I, sec. 8, cl. 18. For support of this view, Scalia relied upon a recent law review article arguing that in order for a law to be upheld under the Necessary and Proper Clause, it must not only be "necessary," but it must be "proper." Moreover, the authors narrowly construed the word "proper" to mean "peculiar," not simply "appropriate." See Gary Lawson and Patricia B. Granger, "The 'Proper' Scope of Federal Power: A Jurisdictional Interpretation of the Sweeping Clause," *Duke Law Journal* 43 (1993): 267.

166. 521 U.S. at 935–36 (O'Connor, J., concurring); Ibid., 936–39 (Thomas, J., concurring).

167. 381 U.S. 479 (1965).

168. Scalia does say (and rightly so) that the "resolution of a significant constitutional question . . . [can] rest upon reasonable implications." 521 U.S. at 924n13. But if this is the case, then he should not be so critical of the Court's nontextualist opinions regarding other provisions of the Constitution. See, e.g., *Planned Parenthood of Southeastern Pa. v. Casey*, 505 U.S. 833, 979 (1992) (Scalia, J., dissenting) (denying a woman's right to have an abortion).

169. Steven G. Calabresi, "A Constitutional Revolution," *Wall Street Journal*, July 10, 1997, A14.

170. *Garcia v. San Antonio Metro. Transit Auth.*, 469 U.S. 528 (1985).

171. Ibid., 550.

172. Ibid., 556.

173. Ibid., 554.

174. 521 U.S. at 958n18 (Stevens, J., dissenting).

175. Ibid., 957–58 (citing Unfunded Mandates Act of 1995, Pub. L. No. 104-4, 109 Stat. 48 [codified in scattered sections of 2 U.S.C.]).

176. FP (No. 15), 147, 149.

177. Debates, 2:232.

178. In *The Federalist*, Hamilton wrote that "I acknowledge my aversion to every project that is calculated to disarm the government of a single weapon, which in any possible contingency might be usefully employed for the general defense and security." FP (No. 37), 240–41. In comparing the framers' constitutional system to the one established under the Articles of Confederation, Hamilton also spoke of extending the authority of the federal government and not "confin[ing it] to the collective bodies of the communities." FP (No. 15), 149; see also FP (No. 27), 203. This language seems to suggest that he did not think that the newly conferred powers on the national government were a substitution for those it had under the Articles of Confederation, but rather they were an addition to them.

179. FP (No. 27), 203.

180. Ibid., 203–4.

181. This interpretation of *Federalist* 27 is also consistent with Hamilton's constitutional plan of government, which called for a unitary executive in which the governor of each state would be appointed by the general government and would have a veto over all laws passed by the state legislatures. PAH, 4:178–211. Thus, while Hamilton's

concerns about having a coercive authority over the states were undoubtedly real, he always defended some sort of federal control over the actions of state officials.

182. See, e.g., G. A. Phelps, *George Washington and American Constitutionalism* (Lawrence, KS: University Press of Kansas, 1993), 132. In a letter to Oliver Wolcott Jr., Hamilton confirms this view:

> It is a good principle for the Government of the UStates to employ directly its own means—only do not let this be carried so far as to confine it to the use of inadequate means or to embarrass the auxiliary means which circumstances may require. The idea of the late Presidents [*sic*] administration of considering the Governor of each State as the first General of the Militia & its immediate organ in acting upon the Militia was well considered & in my opinion wisely adopted—and well to be adhered to. In its general operation it will obviate many difficulties & collisions & by enhancing their importance tend to draw the State executives to the General Government. (PAH, 22:574–75)

183. Letter from Edmund Randolph to Thomas Mifflin (in the handwriting of Alexander Hamilton) (August 7, 1794), PAH, 17:65 (emphasis added).

184. Ibid., 71 (emphasis added).

185. 521 U.S. 898, 919 (quoting *Records of the Federal Convention of 1787*, 2:9 [M. Farrand ed., 1911]).

186. FP (No. 45), 295.

187. PJM, 9:369.

188. Records, 1:356–58, 449.

189. PJM, 9:353–57.

190. PJM, 10:163–64.

191. In *Federalist* 39, Madison wrote, "In several cases, and particularly in the trial of controversies to which States may be parties, they must be viewed and proceeded against in their collective and political capacities only." FP (No. 39), 258.

192. *Printz*, 521 U.S. at 973 (Souter, J., dissenting).

193. FP (No. 44), 291–92. In response to this statement by Madison, Justice Scalia remarked that it is surprising that he did not go on to say that the states were required to carry out federal laws. Instead, Madison mentioned how the states would be important in the selection of federal officials. *Printz*, 521 U.S. at 915. One answer to Scalia's concern is that it would have been imprudent for Madison to do so. Madison did not want to provoke unnecessary hostility from the states before the ratification of the Constitution. The other answer is provided by Justice Souter: Madison (as indicated by earlier language) was supplying only one example of the role of the states in giving effect to the Constitution; there were other roles that he assumed state officials would perform, including assisting the national government in carrying out federal programs. Ibid., 970n2 (Souter, J., dissenting).

194. Debates, 3:306.

195. For example, the Anti-Federalist "Agrippa" objected to the Constitution because "[t]hese provisions [the Supremacy Clause and oath requirement] cannot be understood otherwise than as binding the state judges and other officers, to execute the continental laws in their own proper departments within the state." CA, 4:78.

196. In correspondence discussing his views on the subject of federalism, Jefferson said that "the Governor [of a state] must be subject to receive orders from the war department as any other subordinate officer would." He also said that, "as to the portions of power within each State assigned to the General Government, the President is as much the Executive of the State, as their particular Governor is in relation to State powers." WTJ, 10:267, 15:382–83.

197. Although Justice Scalia is not entirely clear on this point, he appears to argue that because the president does not have the authority to remove state governors at his discretion, he cannot control the actions that they take. For example, in discussing the Selective Service Act of 1917, Scalia maintained that President Wilson lacked the authority to require the assistance of state governors in registering people for the draft during World War I. *Printz*, 521 U.S. at 917.

198. Several constitutional historians have also argued that the framers believed the federal government could conscript state officials into carrying out federal laws. See, e.g., Samuel H. Beer, *To Make a Nation: The Rediscovery of American Federalism* (Cambridge, MA: Harvard University Press, 1993), 252; Edward S. Corwin, *The Constitution and What It Means Today* (Princeton, NJ: Princeton University Press, 1974), 229; Evan H. Caminker, "State Sovereignty and Subordinancy: May Congress Commandeer State Officers to Implement Federal Law?" *Columbia Law Review* 95 (1995): 1001; Saikrishna Prakash, "Field Office Federalism," *Virginia Law Review* 79 (1993): 1957; and H. Jefferson Powell, "The Oldest Question of Constitutional Law," *Virginia Law Review* 79 (1993): 633.

199. *Printz*, 521 U.S. at 936 (O'Connor, J., concurring).

200. In fact, Scalia does express concern that if the Court upholds the Brady Bill, Congress could pass the costs of federal programs to the states without bearing its share of the responsibility. As he put it, "Under the present law . . . it will be the CLEO and not some federal official who stands between the gun purchaser and immediate possession of the gun. And it will likely be the CLEO, not some federal official, who will be blamed for any error (even one in the designated federal database) that causes a purchaser to be mistakenly rejected." Ibid., at 930.

201. See, e.g., *BMW of North America, Inc. v. Gore*, 517 U.S. 559, 599–600 (1996) (Scalia, J., dissenting); *United States v. Eichman*, 496 U.S. 310 (1990); *Maryland v. Craig*, 497 U.S. 836, 860 (1990) (Scalia, J., dissenting); *Arizona v. Hicks*, 480 U.S. 321 (1987).

202. *Printz*, 521 U.S. at 915n9.

203. "Whose Law, Whose Order?" Fred Friendly Seminar, December 14, 1996. Films for the Humanities & Sciences.

# Conclusion: Scalia's Personality and Statesmanship

All too often the majority of justices on the Rehnquist Court were referred to as "conservative," without the recognition that there were significant differences in outlook among them. Just as with the "liberals" of the Warren Court, the Rehnquist Court conservatives were not all of one political stripe. In fact, in some of the most controversial cases that came before this Court, it was the differences *among* the conservatives that were the decisive factor in determining how the Court ultimately ruled in the case.[1] This book has attempted to show that Justice Antonin Scalia is a different sort of conservative: he is a Hamiltonian. Like Hamilton, Scalia supports a formalistic interpretation of separation of powers, which protects the powers of the least dangerous branches of government against encroachment by Congress; he defends a strong and unitary executive, which is the sole organ in foreign affairs and has substantial implied and inherent powers under Article II; he advocates a theory of administration that is based on politics, not science, and which features the Hamiltonian characteristics of unity, discretion, and policy making; he supports a strong and independent federal judiciary that stands ready to strike down federal and state laws that violate the Constitution, but which is still the least dangerous branch of government; and he supports an understanding of the federal system whereby the national government is regarded as supreme, and the states are protected primarily by the political process and the structural provisions of the Constitution. Not only do Hamilton and Scalia share these same political principles, but they also exhibit similar personality traits, including brilliant intellectual abilities, dramatic literary styles, a high sense of character, and uncompromising temperaments.

## INTELLECTUAL PROWESS

Hamilton and Scalia have both been lavishly praised (by friends and foes alike) for their intellectual talents and abilities. Thomas Jefferson, Hamilton's chief political nemesis during his life, referred to him as a "colossus to the anti-republican party—without numbers, he is a host within himself." More than once, Jefferson would plead with Madison, "We have had only middling performances to oppose him—in truth, when he comes forward there is nobody but yourself who can meet him."[2] Similarly, Justice Scalia has been widely praised for his intellectual abilities. During his 1986 confirmation hearings to be an associate justice to the Supreme Court, Senator Edward M. Kennedy (D-MA), who was no political ally of Scalia's, remarked, "As a scholar, public official, federal judge, Mr. Scalia has demonstrated a brilliant legal intellect and earned the respect and affection of colleagues whose personal philosophies are far different from his own."[3] After taking his seat on the high court, the praise for Scalia's intellectual talents has continued unabated. As a writer, he has been compared to two of the greatest stylists who have served on the Supreme Court: Justice Oliver Wendell Holmes and Justice Robert Jackson.[4] And his substantive contributions to the law—while by no means uncontroversial or widely shared by either his colleagues or academics—have been quite significant. Although he has lost many of the major Court battles over such issues as government support of religion, abortion, homosexual rights, and capital punishment, he has written pathbreaking opinions in the areas of religious freedom, property rights, and legal standing. Moreover, his textualist approach to interpreting laws, as well as his rule-based approach to deciding cases, has sparked scholarly debate over the proper role of courts in a democratic system of government. On this basis, several of Scalia's most ardent admirers have made large claims for him. He has been favorably compared to the "Great Chief" John Marshall, and described as someone who will someday "take his place among the Court's giants."[5]

## DRAMATIC LITERARY STYLES

Hamilton and Scalia also share remarkably similar writing styles: clear, direct, passionate, and logical. In fact, it would be difficult to mistake a Scalian or a Hamiltonian opinion. Each of their opinions comes with a distinct personal stamp. For both men, style is a way to communicate at a more personal level. Their writings convey not only their thoughts and the process by which they arrived at their decisions, but their innermost passions and feelings. It is also evident that both men have a decided penchant for hyperbole and drama. One dramatic theme that has surfaced in both men's writings is a deep skepticism about and alienation from the social values held by a certain segment of the population. For Hamilton, this sense of alienation came in relation to the views of the masses. One of Hamilton's principal weaknesses as a statesman was that he did not relate well to the common person. He did not understand the values of the common man, nor did he appear to want to learn about them. Since Hamilton worried that the masses threatened the stability of republican government, he argued at the Constitutional Convention that the "rich and well born" should have a "permanent share in the government."[6] For this reason, Woodrow Wilson referred to Hamilton as "a very great man, but not a great American."[7] Two years prior to his death, and shortly after his son Philip was tragically killed in a duel, Hamilton remorsefully remarked,

Mine is an odd destiny. Perhaps no man in the UStates has sacrificed or done more for the present Constitution than myself—and contrary to all my anticipations of its fate, as you know from the very begginning [sic] I am still labouring to prop the frail and worthless fabric. Yet I have the murmurs of its friends no less than the curses of its foes for my rewards. What can I do better than withdraw from the Scene? Every day proves to me more and more that this American world was not made for me.[8]

Justice Scalia has also expressed a similar feeling of alienation from the social values held by a certain segment of the population. In contrast to Hamilton, however, Scalia's sense of alienation derives from the values of "elite" federal judges, drawn from the "lawyer class," whom he claims are seeking to impose their own moral values on the people. As Scalia sees it, judicially created rights threaten the democratic process and make the Constitution less flexible. The Court's 1995–1996 term was particularly difficult for Scalia. During that term, he filed vigorous dissenting opinions in cases where the Court held that Virginia Military Institute's all-male admissions policy violated the Equal Protection Clause;[9] that a state constitutional amendment withdrawing the protection of antidiscrimination laws from homosexuals violated the Equal Protection Clause;[10] and that state and local governments violate the Free Speech Clause when they retaliate against independent contractors because of their political views.[11] In a reply letter to his former colleague Harry Blackmun, who had retired in 1994 and had written Nino to cheer him up after the 1995–1996 term, Scalia acknowledged that he was "more discouraged [that] year than [he] had been at the end of any of [his] previous nine terms" on the Court. He also said that he was beginning to repeat himself and that he did not see much use in it anymore.[12] In the two political patronage cases, where the Court extended First Amendment protection

CHAMBERS OF
JUSTICE ANTONIN SCALIA

July 2, 1996

Dear Harry,

How kind of you to write the nice note you did! You are right that I am more discouraged this year than I have been at the end of any of my previous nine terms up here. I am beginning to repeat myself, and don't see much use in it any more.

I hope I will feel better in the fall. A cheering note from an old colleague — and one whom, God knows, I was not always on the same side with — sure does help. Many thanks — and have a pleasant summer.

Respectfully,

Nino

*Letter from Antonin Scalia to Harry Blackmun, July 2, 1996, HABP, box 1408* to independent contractors who work for the government, Scalia's dissenting opinion, filed for each of the cases, struck a similar chord of alienation as that expressed by Hamilton in 1802:

> The people should not be deceived. While the present Court sits, a major, undemocratic restructuring of our national institutions and mores is constantly in progress. . . . The Court must be living in another world. Day by day, case by case, it is busy designing a Constitution for a country I do not recognize.[13]

## HIGH SENSE OF CHARACTER

Alexander Hamilton and Antonin Scalia also place great importance on personal and public character. Hamilton lived during a time when a direct challenge to one's honor could result in a duel, and he himself was involved in the preliminaries of six duels before the fatal one with Aaron Burr. In *A Sketch of the Character of Alexander Hamilton*, Fisher Ames made the following observation about his subject: "[N]ot the Roman Cato himself, was more inflexible on every point that touched, or only seemed to touch, integrity and honour."[14] Perhaps as a way of compensating for his illegitimate birth and impoverished boyhood in the West Indies, Hamilton was exceedingly sensitive to slights on his character and was willing to do whatever it took to protect his reputation. When he believed, for example, that James Monroe had leaked information to the press about his adulterous affair with Maria Reynolds, Hamilton was livid and immediately challenged Monroe to a duel. "I will meet you like a gentleman," an irate Hamilton told Monroe.[15] Hotheaded and inflexible, Hamilton was incapable of turning the other cheek when his character was in any way challenged.

Similarly, Justice Scalia assigns tremendous weight to personal and public character. His father, Eugene, would often say: "Brains are like muscles—you can hire them by the hour. . . . The only thing that's not for sale is character."[16] For Scalia, intelligence does not lead to a virtuous life. What makes a person good is personal integrity and upstanding moral character. The importance Scalia places on personal character is evident in at least one area of his jurisprudence. As a court of appeals judge, Scalia was a sharp critic of the Supreme Court's libel jurisprudence and, in particular, its landmark 1964 decision *New York Times v. Sullivan*.[17] In *Sullivan*, the Court required proof of "actual malice" before public officials could win their libel suits. Sitting as a Court of Appeals judge, Scalia filed a sharply worded dissent in a libel case in which he characterized an article written by the syndicated columnists Rowland Evans and Robert Novak as "a classic and cooly crafted libel," and ridiculed the attack-dog journalism represented by the "Media Age."[18] Scalia also took strong exception to the "public bumping" and heavy burden placed on public officials to win libel cases, which he said is "fulsomely assured" by the Court's decision in *Sullivan*. Underlying Scalia's criticism of *Sullivan* was the belief that the press has too much license to destroy the reputations of public officials. In his dissenting opinion in *Ollman v. Evans*, Scalia wondered whether those persons

> are right who discern a distressing tendency for our political commentary to de-
> scend from discussion of public issues to destruction of private reputations; who
> believe that, by putting some brake upon that tendency, defamation liability un-
> der existing standards not only does not impair but fosters the type of discussion
> the first amendment is most concerned to protect; and who view high libel judg-
> ments as no more than an accurate reflection of the vastly expanded damage that
> can be caused by media that are capable of holding individuals up to public
> obloquy from coast to coast and that reap financial rewards commensurate with
> that power.[19]

Interestingly, and perhaps out of concern about how the press covers his speeches, Scalia had a strict policy against audio- or video-taping of his own public addresses. A controversy over this policy arose in 2004 when, without Scalia's authorization, a U.S. deputy marshal erased the digital recordings of two reporters at one of his speeches, even though an announcement about the ban had not been made prior to the address. Scalia immediately issued an apology to the reporters and has since changed his policy to allow the press to audiotape his speeches.[20] As a result of his libel decisions as a court of ap-peals judge, as well as his 1982 article criticizing the Freedom of Information Act, syndicated columnist William Safire referred to Scalia in 1985 as "the worst enemy of free speech in America today."[21]

Justice Scalia has also shown a heightened sensitivity to press coverage of his conduct that touches on his personal character. In September 2000, the *Legal Times* published a front-page story insinuating that Scalia was the driving force behind a proposed bill to eliminate the ban on honoraria for federal judges. The federal ban, passed in 1989, prohibits federal judges from accept-ing honoraria for speaking engagements in order to protect them from im-proper influence by interest groups. Referring to the proposed legislation to lift the ban as the "Keep Scalia on the Court" bill, Tony Mauro and Sam Loewen-berg cited unnamed congressional staffers who had heard that the primary rea-son for the bill was to allay Scalia's frustration over the honoraria ban, which Scalia regarded as prohibiting a legitimate source of extra income for under-paid judges, leading him to publicly muse from time to time about leaving the Court.[22] In a rarity for a Supreme Court justice, Scalia fired off an acerbic let-ter to the editor denying that he was the moving force behind the legislation and disputing "the mean-spirited attack upon my personal integrity." Taking a personal shot at Mauro, a Supreme Court correspondent for American Lawyer

Media and *Legal Times*, Scalia wrote, "All this makes gossipy, titillating (and thus characteristically Mauronic) copy, but in fact the honorarium ban makes no difference to me. For many years, all of my outside earned income has come from teaching, which is not covered by that ban, and that is the only compensable extrajudicial activity I am interested in pursuing."[23]

## Duck Hunting with Vice President Dick Cheney

The best evidence of Scalia's sensitivity to press coverage of his conduct came in his twenty-one-page memorandum defending his decision not to recuse himself from the 2004 case involving Vice President Dick Cheney. On January 5, 2004, three weeks after the Court agreed to hear *Cheney v. United States Dist. Court*,[24] Scalia was caught by the media on the front end of a several-day[25] duck-hunting trip with his longtime friend Vice President Dick Cheney, a named party in the case. The two men were guests of Wallace Carline, a friend of Scalia's who owns Diamond Services Corporation in Amelia, Louisiana, which is a provider of services and rental equipment to oil rigs in the Gulf of Mexico. On behalf of Carline, Scalia invited the vice president to take part in the Scalia-Carline annual duck hunt in the spring of 2003, and the vice president accepted the invitation in the summer of 2003. Vice President Cheney offered to fly Scalia, his son, and his son-in-law down to Louisiana on a government plane, which they accepted. Upon landing in Patterson, Louisiana, the men were photographed getting into cars that took them to a dock, where they embarked on a twenty-minute boat ride to Carline's hunting camp.[26] Although the duck hunting reportedly was "lousy," the media had a field day with this story, and Scalia was the brunt of late-night-comedian jokes. Congressional Democrats inquired about the Supreme Court's recusal process, and twenty out of thirty of the nation's largest-circulation newspapers asked for Scalia to step aside in the case.[27] The Sierra Club, one of the parties in *Cheney*, made a formal request for the justice to recuse himself, but Scalia refused. In a twenty-one-page memorandum, Scalia defended his actions and argued that there was no reason for him to recuse himself from participating in the case. Under Supreme Court rules, the decision to recuse lies with the individual justice, and the standard is whether a justice's impartiality in a case might reasonably be questioned. In Scalia's view, his impartiality could not reasonably be questioned since there was no court precedent stating that a judge could not sit in a case involving a friend when that person is being sued in his official (as opposed to private) capacity. Scalia noted that justices have often dined with presidents and vice presidents, and he mentioned two instances in which a president (or other top-level executive official) went on a trip with a Supreme Court justice at a time when an important case for the administration was pending before the Court.[28] Scalia also argued that the presumption of recusal in lower courts does not apply at the Supreme Court, where the absence of a justice can have a dramatic impact on the institution's decision-making process. Saving his sharpest barbs for the press, however, Scalia observed that recusal in this instance would hurt the integrity of the courts by allowing "elements of the press a veto over participation of any Justices who had social contacts with, or were even known to be friends of, a named official."[29] Scalia blasted the press for inaccurately reporting the duck-hunting trip and misleading the public, and sarcastically stated that "[i]f it is reasonable to think that a Supreme Court Justice can be bought so cheap, the Nation is in deeper trouble than I had imagined."[30]

Prior to declining Sierra Club's recusal motion, Scalia poked fun at his detractors on the lecture circuit. In February 2004, Scalia explained at an address at Amherst College, where some demonstrators in the audience dressed up like ducks, that he had done nothing wrong because the case was against Cheney's office, not against the vice president personally. "It's acceptable practice to socialize with executive branch officials when there are not personal claims against them," Scalia told the large audience of six hundred people. But, unable to resist taking a shot at the demonstrators in the audience, Scalia concluded, "That's all I'm going to say for now. Quack, quack."[31] In October 2004, after the Court handed down its decision in *Cheney*, Scalia was asked by a student at Harvard Law School about his involvement in the case, and he responded (consistent with his twenty-one-page memorandum) that there was no court precedent requiring his recusal in the case. Evidencing an ongoing hostility toward the press, Scalia continued, "I'll be doggone if I'm to get hounded off the case by newspaper editorials."[32]

Justice Scalia's public musings about other legal matters and cases have also attracted criticism and recusal requests. When the Court agreed to hear *Bush v. Gore*[33]—a decision that gave George W. Bush the 2000 presidential election by stopping the hand recount in Florida—Scalia filed a rare concurring opinion to the order granting review, where he provided early indications of his views in the case: "The counting of votes that are of questionable legality does in my view threaten irreparable harm to [Bush], and to the country, by casting a cloud upon what he claims to be the legitimacy of his election. Count first, and rule upon legality afterwards, is not a recipe for producing election results that have the public acceptance democratic stability requires."[34] And after giving a speech at a Knights of Columbus event in Fairfax, Virginia, in January 2003, during which he criticized the Ninth Circuit's decision striking down the recitation of the pledge of allegiance in public schools, Scalia was asked by Michael Newdow, the person who challenged the California school district policy, to recuse himself from hearing the case on appeal. Because Scalia had already expressed an opinion on the constitutional issue in the case, he had little choice but to recuse himself from sitting in *Elk Grove Unified Sch. Dist. v. Newdow*.[35] While Scalia's decision to participate in *Cheney* can certainly be criticized,[36] the nature of how he reacted to the groundswell of controversy surrounding his duck-hunting trip with Vice President Cheney is also interesting. Not unlike Hamilton, Scalia revealed a heightened sensitivity to criticism of his personal character. Scalia's reaction to the *Cheney* flap was not unlike what Alexander Hamilton did when his honor was put into question. He aggressively fought back.

## Uncompromising Temperaments

Alexander Hamilton and Antonin Scalia also exhibit similar temperaments, one aspect of which is their high sense of being principled. Compromise is not a popular word in their vocabularies. Hamilton regarded compromise as the mark of either "a weak and versatile mind, or of an artificial and designing character"[37] Gouverneur Morris, one of Hamilton's closest friends, once remarked that a central characteristic of Hamilton's personality was "the pertinacious adherence to opinions he had once formed."[38] Hamilton's principled nature was prominently displayed in the fatal duel with Aaron Burr, where (unlike in the preliminaries of the six other duels in which he had been involved) Hamilton acknowledged some wrongdoing on his part, but could not allow himself to issue a general apology.[39] In his statement explaining why he proceeded with the duel, Hamilton admitted that on numerous occasions he had censured Burr's public and private character, and, while he regarded much of what he had said as true, he confessed that some of his statements "may have been influenced by misconstruction or misinformation." Rather than issue a general apology, Hamilton decided before the fatal "interview" with Burr that he would "*reserve* and *throw away* [his] first shot." Hamilton had gambled on the mistaken belief that Burr would not shoot to kill, but he was not unaware that he could be killed. Hamilton gave as one explanation for why he went through with the duel that his honorable death might be useful to the country "in resisting mischief or effecting good, in those crises of our public affairs, which seem likely to happen."[40]

Similarly, as a member of the Supreme Court, Scalia has shown an aversion to compromise. Prior to his appointment to the Supreme Court, Scalia was touted as someone who, like Justice William Brennan on the left, would be able to forge majority coalitions with his conservative colleagues on the right. This, however, has not turned out to be the case. Scalia relishes a go-it-alone attitude in which he sees little need to accommodate the views of his colleagues. In a 1994 lecture to the Supreme Court Historical Society, Scalia defended the importance of dissenting opinions. Aside from the usual reasons given for their significance, Scalia observed that the most important reason to file dissents was the personal satisfaction they give the judge who authors them: "To be able to write an opinion solely for oneself, without the need to accommodate, to any degree whatever, the more-or-less-differing views of one's colleagues; to address precisely the points of law that one considers important and *no others*; to express precisely the degree of quibble, or foreboding, or disbelief, or indignation that one believes the majority's disposition should engender—that is indeed an unparalleled pleasure."[41] Scalia's unwillingness to compromise is also reflected in the premium he places on being principled or consistent as a judge. In a revealing 1989 speech at Case Reserve University School of Law, Scalia took issue with Ralph Waldo Emerson's aphorism "a foolish consistency is the hobgoblin of little minds, adored by little statesmen and philosophers and divines." In "Self-Reliance," Emerson contended that complexity is the mark of great souls. "With consistency a great soul has simply nothing to do," wrote Emerson, adding, "To be great is to be misunderstood." Scalia strenuously objected to this view, particularly as applied to legal analysis. For Scalia, "Consistency is the very foundation of the rule of law," and the "the mother of consistency" is logic. He criticized Oliver Wendell Holmes and the legal realists for "pointing out that all these legal fictions were fictions: Those judges wise enough to be trusted with the secret already knew it." As Scalia viewed it, insistence upon logic and consistency is an important check on judicial arbitrariness in making decisions. Even if judges do not care for a particular outcome in a case, Scalia maintained that they must follow the "binding abstractions" of the law. In contrast to Emerson, Scalia argued that the mark of a great soul is not to be misunderstood:

> [T]he person who finds himself repeatedly in that situation—who quite readily speaks today what he thinks today, and tomorrow what he thinks tomorrow, with no concern for, with "simply nothing to do" with, the inconsistency between the two—is rightly regarded, it seems to me, not as a "great soul," but as one who habitually speaks without reflection, that is to say, a right fool.[42]

Hamilton's and Scalia's unwillingness to compromise on basic political and legal principles has earned them great praise from their most ardent admirers, but it is also a character trait that has had its destructive aspects. Hamilton's widely publicized and intemperate criticism of John Adams's character as president of the United States was a principal reason for his marginalization within the Federalist Party and his early retirement from politics.[43] And his repeated attacks on Burr's character (as well as his unwillingness to issue a general apology) were the reasons for his untimely death. Richard B. Morris, another of Hamilton's excellent biographers, ably described the debilitating aspects of Hamilton's personality in this way:

Hamilton's failures as a statesman are attributable more to personality and tactics than to basic principles. Hamilton carried courage in politics to the point of self-immolation. If there was any attacking to be done, he did not assign the task to someone else, but took it on himself. . . . Opinionated and self-assured, he lacked that understanding of the art of compromise, the mastery of which is so essential to the aspiring politician. Thus, he was inflexible when a little yielding would have made all the difference. . . . Hamilton lacked terminal facilities. He was candid, but he was also indiscreet. He wrote brilliantly, but he wrote too much and too often. His astonishing attack on President John Adams left Hamilton a party leader without a following.[44]

Similarly, Justice Scalia's personal criticisms of his colleagues have led some to speculate about whether he is jeopardizing his influence on the Supreme Court. Scalia's no-holds-barred approach to deciding cases earned him the nickname "Ninopath" on the D.C. Court of Appeals, and his strident and uncompromising decision-making approach has not mellowed during his tenure as a Supreme Court justice. While acknowledging that Scalia is a brilliant intellect and judicial visionary, political scientist Christopher Smith has argued that Scalia's temperament was a principal reason why the Rehnquist Court's conservative majority was not more successful in such policy areas as abortion, crime, and church-state matters. Smith refers to Scalia as the Court's "anti-strategist" whose inability (and unwillingness) to build coalitions has contributed substantially to the failure of the judicial counterrevolution.[45] While perhaps too much of the lack of unity among the Rehnquist Court conservatives can be attributed to personality differences, as opposed to philosophical disagreements, Scalia's sharp attacks against his colleagues—or what Judge Alex Kozinski has called "verbal hand grenades"[46]—many of which call into question his colleagues' honesty and character, certainly have not helped to build coalitions on the right. After the Court's 1995–1996 term, a number of legal scholars discussed the potential liabilities of Scalia's temperament. Yale law professor Akhil Amar, an admitted admirer of Scalia's, expressed "disappoint[ment] that, in a few cases, [Scalia] was more sharp than he had to be with his colleagues." Scalia's conduct "strategically," according to Amar, "may be a mistake." And Richard Epstein, a onetime colleague of Scalia's at the University of Chicago Law School, observed,

[J]ustices have long memories. That is, this is not a question of one academic hurling artillery shells at another academic at a different institution whom he may not see again for years to come. This is a situation in which you are in collaborative and deliberative association with other justices, and to the extent that you denounce some of their opinions in this particular fashion, it will make it more difficult for you to exert influence and to maintain cordial relationships with them with respect to other opinions.[47]

It is, of course, much too early to be writing judicial epitaphs for a justice of Scalia's caliber. President George W. Bush has successfully appointed John Roberts as the seventeenth chief justice of the United States, and Samuel Alito as an associate justice to replace Sandra Day O'Connor. The president may also have the opportunity to make additional appointments to the Court before his second term ends. All of these changes to the Court's membership may result in Scalia gaining additional support for his positions. Nevertheless, it cannot be denied that Scalia's temperament has adversely affected his influence on the Supreme Court. He is certainly not the consensus builder that he was billed as prior to taking his seat on the nation's high court.

## STATESMANSHIP

Alexis de Tocqueville believed that federal judges must not only be good citizens, "but they must be statesmen, wise to discover the signs of the times, not afraid to brave the obstacles that can be subdued, nor slow to turn away from the current when it threatens to sweep them off, and the supremacy of the Union and the obedience due to laws along with them."[48] In conservative thought, at least two models of statesmanship can be identified. The first is that associated with Edmund Burke. Burke's standard of statesmanship was "[a] disposition to preserve, and an ability to improve." The speculative philosopher "may wish his society otherwise constituted than he finds it," Burke wrote, "but . . . a true politician . . . always considers how he shall make the most of the existing materials of his country."[49] Alexander Bickel, who acknowledged the influence of Burke on his own thought, maintained a similar view of statesmanship. Bickel regarded prudence as an indispensable condition for success in the activities of both the politician and the judge. The forms of practical wisdom for the judge consisted of what Bickel called the "passive virtues" of the Court.[50] Bickel maintained that the Court has three options when it has a constitutional case before it: it may strike down legislation, it may validate it, or it may do neither.[51] The Court has many ways of doing the latter—it may deny that it has jurisdiction; it may dismiss a case for mootness or ripeness; it may refuse to hear a case on the grounds that it raises a "political question"; or the Court may decide the case on narrow grounds. The virtue of these adjudicatory techniques, Bickel claimed, is that they buy the Court some time. In unpopular or politically charged cases, the Court can postpone decision in order for the political branches to work things out. Bickel did not regard these techniques as unprincipled, but rather viewed them as striking a proper balance between constitutional principle and the expediency of the political process.

A second model of conservative statesmanship can be identified with Alexander Hamilton. Hamilton, like Aristotle, believed in the importance of theory to the practice of politics. Although he contended that the business of government differs from the speculation of it, Hamilton insisted that abiding principles are needed in order to guide deliberation and decision. One of the reasons Hamilton preferred Thomas Jefferson to Aaron Burr in the 1800 presidential election was that, even though he and Jefferson strongly disagreed over basic political principles, Jefferson, in his view, at least followed certain principles in politics. By contrast, Hamilton viewed Burr as a mere politician or political opportunist whose politics did not reflect any overarching political theory. "Is it a recommendation to have *no theory?*" Hamilton asked at the time. "Can that man be a systematic or able statesman who has none? I believe not."[52] The problem of statesmanship, as Hamilton saw it, consisted of determining the best arrangements and policies to achieve basic constitutional ends. Hamilton's statesmanship was called into action by the exigencies of fiscal reconstruction and foreign affairs. His style of his leadership was energetic. Under this model of statesmanship, if political or judicial practice get out of kilter with political principles, then the practice may have to be discontinued.

Justice Scalia's statesmanship has more in common with Hamilton than it does with Burke. On some issues, Scalia has exercised a type of Burkean prudent judgment. For example, Scalia differs from libertarian conservatives who want to see a more activist judiciary in the area of economic and property rights. While Scalia has played a major role in reinvigorating the Court's Takings Clause jurisprudence, he has declined to resurrect the sort of "liberty of contract" right that existed during the *Lochner* era. Aside from his view that there is no constitutional ethos to support such a liberty of contract right, Scalia has cited the more practical concern that some of his colleagues might want to protect "less sensible" property interests, such as welfare, social security, and housing, as a prudential reason for not reinventing economic substantive due process.[53] In other respects, however, Scalia has shown a more energetic type of leadership. Since his appointment to the Supreme Court, he has written the most concurring opinions among his colleagues, and the third most dissenting opinions. He has also been actively engaged in the art of selling his jurisprudence through extrajudicial speeches, sending "Ninograms" to his colleagues, and filing dissents from denials of certiorari. In the area of legal standing, Scalia has shown little interest in the Court's prudential doctrine for examining standing claims, but rather has based his opinions on what he regards as the core constitutional requirements of Article III. Moreover, Scalia has disagreed with the Burkean attitude toward precedent. The Burkean judge places great reliance on precedent, or what Burke called "the collected reason of ages," as a means of curbing judicial behavior. In a concurring opinion in

*Orozco v. Texas*, Justice John Marshall Harlan II, who exhibited all of the traits of a Burkean traditionalist judge, provided the following explanation for why he voted to uphold the Court's decision in *Miranda v. Arizona*,[54] a decision in which he had filed a dissent only three years earlier:

> The passage of time has not made the *Miranda* case any more palatable to me than it was when the case was decided. . . . Yet despite my strong inclination to join in the dissent of my Brother WHITE, I can find no acceptable avenue of escape from Miranda in judging this case. . . . Therefore, and purely out of respect for *stare decisis*, I reluctantly feel compelled to acquiesce in today's decision of the Court, at the same time observing that the constitutional condemnation of this perfectly understandable, sensible, proper, and indeed commendable piece of police work highlights the unsoundness of *Miranda*.[55]

Scalia, by contrast, does not feel compelled to follow Court precedents if they do not conform to his understanding of the Constitution. As he explained in a case involving the use of victim impact statements during the penalty phase of a capital murder trial, "I would think it a violation of my oath to adhere to what I consider a plainly unjustified intrusion on the democratic process in order that the Court might save face."[56] In that case, Scalia also approvingly quoted Justice William O. Douglas on the subject of judicial adherence to precedent:

> A judge looking at a constitutional decision may have compulsions to revere history and accept what was once written. But he remembers above all else that it is a Constitution which he swore to support and defend, not the gloss which his predecessors may have put on it.[57]

The frequency with which Scalia has moved to overturn a prior decision of the Court is nothing short of staggering. From 1986–2003, Scalia voted to alter precedent in four percent of the cases in which he cast a vote. Among Rehnquist Court justices, only Justice Thomas exceeded Scalia's level of commitment to altering Court precedent.[58]

Finally, Scalia has demonstrated an energetic type of leadership in his sharp criticism of the common law method of deciding cases. In Scalia's view, this method of deciding cases, in which judges examine "one case at a time taking into account all of the circumstances, and identifying within that context the 'fair' result," gives judges too much discretion. In a 1989 article titled "The Rule of Law as a Law of Rules," Scalia argued that judges should instead base their decisions on general rules. He cited four advantages of such an approach to judicial decision making: (1) it will make the law more uniform and give credence to the idea that all persons receive equal treatment before the law; (2) it will make the law more predictable, which Scalia believes "is the needful characteristic of any law worthy of the name"; (3) it will curb judicial arbitrariness and discretion to do justice in individual cases; and

(4) it will embolden judges to make hard decisions in unpopular cases.[59] Scalia's concurring opinion in the 1989 decision *Webster v. Reproductive Health Services*[60] illustrates his rule of law approach. In that case, the Court upheld several state regulations on the performance of abortions, including a statement in the preamble of the Missouri abortion statute that "[t]he life of each human being begins at conception"; a ban on the use of public funds to perform abortions unless necessary to save the mother's life; a prohibition on the use of public facilities to perform abortions unless medically necessary; and a requirement that viability tests be performed twenty weeks into a pregnancy. In a pivotal concurring opinion, Justice Sandra Day O'Connor, while agreeing with the majority to uphold the four statutory regulations, declined to reexamine the Court's 1973 *Roe v. Wade*[61] decision, which held that women have a constitutional right to obtain an abortion under the Fourteenth Amendment's Due Process Clause. To support this outcome, O'Connor, who also exhibited all of the philosophical and temperamental characteristics of a Burkean traditionalist judge, cited several of the restraint-oriented maxims set forth by Justice Louis D. Brandeis in his concurring opinion in *Ashwander v. TVA*, including that "[t]he Court will not 'anticipate a question of constitutional law in advance of the necessity of deciding it,'" and that it generally will not "formulate a rule of constitutional law broader than is required by the precise facts to which it is to be applied."[62] In O'Connor's view, the facts of *Webster* did not require the Court to reexamine its holding in *Roe v. Wade*, and she argued that it would be imprudent for the Court to go out of its way to do so: "When the constitutional invalidity of a state's abortion statute actually turns on the constitutional validity of *Roe v. Wade*, there will be time enough to reexamine *Roe*. And to do so carefully."[63] In his own concurring opinion, Scalia caustically criticized the Court's and, in particular, Justice O'Connor's "abstemiousness" in deciding the case. According to Scalia, application of the first Brandeisian-prudential doctrine mentioned by O'Connor "cannot be taken seriously," because here the Court is confronted with a constitutional issue, not a statutory question. And while Scalia acknowledged that there was merit to the second Brandeisian-prudential technique—that is, that the Court will not formulate a rule of constitutional law broader than is required by the precise facts to which it is to be applied—he saw no compelling reason to apply such a cautious approach here. For Scalia, *Roe* was wrongly decided in 1973 and should be explicitly overturned in this case. As Scalia saw it, whether a woman has a right to an abortion and to what extent a state can regulate that decision are political, not judicial, questions. The Court's "indecisive decision," Scalia argued, is an open invitation for further litigation and lobbying of the Court in the area of abortion rights, and the effect of the Court's decision is "that the mansion of constitutionalized abortion law,

constructed overnight in *Roe v. Wade*, must be disassembled doorjamb by doorjamb, and never entirely brought down, no matter how wrong it might be." Scalia concluded his concurring opinion with the following observation: "Of the four courses we might have chosen today—to reaffirm *Roe*, to overrule it explicitly, to overrule it *sub silentio*, or to avoid the question—the last is the least responsible." And underscoring his own style of energetic leadership, Scalia criticized the Court's "stingy" holding in the case:

> The outcome of today's case will undoubtedly be heralded as a triumph of judicial statesmanship. It is not that, unless it is statesmanlike needlessly to prolong this Court's self-awarded sovereignty over a field [abortion] where it has little proper business since the answers to most of the cruel questions posed are political and not juridical.[64]

In sum, not only has Justice Scalia defended the same political principles as Hamilton, he has appropriated a Hamiltonian idea of "energetic" statesmanship to the role of judge. It is important, however, to reemphasize the purpose of Scalia's principled statesmanship: to reduce the influence of federal courts in the U.S. democratic system of government. By employing an originalist approach to constitutional interpretation, Scalia can vote to overturn many of the decisions of the Warren and Burger Courts. And with a rule-based decision-making approach, Scalia can continue to criticize the Court's use of balancing tests as well as those instances in which he believes his colleagues have substituted their own policy views for the law. In the post–Warren Court era, Scalia does not want to simply "preserve" or moderate the present constitutional order; he wants to return the Court to a jurisprudence of original principles. In this sense, Scalia is the Court's counterrevolutionary.

## NOTES

1. See, e.g., *Planned Parenthood of Southeastern Pennsylvania v. Casey*, 505 U.S. 833 (1992) (upholding a limited right of abortion); *Lee v. Weisman*, 505 U.S. 577 (1992) (striking down school-sponsored graduation prayers); *Texas v. Johnson*, 491 U.S. 397 (1989) (striking down a state flag desecration statute as violative of the First Amendment's Free Speech Clause); *Grutter v. Bollinger*, 539 U.S. 306 (2003) (affirmative action can be considered a "plus" when individualized treatment is given to each applicant); *Lawrence v. Texas*, 539 U.S. 558 (2003) (laws prohibiting same-sex sodomy violate the liberty provision of the Due Process Clause).

2. PAH, 18:478.

3. U.S. Senate, *The Nomination of Judge Antonin Scalia: Hearings before the Committee on the Judiciary of the United States Senate*, 99th Cong., 2nd. sess., August 5, 1986, 12.

4. See Charles Fried, "Manners Makyth Man: The Prose Style of Justice Scalia," *Harvard Journal of Law & Public Policy* 16 (1993): 529–36; Rodney A. Smolla, "An-

tonin Scalia," in *Supreme Court Justices: A Biographical Dictionary*, ed. Melvin I. Urofsky (New York: Garland Publishing, 1994), 401.

5. Patrick B. McGuigan and Dawn M. Weyrich, *Ninth Justice: The Fight for Bork* (Washington, DC: Free Congress Research and Education Foundation, 1990), xxi; Alex Kozinski, "My Pizza with Nino," *Cardozo Law Review* 12 (1991): 1583–91, 1591.

6. "Constitutional Convention, Speech on a Plan of Government" (June 18, 1787), PAH, 4:200.

7. Ron Chernow, *Alexander Hamilton* (New York: Penguin Press, 2004), 3.

8. Letter to Gouverneur Morris (February 29, 1802), PAH, 25:544.

9. *United States v. Virginia*, 518 U.S. 515 (1996) (Scalia, J., dissenting).

10. *Romer v. Evans*, 517 U.S. 620 (1996) (Scalia, J., dissenting).

11. *Bd. of County Comm'rs v. Umbehr*, 518 U.S. 668 (1996) (Scalia, J., dissenting); *O'Hare Truck Service Inc. v. City of Northlake*, 518 U.S. 712 (1996) (Scalia, J., dissenting).

12. HABP, box 1408.

13. *Bd. of County Comm'rs v. Umbehr*, 518 U.S. at 710–11; *O'Hare Truck Service Inc. v. City of Northlake*, 518 U.S. at 710–11.

14. Chernow, *Alexander Hamilton*, 308 (citing Fisher Ames, *A Sketch of the Character of Alexander Hamilton* [Boston: Repertory Office, 1804], 8).

15. Ibid., 539 (citing PAH, 21:161).

16. Margaret Talbot, "Supreme Confidence," *New Yorker*, March 28, 2005, 43.

17. 376 U.S. 254 (1964).

18. *Ollman v. Evans*, 750 F.2d 970 (D.C. Cir. 1984).

19. 750 F.2d at 1039 (Scalia, J., dissenting).

20. The incident took place during an April 7, 2004 speech at the Presbyterian Christian High School in Hattiesburg, Mississippi. Many regarded it as ironic that during a speech in which Scalia lamented that people no longer revere the Constitution, strong-arm tactics were used by the U.S. Marshals Service to silence the press. While Scalia did not ask the U.S. marshal to take the actions she did, he acknowledged after the incident that his ban on audiotaping was not clear and since then has changed his policy to allow the media to audio record his public addresses to ensure accuracy in their stories. "Scalia Apologizes for Erased Recordings," *Kansas City Star*, April 13, 2004, A2; Joan Biskupic, "Scalia Apologizes for Seizure of Reporters' Tapes," *USA Today*, April 13, 2004, A17.

21. William Safire, "Free Speech v. Scalia," *New York Times*, April 29, 1985, A17.

22. Tony Mauro and Sam Loewenberg, "Who Really Wants to Lift Ban on Fees? Scalia's Frustration Seen as Factor for Reinstating Judges' Honoraria," *Legal Times*, September 18, 2000, 1.

23. "Text of Scalia's Letter on Reinstating Honoraria," *The Recorder*, October 3, 2000, 3.

24. 124 S. Ct. 2576 (2004).

25. Scalia, his son, and his son-in-law hunted ducks and fished for approximately four days, while Vice President Cheney joined them for two of the four days. Memorandum of Justice Scalia in *Cheney v. United States Dist. Court*, 541 U.S. 913, 915 (2004).

26. Ibid., 913–15.

27. Ibid., 923.

28. Ibid., 924–26.

29. Ibid., 927.

30. Ibid., 929.

31. "Supreme Indifference," *The Oregonian*, February 13, 2004, D10; Bill Adair, "Spirited Scalia Not One to Shy Away," *St. Petersburg Times*, April 25, 2004, A1; David Von Drehle, "Scalia Rejects Pleas for Recusal in Cheney Case," *Washington Post*, February 12, 2004, A35.

32. Douglas Belkin, "Scalia Decries Judicial Activism in Harvard Talk," *The Boston Globe*, September 29, 2004, A2.

33. 531 U.S. 98 (2000).

34. *Bush v. Gore*, 531 U.S. 1046 (2000). In a 2004 speech at the University of Michigan Law School, Scalia was asked about whether the Court's decision in *Bush v. Gore* was correct. In response, Scalia sarcastically said, "I am inclined to say, four years and another election later, 'Get over it!'" Talbot, "Supreme Confidence," 43.

35. 124 S. Ct. 2301 (2004).

36. Scalia's participation in *Cheney* was a major mistake in judgment. After the Court had granted certiorari in the case, Scalia should have contacted the vice president and informed him that he could no longer attend the duck-hunting trip. *Newsweek* reports that in retrospect Scalia wishes he had not gone on the trip, but Scalia has not wavered in his view that sitting in the case was proper. See Debra Rosenberg, "It's Hard to Get It Right," *Newsweek*, May 3, 2004, 40. More importantly, Scalia's arguments about why he did not have to recuse himself from the case are not persuasive. A duck-hunting trip is nowhere akin to a Christmas party at the White House or at the home of the vice president, where numerous public officials are usually invited from both sides of the aisle, including *all* of the members of the Supreme Court. And the two previous executive-justice trips cited by Scalia, in which cases were pending before the Supreme Court, stretch back to the 1940s and 1960s, when times were clearly different. For better or worse, the public-private distinction is not what it used to be, and those trips (if uncovered by the press today) would certainly be criticized. While the private activities of presidents like FDR and Kennedy were once unassailable, we learned from the Clinton impeachment investigation that this is no longer the case. At the very least, Scalia should have recused himself to avoid the appearance of impropriety. Even if Scalia and Cheney did not have time to be alone on the duck-hunting trip (as Scalia claims in his memorandum), the possibility was certainly there.

37. "Examination No. XVI," PAH, 25:564.

38. Chernow, *Alexander Hamilton*, 619.

39. Ibid., 680–94.

40. PAH, 26:278–81.

41. Antonin Scalia, "The Dissenting Opinion," *Journal of Supreme Court History* (1994): 33–44.

42. Antonin Scalia, "Assorted Canards of Contemporary Legal Analysis," *Case Western Reserve Law Review* 40 (1989–1990): 581–97.

43. "Letter from Alexander Hamilton, Concerning the Public Conduct and Character of John Adams, Esq., President of the United States," PAH, 25:169–234.

44. Richard B. Morris, *Alexander Hamilton and the Founding of a Nation* (New York: Dial Press, 1957), xii.

45. Christopher E. Smith, *Justice Antonin Scalia and the Supreme Court's Conservative Moment* (Westport, CT: Greenwood Publishing Group, 1993).

46. Kozinski, "My Pizza with Nino," 1586.

47. See "Morning Edition Transcript," *National Public Radio*, July 8, 1996, 13–15.

48. Alexis de Tocqueville, *Democracy in America*, ed. J. P. Mayer (Doubleday & Co., 1969), 150–51.

49. "Reflections on the Revolution in France," SWEB, 2:261–62.

50. Alexander Bickel, "The Supreme Court, 1960 Term—Forward: The Passive Virtues," *Harvard Law Review* 75 (1961): 40.

51. Alexander Bickel, *The Least Dangerous Branch: The Supreme Court at the Bar of Politics*, 2nd ed. (New Haven: Yale University Press, 1986), 69.

52. Letter to James A. Bayard (January 16, 1801), PAH, 25:321.

53. "Economic Affairs as Human Affairs," in *Economic Liberties and the Judiciary*, ed. James A. Dorn and Henry G. Manne (Fairfax, VA: George Mason University Press, 1987), 31–37.

54. 384 U.S. 436 (1966).

55. *Orozco v. Texas*, 394 U.S. 324, 327–28 (1969) (Harlan, J., concurring).

56. *South Carolina v. Gathers*, 490 U.S. 805, 825 (1989) (Scalia, J., dissenting).

57. Ibid., 825 (quoting William O. Douglas, "Stare Decisis," *Columbia Law Review* 49 [1949]: 735, 736).

58. From 1986–2003, the ranking of the Rehnquist Court justices in terms of the frequency with which each justice sought to alter precedent is as follows: Thomas (5.5 percent), Scalia (4 percent), Kennedy (2.5 percent), Rehnquist (2 percent), Breyer (1.5 percent), Souter (1 percent), Ginsburg (1 percent), O'Connor (.5 percent), and Stevens (.5 percent). In computing these frequencies, I relied upon the United States Supreme Court Justice-Conferred Judicial Database: 1953–2003 Terms (Sara C. Benesh and Harold J. Spaeth, Principal Investigators, Michigan State University, 2003). See also Michael J. Gerhardt, "A Tale of Two Textualists: A Critical Comparison of Justice Black and Scalia," *Boston University Law Review* 74 (1994): 25–66.

59. Antonin Scalia, "The Rule of Law as a Law of Rules," *University of Chicago Law Review* 56 (1989): 1175–88.

60. 492 U.S. 490 (1989).

61. 410 U.S. 113 (1973).

62. Ibid., 525–26 (citing *Ashwander v. TVA*, 297 U.S. 285, 346–47 [1936]).

63. Ibid., 526.

64. 492 U.S. at 532–37 (Scalia, J., concurring). See also *Cruzan by Cruzan v. Director, Missouri Department of Health*, 497 U.S. 261, 292 (1990) (Scalia, J., concurring) ("While I agree with the Court's analysis today, and therefore join its opinion, I would have preferred that we announce, clearly and promptly, that the federal courts have no business in this field; that American law has always accorded the State the power to prevent, by force if necessary, suicide—including suicide by refusing to take appropriate measures necessary to preserve one's life").

# Selected Bibliography

Abraham, Henry J. *Justices, Presidents, and Senators: A History of U.S. Supreme Court Appointments from Washington to Clinton*. New and revised edition. Lanham, MD: Rowman & Littlefield, 1999.

Adair, Douglass. *Fame and the Founding Fathers*. Edited by Trevor Colbourn. New York: W. W. Norton & Co., 1974.

Anders, David B. "Justices Harlan and Black Revisited: The Emerging Dispute Between Justice O'Connor and Justice Scalia over Unenumerated Fundamental Rights." *Fordham Law Review* 61 (1993): 895–933.

Arkes, Hadley. *Beyond the Constitution*. Princeton, NJ: Princeton University Press, 1990.

———. *Natural Rights and the Right to Choose*. Cambridge, UK, and New York: Cambridge University Press, 2002.

Austin, John. *The Province of Jurisprudence Determined*. Edited by Wilfred E. Rumble. Cambridge, UK, and New York: Cambridge University Press, 1995.

Baker, Stewart Abercrombie, and Katherine H. Wheatley. "Justice Scalia and Federalism: A Sketch." *The Urban Lawyer* 20, no. 2 (1988): 353–65.

Barnett, Randy E. *Restoring the Lost Constitution: The Presumption of Liberty*. Princeton, NJ: Princeton University Press, 2004.

Beer, Samuel H. *To Make a Nation: The Rediscovery of American Federalism*. Cambridge, MA: Harvard University Press, 1993.

Berger, Raoul. *Executive Privilege: A Constitutional Myth*. Cambridge, MA: Harvard University Press, 1974.

———. *Government by Judiciary: The Transformation of the Fourteenth Amendment*. Cambridge, MA: Harvard University Press, 1977.

———. *Federalism: The Founders' Design*. Norman, OK: University of Oklahoma Press, 1987.

Berns, Walter. "The Meaning of the Tenth Amendment." In *A Nation of States: Essays on the American Federal System*, edited by Robert A. Goldwin. Chicago: Rand McNally, 1963.

——. *Taking the Constitution Seriously*. New York: Simon & Schuster, 1987.

Bessette, Joseph M., ed. *Toward a More Perfect Union: Writings of Herbert J. Storing*. Washington, DC: American Enterprise Institute, 1995.

Bickel, Alexander M. "The Supreme Court. 1960 Term—Foreword: The Passive Virtues." *Harvard Law Review* 75 (1961): 40.

——. *The Least Dangerous Branch: The Supreme Court at the Bar of Politics*. Indianapolis, IN: Bobbs-Merrill, 1965.

——. *The Morality of Consent*. New Haven, CT: Yale University Press, 1975.

Black, Hugo L. *A Constitutional Faith*. New York: Alfred A. Knopf, 1968.

Bloom, Allan, ed. *Confronting the Constitution*. Washington, DC: American Enterprise Institute, 1990.

Boling, David. "The Jurisprudential Approach of Justice Antonin Scalia: Methodology over Result?" *Arkansas Law Review* 44 (1991): 1137–1205.

Bork, Robert. *The Tempting of America: The Political Seduction of the Law*. New York: Free Press, 1990.

——. *Slouching Towards Gomorrah: Modern Liberalism and American Decline*. New York: HarperCollins, 1996.

Bowers, Claude G. *Jefferson and Hamilton: The Struggle for Democracy in America*. Boston: Houghton Mifflin, 1925.

Brennan, William J., Jr. "Address to the Text and Teaching Symposium, Georgetown University." In *The Great Debate: Interpreting Our Written Constitution*. Washington, DC: Federalist Society, 1986.

Breyer, Stephen G. "On the Uses of Legislative History in Interpreting Statutes." *Southern California Law Review* 65 (1992): 845–74.

——. *Active Liberty: Interpreting Our Democratic Constitution*. New York: Random House, 2005.

Breyer, Stephen G., Richard B. Stewart, Cass R. Sunstein, and Matthew L. Spitzer, eds. *Administrative Law and Regulatory Policy: Problems, Text, and Cases*. 5th ed. New York: Aspen Law & Business, 2002.

Brisbin, Richard A., Jr. "The Conservatism of Antonin Scalia." *Political Science Quarterly* 105 (1990): 1–29.

——. "'Administrative Law Is Not for Sissies': Justice Antonin Scalia's Challenge to American Administrative Law." *Administrative Law Review* 44 (1992): 107–29.

——. *Justice Antonin Scalia and the Conservative Revival*. Baltimore, MD: Johns Hopkins University Press, 1997.

Brookhiser, Richard. *Alexander Hamilton*. New York: Free Press, 1999.

Buckley, William F., and Charles R. Kesler, eds. *Keeping the Tablets: Modern American Conservative Thought*. New York: Harper & Row, 1988.

Burke, Edmund. *Select Works of Edmund Burke*. 3 vols. A new imprint of the Payne edition. Indianapolis, IN: Liberty Fund, 1999.

Burt, Robert A. "Precedent and Authority in Antonin Scalia's Jurisprudence." *Cardozo Law Review* 12 (1991): 1685–97.

Calabresi, Guido. *A Common Law for the Age of Statutes*. Cambridge, MA: Harvard University Press, 1982.

Calabresi, Steven G., and Saikrishna B. Prakash. "The President's Power to Execute the Laws." *Yale Law Journal* 104 (1994): 541–665.

Caldwell, Lynton K. *The Administrative Theories of Hamilton & Jefferson: Their Contribution to Thought on Public Administration*. Chicago: University of Chicago Press, 1944.

Caminker, Evan H. "State Sovereignty and Subordinacy: May Congress Commandeer State Officers to Implement Federal Law?" *Columbia Law Review* 95 (1995): 1001–89.

Canon, Bradley C. "Defining the Dimensions of Judicial Activism." *Judicature* 66 (1983): 237–47.

Carey, George W. "Publius — A Split Personality?" *Review of Politics* (1984): 5–22.

Carrese, Paul O. *The Cloaking of Power: Montesquieu, Blackstone, and the Rise of Judicial Activism*. Chicago: University of Chicago Press, 2003.

Cates, Cynthia L. "Splitting the Atom of Sovereignty: *Term Limits, Inc.*'s Conflicting Views of Popular Autonomy in a Federal Republic." *Publius: The Journal of Federalism* 26 (1996): 127–40.

Ceaser, James W. "In Defense of Separation of Powers." In *Separation of Powers: Does It Still Work?*, edited by Robert A. Goldwin and Art Kaufman. Washington, DC: American Enterprise Institute, 1986.

Chernow, Ron. *Alexander Hamilton*. New York: Penguin Press, 2004.

Choper, Jesse H. *Judicial Review and the National Political Process: A Functional Reconsideration of the Role of the Supreme Court*. Chicago: University of Chicago Press, 1980.

Conlan, Timothy J., and Robert L. Dudley. "Janus-Faced Federalism: State Sovereignty and Federal Preemption in the Rehnquist Court." *Political Science*, July 2005, 363–66.

Davis, Mary J. "Unmasking the Presumption in Favor of Preemption." *South Carolina Law Review* 53 (2002): 967–1030.

Davis, Sue. *Justice Rehnquist and the Constitution*. Princeton, NJ: Princeton University Press, 1989.

Dietze, Gottfried. "Hamilton's Federalist — Treatise for Free Government." *Cornell Law Quarterly* 42, no. 3 (1957): 307–28.

Douglas, William O. "Stare Decisis." *Columbia Law Review* 49 (1949): 735–55.

Duxbury, Neil. "Faith in Reason: The Process Tradition in American Jurisprudence." *Cardozo Law Review* 15 (1993): 601–705.

Dworkin, Ronald. *Taking Rights Seriously*. London: Gerald Duckworth & Co., 1977.

———. *Freedom's Law: The Moral Reading of the American Constitution*. Cambridge, MA: Harvard University Press, 1996.

Easterbrook, Frank H. "Statutes' Domains." *University of Chicago Law Review* 50 (1983): 533–52.

———. "Presidential Review." *Case Western Reserve Law Review* 40 (1989–1990): 905–29.

Eastland, Terry. *Energy in the Executive: The Case for the Strong Presidency*. New York: Free Press, 1992.

Edelman, Peter B. "Justice Scalia's Jurisprudence and the Good Society: Shades of Felix Frankfurter and the Harvard Hit Parade of the 1950s." *Cardozo Law Review* 12 (1991): 1799–1815.

Eid, Troy Andrew, and Jim Kolbe. "The New Anti-Federalism: The Constitutionality of State-Imposed Limits on Congressional Terms of Office." *Denver Law Review* 69 (1992): 1–56.

Eidelberg, Paul. *The Philosophy of the American Constitution*. New York: Free Press, 1968.

Epstein, David F. *The Political Theory of the Federalist*. Chicago: The University of Chicago Press, 1984.

Epstein, Lee, Jeffrey A. Segal, Harold J. Spaeth, and Thomas G. Walker. *The Supreme Court Compendium: Data, Decisions, and Developments*. 3rd ed. Washington, DC: Congressional Quarterly, 2003.

Epstein, Richard A. *Takings: Private Property and the Power of Eminent Domain*. Cambridge, MA: Harvard University Press, 1985.

———. "Needed: Activist Judges for Economic Rights." *Wall Street Journal*, November 14, 1985, 32.

Eskridge, William N., Jr. "The New Textualism." *UCLA Law Review* 37 (1990): 621–91.

Eskridge, William N., Jr., Philip P. Frickey, and Elizabeth Garrett. *Cases and Materials on Legislation: Statutes and the Creation of Public Policy*. 3rd ed. St. Paul, MN: West Group, 2002.

Fallon, Richard H., Jr. "The 'Conservative' Paths of the Rehnquist Court's Federalism Decisions." *University of Chicago Law Review* 69 (2002): 429–94.

Flaumenhaft, Harvey. "Hamilton on the Foundation of Government." *The Political Science Reviewer* 6 (1976): 143–214.

———. *The Effective Republic: Administration and Constitution in the Thought of Alexander Hamilton*. Durham, NC: Duke University Press, 1992.

Franck, Matthew J. *Against the Imperial Judiciary: The Supreme Court vs. the Sovereignty of the People*. Lawrence, KS: University Press of Kansas, 1996.

Frankfurter, Felix. *The Public and Its Government*. New Haven, CT: Yale University Press, 1930.

———. "Some Reflections on the Reading of Statutes." *Columbia Law Review* 47 (1947): 527–46.

Fried, Charles. "Manners Makyth Man: The Prose Style of Justice Scalia." *Harvard Journal of Law & Public Policy* 16 (1993): 529–36.

Frisch, Morton J., Jr., ed. *Selected Writings and Speeches of Alexander Hamilton*. Washington, DC: American Enterprise Institute, 1985.

———. *Alexander Hamilton and the Political Order: An Interpretation of His Political Thought and Practice*. Lanham, MD: University Press of America, 1991.

Fuller, Lon L. *The Law in Quest of Itself*. Chicago: Foundation Press, 1940.

———. *The Morality of Law*. New Haven, CT: Yale University Press, 1964.

Gelfand, M. David, and Keith Werhan. "Federalism and Separation of Powers on a 'Conservative' Court: Currents and Cross-Currents From Justices O'Connor and Scalia." *Tulane Law Review* 64 (1990): 1443–76.

Gellhorn, Ernest, and Ronald M. Levin. *Administrative Law and Process in a Nutshell*. 3rd ed. St. Paul, MN: West Publishing Co., 1990.

Gerber, Scott Douglas. *First Principles: The Jurisprudence of Clarence Thomas*. New York and London: New York University Press, 1999.

Gerhardt, Michael J. "A Tale of Two Textualists: A Critical Comparison of Justices Black and Scalia." *Boston University Law Review* 74 (1994): 25–66.

Ginsburg, Douglas H. "On Constitutionalism," *Cato Supreme Court Review* (2003): 7–20.

Goebel, Julius, Jr., ed. *The Law Practice of Alexander Hamilton: Documents and Commentary*. 5 vols. New York and London: Columbia University Press, 1964.

Goldstein, Leslie F. *In Defense of the Text: Democracy and Constitutional Theory*. Savage, MD: Rowman & Littlefield, 1991.

Gwyn, W. B. *The Meaning of the Separation of Powers: An Analysis of the Doctrine from Its Origin to the Adoption of the United States Constitution*. New Orleans: Tulane University Press, 1965.

Hacker, Louis M. *Alexander Hamilton in the American Tradition*. New York: McGraw-Hill, 1957.

Harriger, Katy. *The Special Prosecutor in American Politics*. 2nd ed. Lawrence, KS: University Press of Kansas, 2000.

Harriger, Katy, ed. *Separation of Powers: Documents and Commentary*. Washington, DC: Congressional Quarterly Press, 2003.

Hart, Henry M., Jr., and Albert M. Sacks. *The Legal Process: Basic Problems in the Making and Application of Law*. Edited by William N. Eskridge Jr. and Philip P. Frickey. Westbury, NY: Foundation Press, 1994.

Henkin, Louis. *Foreign Affairs and the United States Constitution*. 2nd ed. Oxford: Clarendon Press, 1996.

Henriot, Peter Joseph. "The Contemporary Influence in the United States of the Political Philosophy of Edmund Burke." Unpublished master's thesis, Saint Louis University, 1963.

Hickock, Eugene W., Jr., Gary L. McDowell, and Philip J. Costopoulos, eds. *Our Peculiar Security*. Lanham, MD: Rowman & Littlefield, 1993.

Hittinger, Russell. *The First Grace: Rediscovering the Natural Law in a Post-Christian World*. Wilmington, DE: ISI Books, 2003.

Hobson, Charles F. "The Tenth Amendment and the New Federalism of 1789," *Virginia Cavalcade* (Winter 1986): 110–121.

Horwitz, Robert H., ed. *The Moral Foundations of the American Republic*. 3rd ed. Charlottesville, VA: University Press of Virginia, 1986.

Hume, David. *Essays: Moral, Political, Literary*. Edited by Eugene F. Miller. Indianapolis, IN: Liberty Press, 1987.

Hunt, Gaillard, ed. *The Writings of James Madison*. 9 vols. New York: G. P. Putnam's Sons, 1900–1910.

Hutchinson, William T., ed. *The Papers of James Madison*. 17 vols. Chicago and Charlottesville: University of Chicago Press and University of Virginia Press, 1962–1991.

Jacobsohn, Gary J. *Pragmatism, Statesmanship, and the Supreme Court*. Ithaca, NY: Cornell University Press, 1977.

———. *The Supreme Court and the Decline of Constitutional Aspiration*. Totowa, NJ: Rowman & Littlefield, 1986.

Jaffa, Harry V. "The Case for a Stronger National Government." In *A Nation of States: Essays on the American Federal System*, edited by Robert A. Goldwin. Chicago: Rand McNally, 1963.

———. *Original Intent and the Framers of the Constitution*. Washington, DC: Regnery Gateway, 1994.

———. *Storm over the Constitution*. Lanham, MD: Lexington Books, 1999.

Jones, Alan Benton. "An Analysis of the Concurring and Dissenting Opinions of Justice Antonin Scalia, 1986–1993 Terms." Unpublished dissertation: University of North Carolina, 1995.

Kannar, George. "The Constitutional Catechism of Antonin Scalia." *Yale Law Journal* 99 (1990): 1301–57.

———. "Strenuous Virtues, Virtuous Lives: The Social Vision of Antonin Scalia." *Cardozo Law Review* 12 (1991): 1845–67.

Kesler, Charles R., ed. *Saving the Revolution: The Federalist Papers and the American Founding*. New York: Free Press, 1987.

Kirk, Russell. *The Conservative Mind: From Burke to Santayana*. Chicago: Henry Regnery Co., 1953.

———. *The Conservative Constitution*. Washington, DC: Regnery Gateway, 1990.

Knott, Stephen F. *Alexander Hamilton and the Persistence of Myth*. Lawrence, KS: University Press of Kansas, 2003.

Konefsky, Samuel J. *John Marshall and Alexander Hamilton: Architects of the American Constitution*. New York: The MacMillan Co., 1964.

Kozinski, Alex. "Foreword: The Judiciary and the Constitution." In *Economic Liberties and the Judiciary*, edited by James A. Dorn and Henry G. Manne. Fairfax, VA: George Mason University Press, 1987.

———. "My Pizza with Nino." *Cardozo Law Review* 12 (1991): 1583–91.

Kozinski, Alex and Stuart Banner. "Who's Afraid of Commercial Speech." *Virginia Law Review* 76 (1990): 627.

Kronman, Anthony T. "Alexander Bickel's Philosophy of Prudence." *Yale Law Journal* 94 (1985): 1567–6016.

———. "Precedent and Tradition." *Yale Law Journal* 99 (1990): 1029–68.

Landis, James M. *The Administrative Process*. New Haven, CT: Yale University Press, 1938.

Lazarus, Richard James. "The Measure of a Justice: Justice Scalia and the Faltering of the Property Rights Movement within the U.S. Supreme Court." *Hastings Law Journal* 57, no. 4 (Winter 2006).

Lind, Michael, ed. *Hamilton's Republic: Readings in the American Democratic Nationalist Tradition*. New York: Free Press, 1997.

Lipscomb, Andrew A., and Albert Ellery Bergh, ed. *The Writings of Thomas Jefferson*. 20 vols. Washington, DC: Thomas Jefferson Memorial Association, 1903–1904.

Lofgren, Charles A. "The Origins of the Tenth Amendment: History, Sovereignty, and the Problem of Constitutional Intention." In *Constitutional Government in America*, edited by Ronald K. L. Collins. Durham, NC: Carolina Academic Press, 1980.

Loss, Richard. "Alexander Hamilton and the Modern Presidency: Continuity or Discontinuity." *Presidential Studies Quarterly* 12, no. 1 (1982): 6–25.

Lynch, Joseph M. *Negotiating the Constitution: The Earliest Debates over Original Intent*. Ithaca, NY: Cornell University Press, 1999.

Macedo, Stephen. *The New Right v. the Constitution*. Washington, DC: Cato Institute, 1986.

Madison, James, Alexander Hamilton, and John Jay. *The Federalist Papers*. Edited by Isaac Kramnick. New York: Penguin Books, 1987.

Malbin, Michael J. "Federalists v. Antifederalists: The Term-Limitation Debate at the Founding." In *Limiting Legislative Terms*, edited by Gerald Benjamin and Michael J. Malbin. Washington, DC: Congressional Quarterly, 1992.

Mansfield, Harvey C., Jr. "Edmund Burke." In *History of Political Philosophy*, edited by Leo Strauss and Joseph Cropsey. 3rd ed. Chicago: University of Chicago Press, 1987.

———. *Taming the Prince: The Ambivalence of Modern Executive Power*. Baltimore, MD: Johns Hopkins University Press, 1989.

———. *America's Constitutional Soul*. Baltimore, MD: Johns Hopkins University Press, 1991.

Mason, Alpheus T. "*The Federalist*—A Split Personality." *American Historical Review* 57, no. 3 (1952): 625–43.

Matthews, Richard K. *The Radical Politics of Thomas Jefferson: A Revisionist View*. Lawrence, KS: University Press of Kansas, 1984.

———. *If Men Were Angels: James Madison and the Heartless Empire of Reason*. Lawrence, KS: University Press of Kansas, 1995.

Maveety, Nancy. *Justice Sandra Day O'Connor: Strategist on the Supreme Court*. Lanham, MD: Rowman & Littlefield, 1996.

Mayer, David N. *The Constitutional Thought of Thomas Jefferson*. Charlottesville: University Press of Virginia, 1994.

McAllister, Stephen R. "An Eagle Soaring: The Jurisprudence of Justice Antonin Scalia." *Campbell Law Review* 19 (1997): 223–309.

McDonald, Forrest. *Alexander Hamilton: A Biography*. New York: W. W. Norton & Co., 1979.

McDowell, Gary L. *Equity and the Constitution: The Supreme Court, Equitable Relief, and Public Policy*. Chicago and London: University of Chicago Press, 1982.

Meese, Edwin. "Toward a Jurisprudence of Original Intent." *Benchmark* 2 (1986): 1–10.

Miroff, Bruce. *Icons of Democracy: American Leaders as Heroes, Aristocrats, Dissenters, and Democrats*. New York: Basic Books, 1993.

Monaghan, Henry P. "Our Perfect Constitution." *New York University Law Review* 56 (1981): 353–96.

Montesquieu, Charles de Secondat. *The Spirit of the Laws*. Edited by Anne M. Cohler, Basia Carolyn Miller, and Harold Samuel Stone. Cambridge, UK: Cambridge University Press, 1989.

Morel, Lucas E. "Scalia contra Common Law Adjudication." *Perspectives on Political Science* 28, no. 1 (Winter 1999): 11–14.

Morris, Richard B., ed. *Alexander Hamilton and the Founding of a Nation*. New York: Dial Press, 1957.

Muller, James W., ed. *The Revival of Constitutionalism*. Lincoln: University of Ne-
braska Press, 1988.

Nagareda, Richard. "The Appellate Jurisprudence of Justice Antonin Scalia." *University of Chicago Law Review* 54 (1987): 705–39.

Nichols, David K. *The Myth of the Modern Presidency*. University Park, PA: Pennsylvania State University Press, 1994.

Noonan, John T., Jr. *The Lustre of Our Country: The American Experience of Religious
Freedom*. Berkeley and Los Angeles, CA: University of California Press, 1998.

———. *Narrowing the Nation's Power: The Supreme Court Sides with the States*.
Berkeley and Los Angeles, CA: University of California Press, 2002.

Norton, Ann. *Leo Strauss and the Politics of American Empire*. New Haven: Yale University Press, 2004.

O'Brien, David M. "The Rehnquist Court and Federal Preemption: In Search of a
Theory." *Publius: The Journal of Federalism* 23 (1993): 15–31.

O'Connor, Sandra Day. "Our Judicial Federalism." *Case Western Reserve Law Review* 35 (1984–1985): 1–12.

———. "The Judiciary Act of 1789 and the American Judicial Tradition." *Cincinnati
Law Review* 59 (1990): 1–13.

———. *The Majesty of Law: Reflections of a Supreme Court Justice*. New York: Random House, 2003.

Peller, Gary. "Neutral Principles in the 1950's." *University of Michigan Journal of
Law Reform* 21 (1988): 561–622.

Petracca, Mark P. "Rotation in Office: The History of an Idea." In *Limiting Legislative Terms*, edited by Gerald Benjamin and Michael J. Malbin. Washington, DC:
Congressional Quarterly, 1992.

Pickerill, J. Mitchell, and Cornell W. Clayton. "The Rehnquist Court and the Political
Dynamics of Federalism." *Perspectives on Politics* 2 (2004): 233–48.

Pontuso, James F. "Political Passions and the Creation of the American National
Community: The Case of Alexander Hamilton." *Perspectives on Political Science*
22, no. 2 (1993): 70–83.

Posner, Richard A. *Overcoming Law*. Cambridge, MA: Harvard University Press, 1995.

———. *Law, Pragmatism, and Democracy*. Cambridge, MA: Harvard University
Press, 2003.

Powell, H. Jefferson. "The Compleat Jeffersonian: Justice Rehnquist and Federalism." *Yale Law Journal* 91 (1982): 1317–70.

———. "The Original Understanding of Original Intent." *Harvard Law Review* 98
(1985): 885–948.

———. "The Oldest Question of Constitutional Law." *Virginia Law Review* 79 (1993):
633–89.

———. "Enumerated Means and Unlimited Ends." *Michigan Law Review* 94 (1995):
651–73.

Powell, Lewis F. "Stare Decisis and Judicial Restraint." *Washington & Lee Law Review* 47 (1990): 281–90.

Redish, Martin H. "Doing It with Mirrors: *New York v. United States* and Constitutional Limitations on Federal Power to Require State Legislation." *Hastings Constitutional Law Quarterly* 21 (1994): 593–610.

———. *The Constitution as Political Structure*. New York: Oxford University Press, 1995.

Rehnquist, William H. "The Notion of a Living Constitution." *Texas Law Review* 54 (1976): 693–706.

Reisman, Daniel N. "Deconstructing Justice Scalia's Separation of Powers Jurisprudence: The Preeminent Executive." *Albany Law Review* 53 (1988): 49–94.

Rives, William C., and Philip R. Fendall, ed. *Letters and Other Writings of James Madison*. 4 vols. Philadelphia: J. B. Lippincott & Co., 1865.

Rosen, Gary. *American Compact: James Madison and the Problem of Founding*. University Press of Kansas, 1999.

Rossiter, Clinton. *Conservatism in America: The Thankless Persuasion*. 2nd ed. New York: Alfred A. Knopf, 1962.

———. *Alexander Hamilton and the Constitution*. New York: Harcourt, Brace & World, 1964.

Rossum, Ralph A. "The Textualist Jurisprudence of Justice Scalia." *Perspectives on Political Science* 28, no. 1 (Winter 1999): 5–10.

———. "Text and Tradition: The Originalist Jurisprudence of Antonin Scalia." In *Rehnquist Justice*, edited by Earl M. Maltz. Lawrence, KS: University Press of Kansas, 2003.

Rozell, Mark J. *Executive Privilege: The Dilemma of Secrecy and Democratic Accountability*. Baltimore, MD: Johns Hopkins University Press, 1994.

Rubin, Thea F., and Albert P. Melone. "Justice Antonin Scalia: A First Year Freshman Effect?" *Judicature* 72, no. 2 (1988): 98–102.

Sargentich, Thomas O., ed. *Administrative Law Anthology*. Cincinnati, OH: Anderson Publishing Co., 1994.

Savage, David G. *Turning Right: The Making of the Rehnquist Supreme Court*. New York: John Wiley & Sons, 1992.

Scalia, Antonin. "Don't Go Near the Water." *Federal Communications Bar Journal* (1972): 111–20.

———. "Vermont Yankee: The APA, the D.C. Circuit Court, and the Supreme Court." *The Supreme Court Review*, 1978, 345–409.

———. "The Disease as Cure." *Washington University Law Quarterly*, 1979, 147–57.

———. "The Legislative Veto: A False Remedy for System Overload." *Regulation* 3, no. 6 (1979): 19–26.

———. "The Judges Are Coming." *Congressional Record* 126 (July 21, 1980): 18920–22.

———. "Regulatory Reform—The Game Has Changed." *Regulation* 5, no. 1 (1981): 13–15.

———. "Rulemaking as Politics." *Administrative Law Review* 34, no. 3 (1982): v–xi.

———. "The Freedom of Information Act Has No Clothes." *Regulation* 6, no. 2 (1982): 14–19.

———. "Reagulation—The First Year. Regulatory Review and Management." *Regulation* 6, no. 1 (1982): 19–21.

———. "The Two Faces of Federalism." *Harvard Journal of Law and Public Policy* 6 (1982): 19–22.

———. "The Doctrine of Standing as an Essential Element of the Separation of Powers." *Suffolk University Law Review* 17 (1983): 881–99.

———. "Historical Anomalies in Administrative Law." *Supreme Court Historical Society Yearbook* (1985): 103–11.

———. "Use of Legislative History: Judicial Abdication to Fictitious Legislative Intent." Unpublished speech delivered to various law schools in 1985–1986. On file with the author.

———. "Morality, Pragmatism and the Legal Order." *Harvard Journal of Law and Public Policy* 9 (1986): 123–27.

———. "The Role of the Judiciary in Deregulation." *Antitrust Law Journal* 55 (1986): 191–98.

———. "Economic Affairs as Human Affairs." In *Economic Liberties and the Judiciary*, edited by James A. Dorn and Henry G. Manne. Fairfax, VA: George Mason University Press, 1987.

———. "A House with Many Mansions: Categories of Speech under the First Amendment." In *The Constitution, the Law, and Freedom of Expression 1787–1987*, edited by James Breyer Stewart. Carbondale: Southern Illinois University Press, 1987.

———. "The Limits of the Law." *New Jersey Law Journal* 119 (1987): 4–5, 22–23.

———. "Responsibilities of Federal Regulatory Agencies under Environmental Laws." *Houston Law Review* 24 (1987): 97–109.

———. Remarks of Justice Antonin Scalia at Washington D.C. Panel Discussion on Separation of Powers. C-SPAN broadcast, November 5, 1988.

———. "Reflections on the Constitution." Speech to Kennedy Political Union at American University. C-SPAN broadcast, November 17, 1988.

———. "The Courts and the Press." The Francis Boyer Lecture on Public Policy, presented at the American Enterprise Institute for Public Policy Research, Washington, DC, 1989.

———. "Is There an Unwritten Constitution?" *Harvard Journal of Law and Public Policy* 12 (1989): 1–2.

———. "Judicial Deference to Administrative Interpretations of Law." *Duke Law Journal* (1989): 511–21.

———. "Originalism: The Lesser Evil." *University of Cincinnati Law Review* 57 (1989): 849–65.

———. "The Rule of Law as a Law of Rules." *University of Chicago Law Review* 56 (1989): 1175–88.

———. "Assorted Canards of Contemporary Legal Analysis." *Case Western Reserve Law Review* 40 (1989–1990): 581–97.

———. "The Dissenting Opinion." *Journal of Supreme Court History* (1994): 33–44.

———. "Of Democracy, Morality and the Majority." *Origins: CNS Documentary Service* 26, no. 6 (June 26, 1996): 81–90.

———. *A Matter of Interpretation: Federal Courts and the Law*. Edited by Amy Gutmann. Princeton, NJ: Princeton University Press, 1997.

———. "God's Justice and Ours." *First Things: A Monthly Journal of Religion and Public Life* 123 (May 2002): 17–21.

Schambra, William A., ed. *As Far as Republican Principles Will Admit: Essays by Martin Diamond*. Washington, DC: American Enterprise Institute Press, 1992.

Schauer, Frederick. "The Jurisprudence of Reasons." Book review. *Michigan Law Review* 85 (1987): 847–70.

———. "Is the Common Law Law?" Book review. *California Law Review* 77 (1989): 455–71.

———. *Playing by the Rules*. New York: Oxford University Press, 1991.

Schultz, David A., and Christopher E. Smith. *The Jurisprudential Vision of Justice Antonin Scalia*. Lanham, MD: Rowman & Littlefield, 1996.

Schwartz, Bernard. *The New Right and the Constitution: Turning Back the Legal Clock*. Boston: Northeastern University Press, 1990.

———. 1995. "'Shooting the Piano Player'? Justice Scalia and Administrative Law." *Administrative Law Review* 47 (1995): 1–57.

Sedgwick, Jeffrey Leigh. "James Madison & the Problem of Executive Character." *Polity* 21, no. 1 (1988): 5–23.

Sheehan, Colleen A. "Madison v. Hamilton: The Battle over Republicanism and the Role of Public Opinion." *American Political Science Review* 98, no. 3 (2004): 405–24.

Shklar, Judith N. *Legalism*. Cambridge, MA: Harvard University Press, 1964.

———. "Political Theory and the Rule of Law." In *The Rule of Law: Ideal or Ideology*, edited by Allan C. Hutchinson and Patrick Monahan. Toronto: Carswell, 1987.

Siegan, Bernard H. *Economic Liberties and the Constitution*. Chicago: University of Chicago Press, 1980.

Silverstein, Mark. *Constitutional Faiths: Felix Frankfurter, Hugo Black, and the Process of Judicial Decision Making*. Ithaca, NY: Cornell University Press, 1984.

Smith, Christopher E. "Justice Antonin Scalia and the Institutions of American Government." *Wake Forest Law Review* 25 (1990): 783–809.

———. *Justice Antonin Scalia and the Supreme Court's Conservative Moment*. Westport, CT: Praeger Publishers, 1993.

Smolla, Rodney A. "Antonin Scalia." In *Supreme Court Justices: A Biographical Dictionary*, edited by Melvin I. Urofsky. New York: Garland Publishing, 1994.

Staab, James B. "The Tenth Amendment and Justice Scalia's 'Split Personality,'" *Journal of Law & Politics* 16, no. 2 (2000): 231–379.

———. "Conservative Activism on the Rehnquist Court: Federal Preemption is No Longer a Liberal Issue." *Roger Williams University Law Review* 9, no. 1 (2003): 129–85.

Stanlis, Peter J., ed. *The Relevance of Edmund Burke*. New York: P. J. Kennedy & Sons, 1964.

Storing, Herbert. "The Problem of Big Government." In *A Nation of States: Essays on the American Federal System*, edited by Robert A. Goldwin. Chicago: Rand McNally, 1963.

———. *The Complete Anti-Federalist*. 7 vols. Chicago: University of Chicago Press, 1981.

———. "The Constitution and the Bill of Rights." In *How Does the Constitution Secure Rights?* edited by Robert A. Goldwin and William A. Schambra. Washington, DC: American Enterprise Institute, 1985.

Story, Joseph. *Commentaries on the Constitution of the United States*. 2 vols., 5th ed. Boston: Hilliard, Gray, and Co., 1905.

Stourzh, Gerald. *Alexander Hamilton and the Idea of Republican Government*. Stanford, CA: Stanford University Press, 1970.

Strauss, David A. "Tradition, Precedent, and Justice Scalia." *Cardozo Law Review* 12 (1991): 1699–1716.

Sullivan, Kathleen M. "The Supreme Court 1991 Term: Foreword: The Justices of Rules and Standards." *Harvard Law Review* 106 (1992): 22–123.

———. "Dueling Sovereignties: *U.S. Term Limits, Inc. v. Thornton*." *Harvard Law Review* 109 (1995): 78–109.

Sunstein, Cass R. "Constitutionalism after the New Deal." *Harvard Law Review* 101 (1987): 421–510.

———. "What's Standing after *Lujan*? Of Citizen Suits, 'Injuries,' and Article III." *Michigan Law Review* 91 (1992): 163–236.

———. "Justice Scalia's Democratic Formalism." *Yale Law Journal* 107 (1997): 529–67.

———. *Radicals in Robes: Why Extreme Right-Wing Courts are Wrong for America*. New York: Basic Books, 2005.

Syrett, Harold C., ed. *The Papers of Alexander Hamilton*. 27 vols. New York: Columbia University Press, 1961–1987.

Talbot, Margaret. "Supreme Confidence." *New Yorker*, March 28, 2005, 40–55.

Tanielian, Matthew J. "Separation of Powers and the Supreme Court: One Doctrine, Two Visions." *Administrative Law Journal of the American University* 8 (1995): 961–1002.

Thach, Charles C., Jr. *The Creation of the Presidency 1775–1789: A Study in Constitutional History*. Baltimore, MD: Johns Hopkins University Press, 1922.

Thomas, Clarence. "An Afro-American Perspective: Toward a 'Plain Reading' of the Constitution—The Declaration of Independence." *Howard Law Journal*, 1987, 691–703.

———. "Why Black Americans Should Look to Conservative Policies." *The Heritage Lectures* 119 (June 18, 1987): 1–9.

———. "The Higher Law Background of the Privileges or Immunities Clause of the Fourteenth Amendment." *Harvard Journal of Law & Public Policy* 12 (Winter 1989): 63–68.

Tocqueville, Alexis de. *Democracy in America*. Edited by J. P. Mayer. Garden City, NY: Doubleday & Co., 1969.

Tribe, Laurence H., and Michael C. Dorf. "Levels of Generality in the Definition of Rights." *University of Chicago Law Review* 57 (1990): 1057–1108.

Tushnet, Mark V. "Following the Rules Laid down: A Critique of Interpretivism and Neutral Principles." *Harvard Law Review* 96 (1983): 781–827.

———. *A Court Divided: The Rehnquist Court and the Future of Constitutional Law*. New York: W. W. Norton & Co., 2005.

Uhlmann, Michael M. "Justice Scalia and His Critics." *Perspectives on Political Science* 28, no. 1 (Winter 1999): 29–31.

Vile, M. J. C. *Constitutionalism and the Separation of Powers*. 2nd ed. Indianapolis, IN: Liberty Fund, 1998.

Walling, Karl-Friedrich. *Republican Empire: Alexander Hamilton on War and Free Government*. Lawrence, KS: University Press of Kansas, 1999.

Wechsler, Herbert. "Toward Neutral Principles of Constitutional Law." *Harvard Law Review* 73 (1959): 1–35.

Wellington, Harry H. *Interpreting the Constitution: The Supreme Court and the Process of Adjudication*. New Haven, CT: Yale University Press, 1990.

West, Robin. "Progressive and Conservative Constitutionalism." *Michigan Law Review* 88 (1990): 641–721.

White, G. Edward. "The Evolution of Reasoned Elaboration: Jurisprudential Criticism and Social Change." *Virginia Law Review* 59 (1973): 136–63.

White, Leonard D. *The Federalists: A Study in Administrative History*. New York: The MacMillan Co., 1961.

White, Morton. *Philosophy, The Federalist, and the Constitution*. New York: Oxford University Press, 1987.

Wilson, Bradford P., and Peter W. Schramm, eds. *Separation of Powers and Good Government*. Lanham, MD: Rowman & Littlefield, 1994.

Wilson, James G. "Justice Diffused: A Comparison of Edmund Burke's Conservatism with the Views of Five Conservative, Academic Judges." *University of Miami Law Review* 40 (1986): 913–75.

———. "Constraints of Power: The Constitutional Opinions of Judges Scalia, Bork, Posner, Easterbrook and Winter." *University of Miami Law Review* 40 (1986): 1171–1265.

Wilson, Woodrow. "The Study of Administration." *Political Science Quarterly* 11, no. 2 (1887): 198–222.

Wiltse, Charles M. *The Jeffersonian Tradition in American Democracy*. New York: Hill and Wang, 1960.

Wolfe, Christopher. *The Rise of Modern Judicial Review*. New York: Basic Books, 1986.

———. *How to Read the Constitution*. Lanham, MD: Rowman & Littlefield, 1996.

Wright, J. Skelly. "Professor Bickel, the Scholarly Tradition, and the Supreme Court." *Harvard Law Review* 84 (1971): 769–805.

Wyszynski, James Edward, Jr. "In Praise of Judicial Restraint: The Jurisprudence of Justice Antonin Scalia." *Detroit College Law Review* 1 (1989): 117–62.

Yarbrough, Tinsley E. "Mr. Justice Black and Legal Positivism." *Virginia Law Review* 57 (1971): 375–407.

Young, Ernest. "Rediscovering Conservatism: Burkean Political Theory and Constitutional Interpretation." *North Carolina Law Review* 72 (1994): 619–724.

Zeppos, Nicholas S. "Justice Scalia's Textualism: The 'New' New Legal Process." *Cardozo Law Review* 12 (1991): 1597–1643.

Zimmerman, Joseph F. *Federal Preemption: The Silent Revolution*. Ames: Iowa State University Press, 1991.

# Index

343

federalism, 227, 235, 238, 260–261;
Madisonian interpretation of the
General Welfare Clause, 235;
medicinal use of marijuana, 271,
298n59; plain statement rule,
260–262, 295n13; parental rights
case, 213–214; preemption, 241–242,
256n111, 256n113; executive
immunity from judicial process, 121;
separation of powers; states' rights,
227; Tenth Amendment, 288; term
limits, 272; votes to alter precedent,
327n58; voting behavior in
administrative law cases, 164n61;
voting behavior in federalism cases,
243t; voting behavior in preemption
cases, 243t
Office of Legal Counsel, 9–13, 69
Office of Management and Budget, 15,
59, 140–141
Office of Telecommunications Policy, 6,
7–8, 29n26
Office of the President, 116, 123, 125
*Office of the President v. Office of the
Independent Counsel*, 135n140
Office of Special Counsel, 143
Office of the Vice President, 118
*O'Hare Truck Service Inc. v. City of
Northlake*, xxxi–xxxiin9, 28–29n10,
224n117, 325n11, 325n13
*Ollman v. Evans*, 314, 325n18
Olson, Theodore B., 69, 70, 71
Operations Advisory Group, 12
Original intent, xix, 191
Originalism, xix–xx, 205–206
*Orozco v. Texas*, 322, 327n55
Ostrow, Ronald J., 29n18, 29n27, 32n58
*Owen v. Owen*, 257n138

"Pacificus." *See* Hamilton, Alexander
Padilla, Jose, 111
*Panama Refining Co. v. Ryan*, 130n39
Panaro, Eva A., 1
Panaro, Pasquele, 2
Panaro, Vincent R., 2

Parental rights, 213–214
Parole Commission, 86n89
"Passive virtues," 27, 320
Patronage, 26, 207, 311, 313
Paul, John, II (Pope), 4, 29n14
"Pay Book of the State Company of
Artillery," (Hamilton) xxxvn65
Penner, Rudolph G., 14
*Pennsylvania v. Union Gas Co.*, 218n7,
220n54, 223n105
Pension Benefit Guaranty Corporation,
147
*Pension Benefit Guaranty Corp v. LTV
Corp.*, 147–148
Pentagon Papers, 20
Penumbra theory, 288
Perino, Michael A., 32n82, 57n62
Peterson, Peggy Kay, 47
Petracca, Mark P., 302n103
Phelps, G. A., 306n182
"Phocion." *See* Hamilton, Alexander
Physician-assisted suicide. *See* Right to
die
Pinckney, Charles, 275
Plain Statement Rule, 260–264, 295n14,
295n15, 296n22, 295n23, 295n27
*Planned Parenthood of Southeastern
Pennsylvania v. Casey*, xxxin7,
xxxin9, 28n10, 34n114, 224n122,
305n168, 324n1
Plato, 217
*Plaut v. Spendthrift Farm*, 55n8,
180–181
Pogue, Richard W., 5, 6
*Pollock v. Farmers' Loan & Trust Co.*,
236
Pope, Alexander, 40
Posner, Richard A., xvi, xxxin3
Powell, H. Jefferson, xxxiiin28, 253n34,
267, 297n48, 307n198
Powell, Lewis F., xvi, xxxin1, 158, 249
*Powell v. McCormack*, 272, 273, 276
Prakash, Saikrishna, 307n198
Preemption, xxvii–xxviii, xxx, 227,
241–251, 259, 294

# About the Author

James B. Staab is a professor of political science at Central Missouri State University. He received his J.D. from Richmond University and his Ph.D. from the University of Virginia. His scholarly writings are in the fields of constitutional law, civil rights and liberties, judicial politics, and jurisprudence.